WINNING PITCH

The Jim Perry Story

Forging Success from the Ballfield to the Boardroom

BRAD **K**ULLMAN

Discernment Press

Published by Discernment Press
Sarasota, Florida

Publisher's Cataloging-in-Publication data

Names: Kullman, Brad, author.
Title: Winning pitch : the Jim Perry story -- forging success from the ballfield to the boardroom / Brad Kullman.
Description: Includes bibliographical references and index. | Sarasota, FL: Discernment Press, 2023.
Identifiers: LCCN: 2023901896 | ISBN: 978-1-946324-31-3 | 978-1-946324-32-0 | 978-1-946324-33-7
Subjects: LCSH Perry, James. | Baseball players--United States--Biography. | Baseball--United States--History. | BISAC Biography & Autobiography / Sports | Sports & Recreation / Baseball / History | Sports & Recreation / Baseball / Statistics
Classification: LCC GV865.P47 K85 2023 | DDC 796.357/092--dc23

Cover design by Angie Siefring

Cover photo courtesy of James Perry Foundation

Printed in the United States of America

First Edition 2023

For further information on the topics in this book and the author, please see BradKullman.com

To my father, David. Thank you for always being such a great role model of what a man should be. Your teachings in actions, words, and deeds made it so easy for me to see those same qualities in the subject of this book.

Contents

Introduction   vii

1. Subtle Star   1

2. Validation   21

3. Farm Bred   51

4. Old School Cross-Training   65

5. Love and Life   75

6. Beating the Bushes   83

7. Here to Stay   93

8. Settling In   111

9. 9,999 More Lakes   125

10. Déjà Vu All Over Again   147

11. Good to Great   173

12. Veteran Leader   209

13. Tower of Strength   231

14. The Heist   255

15. Brothers in Arms   281

16. Beginning of the End   319

17. Dialing Up Success   337

18. Giving Back   359

Notes   373

Index   395

Introduction

From winning baseball pitches to winning sales pitches, Jim Perry is one of the most understated superstars of his generation. While those who merely count numbers might fail to appreciate his greatness, the stories in this book illustrate the many ways Jim Perry was a self-made winner and leader, both on and off the field. A model of consistency and reliability, he did not spend a single day on the disabled list throughout a 17-year MLB career.

Hall-of-famer Bert Blyleven called him "the master of our staff" and said "he helped the younger players tremendously." Another hall-of-famer, Jim Kaat, said "We're fortunate to have a man as good as Perry is..." Marvin Miller, inducted to the baseball hall of fame for his work as the head of the MLB Players Association, called Perry "a tower of strength" after Jim's work in leading the players through their first organized strike. Minneapolis sports writer Dick Cullum wrote, "Perry is always there when someone else who should be there isn't." A description of Jim Perry can be summed up in one simple word—*dependable*.

Jim Perry is not flashy, perhaps not "exciting," but absolutely dependable. Is there not greatness in that? If not greatness, there surely is honor, and Jim Perry is truly an honorable man who performed with great dedication and determination, both on and off the field.

His muted greatness would have undoubtedly been more celebrated had he played in a larger media market. It would also have helped if more luck went his way. After all, arguably the best game he ever pitched in the majors was lost to the annals of history. A no-hitter in which he had struck out eight of the game's first 13 batters was suddenly washed away by rain in the fifth inning, leaving it an unofficial game and erased from the record books. The box score shows he gave up a grand slam home run in the playoffs, but it does not reflect that gale force winds blew fair a ball that appeared to be so far foul, the right fielder neglected to give chase until it was too late. The swirling—and catchable—fly ball dropped into the front row of seats just inside the foul pole. These stories and many others, from the maddening to the amazing are detailed on the following pages.

Do not be fooled, however. While he may have been dogged by some bad breaks, that is precisely what makes the Jim Perry story such a great one. Growing up the son of a poor sharecropper, Jim learned the value and necessity of hard work. He literally worked his way out of the tobacco fields all the way to the big leagues, arriving well before anyone's expectations (except his own). He paved the way for younger brother, Gaylord, both as a role model and as a confidant. He found success following his playing days by selling a product that was not flashy or exciting, but was simply a reliable improvement on an existing product that could save people money. He married a beautiful, supportive woman, who stated, "He's so strong about all things... He always did whatever it took to support his family."

Jim said of wife, Daphne, "She is a wonderful mother *and* father. She has to be when I am away." Together, they raised a terrific family of three children. I am blessed to be part of this family, married to their amazing daughter, Pam, who perfectly exemplifies those same dependable traits.

Indeed, if there is ever a hall of fame for dependability, Jim Perry will most certainly be included in the inaugural class. It has been a tremendous pleasure to know him, and I hope that this book will help others, as well, to better know and appreciate the man and his remarkable life.

BRAD KULLMAN

1
Subtle Star

As he joined his teammates storming the field in celebration on the late afternoon of September 20, 1969, Jim Perry had a tremendous feeling of satisfaction. Arms raised in jubilation, he almost collided with teammate Rod Carew, who had just raced around the bases, scoring the game-winning run all the way from first on Tony Oliva's line drive double into the left-center field gap. Not only did Carew's run give the Minnesota Twins a thrilling 3-2 victory over the Seattle Pilots in the bottom of the ninth inning, but it made Perry a twenty-game winner for the first time in his major league career.

Reaching the twenty-win plateau has long been considered the gold standard for a pitcher in Major League Baseball. For Perry, however, getting twenty starts in a season had been a challenge, let alone winning that many games. Over the first ten years of his major league career, Jim averaged 21 starts and 17 relief appearances every season. Since starting every one of his 35 games in his third season, in fact, the tall, slender righthander had relieved (18.4 games per season) more than he had started (18.0). Make no mistake, this was through no fault of his own. Rather he was an unwitting victim of his own success.

Jim Perry was literally so valued for his ability to handle any role on the pitching staff that his managers largely felt uncomfortable committing him to any specific role. When asked if Perry might be a candidate to be traded after Minnesota acquired starting pitcher Dean Chance following the 1966 season, manager Sam Mele explained why Jim was more valuable to him than any conventional pitcher.

"Perry has shown me too much. He can do too many things, and you need pitchers like that. He can start regularly, he can spot start and he can relieve.

"When injuries start popping up," Mele continued, "a man who can do all those things can really help. Twice last summer Jim started with two days of rest. And I haven't forgotten it. I don't want to trade Perry. He's too valuable."[1]

Perry's versatility and dutiful willingness to do whatever his team needed—and do it well—was both a blessing and a curse. Always the good soldier, Perry explained his exasperated perspective at the time.

"I think I have made myself into a valuable member of our pitching staff. Not many guys will start and relieve as I have done. I'll still do anything the Twins ask," said the loyal hurler. "But I prefer to be a regular starter, and I'm not going to give up easily on that."[2]

Try, Try Again

Just as he promised, there was no give-up in Perry. Forced to begin the season in the bullpen once again in 1967, he remained ready and reliable no matter when his name was called. Just as the Twins had done in 1965 and '66, however, when the pennant race heated up, they counted on the reliable six-foot-four workhorse to cover big innings as a starter.

Perry posted a sparkling 2.15 ERA in five August starts, four of them wins, as the team reeled off 20 wins in a 29-game span to vault from fourth place into the American League lead. Perry's mastery was highlighted by back-to-back shutouts in early August. On August 10 against Washington, he fired a five-hitter, limiting the Senators to just a pair of walks while striking out eight. After the game, Perry explained the difficulty in bouncing between starting and relieving.

"Any pitcher would rather start than relieve, and long relief in the middle innings is the toughest job in baseball. As a starter, you know when you are pitching and you can work accordingly. I'm not real sharp yet, but I had an idea where the ball was going today and I can feel my control getting better already."[3]

His assertion proved prophetic when five days later, he turned the trick again. On the road in Anaheim, Perry limited the California Angels to six hits and three walks while racking up ten whiffs in the whitewashing. Once again, he let his feelings show, while at the same time maintaining respect for his manager and the greater good of the team.

"I feel I did a good enough job last year—the record shows it—and earned a chance to be a starting pitcher. But I'm not asking to be traded," Perry clarified. "I want to do what I can to help this team."[4]

He would win three more games down the stretch, but the team lost a pair of heartbreakers to the "Impossible Dream" Boston Red Sox on the final weekend of the season, causing the Twins to fall one game short of the World Series.

Perry reported to spring training in 1968 determined to win a spot in the Twins starting rotation. Again, however, events threatened to deny his quest. Despite a strong spring on the mound, Minnesota pitching coach Early Wynn announced that the Twins would begin the season with a four-man rotation, leaving Perry the odd man out. Not only was Jim considered the number five starter, but Wynn knew this left him a protective security blanket in the event his plan went awry.

"If we get into trouble there," the pitching coach explained, "Perry's still able to start…"[5]

Mister Dependable

Of course he is. Dependable Perry was always there to bail the team out of a jam. The casual fan who only followed the game through the highlights on the nightly news broadcast or the headlines in the morning newspaper might not have realized it, but anyone who followed the Minnesota Twins closely could see that Jim Perry was one of the team's most valuable players. Sports columnist Dick Cullum of the *Minneapolis Tribune* was one such astute observer who took notice. Just a little more than a week before the 1968 season was to begin, Cullum devoted a portion of his column to the Twins unsung star under the subhead, *Be Grateful for Perry.*

"Again, Twins fans must be grateful for Perry," wrote Cullum.

"He has never been fully appreciated because he has never had a set place in the pitching rotation. He has done what had to be done at a given moment and has done it well.

"Don't try to count the critical situations he has handled during his years with the Twins. Just keep in mind that he is always there when someone else who should be there isn't, whether it be in the bullpen or in the starting rotation."[6]

> Perry is always there when someone else who should be there isn't.
> — Dick Cullum
> SPORTS COLUMNIST

As if on cue, Jim Kaat, one of the four starters, pulled up lame with a balky elbow as the 1968 season prepared to open, giving Perry his chance to open as a starter. He would not disappoint.

On Saturday, April 13, Jim held the New York Yankees to only four singles, didn't allow a runner to reach third base and only one as far as second as he tossed a 6-0 shutout in Yankee Stadium. He struck out seven while walking only one in the 17th shutout of his career. Perry's sixth strikeout, a whiff of Gene Michael, marked the 800th of his major league career, and the victory was career number 99.

To top things off, Perry even hit a home run, though it was not without some controversy. Already up 5-0 in the top of the ninth inning, the left-handed swinging switch-hitter lofted a deep fly ball to the opposite field down the line. The ball ricocheted off the wall, but umpire Larry Napp ruled that it hit the screen attached to the left field foul pole, making it a home run. Yankees left fielder Tom Tresh went berserk, leading to an argument that delayed the game for a good five minutes while Perry was able to towel off in the dugout and prepare to finish his masterpiece. The homer marked the third consecutive season Perry had gone deep.

A feature that ran in the *Minneapolis Tribune* later in the week once again lamented the plight of the talented and versatile veteran.

"Jim Perry's versatility may be his biggest detriment. The crew-cut right-hander, 31, ranks fifth among active American League pitchers in number of victories, 99. And he is fourth to Camilo Pascual, Dean Chance and Bill Monbouquette in shutouts with 17, despite the fact he hasn't pitched a full season as a starter since coming to Minnesota in 1963.

"When Perry blanked New York 6-0 Saturday, it marked the

fourth consecutive year he had entered the starting rotation with a shutout."[7]

Once again, Jim pleaded his case. "There's no question in my mind about preferences," said the winning pitcher to reporters in the locker room following his shutout. "I'd rather be a starter. I can relax days between starts and prepare myself mentally for the game."[8]

The story continued, detailing the skill that was both Jim's blessing and his curse. "Because Perry had the rare baseball talent to perform equally well as a starter and reliever (long and short), his impressive performances as an emergency starter were often rewarded with long spells in the bullpen."[9]

"I've always kept myself in good shape," said Perry, explaining the secret to his success. "Sometimes, like in 1965 when they weren't using me at all, I'd pitch 15 minutes in the bullpen and throw batting practice when they told me not to. I'd look at the opposition and who our starter would be and take a chance that they weren't going to use me. I just had to throw to keep my arm ready.

"Sometimes I got called on to pitch when I'd thrown 15 minutes of batting practice the day before. I was lucky, I guess, but I always did all right."[10]

More background was shared in regard to what set Jim apart from other players. "Perry's pitching philosophy is relatively simple. He mixes up his pitches—fastball, slider, changeup and sinker—and tries to keep the batter from working out any formula against him. Nobody worked harder than Perry in spring training and, following past performances, it was he who got the call when Jim Kaat went on the disabled list with arm trouble.

"Like his roommate, Al Worthington, Perry leads a good life off the field. While other players celebrated the Twins' third consecutive win with dinner and liquid refreshments [i.e. beer and liquor] at New York eating spots Saturday [following Jim's great game], Perry went to a local bar where he devoured a dish of ice cream. High on the list of things he credits to his success are his abilities as a hitter (better than a .210 lifetime average with at least a home run a year) and his wife's home cooking."[11]

The story ended with a declaration by the newest member of the Twins rotation. "I wanted to start this year," Perry said with a grin, "and I'm going to stay there this time"[12]

Tribune sports columnist Dick Cullum, who had long been an ardent Perry supporter, shared a cogent thought that would prove prophetic in his column a couple days later. "You hear it said repeatedly, in sympathy for pitcher Jim Perry, that he has been of greater value to the Twins than is generally realized. True!

"It is intimated that he should have been used in some different way. But if he has been of such great value all these years, it must show that he has been used wisely.

"And may he continue to be used wisely."[13]

Jim would proceed to start nine more times over the next two months. Luck was not always on his side, unfortunately. He took his first loss of the season on April 20 when a wind-blown home run and four errors were the difference in a 4-2 defeat. He lost another tough one on May 3 when the offense gave him zero runs of support and Lady Luck once again frowned on his exploits. Manager Cal Ermer lamented the rough day.

"Those guys had radar working for them against Perry," said the Twins skipper. "They got a foul-pole homer ('one inch above the glove of a leaping Bob Allison'), two bloops and a seeing-eye double play. Some nights the other guy has all the luck."[14]

Hit to Win

Recall that one of the reasons Jim gave for his success as a pitcher was his ability to contribute as a *hitter*. A switch-hitter who took pride in his ability to both hit and bunt proficiently, it is interesting to note how much the game has changed. The movement for change was just beginning at this time in 1968, as columnist Sid Hartman highlighted in his May 15 column in the *Minneapolis Tribune*.

Hartman discussed how MLB owners had an upcoming meeting in June during which the New York Yankees were reportedly going to "advocate adding a 10th man to the starting lineup" who would "hit on the pitcher's turn to bat." It was to be a discussion of implementing what we today routinely call the designated hitter or DH, though the term had not yet been coined.

What is of particular interest in regard to this upcoming debate was the perspective of Minnesota Twins president Calvin Griffith, which once again highlights the understated greatness of Jim Perry. Griffith told Hartman that he was "in favor of the rule, providing it isn't compulsory to eliminate the pitcher as a hitter." In other words, he wanted to maintain the ability to have his pitchers bat instead of a designated hitter.

"Most pitchers make a farce out of hitting," Griffith explained. "But I don't want to see us eliminate the good-hitting pitchers like Dave Boswell, Jim Kaat and Jim Perry of our staff and Gary Peters, whom the Chicago White Sox use as a pinch hitter."[15]

The switch-hitting Perry batted an even .300 as a rookie in 1959 and recorded double-digit hits in ten of the 14 seasons that he played before the designated hitter rule was finally implemented in 1973.

Perry was at work helping himself with the bat again in 1968 during his start at home against the Detroit Tigers on Wednesday night, May 22. Batting right handed against lefthander Mickey Lolich, Perry came to the plate with two men on base and two outs in the bottom of the second inning. When he got a pitch to his liking, Perry turned on it and launched a blast deep into the left field bleachers, giving himself and the Twins an early three-run lead.

Unfortunately, some bad luck would cost Perry the victory. His home run was the only offense the team could muster, and when Gates Brown managed a one-out triple in the top of the eighth, manager Cal Ermer elected to bring on reliever Ron Perranoski in an attempt to protect a slim 3-2 advantage. Perranoski promptly served up a game-tying base hit to Al Kaline, which cost Perry the chance at picking up another win. Harmon Killebrew would put the Twins back on top in the Twins half of that inning, driving in Tony Oliva with a sharp single to the opposite field, beating an aggressive Detroit shift.

When Al Worthington closed out the save in the ninth, Perranoski got credit for the win, but there was no doubt that Perry's hitting, along with 7⅓ innings of four-hit pitching during which he struck out seven batters while walking just one were the keys to the Minnesota victory.

Farm-Raised Tough

Growing up on the farm, Jim learned early on that the work needed to get done even on days that he might not have felt his best. Not only did that help him to develop his superior work ethic, but it also gave Jim the mental and physical strength to deal with adversity. This training would show through as he faced yet another hurdle in his attempt to gain a foothold in the Twins starting rotation.

On May 28, 1968 against Cleveland, Jim got another three early runs of support, this time courtesy of his teammates. Once again, the Minnesota bats went dormant after that, going hitless over the final eight innings. Jim was ready this time, however. Just as he had in the hard-luck no-decision his prior start, Jim held the lead as he pitched into the eighth inning. With two outs and a runner on first, Tony Horton, who had doubled in Cleveland's only run back in the first inning, once again stepped up to the plate.

Knowing that Horton was an aggressive hitter who liked the ball up, Perry drove hard down the mound in an effort to run his sinker down hard and away from the right-handed hitter. As his left foot planted in the ground, Jim felt a sharp twinge shoot through his right upper thigh. Horton got just enough of the pitch to ground it through the hole on the right side of the infield for a single.

"I over-strided myself trying to keep the ball low to Horton," Perry would later explain.[16] Sensing something was not right with his pitcher, manager Ermer elected to get Perry out of the game and into the safety of the dugout. The move also allowed Ermer to bring in the fresh arm of Al Worthington, who was the early American League saves leader. Worthington got the final out in the eighth and then retired the side 1-2-3 in the ninth to secure his league-leading tenth save, along with Perry's team-high fifth win of the campaign.

Five days later, with a thick wrap covering his entire upper thigh, Perry gutted out six tough innings in Chicago against the White Sox. His only blemish on the day was a soft jam-shot flare off the bat of White Sox second baseman Tim Cullen. The blooper ticked off the outstretched glove of third baseman Rich Rollins, rolling into foul territory and allowing two runs to score. The Twins came up short, falling 3-2, and giving Perry another hard-luck loss, dropping his record to 5-4.

While Ermer surely appreciated the gutsy effort of Perry, he made the determination that risking further injury to his hottest pitcher was not a sensible gamble at this early stage of the season. Though he avoided the disabled list, Perry would not see the mound again for more than two weeks. Finally, on June 17, Ermer announced that Perry was ready to go, but his proclamation carried an ominous tone. "Jim Perry is physically okay now and ready to pitch," Ermer told reporters. "We'll use him in relief before starting him again."[17]

For Jim, it was yet another setback in his quest to become a regular starter. The only difference this time was that he was not simply battling four other pitchers, as had been his persistent nemesis. For the first time in his career, the 32-year old was battling his own health.

Two days later against Washington, just as his manager had promised, Perry was called upon out of the bullpen, though it was not the kind of low-pressure, get-your-feet-on-the-ground, mop-up work one might expect. Rather, it was quite the opposite. Bullpen ace Al Worthington, who did not have his good stuff on this night, had been touched up for three straight hits as he failed to protect a slim 7-6 ninth inning lead. With the Senators suddenly on top, 8-7, and with two runners on base and only one out, Ermer was hoping Perry could somehow snuff out the rally and give the Twins a chance.

As usual, despite not having pitched in game competition in 16 days, Dependable Perry was ready. Washington catcher Paul Casanova rolled over on a hard sinker and grounded into a tailor-made 6-4-3 double play. When Frank Quilici laced a game-tying triple in the bottom of the ninth and then came home with the winning run two batters later, it made Perry the winning pitcher, despite facing only one batter. Following his successful return to the mound, it would seem that all signs pointed to one of the team's best pitchers to this point in the season returning to the starting rotation. But it never seemed to be that easy for Jim Perry.

Rainmaker

Before the creation of domed stadiums, artificial turf, or extensive drainage systems underneath what otherwise appear to be normal grass fields, fighting the weather was a far more difficult proposition than it has become today. Such was the case in the mid-twentieth century, even at the highest level of the professional ranks. Seeing the other hurdles he faced, is it any surprise that Jim had to wrestle Mother Nature, as well?

Although it has been lost to the annals of history, the fact that Jim Perry was pitching arguably the best game of his career on Friday, May 17 of the 1968 season is without question. With the Twins at home against the California Angels, Perry had fired four no-hit shutout innings when the skies suddenly opened. A first inning walk of Roger Repoz was his only blemish to that point. Even more notably, the groundball specialist had just finished off a fourth inning in which he struck out the side in order. That gave Perry a very uncharacteristic six strikeouts of the previous seven batters he had faced, and eight of 13 overall.

As more of a control artist than a big strikeout pitcher, Jim came into the game that night having amassed just 21 strikeouts over 46 innings on the season. To be missing bats at a rate like that showed his stuff was really electric on this night. After a 58-minute delay, however, with no signs of encouragement from the Weather Bureau that the rain would be letting up any time soon, the umpires finally called the game. The decision left Jim's masterpiece, sadly, to be washed away, as well, just as if it had never taken place at all. Although not prone to foul language, a frustrated Perry let his best four-letter words fly while baring his emotions in the clubhouse.

"Darn it, that was the best stuff I've had all season," he said. "My fastball was really moving. Maybe I'll have some more like that one. That one was sure wasted"[18]

Teammate Harmon Killebrew, who was playing first base, remarked that Perry's ball was moving so much, it was even hard to handle his throws over to first! "He was throwing me sinkers when he tried to pick Repoz off first."[19]

Perry lamented his lack of luck with the weather. "It rains more when I pitch and when I'm scheduled to pitch than anybody I've ever heard of." Having grown up working on the farm, however, he knew better than to curse the precipitation too much.

"I'm not complaining," Perry explained. "There's nothing you can do about rain. But I'm a regular rainmaker."[20]

All Wet

As the morning of Tuesday, June 25 broke, Jim was looking forward to making his first start in more than three weeks against the Chicago White Sox. The weather, however, told a different story. As relentless rain poured down all day, a frustrated Perry paced the lobby of the Chicago-Sheraton hotel.

"Just my luck," he lamented. "I was ready to go to work."[21]

The constant rain continued into the following day, forcing the postponed game to be pushed back to late August as part of a doubleheader. More significantly, the sudden back-to-back off days were threatening to throw the entire Minnesota pitching rotation out of whack. As the Twins skipper considered his options, the best one he could come up with, not surprisingly, involved relying on the most versatile pitcher on the staff.

"I don't think I can back up the whole rotation to use Perry Thursday," Ermer explained. "That would throw everyone off. I'll probably stick with Dave Boswell Thursday and put Perry back in the bullpen."[22]

Ah, but, of course. Whenever the team is in a jam, *we'll just move Dependable Perry to wherever is needed.* It had become the most consistently reliable strategy employed by Minnesota managers since the long, lean righthander had come to town.

Always a leader on the team simply by the way he carried himself, the quiet veteran pitcher never put up a fuss, no matter how disheartened he might be on the inside. During the team's trip from Chicago to Baltimore for a weekend series with the Orioles, Ermer sat down with Perry to provide some reassurance that he was still an important part of the pitching staff.

"He explained that I'd be the first long-relief man used," related Perry. "And he told me why he couldn't upset his rotation to start me in this series. I understand. I'll just have to work myself back into a regular spot."[23]

Always positive. Always working to be the best he could be. Always putting the interests of the team's success ahead of personal glory. Jim Perry epitomized what leadership on the athletic playing field is all about.

Perry's teammates appreciated his value to the team, as well. Though the Twins gained a split of the four-game series in Baltimore, the pitching staff was uncharacteristically wild throughout the weekend, issuing 22 walks over 30 innings. (Two of the games were shortened by rain from the same storm system that washed out their final game in Chicago.) Lefthander Jim Kaat, who was not only a Twins starting pitcher, but also a thoughtful student of the game, shared his theory on the staff's collective wildness. Kaat's theory is especially interesting, considering the evolution of five and even six-man rotations, accompanied by arbitrary pitch counts that have pitchers focused more on resting than pitching.

"It's the lack of work," Kaat explained. "Last week we had two five-inning games, a rainout and an open date in four days. The Friday game was my first start in six games. I've got to go every fourth day. I think any starter feels that way."[24]

Kaat illustrated how the Cleveland pitching staff, which ranked as the best in the American League at that point, had finally reached their potential because of the way their new manager was handling the starters.

"I remember that Birdie Tebbetts (the previous manager) used to shift his starters all the time. He was always experimenting. A guy would never know when he would pitch. Now they've got Alvin Dark and he's got the staff straightened around. He goes with four starters and a fifth man for spot duty. This is ideal."[25]

Expounding how this strategy could be translated to the benefit of the Twins pitching staff, Kaat detailed how he felt the Twins would be stronger with four consistent starters. However, he also clarified that the success of the plan depended upon one key piece that the Twins should be grateful they already had in place.

"We're fortunate to have a man as good as Perry is for spot starts," Kaat pointed out. "He really makes a contribution to our staff."[26]

Chin Music

There is another little-known and underappreciated aspect of Jim Perry's success on the mound. Because excellent control was a major part of his game, the kind-hearted, soft-spoken pitcher needed to make sure opposing

> We're fortunate to have a man as good as Perry is... He really makes a contribution to our staff.
>
> — Jim Kaat
> TEAMMATE AND
> HALL-OF-FAME PITCHER

hitters did not get too comfortable digging into the batter's box to face him. So, how does a pitcher with superior control keep a batter from patiently waiting for a perfect pitch to his liking? You give him an occasional high, hard one. It's what's referred to in the business as a "close shave" or "chin music."

A good fastball in off the plate, between the hands and the chin is enough to make even the most confident of batters a bit more wary about leaning over the plate to mash a pitch down low and away. This is where Perry made his living, so playing a little chin music from time to time kept hitters honest. It could also lead to some extracurriculars breaking out on the field. That's what happened in a relief appearance on July 1 of that 1968 season.

Called on in relief of Dave Boswell in the sixth inning with the Twins trailing Cleveland by a score of 4-0, it was clear to Perry that the Indians hitters were feeling a little too comfortable at the plate. They had tagged Boswell for nine hits, including a pair of home runs, and Jim was determined to avoid a similar fate. With runners on first and second, Perry fired a good fastball up and in on right-handed-hitting Max Alvis, which grazed his shoulder as he ducked his head safely out of harm's way, While this loaded the bases, the strategy worked to perfection, as the next batter, Lou Johnson, pulled off an outside breaking ball just enough to loft a harmless inning-ending fly ball into the glove of right fielder Tony Oliva. While Perry did his job, the aggressive manner in which he got it done set the stage for what was to come next.

Bob Allison, who led off the top of the seventh inning, was the first Twins hitter to bat following Perry's chin music. No sooner had Allison dug in for his at bat when Cleveland pitcher Sam McDowell sent him sprawling to the dirt with a high, hard tune of his own. Allison scrambled to his feet and took off toward the mound, bat in tow, in an effort to confront McDowell for what he felt was clearly a purposeful retaliatory shot. Though no physical blows ensued, Allison got off some verbal jabs.

"I can't tell you what I said to him," Allison declared after the game, "but it was a warning not to try that again."[27]

Twins manager Cal Ermer, who was plenty upset about the purposeful bean ball in response to what he considered Perry's good, aggressive pitching, was more forthcoming. "Allison told McDowell that if he ever did that again he'd wrap a bat around his head. That's all," Ermer explained.[28]

When pressed by reporters if he thought the pitch by McDowell was intentional once he had time to calm down and was not in the heat of the moment, Allison maintained his view. "He threw at me all right," the Twins left fielder protested. "It was a half-humped fastball."[29]

Similarly queried about the pitch that started the fracas, Perry denied that it was anything more than a tough, inside pitch–chin music–which had long been considered an accepted part of the game. "I'm sure Max would back me up," Perry added, which, indeed, Max Alvis did.[30]

This incident simply serves as yet another example of how Jim Perry played the game hard, yet played the game right. While he gave no quarter to his opponent, Jim Perry always respected him as a man and as a fellow human being.

Answering the Call

After a month of short outings in which he never pitched more than three innings at a time, opportunity finally knocked again on July 21. With a double-header on the schedule, the Twins needed a fifth starter and—as usual—Dependable Perry was ready. After Minnesota beat Oakland 7-5 in game one, Perry completed the sweep with an eight-hit complete game shutout. He even shot an RBI single past the shortstop for good measure to help the cause in the 10-0 laugher. The win gave Perry seven on the season, which tied Jim Kaat for the team lead.

While he did not specialize in missing bats, Jim Perry excelled in getting hitters to make soft contact. Whether using his power sinker or his sharp-biting slider, Jim consistently found a way to miss the bat's sweet spot, often turning a bat into splinters as it broke. While this frequently led to weak ground balls or lazy flies, sometimes those mishits could fall in, which is quite maddening. Such was the case on this day, forcing Jim to work around several jams, even as he issued only one walk while striking out four A's.

"I've never seen so many broken bat hits," he lamented after the game. "Why, Sal Bando got two of them."[31]

The great outing forced manager Cal Ermer to consent to another start for his dutiful righthander, but he did it begrudgingly. The skipper promised Perry another start against the same A's, this time when the team traveled to Oakland, but "beyond that I don't know," he cautioned.[32]

Before the team ever got out of town, however, duty called once again. Just two days after Perry had pitched a complete game shutout, Ermer called for his security blanket. Rookie Ron Keller was called up from triple-A Denver to make his major league debut in game one of a doubleheader with the California Angels on Tuesday, July 24. Keller was tagged for a pair of runs in the first inning, but he somehow worked around eleven hits while allowing only one more run over six innings.

With Minnesota trailing 3-1 and a second game still to follow, Ermer asked Perry to keep the game close and help save the bullpen. Amazingly, on just one day of rest following his complete game effort, Jim gave the team two more perfect innings, striking out two of the six batters he faced. A feat that would merit headlines in today's era of carefully monitored pitch counts and mandated rest was a mere side note in the game story carried in the local paper. Jim continued to quietly do yeoman's work that was barely noticed, save for his teammates and a handful of observant pundits.

Three days after his spotless relief appearance, true to his word, Ermer had Perry on the mound again, starting in Oakland. The rest of the team, however, was a skeleton crew, as stars Harmon Killebrew, Tony Oliva, and Rod Carew were all nursing injuries. Another regular, first baseman Rich Reese, was missing due to a military obligation. Beat writer Dave Mona described it as a starting "lineup which looked like a hangover from spring training."[33]

Despite being short-handed and outmanned, Perry and the Twins had battled to a 2-2 tie going into the bottom of the fifth. Dave Duncan led off the inning with a single. When Catfish Hunter attempted a sacrifice bunt, Minnesota first baseman Bob Allison tried to get Duncan at second, but the throw was late and suddenly there were two runners on with nobody out. After leadoff man Bert Campaneris advanced both runners with a sac bunt of his own, Perry induced a soft ground out by John Donaldson that left him one out away from escaping the jam.

With the left-handed-hitting Rick Monday coming to the plate, manager Cal Ermer ordered him intentionally walked in order to face the right-handed bat of Sal Bando. Jim pitched him tough, but Bando put a nice swing on an outside fastball and sliced it into right field for a two-run single. The hit sent Jim to the showers on a day that he certainly had to battle without his best stuff. His location was off, to be sure, as he uncharacteristically walked three while recording no strikeouts.

Another Setback

Despite the rough outing, Ermer must have seen something he liked, because five days later the manager had Perry back on the mound again August 1 for a start at home against the Chicago White Sox. With the team struggling so badly at this point that Ermer held a closed-door locker room session before the game, the start was especially big for Perry. As usual, he rose to the occasion.

Scattering seven hits over the first eight innings, Jim held a 4-1 lead, headed for his fourth complete game of the season. When Dick Kenworthy of the Sox led off the ninth inning with a hard bouncer up the middle, the slick-fielding Perry made a diving grab to snare it and throw Kenworthy out at first. He retired the next batter, Ken Berry on a fly ball to right field, but something wasn't right. Trainer Doc Lentz came to the mound along with manager Ermer and made the determination that it was not prudent for Jim to go after the final out.

"Perry wanted to stay in the game," explained Lentz, "but he could have hurt himself worse by throwing any more."[34]

The diagnosis was a pulled muscle on his left side, suffered when making the diving grab of Kenworthy's chopper. It was yet another unfortunate development in Jim's quest to lock up a consistent role in the starting rotation, as Ermer waited 16 days before using him again. Jim immediately went to work dutifully soaking in the whirlpool, hoping the pulsating water would help his muscle to loosen up. While the injury kept him from taking the ball for more than two weeks, he once again managed to avoid the disabled list. The combination of Jim's value to the team plus the hope that he could heal quickly led the club to decide against formally shelving him.

When Perry finally did return to the mound in relief of Jim Roland on August 17 against the Orioles, the pain in his side acted up again. Jim was forced out of the game during his third inning of work when he became uncharacteristically wild, walking the light-hitting Mark Belanger on four pitches to begin the sixth inning. Three days later, however, Jim showed he was ready to go with a perfect relief outing against the Yankees as he retired all five batters he faced. The manager again took notice.

Family Night

On Monday, August 26, the Twins were in Washington D.C. for a doubleheader with the Senators. As Jim's brother Gaylord was pitching a one-hitter against the Cubs in San Francisco, Jim was virtually matching him in one of his best starts of the year. While the Giants supported Gaylord with three runs of offense, however, the Twins could not do the same for Jim.

When he struck out Ken McMullen and Mike Epstein back-to-back to end the first inning, it was clear that Perry had his good stuff working on this night. He mowed down the entire Washington lineup, retiring the side in order each of the first three innings. Even when the Senators finally did get a runner to reach with Del Unser's infield single, Jim quickly erased him by inducing a tailor-made 6-4-3 double play. When he retired McMullen again on a ground out for the second out in the seventh inning, Jim had faced the minimum 20 opposition batters to that point. A single to left by Epstein—the first *clean* hit by Washington—broke the string, but Jim promptly whiffed big Frank Howard to send the game to the eighth inning, still scoreless.

Jim would issue his only base on balls of the night to Bernie Allen in the eighth inning, but followed that up with an inning-ending strikeout of pinch-hitter Gary Holman. In the ninth, it was 1-2-3, including a strikeout of McMullen, which should have put the stamp on a fantastic complete game win for the once-again-healthy Perry. Unfortunately, lefthander Frank Bertaina was having similar success against Minnesota hitters.

Though he had faced only two over the minimum through nine sterling innings, and he certainly still appeared to be going strong after the clean ninth, Ermer decided against pushing a key member of his staff. Fearful that Jim might be apt to overexert himself as he became fatigued and that might leave him prone to reaggravating his tender side muscle, Ermer brought on the fresh arm of Al Worthington. The move worked, as Worthington delivered three hitless innings, but when he finally tired, Twins pitchers could carry their anemic-hitting teammates no longer. Ron Perranoski coughed up a pair of walks and a hit before allowing the game-winning single to Tim Cullen.

While the win eluded Jim, August 26, 1968 was still an incredible night for the Perry family. Brothers Jim and Gaylord combined to throw 18 shutout innings, allowing only three hits—all singles—and only one walk, while racking up 12 strikeouts, including nine by Jim. Mamma Ruby and Daddy Evan had to be proud to hear the news back home in Williamston, North Carolina.

Strong Finish

After a scoreless two inning relief appearance on the first day of September, Jim got the call for another start on Sunday, September 7 at Detroit. He scattered six singles and three walks over seven innings, but the only other hit he allowed was a solo home run to Don Wert. Sadly, the one run was enough to stick Jim with yet another no-decision, as the Minnesota offense could only manage a single run of its own before rookie Graig Nettles hit his second home run of the game in the ninth inning to help the Twins squeak out a 2-1 win.

Jim would get the ball again in Cleveland four days later to make what would turn out to be his final start of the season. The Twins, who had been languishing at the bottom of the standings since shortly after the all-star break, had finally been mathematically eliminated from the race the day before Jim's previous start, so they would be looking at some youngsters during their final games. On September 11, however, Jim painted one more masterpiece, scattering eight hits and issuing no free passes while striking out five Indians as he pitched a phenomenal ten shutout innings.

Once again, however, his teammates came up empty in support. Ermer sent up a pinch-hitter for Jim in the bottom of the tenth inning and Minnesota eventually lost it 1-0 in the twelfth. The game story the following morning in the *Minneapolis Tribune* referred to Perry as "the luckless Minnesota starter."[35]

One thing about Jim Perry, no matter what might be transpiring around him, he always excelled at staying focused on just what he could control. And so it went as the team played out the string in the final days of a disappointing lost season. Jim was limited to only four relief appearances over the final two-and-a-half weeks following his ten inning masterpiece, but he quietly continued his outstanding pitching with four more shutout innings to finish the season.

When the 1968 season mercifully ended for the Twins with a 4-3 win over the Oakland A's on September 29, Jim made his final scoreless relief appearance to cap off a finish that was furtively amazing. Over Minnesota's final 40 games, Perry pitched 34 innings while allowing only one run for a remarkable 0.27 ERA. He allowed just 21 hits and walked only five against 20 strikeouts. Just as inconceivably depressing, the team could manage just two runs during the time Jim was on the mound over that stretch. As a result, he did not get credit for a single victory during that time, despite his stellar work.

During the final days of the season, the Twins players voted among themselves for tongue-in-cheek awards meant to emulate the Emmys that they called the "Nummies." Bullpen coach Bob Oldis served as master of ceremonies and Jim received an appropriate award to sum up his frustrating season. For bad luck with his body as much as his lack of run support, Perry was bestowed the "Purple Heart Award" for his outstanding performance in "Grimace on the Hill."[36] It was a light-hearted touch to wrap up a frustrating season, but one that Jim used to set the stage for something bigger.

Overall, Jim finished the 1968 season with a team-leading 2.27 ERA. While he may have been flying under the radar to the casual fan, his exceptional finish was a sign of things to come.

2
Validation

It is amazing how you can want something so bad yet nothing you do seems to make it happen, so you step back, change course, and suddenly things fall into place. After spending his first six years with the Twins desperately fighting to become a full-time member of the starting rotation, that is exactly what Jim did. He had continually been yanked back-and-forth between starting and relieving, making 99 starts and 116 relief appearances over those six seasons. Continually denied a consistent role despite posting a sterling 2.89 ERA while doing everything his managers had asked, Jim finally decided it was time for a new tack.

The 1969 season promised to be a time for new beginnings for the entire Twins team, as there would be a new leader in the dugout. Manager Cal Ermer was fired the morning after a disappointing 1968 season had come to a close, and he was replaced less than two weeks later by a feisty competitor who pundits and fans alike felt could bring out the best in the Minnesota Twins. When Twins president Calvin Griffith introduced the new manager to the media, he said, "I feel that Billy has the ability to be another Casey Stengel."[37]

Stengel, of course, was not only a hall-of-fame manager, but he had also served as a mentor during Billy Martin's seven years as a player with the Yankees. While Martin is generally thought of as a

Yankees player, he bounced around between six different teams during the last five years of his career. He had been in the Twins organization since playing his final year in Minnesota in 1961. Martin was a scout from 1962-64 and became third base coach for the major league club in the World Series season of 1965.

Despite being considered one of the best third base coaches in the game, Martin headed to the minor leagues early in the 1968 season to take over as manager of the Twins struggling triple-A affiliate. The Denver Bears had begun the 1968 season by losing 22 of their first 29 games, but they suddenly turned things around under Martin's fiery leadership and went 66-50 the rest of the way.

So many Minnesota pundits felt Billy Martin could work the same magic for the big club that at Martin's introductory press conference, Griffith credited the media for the new hire. "I'd never seen such a campaign in my life about one personality," said the Twins president. "I say personality because Billy is a personality. He's one of the better known men in baseball, and I feel that under Billy's guidance and leadership we can produce a winning team."[38]

In addition to the new skipper, Jim Perry saw a void at the back of the bullpen, where 40-year old closer Al Worthington had announced his retirement after leading the American League with 18 saves in 1968. Jim's reputation as an unflappable competitor was very similar to that of Worthington, his former roommate. Figuring he would be a perfect fit as a replacement, Jim went to Griffith and Martin with the request to have first crack at filling the role.

As 1969 spring training neared, however, the first organized labor dispute in MLB was brewing. Marvin Miller, the new head of the MLB Players Association had encouraged players to avoid signing their contracts and refrain from reporting to camp in order to get the owners to increase contributions to the players' pension fund. The players were fighting for a greater share of the lucrative new television contract MLB had just signed, as well as more money coming into the league from the addition of four new expansion teams.

With many veterans holding out, Martin was forced to begin his first camp filled with youngsters. By the time Jim finally agreed to sign his contract (for just under $30,000, tenth highest on the team[39]) and report to camp, the start of the Grapefruit League exhibition season was only a day away. As usual, however, Jim reported in excellent shape, ready to grab hold of the vacant closer role.

"I knew spring training was going to be short because of the pension trouble," Perry explained. "So I started working out at home in Bloomington, Minnesota. I wasn't taking any chances. I was getting up at 6 a.m. and working out at 7 a.m. for an hour or so. Then I'd go to work. It wasn't easy, but you have to have enough pro stuff in you to push yourself.

"You have to push yourself to stay in shape," the wise veteran continued. "You can't have someone watching you all the time. You've got to punish yourself. I have a routine and try to do it every day. That way it doesn't get any harder as I get older."[40]

Slice of Good Fortune

On March 15, just ten days after reporting to camp, Jim made his Grapefruit League debut, pitching two perfect innings as part of a combined shutout over the Atlanta Braves. Jim was still yet to allow his first baserunner through five spring innings, in fact, when his fortunes suddenly took a turn. On March 24, only two weeks before Opening Day, a freak accident drastically altered the dynamics of manager Billy Martin's plan for his new team.

Dave Boswell, slated to be the number three starter after Dean Chance and Jim Kaat, was cleaning fish when the knife slipped and he cut his left hand. Though it was his non-pitching hand and the slice required just eight stitches, Boswell had severed two tendons in the little finger. Team physician Harvey O'Phelan determined Boswell would not regain use of the finger until surgery could be performed following the conclusion of the baseball season. While Boswell could still throw fine, O'Phelan and Martin agreed it was best to keep the injured pitcher out of action until the wound healed up enough to effectively catch a baseball with his remaining healthy digits.

Four days later, Martin stated that he was considering nixing the plan to use Jim as a short reliever. The new skipper explained that he valued the consistent stamina Perry could provide as Boswell's replacement over more intermittent short relief stints. Early the next morning, the dutiful, hard-working hurler hopped on the bus for the

60-mile trip up to Daytona Beach with the Twins B team, determined to take advantage of this sudden opportunity. Despite the fact he had been working only brief 1-2 inning stints in preparation for the closer role, Jim pitched a remarkable seven innings against the Dodgers. Just say the word, and Jim Perry is ready to go!

As the 1969 season approached, Martin envisioned a four-man rotation consisting of righthanders Dean Chance and Jim Perry, along with southpaws Jim Kaat and Tom Hall. Once Boswell's hand was fully healed and he was back up to speed, Boswell would replace Perry, who would return to the bullpen.

With opportunity beckoning, however, Jim was getting the itch. "Even though I'm willing to do anything necessary to help the club, I'd much rather be a starter," Perry admitted just before Opening Day. "I feel if I could start right from the beginning of the season I'd have a chance to win 15 or 20 games."[41] It was a prescient statement.

The new Minnesota skipper must have been having thoughts along those lines, as well. When Boswell impressed pitching coach Early Wynn with seven strong innings in a minor league spring training game just before the big league club broke camp, the Twins decided against putting him on the 21-day disabled list. Despite the fact Martin now had his original four starters ready for the start of the season, he had been so impressed with Jim's work and the way he went about his business that he quietly elected to begin the season with five starters.

The manager wasn't the only one impressed with Jim Perry in the spring of '69. Minnesota team president Calvin Griffith was also becoming a big fan. Jim's final spring tune-up came in New Orleans two days before the opener. When he struck out seven New York Mets in just three and two-thirds innings, Griffith was wowed. "I thought Perry had great stuff," the boss enthusiastically exclaimed.[42]

A Bigger Chance?

Jim's opportunity seemed to grow even larger with news concerning another Minnesota starter. Righthander Dean Chance, originally projected to be the Opening Day starter, reported late to camp, as did many players, due to the holdout. Chance's arrival was even later than most, however, as he was upset about receiving a $5,000 pay cut from the prior season. When he finally did report, Chance tried to get in shape quickly, which proved a costly tactic. With only two spring starts under his belt and the season just five days away, Sid Hartman of the *Minneapolis Tribune* reported, "Dean Chance, slated to be the opening day pitcher in Kansas City, has a slightly pulled groin muscle, but he still will go as far as he can today against the Washington Senators in the final exhibition game in Orlando."[43]

That start did not go well. Chance was pounded for seven runs on eight hits as he labored through seven long innings. Among the hits was a mammoth 450-foot home run by Washington Senators slugger Frank Howard. After the game, Twins catcher John Roseboro was asked about the presumptive Opening Day starter. "Chance is not by any means throwing as hard as he did a year ago during the season," his batterymate remarked.[44] The performance was enough to convince Martin to instead go with 150-pound Tom Hall for the opener. Nicknamed "The Blade" because the six-foot lefty was so skinny, Martin said he was going with Hall on Opening Day "because he is in the best condition of our starting pitchers."[45] (Obviously the supremely conditioned Perry was still not considered anything more than a temporary "starting" pitcher.)

After the Twins lost their first two games in Kansas City, Chance was scheduled to start game three in California against the Angels. The morning of that game, however, word came out that Chance had developed a "dead arm" trying to get ready too fast. Jim was tabbed for the start in his place, but unfortunately, he was tagged for a pair of home runs and was lifted in the fourth inning of a 5-3 loss.

With Dave Boswell's glove hand now deemed healed enough to catch, he started the next day and Dean Chance was surprisingly inserted back in the rotation the next time his turn came around. Between numerous early season off days built into the schedule accounting for potential rain, which had not been a problem early in the '69 season, and return to health of the original four starters, Jim suddenly found himself back in the bullpen, but it was not in the closer role he had hoped for prior to the season.

Veteran lefthander Ron Perranoski, who had come over from the Los Angeles Dodgers prior to the 1968 season, got off to a great start in '69, quickly earning the manager's trust at the back end of close games. Perranoski did not allow a run while racking up three wins and two saves, as he appeared in nine of the Twins first 14 games.

The combination of Perranoski's success plus Jim being sufficiently stretched out left Martin turning to Perry for longer middle relief work during the two week stretch following his rough first start. Never one to let circumstances get him down, however, Jim turned his workmanlike attitude to the job at hand. He hurled 11 highly effective innings over five mid-April outings, including four games in a row. He struck out 13 and limited opposing hitters to a .143 batting average while posting a sparkling 1.64 ERA.

Opportunity Knocks

With the first game of a quick two-game set against the Kansas City Royals set for an early 1:30 p.m. start on Monday, April 28, Tom Hall was scheduled to start. Unfortunately, a weekend military commitment with the Marines in Charlotte, NC delayed his return to Minnesota until just minutes before the scheduled start of the early afternoon game. As Billy Martin sat in his office less than two hours before gametime filling out his lineup card with Hall yet to arrive, the manager scrambled to pick a replacement. He later explained the method for his choice. "The selection process was really quite simple. Perry was the only possibility."[46]

As Twins beat writer Dave Mona explained, the choice of Perry on short notice reeked more of desperation than any sound strategy. "The odds were against Perry's doing very well. He had a cold picked up over the weekend in Chicago. He had two days rest, but had worked in four straight games before that."[47]

Of course, Jim had a way of making his manager look smart and he did not let Martin down. "Armed with those two tailor-made excuses for a bad performance," Mona continued, "the 32-year old righthander used only 103 pitches in his seven-hit, 4-0 victory over the Royals. The victory was Perry's 19th major league shutout.

"Perry's performance was typical of what he has done every year since joining the Twins in 1963 in a trade for Jack Kralick," Mona attested. "In his years with the Twins he has a 55-39 record compiled both as a starter and reliever.

"He is in the unique position of being able to perform equally well at either job, something that has kept him out of the starting rotation more than in it."[48]

While Martin gushed about Jim's performance after the game, the skipper kept his options open as to how he would deploy his versatile weapon going forward. "I've always had confidence in Jim," the manager explained. "He pitched one helluva game today but his position is still up in the air."[49]

Another interesting note about this game was the perspective shared by the manager sitting in the opposing dugout. Royals manager Joe Gordon had previously been at the helm of the Cleveland Indians ten years earlier when he brought in a young righthander for his major league debut. This gave Gordon a unique view to compare and contrast the two versions.

"Perry was a little quicker then but not much," Gordon recalled. "Then he just had a fast ball that was the sneaky type and came out of his uniform in some way to make the ball hard to pick up. Now he is a matured pitcher with a slider, a sinker and a good curveball. Jim looked like the pitcher who won 12 games for me in 1959 and in 1960 when he had a 18-10 record for me. He looked stronger at the finish than he did at the start.

"I remember the first time he pitched a major league game was in Yankee Stadium," Jim's former skipper continued, "when we relieved with him with the bases loaded and Mickey Mantle, Yogi Berra and Moose Skowron—the heart of the Yankee batting order—coming up. He struck out two and forced the third to pop up for the final out. The following year Perry was one of the best pitchers in the American League."[50]

Five days later, with Kaat (nursing a sore groin) and Chance (building up stamina) both skipped in the rotation, Martin called on Perry once again to face the White Sox. After scattering three harmless singles over the first five innings, Jim ran into trouble in the sixth. Perranoski continued his strong relief work, holding Chicago to only one hit over the final four innings, preserving Jim's second straight win. Despite his success, upcoming off days plus the return of both Kaat and Chance to the rotation bounced Perry back to the bullpen yet again. That assignment lasted all of three weeks until Chance once again encountered problems.

Seize the Chance

After a rough outing on May 17 against Detroit in which he lasted only three innings while being pummeled for eight hits and four runs, Dean Chance was pulled from the rotation a second time. Martin announced that, rather than pitching in games, Chance would throw daily batting practice for the next week in an effort to get his arm in condition. Rather than excessive rest, the cure for many arm issues back then was to throw your way into shape.

"We're pretending this is the start of spring training for Chance," his manager explained. "He's no good to us the way he is so we're going to give him the time off to get in shape."[51]

Who would Martin tap to fill the void? Dependable Perry, of course. This time, Jim was ready to seize the opportunity and show the boss that he could not afford to limit Perry to relief work.

On May 22 in Baltimore, Jim had a shutout going until Frank Robinson took him deep to begin the sixth inning. When Mark Belanger doubled to lead off the seventh, Martin called on Perranoski to protect a slim 2-1 advantage. It was the fifth consecutive game the manager had gone to his sizzling bullpen ace. Now running on fumes, however, the lefty finally hit the wall. Not only did he allow Belanger to score, but Perranoski proceeded to cough up four runs of his own, as Minnesota fell by a score of 6-2. It was the 21st time in the team's first 35 games that the overworked Perranoski had been called upon.

With the realization that he could not afford to keep working Perranoski so hard, Martin pleaded for reinforcements. Two days later, the team announced 40-year old Al Worthington, who had led the American League in saves the previous year, was coming out of retirement. "We need a right-handed relief pitcher," Calvin Griffith explained, "and rather than give up a number of our young players in exchange for somebody who might not do the job, I decided to take Martin's suggestion and we are going to re-activate Worthington."[52]

For Jim, this was a welcome development in several regards. Not only did another key righthander in the bullpen reduce Martin's need for Perry in that spot, but Worthington had been one of Jim's closest friends on the team and regular road roommate prior to his retirement. "I can remember the two of us turning in at night on the road and saying a prayer together," Jim recalled. "We would give thanks and say, 'Ain't it good the good Lord is looking after us.'"

After the first game following his return to the team, Worthington slipped into his regular seat on the bus next to Jim and seamlessly joined the post-game conversation. "You know," Worthington mused aloud, "it doesn't feel like I've ever been away."[53]

With Chance still deemed not ready for starting work and bullpen reinforcements on the way, Jim could smell blood in the water. On top of that, Tom Hall had an impending two-week military service commitment in mid-June. Jim could see this was his chance to tighten his grip on a rotation spot. On May 26 in Washington, D.C., Minnesota rolled to a 7-1 win over the Senators, as Rod Carew knocked a pair of home runs and Jim hurled a complete game. He gave up nine hits, but did not walk a batter. The only hit that did any damage was a solo home run by Frank Howard after the Twins were comfortably ahead by seven runs. There was certainly no shame in giving up a solo home run to the gargantuan Howard, whose 48 long balls would rank second in the league that season.

Perry's record now stood at 4-1, while his ERA had been whittled down to 2.70. Even more significant was the fact that over his four most recent starts since his rough first outing back on April 11, Jim had allowed only four runs in 29 innings for a microscopic 1.24 ERA. Most importantly, the victory pushed the now first place Twins out to a two game lead over second place Oakland in the newly created American League West Division.

The next three starts were tough ones for Jim, as he was unable to make it through the sixth inning in any of them, suffering a pair of defeats in the process. On June 16 against California, however, he had everything working. Not only did he hurl another complete game with a season high nine strikeouts in an 8-2 Minnesota romp, but Jim led the offensive attack, as well.

In the second inning, batting left-handed, Jim poked a single into left field. Unfortunately, he was nabbed off first base for a double play when pitcher Tom Murphy snared a line drive off the bat of the next hitter, leadoff man Ted Uhlaender. The next time up in the fourth inning, Jim pulled a single into right field, but he was left stranded at first base. His handiwork with the bat finally inflicted some damage when he came up with nobody out and the bases loaded in the sixth and got the job done with a sacrifice fly to center field, scoring Cesar Tovar. Jim put the capper on a great night at the plate when he came up in the bottom of the eighth and socked a double to left off reliever Pedro Borbon. It was a great night all around for the solid-hitting pitcher, who had been taking a little ribbing about having only one hit in his prior 17 at bats going into the game.

Of course, Perry's pitching and another win for the Twins, who edged back into first place by a half-game, were the most important aspects of the night. "I was glad to get over the hump after three failures to win my fifth game," the slender right-hander told reporters after the game. "The big thing was that I stayed ahead of the hitters and kept the ball down. I hope Billy keeps on starting me."[54]

Squeeze Out a Win

Billy did keep on starting him, but that doesn't mean the manager wouldn't hesitate to deploy his versatile weapon as necessary to win a game. Five days after going the distance, Jim worked into the sixth inning in his next start on June 21 at division-rival Oakland. He came out after he clipped Oakland catcher Larry Haney in the jaw with a pitch, loading the bases with one out and a tight 3-2 lead. Ron Perranoski came on and escaped the jam, but the A's managed to tie it up in the bottom of the eighth on a Danny Cater home run. When neither team scored in the ninth, Minnesota was faced with a second straight night of extra innings. They had just played into the wee hours of the morning in a 14-inning marathon the night before. Thankfully, and amazingly, the offense erupted with an 11-run explosion in the top of the tenth inning, as the Twins pulled out a 14-4 win.

The quick extra-inning ending was especially helpful to the Twins in light of a Sunday afternoon double-header scheduled between the two teams the following day. Minnesota dropped game one of the double dip by a score of 7-3, running through four pitchers in the process. Starter Jim Kaat was pounded for back-to-back-to-back home runs in the third inning by Ted Kubiak, Reggie Jackson, and Sal Bando. He was knocked out the next inning after loading the bases with nobody out. This taxed the bullpen before the second game even began.

In the nightcap, Rod Carew put the Twins on top early with an RBI single in the top of the first. Oakland evened the score at one in the second and then pulled in front in the fourth, with a pair of one-run singles of their own. When Rick Monday followed Danny Cater's RBI hit with another base knock to put two on with only one out against Minnesota starter Bob Miller, manager Billy Martin was compelled to turn to his depleted bullpen once again in an effort to avoid dropping three of four to the team they were battling for the division lead.

Three relievers later, including three and a third shutout innings by bullpen stopper Ron Perranoski, the game was tied at three and in the midst of extra innings for the third time in the three-day, four-game series. With the critical game against the division-leading A's up for grabs and his bullpen completely depleted, Martin had no choice but to turn to his ace in the hole, the versatile (*dependable*) weapon the rookie manager was quickly learning he could always count on.

Despite having thrown close to 90 pitches the day before, Dependable Perry was called on to keep the A's at bay until the Twins could find a way to score. Jim had worked through two scoreless innings, allowing only a harmless single, when Minnesota finally generated a rally. Tony Oliva led off the top of the 13th inning with a sharp double up the left-center field gap. Graig Nettles then pulled a grounder to first, moving Oliva to third with the go-ahead run. With Jim on deck, Oakland manager Hank Bauer elected to intentionally walk Charlie Manuel in hopes of setting up a double play.

The strategy was to force Perry out of the game by inducing Martin to send up a pinch-hitter. With no one else to turn to on the mound, however, plus his confidence in Jim's quite capable plate skills, the Twins manager sent his multifaceted weapon up to bat. Martin's confidence was rewarded when Jim executed a perfect suicide squeeze bunt that left pitcher Rollie Fingers no chance to get Oliva as he scampered across home plate with the go-ahead run. Now running on fumes and having done his job both on the mound and at the plate, Martin let Jim rest, amazingly turning back to game one starter Jim Kaat for the final three outs to secure the win.

After the game, the Twins skipper relished the perfect execution of the game-winning play by Tony Oliva and his expert bat-wielding pitcher. "Oliva waited for just the right moment to break for home—when the pitcher was at the top of his motion—and Perry did the rest, Martin explained.[55]

In addition to highlighting Jim's great versatility, the curious usage of both Perry and Kaat to win a critical game demonstrates the remarkable ways the game has changed over the last fifty years. Pitchers were much more durable and the willingness to do virtually anything to help the team certainly made for a different atmosphere. In fact, it was no surprise (in that era) that Jim took his regular turn in the rotation just three days later, working into the seventh inning in a game the Twins would pull out 3-2 with a late run.

Fooling the Experts

As June came to an end, Jim had one of his rougher outings, getting tagged for eight hits and four runs in just three and a third innings in a 7-2 loss at Kansas City. With his record now at 6-4, columnist Paul Foss of the *Minneapolis Tribune* had a curious take on the Twins starting pitching situation.

"Reliable Jim Perry, of course, has done a big job. He'll win nine games, a big help. But somewhere, Calvin Griffith has to come up with a couple of starting pitchers to aid Jim Kaat and Dave Boswell…"[56] As Jim had been a winner of eight-games each of the prior two seasons, Foss was assuming that his six-wins over the season's first half might get him to one win higher by the end of the year. Jim Perry, however, had other plans.

Another rough start for Perry in Chicago on July 1 caused some to wonder if his time in the rotation was running short, just as it had in seasons past. Four days later, however, he got the ball again for a nationally televised home game against the division rival Oakland A's. In the top of the first inning, Jim was tagged for a long home run by Reggie Jackson, but he proceeded to limit Oakland hitters to just four harmless singles the rest of the way. Twins bats pounded out 16 hits in support en route to a 13-1 drubbing. After the complete game effort, Perry credited his catcher for a key adjustment to his approach.

"John Roseboro pointed out that I had been starting my sinker out too low," Jim explained, "and most guys were taking it for a ball.

I moved it up and they were hitting a lot of ground balls off me. I was letting the fielders do my work."[57] The change helped Jim generate 11 ground ball outs, including a 6-4-3 double play off the bat of Phil Roof to close out the win.

In classic Perry fashion, he shared his appreciation of his manager's confidence despite back-to-back un-Perry-like outings. "I'm grateful for Martin sticking with me and giving me the chance to pitch today after two bad games."[58]

As for the prodigious first inning blast by Jackson, it was considered by many to be the longest home run hit in the history of Metropolitan Stadium up to that time. Aided by a 14 mile per hour wind blowing out, the towering fly hit a beer sign 55 feet above the ground on the right field scoreboard positioned 442 feet from home plate. Estimates speculated the ball would have traveled some 515 feet had the scoreboard not been located there, with some surmising it might have been the first fair ball to carry all the way out of the Met. Twins manager Billy Martin, longtime teammate of renowned slugger Mickey Mantle and thus no stranger to colossal clouts, called it "one of the three longest I've ever seen."[59]

Not only did Perry not let the monstrous first inning shot get him off his game, but he provided an insightful look at how he handled giving up such a notable home run. "The pitch to Jackson was a mistake," he explained. "It was a fast ball away from him. One nice thing was that it counted only one run and it will just be listed as a home run with a number after it in the record books. It doesn't really matter how far they go." The wise perspective revealed how Jim Perry maintained such an even keel throughout a career filled with many ups and downs. In this case, it enabled him to quickly move past the moment and focus on getting the next 25 outs needed to polish off another fine victory.

Resilient Team Player

As the summer of '69 wore on, the arms of the Minnesota rotation were buckling, forcing manager Billy Martin into a daily juggling act. Dean Chance had been out with a sore shoulder since the end of May, Opening Day starter Tom Hall missed time due to his mid-summer military commitment, and Jim Kaat was slumping with a 5.34 ERA over his last six outings. The one reliable constant from the season-opening foursome was Jim Perry. On July 9 Jim worked into the sixth inning in a 4-3 loss versus Kansas City. After the game Martin announced that Kaat would receive an extra two days of rest "because of all the warm weather pitching he has done lately."[60]

With the minor leagues offering no viable reinforcements, who would Martin turn to in this pinch? His most reliable weapon, of course, who it should be noted had similarly been pitching in the same "warm weather." Working on just two days rest and making his fifth start in 14 days, Jim Perry took the mound for a Saturday afternoon game at the Met in 90-degree sunshine. Once again, the slender righthander put the team on his back, hurling a staff-saving five-hit complete game, as Minnesota rolled over the Seattle Pilots by an 11-1 score.

While he only tallied three strikeouts, Jim was able to effectively maintain his recent adjustment, inducing a dozen ground outs, two of which were converted into inning-ending double plays. Game reports confirmed that "he kept most pitches low and made his infielders do most of his work."[61] Jim was even in the middle of the offensive outburst, plating a pair during a five-run fifth inning rally when he knocked a bases-loaded single up the middle. Not only was it a big win for the team, but it also marked the beginning of a tremendous run for Jim Perry.

Man on the Moon

While Jim was considered an excellent hitter among major league pitchers, his younger brother Gaylord was viewed closer to the other end of the spectrum, especially in his early years. Of 60 hits over his first seven big league seasons, 56 of them were singles, and Gaylord showed little signs of power. "He just didn't have the snap of the bat to where (a batted ball) would jump out of the ballpark," explained teammate Bobby Bolin.[62]

During Gaylord's rookie season in 1962, "we were just sitting around the (batting) cage," said Bolin. "It was pitcher's batting practice, and Gaylord was trying to hit one out. Somebody was talking about hitting home runs..."[63]

At that point, Harry Jupiter, a Giants beat writer in his first year covering the team for the *San Francisco Chronicle*, joined in with a comment to Giants manager Alvin Dark. "I said to Dark, that guy looks like a pretty good hitter," said Jupiter. "And Dark says, 'Harry, there will be a man on the moon before (Gaylord Perry) ever hits one out of the park.'"[64] He would prove to be quite prophetic.

Fast forward to 1969 as the Twins completed a four-game series sweep of the Chicago White Sox with an 8-5 win on the night of Thursday, July 17. The sweep capped off a fantastic two-week homestand that saw Minnesota win 14 out of 15 games. As they packed their bags for a weekend series in Seattle, however, things were about to get bumpy.

To begin with, the flight crew for the plane that would take the team to Seattle was late arriving from Chicago. This left the team's flight delayed 90 minutes on the ground. Despite enjoying the long homestand, the team had still crammed 15 games into 14 days, including a doubleheader the day before, in which Jim had picked up his ninth win, falling just one out short of a complete game.

When the team finally got airborne for the three-plus hour flight to the West Coast, it was already after midnight. By the time they landed, bused to the hotel, and got checked into their rooms, it was 3 a.m.—Seattle time. That is 5 a.m. (Minneapolis time) as far as their internal body clocks were concerned. Unlike today, where such travel would almost surely be met with an off day to get adjusted, Minnesota had to gear up for not one game, but a Friday twi-night doubleheader beginning at 5 p.m.

Not surprisingly, the Twins appeared sluggish as they dropped both ends of the doubleheader, each by a heartbreaking single run. Losing the weekend series to the expansion Pilots would be a devastating blow for the first-place Twins, increasing the importance of the final two games.

Minnesota came out swinging on Saturday night, as leadoff man Ted Uhlaender drove in five of their first six runs, giving the Twins a 6-0 lead in the sixth inning. With the game seemingly in hand, manager Billy Martin gave Jim, who was scheduled to start the following day's matinee, permission to leave and get a good night's sleep. With his Saturday evening suddenly free, Jim took advantage of the opportunity to enjoy dinner with wife Daphne, who had accompanied him on the trip, at the restaurant atop the Space Needle.

Before Jim and Daphne could begin enjoying their entrees, however, the Pilots were already fighting back. Jim was pacing the floor of the rotating restaurant with his ear to his transistor radio as Ron Perranoski struggled to squelch a three-run ninth inning rally that sent the game into extra innings. Perranoski and Seattle's Gene Brabender traded zeroes over the next four innings as the game approached midnight.

With Perranoski on fumes after four and two thirds innings of relief work, Martin turned to Jim Kaat to begin the 14th inning. Kaat had been the starting and winning pitcher just two days earlier, working 5⅔ innings in the final game of Minnesota's homestand. He was the only available arm remaining at the ballpark. Back in their hotel room, Jim remarked to Daphne, "Billy might need me to come back to the park before this is all over."

The Twins finally scratched a run across in the top of the 15th inning, and it looked as if they might pull it out, but the Pilots' Jim Pagliaroni drilled a home run into the left field bleachers off of Kaat to tie it back up and keep the game going. Both teams came up empty in the 16th and play was finally halted at 1:05 a.m. due an American League curfew rule that no new inning could begin after 1 a.m. As the game story in the *Minneapolis Tribune* pointed out, the morning sun appeared over the horizon back home just two hours and 41 minutes after play was mercifully stopped in Seattle.

With the suspended game due to resume prior to Sunday's regularly scheduled game and lacking any other viable options on their depleted staffs, both managers elected to use Sunday's scheduled starters to begin the completion of Saturday night's suspended game. "When I got to the ballpark, Billy told me 'you'll start this suspended game, give us two good innings and we'll win it. Then, you will start the regularly scheduled game and go as far as you can.'"

Jim retired the Pilots 1-2-3 in the bottom of the seventeenth, then took matters into his own hands. Jim lashed a one-out double off the right field wall to open the top of the 18th inning. Ted Uhlaender beat out an infield single and Rod Carew worked a walk to load the bases. When opposing pitcher John Gelnar balked, Jim trotted home with the go-ahead run. The Twins would tack on three more before Perry methodically retired the side in order a second time to seal the 18-inning win. Including the extended action from the prior night, the game checked in as the longest in team history at an official playing time of five hours and 41 minutes.

After a brief break, the two teams began preparation for the regularly scheduled game. At 1:17 p.m. Pacific Daylight time on Sunday, July 20, 1969, Apollo 11 touched down on the moon. Although the landing was televised nationally, Jim was unable to watch, as he was in the bullpen getting loosened back up for the next game. "I'll see it tonight on the news," he wisely observed. "I can't help (the astronauts). I've got to get my stuff together for the next game out there."[65]

Moon Shot

At the same time some 800 miles down the coast in San Francisco, Jim's brother Gaylord was getting roughed up by the Dodgers, who were in the process of batting around in the top of the first inning. With the bases loaded and three runs already in for Los Angeles, the Candlestick Park public address announcer interrupted the action to ask the crowd for a moment of silence for the Apollo 11 astronauts who had just landed safely on the moon. When play resumed, Gaylord suddenly righted the ship, retiring the next two batters to escape any further damage.

Gaylord retired six of the next seven batters he faced, maintaining the 3-0 deficit when he came up to bat with two outs in the bottom of the third inning. Dodgers starter Claude Osteen delivered a high fastball and Gaylord made solid contact, sending the ball soaring through a biting wind out toward center field. Sure enough, in his 485th major league at bat, just as former manager Alvin Dark had unwittingly predicted, precisely 34 minutes after man had finally landed on the moon, Gaylord Perry hit his first major league home run.

He would go on to pitch six more fantastic innings, allowing only a harmless single the rest of the way as the Giants came back to win 7-3, giving Gaylord his 12th win of the season. Incidentally, Gaylord would proceed to hit five more home runs in his 22-year career, including one in each of the three subsequent seasons.

Meanwhile, back up in Seattle, Jim picked up right where he left off in winning the suspended game, as he continued to follow his special recipe of throwing strikes and getting ground balls. While the offense managed only one run through the first seven innings, Perry kept the Pilots at bay, scattering eight harmless singles and one double. He issued no walks and only allowed one runner as far as third base on the way to a masterful nine-hit shutout. Jim even helped the offense as he singled and scored one of three big eighth inning insurance runs.

Seattle manager Joe Schultz spoke with admiration of Perry's dominant performance. "The way Jim Perry was pitching," bemoaned the exasperated Schultz, "we wouldn't have scored a run if the makeup game and the regulation game went 50 innings."[66]

When the day finally ended, not only had man landed on the moon and Gaylord socked his first big league homer, but Jim had pitched a remarkable 11 shutout innings and won two games in less than three hours while saving the exhausted Twins pitching staff. He also contributed two of the team's nine hits on the day and scored two of the team's eight runs, including a game-winner. July 20, 1969, the day man first landed on the moon, was a great day for America and a great day for the Perry brothers.

A Star is Born

The three-day MLB all-star break followed "Moon Day" and it was a welcome respite for the worn out Twins. They began the second half in Cleveland where Dave Boswell got knocked out in the fourth inning of a 6-5 loss. For the next game, Martin turned to Dependable Perry in hopes of re-starting the team's winning momentum.

As he had been making a regular habit, Jim served up a healthy dose of strikes and induced a plethora of ground balls. He had scattered only four meaningless singles and issued one walk when he was relieved by Al Worthington in the seventh inning with the Twins nursing a 2-0 lead. Worthington struck out Chuck Hinton to end the seventh inning, but he later surrendered a game-tying home run to Duke Sims in the bottom of the ninth, costing Jim his 12th win of the season.

Minnesota would eventually pull it out thanks to a two-run double by Rod Carew in the 16th inning. Ron Perranoski had his most impressive outing since suffering a pulled hamstring back in early June. He worked the final 5⅔ innings, allowing only one single and no walks while striking out six and keeping Cleveland at bay until the Twins could score.

Before the Twins next game, Sid Hartman, prominent *Minneapolis Tribune* sports columnist, sat down with Jim to discuss the keys to a scoreless pitching streak that had now reached 17⅔ innings.

"I've started seven or eight times in a row—more than ever since I joined the Twins in 1963," Jim explained. "Billy Martin has been quoted as saying that my one problem is I don't challenge hitters at times. He wants me to throw as hard as I can for as long as I can and then get relief if I need it. I admit that when I get a lead, I try to change speeds and do some things to try to hold something in reserve. But of late I've challenged the hitters. Sometimes it may not look that way to the bench."[67]

Jim also revealed his remarkable ability to remain focused on the present even as he mentioned the existence of a personal season-long goal. "I'd like to win twenty games," Jim explained. "But right now all I'm going to do is get ready physically and mentally for one game at a time."[68]

After splitting the four-game series in Cleveland, the Twins returned home for a series with Detroit, who was second in the American League East division. The four-game set would begin with a Tuesday night doubleheader against the dynamic Tigers duo of Mickey Lolich and Denny McLain. The pair had led Detroit to a World Series championship the previous year and currently held a combined 1969 record of 29 wins and only 7 losses. Jim got the ball in game one, going up against the left-handed Lolich, who was 14-2.

While the Twins offense was putting up three runs in the third and two more in the fifth inning, Jim was busy working on extending his scoreless streak. He was filling up the strike zone once again, not walking a single batter while limiting Detroit to four harmless singles and a double through eight scoreless innings. In the ninth inning, pitching with a 5-0 lead, Jim's outstanding run of 25⅔ consecutive innings without allowing a run finally came to an end.

Three consecutive singles to open the ninth inning ended the streak, as a potential double-play grounder off the bat of Jim Price eluded the glove of Twins shortstop Leo Cardenas, rolling into center field and allowing Willie Horton to score. Billy Martin promptly called on Al Worthington to wrap up the win. Although Jim was charged with a second run that scored on a groundout, he still captured his sixth consecutive victory to push his record to 12-4.

In the following morning's *Minneapolis Tribune*, Sid Hartman was once again extolling the underappreciated virtues of Jim's contributions since coming to Minnesota. "Now Perry has developed into the star of the crippled Twins pitching staff," the columnist wrote.[69]

In the same column Jim shared how he was able to stay ready even as the players held out at the beginning of spring camp. "It helped me to run every morning at 7 a.m. for two weeks before I went to spring training. When I reported I was in shape even though we started two weeks late because of the player pension disagreement."[70]

Jim also credited his manager. "Then too, manager Billy Martin stayed with me even after a couple of bad outings. My sinker ball is improved and it helped me against Detroit. I got a little tired in the ninth but the big thing is we won."[71]

Jim only worked into the fourth inning in his next start, but did not factor into the decision, as the Twins lost to Baltimore by a score of 6-5. The short outing did nothing to dampen Martin's confidence in his new ace as the team prepared for what was billed as its "longest, hardest and most important road trip of the 1969 season."[72] The trip would encompass 15 games in 17 days against tough A.L. East division opponents and Martin stated that he had "hopes of going with a basic four-man pitching rotation of Dave Boswell, Jim Perry, Jim Kaat and Dean Chance."[73]

Not Easy Looking Easy

After splitting the first two games of the trip in Detroit, Jim took the mound for game three, once again going up against Mickey Lolich. A run in the first and another in the second off the Tigers lefty would be all Jim would need, as he hurled a complete game three-hitter. Jim retired the last 11 batters of the game, cruising to his

13th win of the year, while sticking the All-Star Lolich with the loss for the second time in just over a week.

Sportswriter Dick Cullum described the easy manner in which Jim methodically controlled the game. "His pitching was so effortlessly effective that his mates did not need to make a single difficult play. Everything was strictly routine."[74]

When told that he made his smooth outing seem easy, Jim shared some insightful wisdom that is just as true in virtually every area of life as it is on the pitcher's mound. "It is never easy to make it look easy."[75]

On August 10, Jim made his next start in Baltimore against the Orioles. It was a matchup of the American League's two first-place teams with the newly created division format. While Minnesota was leading Oakland by a game-and-a-half in a tight American League West division race, Baltimore was in first by 14½ games in the East. Perry was on his game once again, limiting Baltimore to just four hits over seven innings. Unfortunately two of the hits landed over the outfield fence. Boog Powell hit an opposite-field home run in the fourth inning and Elrod Hendricks added another long ball in the seventh.

> It is never easy to make it look easy.
>
> — Jim Perry

The pair of solo homers were all that was needed for Orioles red-hot lefty Mike Cuellar, who narrowly got the better of the Twins in a classic pitcher's duel. In the midst of a personal seven-game winning streak, Cuellar fired a one-hit shutout. The Twins were three outs away from being no-hit when Cesar Tovar lined a single into left field to open the ninth inning. The next three hitters were quickly retired in order, however, and Jim was stuck with his fifth loss, despite lowering his ERA by two more points to a sparkling 2.87.

Five days later, the Twins were in Washington D.C., where Jim was not able to make it look as easy as he had recently, but still managed to achieve the same result by battling through seven shutout innings. He retired the Senators in order in the first inning, but had runners on base every inning after that. Jim again found success, however, by keeping the ball on the ground. He held the Senators at bay throughout the night, scattering six singles and a double, to go with two walks. Closer Ron Perranoski finished up for his 22nd save, as Jim earned win number 14.

No Alibi

With the rest of the Minnesota starting rotation ailing in both health and effectiveness, *Minnesota Tribune* columnist Paul Foss pointed out Jim's starring role in quietly holding the staff of the first-place Twins together. He also provided cogent insight into the nature of Jim Perry that made him such a success.

"It's a miracle that the Twins are in the West Division where the Oakland Athletics are their only competition for the playoff spot," wrote Foss. "Talk about a team fighting for a title with limited pitching—the Twins haven't got a pitching staff.

"Excuse me, we do have Jim Perry . . . Jim goes his way, pitching good ball, not alibiing, not beefing, not fighting, not worrying about injuries. When the Twins get him a few runs he wins. He's a real pro—one of the greatest highlights of the 1969 season."[76]

> *Jim goes his way, pitching good ball, not alibiing, not beefing, not fighting, not worrying about injuries. He's a real pro.*
>
> — Paul Foss
> SPORTS COLUMNIST

As the Twins wrapped up their roadtrip in Boston, Jim was not as sharp as he had been recently. He walked three batters for the first time in a month-and-a-half, but the biggest blow was a grand slam off the bat of Sox slugger Carl Yastrzemski. The left-handed hitter got just enough of a high fastball on the outer part of the plate to poke it over the green monster in left field. Thankfully, Harmon Killebrew answered back with a game-winning ninth inning home run to give the Twins a win that salvaged a 6-9 road trip. The team had left home in first place by 3½ games and returned still up by a game-and-a-half over Oakland, despite the losing record on the grueling eastern swing.

Upon their return to the friendly confines of Metropolitan Stadium, Minnesota faced a weekend series with the Yankees. After a 6-0 win on Friday night, Jim faced off with New York's ace 16-game winner Mel Stottlemyre. Surprisingly, the presumed pitcher's duel never materialized, as the Twins jumped on Stottlemyre for six hits, including three doubles and a Killebrew home run to deliver a first-inning knockout punch. The early cushion enabled Jim to do what he does best—throw strikes and generate a plethora of routine outs.

He did receive a visit from manager Billy Martin when he

issued a one-out fourth inning walk to Yankees five-hole hitter Bobby Murcer with an 8-0 lead. Martin explained that it was just a routine maintenance visit to remind Jim of a sometimes troublesome tendency.

"I just told him to throw the ball over the plate," Martin explained. "Jim has a habit of working too fast when he gets into trouble and I wanted to slow him down just a little."[77]

His only difficulty of the night came in the sixth inning with the Twins leading by eight when New York strung together four consecutive hits. The biggest of the hits was a fluke. Center fielder Ted Uhlaender slipped and fell charging a low liner, which allowed the ball to roll all the way to the wall for a two-run triple. Perry quickly recovered and cruised the rest of the way. He retired ten of the last eleven batters to finish off a complete game 8-3 win and notch his team-leading 15th victory of the season.

Talk of Twenty

Suddenly sporting a 9-1 record in his last 14 outings over the previous six weeks, talk in the clubhouse after the game centered around Jim's chances of becoming only the sixth pitcher in Twins history to be a 20-game winner. Ever humble and in-the-moment, Jim did not give in to the talk. "Right now I'm just concentrating on number 16," he told the reporters surrounding his locker.[78]

Manager Billy Martin, saying he was "very pleased" with Perry's efforts, assured reporters that his new ace could count on "working every four days" the rest of the way.[79] It was the first time Jim had enjoyed such confidence from a Minnesota manager.

Sports columnist Sid Hartman shared some background on Jim's 1969 success: "Perry figures that the sinker or screw ball he has developed the past two years has made him a lot more effective against left-handed hitters. The Twins pitcher feels he is a much smarter pitcher and has more pitches than he had in 1960 when he won his career high of 18 games for the Cleveland Indians."[80]

"My arm is as strong as it ever was," Jim explained, "because I always take care of myself. But the big edge I have now is that I know the hitters so much better."[81]

Minnesota would complete a weekend sweep of the Yankees the

following day when George Mitterwald singled with the bases loaded in the bottom of the ninth. They then welcomed the Washington Senators to town. As promised, four days after his previous start, Martin gave Jim the ball and for good reason, of course. His ace righthander was on a roll, and on this August 27 night, it was the same recipe for success. The Twins jumped on top early and Jim took it from there.

The Twins greeted Senators starter Joe Coleman with three hits, a pair of walks, and a hit-by-pitch to put a four spot on the board in the first inning. That was more than enough for Perry, who cruised to his ninth complete game and win number 16. Once again, Jim finished strong, retiring the final eleven batters of the 4-2 four-hitter. "It's always easier to work with a lead like that," he admitted after the game. "But I felt really strong tonight. It was as good as I've felt all year. The combination of feeling good, having that support and pitching in almost perfect weather (83 degrees, with a nice 14 mph breeze at gametime) is a great thing. Now I can start worrying about number 17."[82]

Jim did not have to worry for long, because he was on the mound again four days later and kept the beat going against the Boston Red Sox. After a base hit into right field by Carl Yastrzemski, the third batter of the game, Jim gave up only two infield hits and did not walk a batter over the next six innings. He finally lost his shutout and bid for a third straight complete game when he tired in the eighth, but Ron Perranoski came on to finish up and secure Jim's 17th victory. It was another fantastic all-around effort, as Jim even contributed two of eight Minnesota hits on the day—one from each side of the plate.

After the Twins swept Cleveland to wrap up an excellent 10-2 homestand, they headed to Oakland for a big four-game showdown with the A's. The series could almost lock up the division if Minnesota could build on their now 6½ game lead. Unfortunately, Jim was about to experience a rough patch, or more accurately, the defense behind him was about to hit a slump.

In the first game at Oakland on September 4, the defense made three errors behind Perry, plus a botched double play ball that forced manager Billy Martin to go to the bullpen in the fourth inning. The Twins came back to win in extra innings as Cesar Tovar blasted a tenth-inning grand slam, but Jim would need to wait until his next time out to go for win number 18.

The Twins would win three out of four against the second-place A's, effectively putting them in the driver's seat for the west division championship. Next, they headed down the coast where the defense behind Jim once again faltered. A passed ball, another error, and a couple of errant throws that don't show up in the box score—one to the wrong base and one that missed the cutoff man—let him down. For the second straight start, Jim failed to make it through five innings. This time he was charged with his sixth loss on the season, just the second in his last 13 decisions.

As he had done all season whenever he had a tough spell, Perry quickly got things turned back in the right direction. On Friday, September 12 in Kansas City, Jim whitewashed the Royals, hurling a brilliant six-hit shutout. He walked just one while striking out six and again finished strong, allowing only two baserunners—both on harmless singles—over the final five innings. Asked after the game if he was down about failing to capture win number 18 in either of his previous two starts, Jim pointed out that it was just the nature of the game.

"It was cold the night I pitched in Oakland and I didn't feel right," he explained. "I threw well in Anaheim, but it was just one of those nights when their hits fell in. I didn't have any reason to feel bad."[83]

Note that he also never placed any blame on the obviously shaky defense behind him in those two very atypical outings. It was just another example of the subtle leadership Jim Perry brought to the clubhouse. He never called out a teammate, no matter how deserving.

Oakland came to town next, giving Jim a chance for redemption and he was ready, along with the rest of his teammates. Harmon Killebrew blasted a three-run home run in the bottom of the first inning and Jim took it from there, grinding out a workmanlike 147-pitch complete game to record his career-best 19th win. He was not as sharp as usual, allowing ten hits and matching a season-worst four free passes, but he never surrendered the early lead. Aside from a second inning triple by Dick Green, all of the hits Jim allowed were singles. In what was quickly becoming a trend, Perry again finished strong, retiring seven of the last eight batters he faced.

In the clubhouse after the game, Jim finally admitted that he could think about the topic he had been avoiding with reporters in recent weeks. "Okay, now I can concentrate on winning twenty," said the smiling pitcher.[84]

Game of Accomplishments

Saturday afternoon, September 20 things looked dicey early against visiting Seattle. Perry gave up back-to-back singles to open the game, but proceeded to strike out the next three in a row to escape the early trouble. Among the first inning punch-outs was the milestone 1,000th of Jim's career. In the second, he was not so fortunate, however, as Pilots third baseman John Kennedy followed a leadoff walk by pulling a fastball into the left field bleachers for a two-run homer, the first home run Jim had permitted in his last six starts. When Perry then walked Ron Clark, the eight-hole hitter, that elicited an early mound visit by manager Billy Martin.

"He told me that I wasn't throwing the way I was when I won the first 19," Jim revealed after the game. "But he told me to settle down because he knew I was going to win 20."[85]

Whether it was Martin's pep talk or the normal pattern of Perry getting stronger as he worked, Jim quickly got back on track. He induced a pair of easy grounders including one for a double play that prevented any further damage. A base hit in the third inning and back-to-back one-out singles in the fourth were inconsequential, but Minnesota continued to trail. As Jim settled in, however, the Minnesota offense fought back, scratching together a pair of runs in the seventh inning to tie the game at two and set the scene for a wild finish.

After Jim sent down the Pilots in 1-2-3 fashion in the top of the ninth, he had retired 17 in a row, but was still looking at a no-decision. Pilots ace reliever Diego Segui, who was in his third inning of work, struck out Ted Uhlaender to begin the bottom of the ninth. Rod Carew came up next and sliced one of his patented opposite-field line drives in front of left fielder Danny Walton for a one-out single. That brought up three-hole hitter Tony Oliva.

As the left-handed hitting all-star dug into the batter's box, Jim noticed an opening in the Seattle defense—Walton was playing straight away in left field, while center fielder Steve Hovley had shifted over toward right, playing Oliva to pull. Sitting next to catcher John Roseboro on the Minnesota bench, Jim pointed to the open gap between the two outfielders and predicted that Oliva, who was a superb all-fields hitter, could win the game by driving a shot up the gap. No sooner had Jim made his prediction to Roseboro when Oliva drilled a line drive over shortstop Ron Clark, headed toward that very gap.

"I saw the ball go over the shortstop's head and I just knew it was through," an elated Perry recalled after the game. "I was pushing Rod around the bases."[86]

Jim Perry had finally joined the exclusive ranks of 20-game winners, and he did it by finishing with a flourish. After posting a record of 6-4 through the first half of the season, Jim proceeded to go 14-2 with a sparkling 2.40 ERA over his next 21 outings, including a phenomenal nine complete games out of twenty starts during that span.

The Twins clinched the division title two days later on September 22, making the final week-and-a-half a rather anticlimactic tune up for the playoffs. Jim started again in Kansas City on September 24 and was in line for the win when he was surprisingly replaced by rookie Dick Woodson after giving up a one-out eighth inning single.

With the pennant locked up, manager Billy Martin was purposefully inserting young players in tough game situations in hopes of preparing them for the pressure of the postseason. On the road with a slim 1-0 lead, this situation certainly qualified. Unfortunately, learning on the job is not always a smooth process and Woodson coughed up a double to Ed Kirkpatrick, the first batter he faced. Lou Piniella followed with a ground ball that shortstop Rick Renick could not get out of his glove, allowing the tying run to score. Not only was the run charged to Perry, but it cost him his 21st win, despite another excellent start.

Jim made his final start on September 30 at home against the Chicago White Sox and again he saw his chance at a 21st victory slip away after being arbitrarily removed from the game. With Martin trying to give his starters some rest and get his pitching lined up for the playoffs he again removed Perry from the game with a slim 2-1 lead after six innings despite the fact he had retired seven of the last eight batters he faced. This time it was Jim Kaat who gave up the tying run only to get credit for the win when Ted Uhlaender came through with a game-winning single in the bottom of the ninth.

Disappointing Conclusion

The Twins traveled to Baltimore to begin the best-of-five American League Championship Series against a powerful Orioles team that had won an MLB-best 109 games. Manager Billy Martin tabbed Jim over fellow twenty-game winner Dave Boswell for the game one start.

The game began as the expected pitcher's duel, with Perry matching Orioles starter Mike Cuellar in hanging zeroes on the scoreboard. Each had limited opposing hitters to a measly single through the first three innings, but Lady Luck shined down on Baltimore in the bottom of the fourth. Baltimore three-hole hitter Frank Robinson pulled a line drive down the left field line that ricocheted off the foul pole for a solo home run.

Minnesota tied it on a Bob Allison sacrifice fly the next inning, but Jim was bitten by some more tough luck in the bottom of the fifth when light-hitting Mark Belanger got just enough of a fly ball for it to carry into the first row of seats in left field. Belanger only hit two home runs in 530 regular season at bats, but this one gave the O's a big 2-1 lead. Jim shut the Orioles down after that, allowing only a harmless single and a pair of walks over three more scoreless innings, while Tony Oliva blasted a two run homer deep into the right-center field stands.

The Twins headed to the bottom of the ninth with a 3-2 lead and Perry looking to close it out strong as he had done all year. Unfortunately, it was not to be on this day. Orioles cleanup hitter Boog Powell led off the ninth and worked the count full. Jim then challenged him with a good inside fastball, breaking his bat, but the big Baltimore first baseman was strong enough to pull it into the right field stands for a game-tying home run.

Powell was surprised that he was able to hit the tough pitch well enough to carry over the fence. "My bat suffered a hairline fracture on that one," he told reporters in amazement after the game.[87]

Ron Perranoski came on in relief, and the game went to extra innings, but Minnesota was unable to score off a quartet of Baltimore relievers. The Orioles finally pulled it out when Paul Blair executed a perfect squeeze bunt with two outs in the bottom of the twelfth inning. Belanger scored from third as Blair streaked safely across the first base bag, the perfectly placed bunt leaving Twins catcher John Roseboro with no play on either man.

Minnesota's disappointment carried over to the following day, as another pitcher's duel again lasted into extra innings. Baltimore's Dave McNally shut out the Twins for 11 innings, while Dave Boswell had done the same against the O's through ten. With two on and two outs in the bottom of the 11th inning, Martin went back to Perranoski, but pinch-hitter Curt Motton lashed a line drive that just eluded the glove of a leaping Rod Carew. Center fielder Tony Oliva fired a strong throw to the plate, but Boog Powell, running from second base, arrived at the same time as the ball. The 6-4, 230-pound Powell sent catcher George Mitterwald sprawling in the ensuing collision, dislodging the ball, leaving Powell safe with the game-winning run.

The series moved to Minneapolis after the pair of heart-breaking losses. The Twins were hopeful that the friendly confines of Metropolitan Stadium would help them bounce back, but it was not to be. Game three starter Bob Miller was knocked out in the second inning of an 11-2 blowout and a great Minnesota Twins season was suddenly over.

Despite the disappointing finish, 1969 was still a great year for Jim Perry. He had not only reestablished himself as a bona fide major league starter, but he had emerged as one of the top starting pitchers in the game. It was a long way from a modest life growing up on a small North Carolina tobacco farm.

3

Farm Bred

Anyone who meets Jim Perry today would have a difficult time even imagining his humble origins. Not that he leads a life of extravagance. Quite to the contrary, Jim and wife Daphne epitomize dignified grace and class, with great appreciation for what has been an amazing journey.

If you've ever heard or used the term "born into a life of privilege," Jim Perry's upbringing was surely the opposite of whatever that might mean. The only "privilege" he and younger brother Gaylord enjoyed was getting a chance to play ball after a long day of manual labor, working the tobacco field in the sultry North Carolina sun. They were raised in a small community of tenant farms referred to as Farm Life, North Carolina, located about 45 miles south of Ahoskie and 35 miles northeast from Greenville. The nearest town was Williamston (pop. 3,966 in 1940), about ten miles to the north—a good two-hour walk for a strapping teenage boy.

As opposed to a town or village with any kind of hub, Farm Life was more of a general area littered with an occasional crossroads store, a schoolhouse, and a handful of churches. Few of the roads were paved, with even less having formal street names. Residents regularly got around by use of well-known landmarks, both natural and man-made. Residents of Farm Life, close to a thousand in number, supplied themselves with more than three-fourths of the food they consumed. From home grown vegetables to dairy (milk and butter) to poultry, eggs, and home-raised pork, Farm Life families were close to self-sufficient. More than driving or riding, the people of Farm Life generally walked to their destination, though that destination was most often the adjoining tobacco fields.

The large farmhouse in which Jim grew up dated back to before the Civil War and had no electricity and no modern plumbing for any kind of bathroom. When nature called, only an outhouse located some 200 feet out back was available. That trip was no fun when the weather turned cold or when nature called in the middle of the night.

Bathing, if you could call it that, was done nightly on the back porch next to a basin of cold water. Armed with a washcloth and a bar of lard soap she had made herself, Mamma Ruby would wipe the day's dirt off of each boy and later sister Carolyn. For a special treat on Saturday night, Mamma might boil up water on the wood stove and fill a big old tub. If the weekday washcloth baths had done their job, the second and third kids in the tub might enjoy water that was still relatively clear. Jim regularly made a point to argue that the oldest should get to go first.

The house had no basement because it was built up off the ground in order to keep snakes and insects from nesting underneath. A wide hallway ran from front to back with two large rooms on each side, leading to a "back porch" breezeway that connected the house to a shed kitchen that was a free-standing structure in order to separate the wood-burning stove from the house. Three of the rooms were bedrooms and the fourth was a living room reserved for company. Filled with pictures, souvenir ashtrays, stuffed furniture, miniature statues, and other "fancy" knickknacks, the door to the living room was mostly kept locked. There was a second floor, which was also kept locked in order to save money. After all, if nobody ever went upstairs, there was no need for it to be heated—or furnished.

The only running water in the house came into the kitchen from a pitcher pump that pulled water up from a 25-foot well and drained back out through a pipe directly onto the ground. It was a simple house in which the Perry family lived a simple life. Jim shared a bedroom—and bed—with Gaylord, who was two years his junior.

He was nine years old when sister Carolyn was born. Despite their meager surroundings, the Perry children grew up never feeling poor or needy in any way. Their parents, Evan and Ruby, ran the farm, as well as the house, with firm, steady hands, ensuring each child felt loved and cared for.

While far from extravagant, the house was kept spotless. Mamma Ruby would rise at four o'clock each morning, knock out a bushel basket of laundry, and get started cooking. She had the evening meal in a pot simmering on the wood-burning stove before the sun came up.

As Ruby got things underway inside, Evan was already at work in the barn, getting a jump on the sunrise. He explained that a farmer's work schedule was "kin 'til kint (from when you just kin see the sun 'til you just kint)."[88] That is, you get out in the field when the sun provides enough light so you can see and then work until it sets and you can't see anymore.

Behind the house were a pair of square barns, each standing 30 by 30 feet and just about as tall. Inside the barns were wood-burning ovens that were used to dry out the tobacco. Once the tobacco was dry, the boys would stack it across wood sticks all the way up to the rafters. Outside the barns were separate sheds for corn, hay, mules, hogs, and chickens. In addition to those, they had a smokehouse where meat was stored and a potato house for vegetables.

The nearest neighbors were more than a mile away, though the telephone kept people connected. It was a community line, shared by several families, each with their own distinctive ring.

Evan was sharecropping for the Roberson family, who provided him with the farmhouse and 25 acres of cleared land, plus 75 more heavily wooded acres. Evan and Ruby were responsible for furnishing the house, growing the crops, and keeping up the farm. Evan split the cost of seed and fertilizer with the landlord and turned over half of everything the crops brought in.

Tobacco was the main money crop for the Perry farm, though they also grew peanuts for a second cash crop, along with corn for the farm and potatoes, both sweet and Irish. They raised a few hogs and some chickens for themselves, along with growing all their own vegetables in a large garden. Most of the clothes were handmade, first used by Jim before being handed down to Gaylord. They may have been worn, but they were undoubtedly clean.

Perhaps because they always had food to eat and a mom and dad who maintained order and discipline, the Perry children never felt like they were going without a need met. While they didn't have much in the way of luxury material goods, they had a tight knit family that worked together for the same cause. You might say it was where Jim Perry first learned what it meant to be a great teammate.

As they gathered for early morning breakfast, the light of the kerosene lamp gave the kitchen a warm glow. The table would inevitably be filled with a bountiful spread of eggs, ham and bacon, hot biscuits and homemade jelly, along with milk and hot coffee, all prepared by Mamma Ruby.

Never was there talk about bills that needed to be paid (of which there were many) or the week ahead. Only a simple focus on the work at hand that day. It was a straightforward, matter-of-fact approach to getting the work done that needed to be done on a farm. It was a classic farm life. There was never longing for more, at least outwardly.

Like Father Like Son

Evan Perry did not have it easy growing up, the difficulties of his youth beginning almost as he breathed his first breath on August 11, 1917. When his mother, Emma died during childbirth, James, his father, panicked and ran off, leaving Evan and a twin sister Mollie behind, along with their young sister, Fannie. Emma's sister, Mary Louise, who went by Ludie, took in the children, along with her husband, William Perry (no relation, despite the same surname), who went by his middle name, Amos. Sadly, Mollie soon fell ill, likely a victim of the 1918 Spanish flu pandemic, and passed away before her second birthday.

With the same surname, by coincidence, as his uncle Amos, memories of Evan's birth father eventually faded away. That is not to imply that Amos took pleasure in adding three more children to care for in addition to his and Ludie's five. Amos treated young Evan rough, putting him to work mule plowing by the time he was five years old. Whether planting, harvesting, or pulling out tree stumps, there was always work to do, and Evan grew up charged with getting it done.

Evan did not do particularly well in the classroom, but he became enthralled with sports, thanks to the encouragement of a high school coach named Frosty Peters, who was something of a local legend in Williamston. With his farm-honed strength, Evan was a good athlete and enjoyed practicing football and baseball after school. The extra-curricular activity, however, left Evan with a four-mile walk home after practice, straight into the fields to tend to the crops until sunset. Uncle Amos, who had little interest in sports, resented the fact that Evan was playing games when there was work to be done on the farm.

Despite little encouragement or support from his foster parents, Evan starred at Williamston High School. Years later, locals still raved about the way Evan Perry ran with the football, as he led the Williamston High School football team to 21 wins against just one loss over three years on varsity. He was also an excellent pitcher, who may have had a chance to play pro ball under different circumstances.

In March of 1935, Evan finally found a way out from under the oppressive thumb of Uncle Amos by marrying his high school sweetheart, Ruby Coletrain following a three-year courtship. Ruby's older sister Mittie had married into the Roberson family, who owned a great deal of the farmland around Farm Life. Mittie's husband, Arnold Roberson, took in Evan as a tenant, starting him with a handful of tobacco acres to farm, plus a square four-room tenant dwelling where Evan and Ruby could live.

Arnold also provided Evan and Ruby a pair of farming mules and a cow for milk, along with some farming equipment, as well as a helpful line of credit at the nearby Roberson family store. As was customary for the arrangement, Evan would "work on halves," splitting the cost of seed and fertilizer with his landlord, Arnold, and then splitting the proceeds evenly following the harvest. Evan used his life savings of $125 to furnish the empty house, which bought a wood-burning stove along with some secondhand furniture.

As he worked the farm trying to make a life for himself and support his family, Evan never lost his love of sports. He continued to play baseball for many years on the Farm Life team in the local semi-pro Beaufort County League where they passed the hat to collect money for equipment. The team never had more than two baseballs for a game, and the game ended early if both balls were lost.

Perry and Slim

Evan teamed up with Slim Gardner to deliver a one-two pitching combo that was good enough to keep most minor league barnstorming teams from coming through the Farm Life area for fear of being embarrassed. Slim Gardner was a lanky six-foot-six righthander who had no teeth, but a blazing fastball. What Slim lacked in teeth, he regularly made up for in his mouth with a giant wad of tobacco, though it is likely that the latter accounted for the former. It was Slim, in fact, who reportedly first introduced Jim's younger brother to the idea of applying moisture to the ball when he showed young Gaylord how he threw his late-diving "tobacco ball." As you might imagine from such a description, Slim's exploits on the baseball diamond were the stuff of legends.

One July Fourth, Beaufort took on the New Bern Bears for a holiday doubleheader. Slim pitched a shutout in the morning game, after which the teams broke for a festive holiday barbecue. After lunch, as the story goes, Slim swam the mile-wide Neuse River, before coming back and shutting out the Bears again in the afternoon game.

Regardless of how tall that tale may be, it is an undisputed fact that Evan would regularly come out of the fields and pitch back-to-back games. Though he may have lacked the overpowering fastball of his toothless moundmate, Evan had a good curveball that he was not afraid to throw in any count. He also threw a baffling knuckler that was said to rival that of MLB great Hoyt Wilhelm.

If Evan's dominance was not the stuff of legend, his endurance and determination certainly was. Decades later, locals still talked about a day back in 1941 that was the hottest on record. With the temperature soaring to over 110 degrees under the mid-summer sun, Evan pitched a pair of complete games, as Farm Life defeated White Post by scores of 4-1 and 9-3. Evan brought that same determination to raising his boys. The day Jim was born, Evan vowed there would always be time to play some ball, no matter how much farm work needed to be done.

Work Before Play

A rural North Carolina farmer's life in the 1940s was a simple, straightforward existence. Work the fields from dawn 'til dusk (Evan's "kin 'til kint") Monday through Friday, and then a half day on Saturday if everything was under control. On Sunday, it was go to worship and then play ball.

Baseball was everything in small town North Carolina back in the mid-20th century. The area was filled with semi-pro hometown teams, which gave rise to the community pitcher, a highly respected man revered at a level similar to that of the town parson or the corner druggist. Evan Perry was a man of stature in the Farm Life community of Williamston, North Carolina. That didn't change the fact that there was work to be done in order to feed his family.

Nearly from the time he could walk, Jim joined Daddy and Mamma tending the tobacco crops by hand. It was a dirty job. Even as advanced fighter jets from nearby Seymour Johnson Air Force Base regularly whistled overhead at the speed of sound, work on the tobacco farm remained remarkably primitive. Whenever her work in the house was caught up for the moment, Ruby would join Evan, bent over at the waist, working the tobacco crops with bare hands, young barefoot Jim, soon joined by Gaylord, in tow. Evan incorporated the same methods that had been in use for the past couple centuries, teaching Jim at an early age to take the reins of their two plow mules, Mollie and Red.

Tobacco Road

The money crop for the Perry family was tobacco—the most demanding crop of all. While an acre of corn could be raised from start to finish with roughly three man-hours, that same acre required more than 500 man-hours of work for tobacco.

Soon after the first of the year, Evan would begin preparing the soil by burning off any undergrowth, which would sterilize the ground while adding ash to the soil. The ash was a good supplement to help the tobacco get started. In February, he would mix small tobacco seeds with some soil and spread them in a special bed where the seedlings were protected while they matured over the next six weeks.

While the seedlings grew, the main fields were prepared for transplanting. Mollie and Red pulled a heavy plow to break up the soil and make furrows. Beginning in early April, weather permitting, the seedlings would be transplanted into the main fields. This was a three-man job, which made the two boys an essential part of Evan's operation. The first man made a hole in the furrow with a hand peg, the second placed a seedling in the hole, and then the third added a water/fertilizer mix to the plant.

As the tobacco plants grew, there was still more work to be done before they could be harvested. The ground had to be continually weeded and the plants needed to be protected from pests. The biggest pest was tobacco worms, which were commonly known as hornworms. The only way to keep hornworm from causing damage was to inspect each plant and remove the worms by hand. This was a job that everyone contributed to, but one that could be especially handled by the children. Jim, Gaylord, and eventually little sister Carolyn spent many hours in their younger days deworming tobacco plants.

The other important job during the growing season was "topping" and "suckering" the tobacco plants. When the plants began to flower, the buds needed to be snapped off the top of each plant. This would cause other buds, called "suckers," to soon appear down lower on the plant. Removing all of the buds conserved the plant's energy by allowing nutrients to go to the leaves instead of the flowers. This helped the plant to keep growing longer into late summer.

As July turned into August, the "easy" part of the tobacco farming process was complete. Now it was time to begin the harvesting process. Every two to three weeks, a few leaves were removed from each plant, working from the bottom up. It might take anywhere from three to five rounds before all the leaves were harvested. The mules would then haul the harvested leaves back to the curing barn where the "loopers," generally women, would loop the tobacco onto sticks.

At the end of the day, Evan and the boys would hang the prepared sticks of tobacco from the rafters of the curing barn and fire up the pair of big wood stoves attached to the barn. For seven days, the fire in the stoves would gradually be increased, causing the tobacco leaves to yellow and dry out. Once this curing process was complete, the stoves would be extinguished and the doors of the curing barn would be opened in order to allow the dried leaves to absorb the humid North Carolina summer air.

Once the tobacco had absorbed enough moisture to become pliable again, it was taken down from the rafters—a particularly messy job—and placed in ordering pits to absorb even more moisture before being taken to the neighboring packhouse barn. At the packhouse, the tobacco was laid out and graded before it was bundled into "hands." Ruby was known as one of the finest tobacco graders around. Not only did she routinely grade the Perry harvest, but she was frequently paid by other farmers to grade their harvest, as well.

Finally, the hands of tobacco were pressed flat and loaded onto a truck to be taken to a nearby warehouse and await the next tobacco auction. Tobacco buyers came to pay extra attention when a crop from Evan Perry was up for bid, as his tobacco became known for being top quality.

After the tobacco left the curing barn, the harvesting process was ready to begin again, working up the tobacco plants until finally there were no leaves remaining. The grading and bundling process took quite a bit of time, so this might still be going on as late as November.

While the work in the fields may have ended by October, there was still no rest for the weary tobacco farmer. The November and December months were generally spent doing important maintenance to equipment and structures around the farm and stocking up on supplies for the following year. One of the most important activities during this time was patching up any seams or holes on the side of the curing barn to make sure it was airtight.

By the time this work was finished, it was inevitably time to start the process all over again. Tobacco farming was truly a full-time job.

Tobacco Ball

By the time he was seven years old, Jim (soon joined by brother Gaylord), worked alongside Daddy from dawn to dusk six days a week, sowing, tending, harvesting, and curing tobacco crops. When they weren't tending to the tobacco, they were plowing fields, pulling out tree stumps, and cutting wood.

"I was always faster at working the crops than Gaylord," Jim recalled. "We'd start out together and I'd soon end up a row ahead of him. 'Course, I was older. Next to his being slow, the thing I remember about Gaylord is that he sucked his thumb until he was nine. He'd come in after working all day on the farm and his whole hand would be black but his thumb would still be white."[89]

The boys were always active, getting through the day throwing stones at trees or hitting clods of mud with broken-off tree limbs. Even catching a quick break from work in the field was no time to rest. If they didn't keep moving, the scorching North Carolina sun on their britches would burn the top of their legs.

The only fun respite from a day of grueling manual labor was when Daddy and the boys took advantage of a break for lunch to play a little 3-man baseball in the neighboring pasture. They would be back at work within the hour, but would try to squeeze in a little more before nightfall if they could. Sunday afternoon following church was the one time of the week specifically set aside to relax and play. They had a bat, a homemade ball, and Daddy's worn out glove. Evan rotated with young Jim and Gaylord between pitching, hitting, and shagging. The glove was usually reserved for whoever was doing the shagging.

Mamma Ruby regularly admonished the threesome for their choice of "break time" activities. "You and the boys are blamed fools, playin' ball in this awful heat," she would exclaim. "You should be restin'!"

Evan calmly explained the method to his apparent madness. "The boys do their work and go to church on Sunday. The least I can do for them is teach them how to play baseball. They need to learn it, so they will be able to enjoy it when they're grown. If they get good enough, there's no telling where playing ball can take 'em."[90]

Evan could see that, unlike when he was younger, changing times were opening up opportunities for young men to leave the farm. While he likely felt there would be an opportunity for his two lanky sons to someday make some money playing ball professionally, even the wildest dreamer would be hard pressed to imagine the enormous impact of those tobacco field lunch break lessons.

Not surprisingly, tobacco field baseball was not played using the finest equipment hard-earned money could buy from the local sporting goods store. The bat might be an old oak root. On the rare occasion they were able to come up with a real bat, it was inevitably held together by a crude combination of nails and tape.

Despite her regular complaints and caring castigation, it was not uncommon for Mamma to take a break from her myriad duties to sew up some old fertilizer sacks for uniforms. She also helped with producing a "ball." The early form was a stocking ball, comprising old socks rolled tightly into a round wad and sewn together. It was very useful for teaching the game to the young boys because it was firm enough to hit but didn't travel so far that the shagger would get worn out.

The two brothers soon figured out how to make more of a crude "regular" ball. "We would get a hard rubber ball from our sister (Carolyn), the kind girls use for jacks," Jim later recalled. "Then we'd wrap it in yarn and thread from our mother's sewing basket and cover it with some black tar paper Dad used to hold tobacco leaves together for curing. It didn't look like much, except it was sort of round. But it did the job and didn't cost anything."[91]

If the boys couldn't come up with one of Carolyn's balls, they might use a walnut, or even a small rock. "You had to pitch to spots with that ball," Jim cautioned. You could make it curve or drop a little, but it hurt your arm (to do so)."[92]

Years later, Daddy Evan would provide an interesting perspective on the impact of these homemade balls on his oldest son's development as a pitcher. "Jim never has had problems with his control and, in looking back, I often wonder if it was because of those balls. There was no way to make them curve and so you had to pitch to spots if you wanted to get anybody out."[93]

Tobacco field baseball may not have been glamorous, but it brought a joyful respite to tough farm life, both for the boys, as well as their hard-working father. Even as she claimed to protest, Mamma

> *You had to pitch to spots (with that homemade ball) if you wanted to get anybody out.*
>
> — Evan Perry
> DADDY

surely took joy in the tight-knit family working and playing together. Daddy was usually the pitcher, allowing the boys to flip-flop between doing the hitting and doing the running to retrieve the ball. They used the potato barn for a backstop and kept score based on how far the ball was hit. When the ball was caught on the fly, the batter was out.

Gaylord later recalled the lessons learned during tobacco field baseball. "Dad was a pitcher and worked with Jim and me. There were two things he preached the most. One was to throw strikes. Make the hitter hit the ball, don't walk him. The other thing was to not give in to the hitter. Make him hit your best stuff. Don't beat yourself."[94]

Farm Life School

The Farm Life community where Jim grew up got its name due to its association with the local education institution. Farm Life School was the rural community answer to conventional schools that focused mainly on the "three Rs" of education. The state of North Carolina began the county-based Farm Life School concept back in 1911 when more than eighty percent of North Carolina's young were considered "country children." In addition to traditional subjects, farm-life schools emphasized agricultural and home economic lessons that would be of particular value to pupils destined for a life on the farm.

Within five years from its implementation, there were 21 farm-life schools operating throughout the state. A 1914 article in the *Western Carolina Democrat* explained the perceived value of this rural-oriented education institution. "The county farm life school, giving to boys instruction in practical agriculture with a real farm for laboratory work, and to the girls, training in the arts of home-making and house-keeping, is becoming one of the most influential agents in North Carolina in making rural education efficient, in refashioning rural living conditions, and in making agriculture scientific, satisfying, and profitable."[95]

As urbanization increased, along with the advent of motorized transportation for students, the federal government passed the Smith-Hughes Act in 1917, which appropriated federal funds for vocational education in public high schools. This lessened the need for a farm-specific curriculum and led to the eventual demise of the farm-life school concept. In the early 1940s, however, the Martin County Farm Life School was still going strong for grades 1-8, and that is where the Perry kids walked for their daily learning (and respite from working in the tobacco fields).

The Martin County Farm Life School was a red brick building that housed four large classrooms with two grades, first through eighth, taught together in each. With an average of 15 students per grade, that made for around 30 per room and 120 for the entire school. The teacher would teach one grade while the kids from the other grade would "coast," working on previously assigned projects. While Jim took his studies seriously, Gaylord tended to take the "coast" aspect of the classroom arrangement more literally.

Farm Life Fun

After a hard week of working the fields, Evan might treat the boys to a Sunday matinee at the Watts picture show. They would pile into the family's 1934 Ford jalopy with its distinctive ahooga horn and drive it some ten miles into the local town of Williamston, backfiring, herking and jerking all along the way. Evan was a big fan of westerns, so the trio usually ended up at a cowboy shoot-'em-up double feature. While Johnny Mack Brown was a popular star of the day and John Wayne was on his way to becoming one, Jim favored Roy Rogers while younger brother Gaylord longed to someday be just like Gene Autry.

If they didn't go to the movies, the boys might tag along with Daddy to Noah Roberson's grocery store, where the kids would gather round the wood-burning pot-bellied stove and sit quietly as they listened intently to the men swapping stories. The talk might range anywhere from some of Evan's big games to local legends like Jimmy Brown, an infielder who grew up in nearby Jamesville and played eight years in the major leagues in the late 1930s and early '40s.

Another popular destination was Nathaniel Coletrain's East Side where the boys would "pull for Cokes." In this game, which could go multiple rounds on a hot summer day, each boy would grab a bottle of Coca-Cola out of the ice-filled barrel and then they would all turn over their bottle at the same time and one by one, announce where their choice was bottled. The boy who grabbed the bottle filled at the most distant location got his drink paid for by the other boys.

During the week, when work was finished for the day and they had been cleaned up with their nightly sponge bath, Jim and Gaylord would often huddle next to their battery operated radio and listen to Bill Stern sports and the Friday night fights. They also enjoyed popular programs of the day, including "The Lone Ranger" and "Amos and Andy." Gaylord especially liked "Gang Busters" which billed itself as "the only program that brings you authentic police case histories."

In the winter, when darkness fell earlier, leaving the boys with more time before bed, Mamma Ruby might roast some chestnuts or pop up some popcorn. Daddy might even pull out the checkerboard for a few games. It was a simple time with simple pleasures, and the Perry children never lamented any luxuries they may have lacked. They simply did not know any different. The family shared the love and support of each other and lived life firmly in the moment.

Farm Life Baseball

One of the underappreciated luxuries most youngsters enjoy today is the opportunity to play in an organized community Little League. This was unheard of in 1940s rural North Carolina, so Jim and Gaylord soon joined up with some other Farm Life boys to create their own "league." After they convinced one of the neighborhood tenant farmers to loan them some land, Jim and Gaylord hitched up their trusty mules, Mollie and Red, and used them to clear a rough baseball configuration and then scrape off an infield. They boys wrangled some pine logs, which they cut up at the saw mill and built a backstop to go with a set of bleachers. They even canvassed neighbors, collecting chickens, hogs, and even occasional cash money, using the combination to trade for equipment.

There were no "travel teams" or local gurus to sell "expert" advice. Jim and Gaylord learned, as did most kids of the day, from their dad. The one advantage the Perry boys did enjoy was a father who was passionate about the game and had a good idea about the basic principles of playing it well. Evan emphasized throwing strikes and keeping your eye on the ball. Though seemingly fundamental words of wisdom, the oft-repeated mantras served to provide the foundation that would carry the boys all the way to the major leagues.

As Jim and Gaylord toiled together, working the tobacco fields in the hot North Carolina sun, they might pass the time discussing their hopes and dreams. Both had visions of careers that would lead them away from the farm. While Gaylord dreamed of becoming a famous cowboy like Gene Autry, Jim had other ideas.

"I wanna be a ballplayer," Jim confessed to his younger brother one particularly sultry afternoon. "Daddy and I were talking. He wanted to be a professional ballplayer when he was a boy, but couldn't because of the farm."

"Well then, how can you ever be one?" young Gaylord queried.

"By practicing ball just as hard as you work in the tobacco field, Daddy says," the big brother explained. "Daddy says that if you are good enough to be a professional ballplayer, you can go on to be anything else you want."[96]

It was a life lesson that served Jim well and guided him the rest of his days.

4

Old School Cross-Training

As he entered his teen years, Jim was particularly big for his age. By the time he reached 14 years old, he was joining Daddy Evan on the Farm Life semi-pro team playing in the Beaufort County League. Jim was not yet a pitcher at that point. Evan handled those duties, of course, while Jim played both second base and right field. It wasn't long before Gaylord, who shared Jim's large stature, joined big brother and Daddy. The team was basically made up of three families. The Griffins, the Hardesons, and the Perrys. Evan handled primary pitching duties while the younger Perrys played behind him in the field.

They would play teams from nearby towns like Ahoskie, Edenton, Tarboro, and Hertford, where another young future MLB star named Jim (not yet "Catfish") Hunter was growing up. Fans would come from all around the area, some in gas-powered jalopies, others on horseback or horse-drawn buggies, and some even by foot to watch the games. They brought along with them all the fixins for a bountiful post-game spread to be enjoyed, win or lose, by the fans and players alike.

With limited bleacher seating at the local fields, crowds sometimes in excess of a thousand people would populate the foul lines and the deep outfield area. While the rivalries between the towns were lively, fans behaved orderly as they cheered on their local nine. "But when the game was on the line," Gaylord explained, "you'd hear the people yelling 'Here's five dollars for a hit,' or 'Here's five dollars for a strikeout,' or 'Two live chickens if you bring in a run!'"[97]

There was no formal admission, but after the game, fans would pass the hat and pitch in money, which the team used for baseballs and any other equipment they might need, though they made the most of what they had. If a bat splintered, they would just tape it together. If it got a good crack, they would use nails for the repair. All options were exhausted before giving up on it.

All this "just made us appreciate it that much more when we got to the big leagues," Jim later recalled. "I'd see them throw out a bat with just a little nick on it and I'd say, 'We wouldn't even have taped that around home.'"[98]

If there was anything left after equipment reinforcements, the players would split it up among themselves. Sometimes the day's pitcher might get twenty dollars for pitching a win or ten dollars for a good effort in a loss. With a Perry frequently on the mound for the Farm Life nine, that little extra was a big help back home.

The rare times Jim and his brother were not playing ball or working on the farm, they could still be found trying to earn a little extra money for the family. Jim and Gaylord both worked part-time at Griffin's Quick Lunch in town. Jim took orders and helped out in the kitchen, while the younger Gaylord was confined to washing dishes for a dollar an hour. Jim also took on another job, one that is unheard of for a student. He drove the school bus!

With drivers not always easy to come by in the Farm Life community, and as one of the few teens with a driver's license, Jim got the job. For much of his sophomore and junior years of high school, Jim would drive the bus route in the morning, picking up classmates on the way into town and then park the bus at school. Another classmate would take the afternoon route ending at his own home, where Jim would walk to pick up the bus after basketball or baseball practice to drive it back to the Perry farm and repeat the process the following morning.

Exciting Times

In 1950, a major event in the community led to a sudden change in the boys' routine. Manning-Gurkin's country store installed Farm Life's first television set. The boys quickly moved their social gatherings to this new location and reveled in being able to see wrestling and boxing matches that previously lived only in their mind as they listened on the radio or read a reporter's recount.

Any other social activity for a young teenage boy in rural North Carolina in the early 1950s inevitably involved church. From tent revival meetings passing through town to picnics at nearby Maple Grove First Christian Church, Jim and his siblings were raised to love, respect, and worship the Lord. Mamma Ruby saw to that. A devout Fundamentalist, she was not fond of either work or play on the Sabbath.

After morning church and afternoon baseball, the Gurkins, Coletrains and other neighbors might come to the house on Sunday evening. The adults liked to play a favorite Carolina card game called "Catch the Five."

One of the landmark events in the Perry family occurred in the spring of 1951 when their tenant farm was finally electrified. To celebrate, Evan bought a used Philco floor cabinet radio, which was a real step up from the boys' battery-operated, hand-held transistor unit. Two years later, in the fall of '53, the Perry family got their own television, a brand new 14-inch RCA model, black-and-white, of course. It was just in time for them to watch the New York Yankees defeat the Brooklyn Dodgers in the World Series. The series star was a scrappy infielder named Billy Martin, who rapped out 12 hits in 24 at bats. Little did Jim realize what a pivotal role Martin would later play in his career.

In addition to baseball, the boys loved to watch big-time wrestling on their new television. "The Perry family went loony over wrestling," Gaylord recalled. "We caught every match we could. We'd get so worked up, we couldn't watch close to meal time."[99]

Next-Level Sport

Jim began high school in the fall of 1952. As the area's premier athlete, he naturally went out for football and showed promise as a young quarterback. There was still much work to be done on the farm in the fall, however, which made practicing football difficult. He was also cognizant of the potential for injury, which might effectively derail his dreams in another sport. After his sophomore year, Jim hung up the helmet and pads for good in order to focus on what he was confident would be his future—baseball.

While baseball may have been his focus, Jim continued to play basketball throughout high school. Not only did the winter schedule avoid interfering with his obligations on the farm, but the conditioning needed for basketball left Jim in great shape when baseball season began in the spring. With his superior conditioning from playing basketball, combined with his farm-strong physique, Jim quickly established himself as an ironman on the mound.

The high school team regularly played its games on Tuesday and Friday afternoons. Jim routinely pitched both of those games, going the distance more often than not. He compiled a 10-1 combined record over his first two high school seasons. Jim quickly became known for his signature pinpoint control, which was highlighted by the fact he walked only one batter during his entire sophomore season.

"James was the type that if he felt like he was doing himself a favor he would work himself to death," recalled Larry Woolard, a teammate on those Williamston teams. Woolard, who came from a family that was better off financially than the Perrys, would take advantage of that disparity to avoid embarrassment on the field. "One year I had to play third base, which I wasn't too good at," said Woolard. "I told James, 'Don't let them hit the ball to me and I'll buy you a milkshake and a hamburger.' I went three games without a chance."[100]

Jim was starring in both sports by the time his younger brother arrived in the fall of '54. Many of the locals were looking forward to seeing what the Perry brothers would do teaming up together. "When I got to Williamston High, Jim was already an all-state center," Gaylord explained. "He was nicknamed Goose for some reason, so I got stuck with the nickname Duck. Anyway, Jim and I had grown up playing two-on-one basketball against Daddy in the backyard, with a hoop attached to the potato barn. Jim and I knew each other's every move."[101]

Unfortunately, the debut of the dynamic brother duo would have to wait. Gaylord went out for football, but that was the year Jim decided it was best to limit his attention to just two sports. While he was hopeful that he might get the opportunity to team up with his big brother on the hardwood, young Gaylord was assigned to the junior varsity as a freshman, much to his dismay.

The spring of '55 finally brought the opportunity Gaylord and many others had been anxiously awaiting. It would not be as a one-two punch on the pitching staff, however. By his junior year, Jim *was* the Williamston Green Wave pitching staff. With Jim easily handling the two-games-per-week schedule and rarely in need of help, Gaylord was happy to handle the duties at third base and slot in behind his big brother in the batting order.

Fresh Arm Needed

Once the regular season concluded, however, the post-season state tournament presented a problem for the ride-Jim's-back pitching formula. The tourney schedule included three games a week, and Jim could not pitch all of them. Gaylord recounted how this predicament gave birth to his pitching career.

"Gaither Cline, our baseball coach that year, called over to me at third base where I was taking infield practice. 'Gaylord,' he said, 'how'd you like to pitch tomorrow against Beargrass?'

"'I don't mind if you don't mind,' I said, 'but you have to know, Coach, I never pitched in a regular game before.'

"'Gaylord, pitching's in your blood. Your daddy is one of the best in these parts still. We all know how good Jim is. I believe you can do it. No infielder in the conference has an arm like yours. And besides, we'll have Jim ready to spell you if you get into trouble.'

"That night at home, Daddy and Jim showed me everything I'd need: how to pitch off the rubber, take a stretch, hold runners on base. It was like cramming for an exam.

"I remember the first two batters went out and I thought to myself, 'What's so hard about this? I'll just shoot the ball a little lower and then experiment with some fancy stuff.' I walked the next three batters on twelve pitches. The coach ran out to the mound. 'Gaylord,' he said,

'I'm not giving up on the Perrys. No, sir. A Perry started this game, and a Perry will finish it. But I'm gonna call on Jim to help you out.'

"Jim, who was playing third base, trotted to the mound and I went to third. It took Jim three pitches to strike out the next Beargrass batter and end the inning. We had a good hitting team—Jim and I both batted over .400—and we took a quick eight-run lead. I went back to the mound the next inning a little wiser. But I loaded the bases in the fifth and again in the seventh. Jim and I exchanged positions each time, and each time he got them out."[102]

Gaylord was awarded his first win as a pitcher that day and the dynamic Perry duo proceeded to carry Williamston to the state finals, dominating their opponents with shutouts in each of their last five games, three by Jim and two by Gaylord. The pair limited opposing hitters to just 12 hits over those five games, allowing not a single runner to even venture past second base.

A recap of the games in Williamston's semiweekly newspaper, *The Enterprise*, included this bizarre highlight from one of the Williamston High wins: "In the fifth things began to happen. Bobby Hardison was safe on an error, Bobby Mobley and Gerald Griffin bunted for infield hits, James Perry sacrificed but was safe on an error, Gaylord Perry and Zack Gurkin bunted safely and the Coopers' catcher walked off the field and did not come back."[103]

Hal Shapiro, reporting for the *Carteret County News-Times* of Morehead City, North Carolina, provided his personal scouting report following Jim's 5-0 shutout of Morehead City that put Williamston one win away from advancing to the state championship series. "The big man for the Williamston nine, their pitcher James 'Goose' Perry, was everything that was said of him and then a little bit more. He hurled a one-hitter and made two hits himself, the first of his hits driving in the run that put his team in the lead and just about gave them the game. This Perry boy can throw that ball with something on it every time.

"In the Friday afternoon encounter everyone in the crowd of 200 was amazed at the control of this high school hurler. Goose had the ball over the plate all afternoon, throwing up fast balls and a wide assortment of curves. His incurve to righthanded batters was something to behold. The ball would seem to be going away from the man at bat and then suddenly reverse its course and come busting in over the inside corner.

"He struck out seven men and walked but one, but it was his ability to get the ball over with men on base that had everyone shouting his praises after the game was over. Perry would look over at first to keep the baserunner from getting a jump on him, and without seemingly looking at the batter at the plate, bust the ball over the middle of the plate.

"This boy could certainly go a long way in professional baseball since he looks and plays like a natural. He's 6'4" and like Ewell Blackwell who used to pitch in the major leagues, is a long lean boy, weighing in at no more than 160 pounds.

> *It was his ability to get the ball over with men on base that had everyone shouting his praises.*
>
> — Hal Shapiro
> LOCAL NC SPORTSWRITER

"Major league scouts are reportedly hot on his trail right now and it could be that either Harry Postove of the Chicago White Sox or Tim Murchison of the New York Giants may have the inside track with him. (Murchison, it is interesting to note, was apparently already building a close relationship with the Perry family, which would pay off when he eventually signed Gaylord.)

"The Eagles (of Morehead City) just couldn't seem to get themselves untracked against the elongated righthander and he had them biting at some mighty wicked hooks.

"Jimmy Willis made the only safety for the Eagles on a liner into right and Jimmy said that he hit the ball on the end of the bat, since it was mighty difficult to get around on the hooks and fastball of Perry."[104]

The five-game shutout streak set Williamston up for a best-of-three series for the state championship against Colfax high school. Colfax was a suburb of Greensboro, located between Greensboro and Winston Salem, some three hours west of Williamston.

"In fact," said Jim, "Gay and I won seven games in a row going into the finals with Colfax High. All you could hear about was how good Colfax was and how their best pitcher, Bobby Simmons, was. Then we met them in two games, a Friday and a Saturday (in a best-of-three series). Well, they wouldn't pitch Simmons against me. They held him out. So I won the first game 9-0, a two-hitter. Then they came back with Simmons on Saturday, and Gaylord beat him 2-0, a three-hitter."[105] Gaylord was the first freshman to ever win a State championship game in the state of North Carolina.

Jim finished the year with a 13-1 record that featured five one-hitters. He allowed only one run and sixteen hits for the entire spring. How he might have actually suffered a loss is a mystery that has been lost to the annals of time. Oh, and the switch-hitter also posted a .400 batting average to boot.

New Challenge

With nothing left to accomplish at Williamston High, Jim enrolled at Campbell College for his senior year. Campbell was a junior college located in Buies Creek, North Carolina, about 30 miles south of Raleigh and some two hours southwest of Williamston. Originally founded in 1887 as a high school named Buies Creek Academy, the institution formally transitioned to a junior college in 1927 and changed its name to Campbell College in honor of its founder, J.A. Campbell. The school continued to offer high school classes until achieving senior college status in 1961.

With Campbell, Jim stepped right in, holding his own with mainly older teammates. First on the hardwood before doing the same on the diamond in the spring. Just as at Williamston High, the conditioning Jim gained playing basketball put him in peak physical shape to begin baseball in the spring. He also got to play for renowned basketball coach Fred McCall.

In the winter of 1955-56, McCall was in his third of sixteen seasons as head basketball coach at Campbell. He would proceed to guide his teams to a combined 221-104 record during that time. Jim Perry was a big part of that, beginning with that first winter on campus as a high school senior.

"Coach (McCall) is one of the finest guys you'd want to meet," Jim later related. "I certainly got a big kick out of playing on two championship teams there."[106]

Jim was a starter on the 1955-56 Campbell team that won the State junior college tournament. He averaged approximately 22 points per game during his basketball career at Campbell.

"Coach McCall would not let us leave practice until we each made 25 free throws," Jim recalled. "Because of that, I really refined my shot. One time, I got on a roll and made 100 free throws in a row. I was making so many without a miss, the other players gave up and left!"

That first spring of '56, Jim played baseball for Campbell as a high school senior under coach Hargrove "Hoggie" Davis. Immediately installed as the starting right fielder, Jim began the season with a pair of multi-hit games and remained a regular in the lineup whenever he was not pitching. He proceeded to hit for a .410 average and had a fine year on the mound, as well.

Jim became fast friends with Morgan Harris, another new player on the Campbell campus. "I can remember our first practice," Jim recalled. "There were six other guys who came out for shortstop. Morgan says to 'em, 'I don't know why you guys are here. I'm gonna be the starting shortstop on this team.' I thought to myself right there, I like this guy." Sure enough, Harris did win the starting shortstop job and he and Jim formed a lasting bond.

Shortly following the conclusion of that first season at Campbell, Jim signed a professional baseball contract with the Cleveland Indians and reported to North Platte, Nebraska. He spent the summer of '56 playing in the Nebraska State League, but when the season was over, he returned to Buies Creek and enrolled in more classes at Campbell. He would repeat the routine for the next three years.

Because the professional baseball season lasted into late September, the fall semester was in full swing by the time Jim made it back to campus. "It puts me behind some but I can usually make up the work in a hurry," he explained.

"When I started in the minor leagues, I gave myself four years to make it to the majors," Jim later recalled. "If I didn't make it, I was going to do something else. And I was going to have a good education. That's why I kept coming back."[107] His fallback plan was to eventually teach and coach at the high school level. Needless to say, life had a far different experience in store for Jim Perry.

Besides his in-class education, Jim also benefited from mentors in men like Coach McCall and Professor A.R. Burkot. Even as Jim was becoming a big man on campus at Campbell, he did not enjoy the luxuries one might expect of a star on the basketball team who was also already a professional baseball player. The modest star even spent one winter living with a handful of other athletes in what would best be described as a large storage closet inside Carter Gymnasium, the same place where he played basketball.

A short article in the *Raleigh News and Observer* during Jim's rookie year in the major leagues related his feelings for the school. The story was titled "Off-Season Student: Jim Fond of Campbell College."[108]

"Campbell College could ask for no better public relations man than Jim Perry," the story began. "Perry, who attends the Buies Creek school during the winter semester, thinks the people at Campbell are just fine and dandy."[109]

"They've really been great to me down there," Jim stated for the story.[110] It was a sentiment he would never lose.

5

Love and Life

Born in 1941, Daphne Snell is more than five years Jim's junior. Growing up in nearby Roper, about 30 miles due east of Williamston, Daphne enjoyed a few more luxuries than Jim. Daphne's father, Ben, was a farmer like Evan, but he also worked at Weyerhaeuser, a company that made wood products and was involved in several aspects of forestry.

Ben and wife Margaret lived in the house of a relative when Daphne was born. Ben farmed the land in exchange for the free housing. Unlike Jim, Daphne's first house had both electricity and indoor plumbing. That would come in handy at the time of Daphne's birth.

"Mom almost died having me," Daphne explained. "There were many cases of babies being switched at the hospital during this time, so Mom made up her mind that she would have her baby at home. Her heart started racing badly during labor and they had to give her something to slow down the labor."

Unfortunately, the medication provided by the doctor who was handling the home delivery caused liver damage that soon led to jaundice. In addition, Margaret had hemorrhaged so badly following the delivery that it left her incredibly weak. The difficult delivery caused Margaret to end up hospitalized, the very place she had taken pains to avoid.

Her infant daughter was fine, but when baby Daphne was brought to the hospital so that her mother could hold her newborn, another problem quickly became apparent. When Margaret reached out for her baby, it was like she was grasping in the dark—the jaundice had caused temporary blindness. Thankfully, Margaret's sight returned after a week, and the jaundice eventually dissipated, as well.

It was such a scary experience for the family that when Margaret became pregnant with Daphne's brother, Mack, six years later, she made clothes for Daphne in the event she would not survive the pending delivery. Margaret also marked up her Bible so that her survivors would know what verses she wanted read at her funeral. Thankfully, that would have to wait, as Margaret would go on to live 84 vibrant years.

Much to everyone's surprise, Margaret would give birth a third time some 19 years after her first. Concerned initially that she was dealing with a gallbladder issue, Margaret soon came to realize that she was carrying a third child—at the age of 44! By that time, Margaret had come to be more trusting of hospitals and Daphne's sister Laura was born without issue.

Health and Wellness

Even once back safe at home, mother Margaret remained protective of her first little girl. Not fully trusting of the safety of indoor plumbing when it came to the health of a little toddler, Margaret painstakingly boiled all the water that Daphne would drink in order to be sure it was safe. "One day she saw me out with Dad giving me water straight from the pump and she about had a fit," Daphne recollected.

When Daphne was five years old, Ben's mother, Daphne's Grandma Snell, died from stomach cancer and Grandpa Snell asked Ben to move his young family back home, approximately three miles to the north and farm the land there. Because Ben stood to eventually inherit this land, he readily accepted the invitation.

The trade off of moving back to Ben's boyhood home, however, saw the Snells return to a home with no electricity or indoor plumbing. "I can remember being in first grade, sitting at the kitchen table with an oil lamp doing my homework," Daphne recalled. Ben soon had plumbing installed and eventually electricity, as well.

Second grade was a difficult time for young Daphne, as she experienced a litany of maladies, including chicken pox, measles, and whooping cough. "Dad became so tired of me looking so unhealthy all the time," Daphne lamented, "that he gave me a homemade elixir of tonic filled with herbs. It tasted worse than castor oil! Well, no, nothing is worse than castor oil, but it was REALLY BAD!"

In the end, Daddy Ben's methods did the job, even if it wasn't the direct work of his concoction. "After that," Daphne recalled, "I was never skinny again. It made me want to eat!"

Skinny or not, Daphne always felt safe as a child, thanks to a pair of English Setters named Betty and Ben. "They were my protectors when I was in my stroller," she later recalled. "One day a neighbor boy came riding up on his bike a little too fast for the dogs' liking and one of them took a chomp on the boy's leg! Needless to say, that boy didn't dare venture close to my stroller again."

Farm Girl Life

Life on the farm lent itself to all kinds of animal pets. Daphne's brother, Mack, had a goat named Lulabelle. "She followed me around like a dog," he said. "She would even come in the house and sit on the couch to watch television with me."

While Ben was not completely reliant on farming, he still did his share, with crops that included tobacco. Growing up on the farm led impressionable Daphne to get herself into some hot water at a young age by her use of some colorful language. "I was about four or five years old," Daphne explained, "and I reacted to something outside just as I had seen Daddy do numerous times. I went out on the porch, put my hands on my hips just like my Dad, and exclaimed, 'the damn pigs are in the garden again!' Mom about fainted."

Like most all youngsters in this part of North Carolina, Daphne also did her share of farm work. She was a tobacco "handler," skilled at bundling the uncured leaves into "hands" before passing them on to the "looper," who put it on sticks to be hung in the barn for curing. Daphne's mother, Margaret, was considered one of the area's most expert loopers.

While Daphne did fine work helping with the tobacco as it was brought in, she felt that she could earn some money by doing more.

Eventually, Daphne and schoolmate Margaret Davenport took a job two farms down "topping" tobacco.

Because a tobacco plant is driven to reproduce, it concentrates most of its energy on making a big, beautiful flower, which grows out of the very top of the plant and contains thousands of tiny tobacco seeds. While tobacco farmers do need some seeds, they want the majority of their crop to grow with a little more kick, so that means removing the flower.

Taking off the flower is known as topping. When a tobacco plant is topped, especially when it's done very early when the flower is but a bud, the tobacco plant concentrates its efforts on the leaves. More energy to the leaves means more power, and stronger tobacco.

In the days before this was handled by machines, farm workers had to go up and down each row under the hot sun topping the tobacco plants manually. Ben did not believe women should be doing this manual labor in the field and when he found out what Daphne was up to, he was not pleased.

"You don't have to work at home like that," Daddy Ben explained to his enterprising daughter, "and if you don't have to do it here, you're darn well not going to do it for somebody else!"

"So we had to quit," Daphne lamented.

Talents Refined

When she wasn't helping around the homestead, Daphne was very involved in her church. Like many families of the area, the Snells were devout in their Christian faith. Perla Brey was the organist at their church (as well as the local postmaster). "If any of the kids showed any kind of talent," Daphne chuckled, "Perla was sure to put them up in front of the congregation. I enjoyed singing, so Perla groomed me from a young age. I was so small at the time, she had to put me up on a stand so the congregation could see me over the rail!"

Like Jim, Daphne decided to finish her high school education at Campbell College. However, she decided to transfer to Campbell following her sophomore year of high school at the tender age of 16, a year sooner than Jim had done. The decision would prove to be serendipitous.

When she began at Campbell in 1957, her first roommate, Helen

Manning, was a junior college sophomore, more than three years older than Daphne. Helen lived in nearby Plymouth and the two had become friends through their involvement in 4H.

Lucky in Love

When Helen heard that Daphne was going to enroll at Campbell, she called Daphne's mother and said she would like Daphne to be her roommate. Helen was on the women's basketball team at Campbell and also dated a player on the men's team, Eley (pronounced "EE-lee") Newsome, who would later become her husband. Helen was also friends with Jim who, of course, was a teammate of Eley's. In addition to that, Helen's grandparents happened to live very close to the Perry farm. This would prove to be a fortuitous connection.

It was not long after Daphne's parents dropped her off at Campbell College that she began to have second thoughts. While she knew the educational aspect of Campbell was positive, she underestimated how much she would miss home.

"The first weekend, you couldn't go home," she explained, "and the next weekend, Mom and Dad would not let me come home because I think they felt if I did that I wouldn't go back, I was so homesick. When I did finally go home for the first time, I mailed them a note saying not to worry, because I was gonna ride with this guy Helen knew named James Perry who lived in Williamston."

With Jim's Farm Life home located only about 20 miles west of Helen's hometown of Plymouth, Jim was happy to have company for the ride, plus a couple dollars toward gas, so he had regularly given Helen a ride, both to and from school whenever he had occasion to return home. When Helen asked if her friend, Daphne, who was a new student at Campbell, could join them, Jim did not realize his good fortune.

Although she was five-and-a-half years younger, Daphne and Jim immediately hit it off. It certainly didn't hurt that she was squeezed into the middle of the big bench seat right next to him for the two-plus hour drive.

"We would all three ride in the front seat of his '56 Oldsmobile," Daphne explained, "because Ruby had washed and ironed every piece of shirt or whatever, and he had one of those rods across the back seat.

Of course, they all had to hang, so they wouldn't get messed up. He was so particular about his clothes."

It was not long after that first road trip before Jim invited Daphne to go with him to some concerts on campus and the pair quickly became an item. Seeing the tall, good looking, star athlete dating a young "high school" girl did not please the older girls on campus, needless to say.

"The older girls were so jealous that he was dating somebody who wasn't his age," Daphne explained. "We only had a phone in the hallway at the dorm. When Jim would call me and somebody would answer that phone, they would yell for me down the hallway in such a condescending way that you knew they just didn't like it at all."

"We hit it off right away," Jim recalled. "We enjoyed doing a lot of the same things and had a lot in common. Other people thought it was great."

Love Detector Test

The new lovebirds quickly discovered, however, that not everyone at Campbell was fond of young love. "Trying to hold hands while walking around campus was a challenge," Jim explained. "If the president of the college saw you, he would tell you to stop."

"The president of the college (Leslie Campbell, son of founder J.A. Campbell) frowned on anything like that," added Daphne.

One of the "same things the pair enjoyed doing" was playing basketball. Like Jim, Daphne played on the Campbell team. Back then, the women's version was a half-court 3-on-3 matchup at each end of the floor. Three players on offense and another three on defense. No players were permitted to cross over the half-court line. A defensive specialist, Daphne was named co-captain, due to the leadership qualities she exhibited both on and off the court. This basketball relationship helped to reveal that the pair's love relationship was far from inconspicuous.

"Shortly after we met, the boys and girls teams were riding the bus together to play Chowan, and Dr. Burkot, the Dean of Students, took the trip with us. Jim and I were seated together, and at that time, Coach McCall didn't know who I was. So he asked Dean Burkot, 'Who is this girl?' like he didn't want me there. And I understood, because Jim was his 'boy.' He had three daughters, and Jim was like a son to him. He wanted to know who this little girl was messing with his boy."[111]

Daphne was never intimidated by her boyfriend's "celebrity status," and Jim, ever humble, surely never gave her any reason to feel that way, but others were not so kind. It was Jim's coaches, especially, who seemed to take great pleasure in teasing his young girlfriend whenever they found the chance.

"Coach McCall was teaching a health class," Daphne explained, "and he called me out in class once saying, 'Ms. Snell, I saw you with Mr. Perry having breakfast this morning. Did he have halitosis? You know what halitosis is, right?' Well, halitosis is bad breath, and of course, he did a good job of embarrassing me in class."[112]

Well-Rounded Student

Daphne did more than just date Jim and play basketball, of course. For one thing, she completed her junior and senior years of high school work in just one year. In her second year at Campbell, Daphne commenced her college study with a major in business education.

In addition to her studies, she was involved in several student organizations, including the Baptist Student Union, the New House Council, Beta Club, May Court, and Future Business Leaders of America. In 1960, Daphne received the Outstanding Student Award, as well as the Vivian Dawson Massey Music Award.

Her fondest memory at Campbell was when she was chosen for the prestigious formal Campbell Touring Choir. Not only did Daphne utilize her beautiful singing voice, but she also contributed her organizational talents while serving as Librarian for the Choir. She relished the opportunity to travel to various cities, including New York City where the Choir performed at one of the elegant Manhattan cathedrals. While there, members of the Choir were able to take in a performance of the Rockettes.

"Just to be in that big city with all those bright lights at only 17 years old was really something," Daphne marveled.

Another highlight came when the Choir received an invitation to perform for the Southern Baptist Convention in Miami, Florida. They became the first junior college program to receive such an honor.

It was during Daphne's second year at Campbell that her mother gave birth to sister Laura. In addition to her studies and extracurricular activities, Daphne made it a point to get back home every weekend she possibly could to help care for her new baby sister, but in the spring of '59 she would have to make the trip home on her own, because the man who normally gave her a ride was no longer around.

One Good Shot

After winning 16 games with a sparkling 2.79 ERA at A-level Reading in 1958, Jim received his first invitation to big league spring training in Tucson, Arizona the following spring. The first person he shared the news with was Daphne.

"I can remember what a thrill it was for him after having played only three years in the minors," Daphne later recalled. "I can also remember how disappointed I was. When Jim told me that he would leave for Arizona in just a few weeks, all I could think of was myself. I knew my geography well enough to know that it was a long way from North Carolina to Arizona.

"I didn't know anything about baseball. I couldn't see what this could possibly mean to him—he would be leaving me!"

Little did young Daphne realize that this break would lead to her ultimate goal—marriage to the love of her life—coming to fruition sooner than Jim had originally planned.

The next person Jim told was his basketball coach and mentor. "Nobody was happier than Coach McCall," Jim recalled, smiling. "He was so excited for me. Then, of course, the first thing he asked was, 'You're still coming back, right?' I told him absolutely."[113]

It was Coach McCall who Jim would credit for his supreme self-confidence that contributed to his surprising success later that summer.

> My coach (McCall) kept telling me I'd make it, and I began to believe him.
>
> — Jim Perry

"My coach kept telling me I'd make it, and I began to believe him," said Perry of McCall's never-ending encouragement. "A lot of guys get one good shot at this thing. I don't figure to miss out on mine."[114]

6

Beating the Bushes

In the spring of 1956, following the conclusion of Jim's first baseball season at Campbell (and thus his "graduation" from high school), several MLB teams were interested in signing him. The New York Yankees, Cleveland Indians, Philadelphia Phillies, and San Francisco Giants were all after him, but there was a catch. Each club wanted Jim to work out with them exclusively for a couple weeks before they would make their final offer.

Jim wisely figured that spending the summer jumping all over the country trying to impress teams was a recipe for a sore arm, so he came up with a better plan. He went to Asheboro, North Carolina where he could work for a hosiery mill earning $500 a month. The work, however, was secondary to the fact that they had a semipro baseball team, for which he would pitch. This gave MLB scouts an opportunity to continue watching him and bidding for his services.

Another complication of the times was the short-lived existence of the convoluted MLB "Bonus Rule." Intended to save teams from themselves by discouraging bidding wars, the Bonus Rule mandated that any amateur player receiving a signing bonus over $4,000 was required to immediately be placed on the active big league roster and remain there for two full calendar years from the signing date. Because these peach-fuzzed youngsters, no matter how talented, were ultimately unprepared to immediately step in and compete against grizzled major league veterans, they inevitably ended up riding the pine for two years before being sent back down to the minors to begin their true development. The fact that this cost these "Bonus Babies," as they were called, valuable minor league development time was not lost on Jim. He was laser focused on making it to the big leagues not to ride the bench and collect a paycheck, but to pitch— for a long time.

4 - 4 = Opportunity

As the competing clubs came at him with offers, young Jim carefully assessed the opportunities with each team. The Yankees, who had played in the World Series six of the prior seven years, wanted him badly and were willing to make him a Bonus Baby. Not only would that have hurt his development by placing him on the bench in the major leagues, but he would also be looking up at a formidable established rotation that included the likes of Whitey Ford (27 years old), Don Larsen (26), Bob Turley (25), and Tom Sturdivant (26).

The team that interested Jim the most was the Cleveland Indians and it was for one big reason. Cleveland was arguably the second strongest team in the American League after the Yankees at that time, but there was one major difference between the two teams, and it happened to be on the mound. While the average age of the Yankees rotation was a mere 26 years old, suggesting many more productive years ahead of the quartet, Cleveland's pitching core was far closer to the end of the line. At 37 years of age, Bob Feller was in the final season of his hall-of-fame career. Early Wynn and Bob Lemon, both of whom would eventually join Rapid Robert in the Hall, were 36 and 35, respectively, while nine-year veteran Mike Garcia was 32. Herb Score at 23, who was easing into Feller's rotation slot, was the only youngster among the group. Jim smelled opportunity. He wisely deduced that if he worked hard and developed on schedule, there would be a great opportunity to crack the rotation in Cleveland within the next few years.

In late June, Jim agreed to a $4,000 signing bonus with Cleveland—the maximum amount he could get and still avoid violation of the Bonus Rule. Roger Thrift, who was Jim's football coach during his brief high school gridiron career, shared how the new pro made use of his modest yet not insignificant windfall.

"Perry is a wonderful kid," Thrift related. "He got a $4,000 signing bonus for signing. First thing on the mind of most youngsters in his position would have been to buy a swanky convertible. Jim took his money and bought a tractor and truck—for his dad's farm."[115]

Go West, Young Man

Jim did manage to pick up a '56 Oldsmobile for himself, as well—the first new car anyone in his family had ever owned. He would need it to make his way westward to his first pro destination in North Platte, Nebraska where he was assigned to play in the Class D Nebraska State League. "I had never seen so many black bugs in my life as the swarm I drove through crossing over the Platte River," Jim recalled. "I had to pull over and scrape them off my windshield just so I could see!"

Jim wasted no time in making his mark as a professional, firing a three-hitter on July first in North Platte's opening game. After allowing a first-inning run, Jim proceeded to retire 21 men in a row before a single with two outs in the ninth inning ended his streak of dominance. He struck out 16 opposing batters in the complete game effort and even added two hits of his own for good measure.

Racking up 40 strikeouts in his first three professional starts, Jim quickly became known as a dependable workhorse who would compete ferociously for nine innings. Even after throwing all spring during Campbell's season, Jim hurled complete games in more than half of his 15 starts during his first summer as a pro. His 120 innings pitched ranked second among pitchers in the Nebraska State League.

An Associated Press summary of a late-season game summarized young Jim's tenacity on the mound: "Jim Perry put down a ninth inning Hastings uprising Friday night and North Platte walked off with a 7-5 Nebraska State League win. Hastings had loaded the bases with one man out but Perry got the next two hitters."[116] That ability to persevere when faced with ominous circumstances would come to characterize Jim's career.

He was also becoming known as a pitcher who could hold his own with the bat. In his final start of the season on August 31, Jim broke up a no-hitter that was being thrown at his team by a fellow future major leaguer, Gary Peters. The bad luck of facing off with a pitcher throwing a no-hitter against his team would unfortunately prove to be another omen.

Spring Into Work

While Jim's 7-8 record to go with a 4.80 ERA in his first pro season were far from dazzling, he certainly showed enough to move up a level from the Class D designation of the Nebraska State League. His first professional spring training camp would make an impression that left no doubt he was more than an ordinary ballplayer.

Jim reported to Cleveland's farm club base in Daytona Beach, Florida in March of 1957 prior to his first full pro season. Observers were immediately impressed by young Perry's maturity. Tony Pianowski, who was administrator of the rookie camp, shared a story that exemplified Jim's thoroughgoing determination.

"Sometimes I think country boys make the best players," said Pianowski. "Perry from the start was one of our hardest workers. Red Ruffing was on our staff then and he was a great believer in running the kids until their tongues were hanging out. Jim would stay right with him, chasing fungoes as long as Red could hit them."[117]

One Step at a Time

Jim moved to the next rung on the developmental ladder for his first full professional season in 1957 as he journeyed to a region that he would later come to call home. He was assigned to Fargo-Moorhead of the Class C Northern League. Located on the border of Minnesota and North Dakota, just a little more than 150 miles due south of the Canadian line, the team represented the neighboring towns of Fargo, North Dakota and Moorhead, Minnesota. Even more prescient was the fact that Jim's first full-season pro team was nicknamed the Twins.

The Fargo-Moorhead Twins played their home games at Barnett Field located on the North Dakota side of the border. The team traveled to its road games in a caravan of three vans. Being an experienced school bus driver, Jim was naturally tabbed to drive one of them. As one might expect in the vast northern regions of Minnesota and the Dakotas, these were not commuter trips. Far from it. The 1957 Northern League schedule included trips to Eau Claire, Wisconsin (a drive of more than 300 miles), Duluth, Minnesota (250), Winnipeg, Canada (225 miles due north), and even Wausau, located almost 450 miles east in the heart of northern Wisconsin.

After finding himself assigned to a North Platte team that would finish with a 24-39 record, good for a seventh place finish in the eight-team Nebraska State League, his first year as a pro, Jim was hoping for a better environment with his first full-season squad. He could not have been too thrilled to join a Fargo-Moorhead club coming off a miserable 49-74 season that saw them finish dead-last in the Northern League the prior season. As the team prepared to break spring training camp in Daytona Beach, Florida, however, things appeared to be shaping up. A pre-season preview printed in the *St. Cloud Daily Times* stated that "Cleveland farm system officials have given new manager Frank Tornay a balanced club featuring strong pitching and good defense."[118]

Headliner

It was the lanky righthander from Williamston, North Carolina who was expected to headline the strong pitching staff. Unlike today's deep rosters of situation specialists, players in the late 1950s were expected to be multifaceted competitors and the rosters reflected that fact. Fargo-Moorhead broke spring training camp with a 19-man roster comprising eight pitchers and eleven position players. Just as he did in his pro debut, Jim burst out of the gates, winning his first two starts.

In addition to gaining the reputation as a reliable workhorse, young Perry was also characterized by his ability to withstand the elements. Of course, he grew up determined to find a way to play ball regardless of how hard he might have already labored in oppressive heat. Spring weather in the Northern League, however, tended to be the opposite of "oppressive heat." Jim got a chance to test his mettle in biting cold conditions in a game in Wausau, Wisconsin on Sunday, May 26 of that 1957 season. According to the *St. Cloud Daily Times*,

Wausau and Fargo-Moorhead played in 45-degree weather with a 40-mile-per-hour northwest wind! How did young Jim fare? He fired a four-hit shutout to push his team into first place in the standings. Oh, and he drove in one of the Fargo-Moorhead runs to help propel the offense in the 8-0 victory.

Perry was 11-6 by the all-star break, his eleven wins tied for the league lead. Unsurprisingly, he was selected for the Northern League all-star game. He hurled two shutouts in eight days in early August, just missing a no-hitter in the second one when a Wausau hitter beat out a slow-rolling dribbler down the third base line.

Fargo-Moorhead would finish the season with a winning record of 65-57, only good enough for fourth place in the eight-team Northern League, but still a much more pleasant experience than Jim's first taste of pro ball the previous summer. More importantly for his future prospects, Jim had not only solidified himself as a dependable workhorse starter, but he had also gained a reputation as one of the top control artists in the league. His 231 innings pitched and 21 complete games were both tops in the league. He also boasted excellent control with just 2.8 walks per nine innings.

Picking Up Steam

Following his strong 1957 season in Class C, the Indians decided to have Jim skip a level and move up to the Class A Eastern League for the 1958 season. After spending his first two years playing in rather shoddy, primitive environments of the low minors, arriving in Reading, Pennsylvania was a pleasant surprise.

"Reading had the best field in the league," said Jim. "To me, it seemed like the major leagues!"

Having just been built in 1951, community owned and operated Reading Municipal Memorial Stadium was one of the newer minor league parks in the country and was the pride of the city. In addition to baseball, the facility hosted high school football in the fall, as well as circuses, concerts and other civic events year-round. The city took great care in maintaining the facility—a fact not lost on minor league players who traveled through.

There was another benefit of playing at the higher minor league classification for Jim Perry. He was no longer charged with driving one of the team vans. He was not in the actual big leagues yet, however, and there were still some parts of the experience that epitomized minor league life, especially when it came to travel.

"Stan Shackler was the team's bus driver," Jim recalled. "He was a big guy, must have weighed about 400 pounds."

The Eastern League was divided into two divisions, Northern and Southern. Reading was in the Southern Division, along with three other Pennsylvania teams that were all within a 90-minute drive. This made many of the road games commuter trips, but also made for some late-night returns.

"We called our team bus the old blue goose," Jim laughed. "I had to sit in the front seat and keep Stan awake driving up the big Pennsylvania hills coming back home late at night."

Another characteristic in those days was that minor league staff members had to handle multiple duties, and Reading was no exception.

"Not only was Stan the bus driver, but he was the trainer, too," Jim explained. "We didn't have any kind of advanced post-game treatment. Heck, we didn't even know about ice. After the game on hot days, Stan would make a swipe on your arm with alcohol to close the pores and you were good to go!"

Unlike his first two seasons as a professional, Jim did not get off to a quick start at Reading. Bouncing between the bullpen and the rotation, perhaps because the Indians jumped him a level, it wasn't until almost a month into the season that he notched his first win. When he finally did capture his first victory of the 1958 season, however, he did it in classic Perry fashion. On May 21 on a chilly 45-degree night in Binghamton, New York, Jim fired a three-hitter, as he went the distance in a 5-1 Reading win.

Ace Advice

As the spring wore on, back home in Williamston, North Carolina Jim's little brother Gaylord was being wooed by scouts with various teams. The oppressive "Bonus Rule" that had arbitrarily held down Jim's signing bonus to $4,000 had just been rescinded and teams were aggressively going after top amateur talent. Gaylord later described how he and father Evan valued Jim's input.

"Jim kept in telephone contact with us. 'Give each club a fair chance,' Jim advised. 'Take every promise that isn't in writing with a grain of salt. Go with the club which offers you the most money, but consider the quality of the organization, the pitching needs of the big club and how fast they bring along their prospects.'

"Most of the clubs dropped out early in the bidding, the Cleveland Indians among them. I thought they would come up with a good offer because they had Jim. But they didn't. Jim hadn't been pitching real well yet and maybe one Perry was all the organization could handle at the time. But to tell the truth, if the Indians had come only close to the others, I would have signed with them just to be with Jim. I think the Indians' best offer was about $7,000. I believe the Indians thought that Jim would sway me into signing with them and that they could get me cheap. Jim told me *not* to be influenced by the fact that he was with Cleveland. Washington came up with a real good offer, not a big bonus but a promise to put me right into the big leagues. The Yankees offer was low. They tried to sell me on the greatness of the Yankee uniform and annual pennant shares. I wanted something substantial.

> If the Indians had come only close to the others, I would have signed just to be with Jim.
>
> — Gaylord Perry

"Finally, four clubs were left... Milwaukee decided to invest $100,000 in Tony Cloninger who was also a high-school senior in North Carolina that year. The Giants were surprised. They'd expected to get Cloninger. They didn't want to lose me, too.

"The negotiations at my house lasted two days, and after overhearing a few other bids and sampling a lot of Mamma's cooking, the Giants made the bid we wanted: a bonus plus three years of salary, all adding up to $73,500—the most the Giants had ever paid a rookie."[119]

As Gaylord got his career started, the two brothers remained as close as ever. Jim would tell people that his favorite baseball player is Gaylord Perry, while Gaylord would brag a similar sentiment about his big brother. Even as their respective professional journeys left many miles between the two, they managed to stay connected.

"We exchange about two letters a week," Jim confirmed. "We keep close tabs on what each other is doing."[120]

Settling In

As the weather heated up, Jim really began to get his feet under him at the new level. On June 5 in a home game against Allentown, he accomplished a rare baseball feat by producing more hits than he allowed. You read that right. After a pair of first inning runs, one due to an error, Jim gave up only two more hits the rest of the night, allowing only one more Allentown runner to get as far as second base. At the same time, he was pacing the Reading 20-hit attack with a team-high four hits of his own! Jim personally rapped out a double and three singles while allowing the entire Allentown team only three measly singles en route to a 17-2 complete game win.

On June 26, Jim struck out ten in another three-hit complete game effort to even his record at 4-4. That win began a stretch in which he posted a 13-4 record over the season's final two-plus months. He was also the winning pitcher in the Eastern League all-star game. After a mid-August shutout, the *Daily Intelligencer Journal* in nearby Lancaster ran a rare game story that provided a perfect description of Jim's secret to success:

"The Reading Indians pounced on Lefty Ron Nischwitz for four hits and three runs in the sixth inning tonight and went on to blank the Lancaster Red Roses 3-0 behind Jim Perry's brilliant hurling… Perry was in plenty of tough spots but always came through with the pitch in the clutch."[121]

Jim finished the 1958 season with a 16-8 record and a 2.79 ERA. He was selected to the Eastern League post-season All-Star team. He also pitched exactly 200 innings, reaching that plateau for the second consecutive season. His durability plus his consistent success was quietly gaining the attention of decision-makers back in Cleveland.

> *Perry was in plenty of tough spots but always came through with the pitch in the clutch.*
>
> — Rare newspaper minor league Class-A game recap

7
Here to Stay

Following his strong finish in Reading, the Indians invited Jim to major league spring training camp for the first time in 1959. The invitation was partly a reward for Perry's strong work since joining the organization, no doubt. It was also common practice for the big league brass to get a good look at top young players before they were reassigned to minor league camp and then dispatched to the appropriate minor league team for the regular season.

For 23-year old Jim Perry, who spent the prior season in Class A, the eventual destination was likely double-A Mobile, Alabama, which was the roster on which he was listed as he reported to his initial big league camp. From any reasonable perspective, a best case scenario—if he had an extremely impressive spring training—might have Perry beginning the year in triple-A San Diego. However, that would be a long shot. Unfortunately, nobody bothered to explain this to the bright-eyed hurler before he arrived at the Indians spring training complex in Tucson, Arizona.

"'I'm here to make this club,' drawled the skinny youngster from North Carolina. 'I don't intend to go anywhere else!'

"Knowing smiles and even snickers might have greeted big, brash Jim Perry when he barged into the Cleveland Indians' spring camp at Hi Corbett Field," wrote Carl Porter of the *Tucson Citizen*. "'He just walked right into camp and said he was going to stay here,' laughed Manager (Joe) Gordon. 'He wasn't really cocky... he just meant it. A lot of guys do the same thing but can't back it up.'"[122]

"I didn't know how good a chance I had of sticking with the Indians," Jim later admitted, "but I knew two things: I was going to report in shape and I was going to work my heart out."[123]

Still, Perry's self-confidence was so apparent that teammate and fellow pitcher Gary Bell soon began calling him "Miller Huggins" in reference to the famed manager of the first great New York Yankees teams because "he seems to know it all."[124] From his first bullpen in late February, however, the youngster backed up his big talk. Joe Gordon, the Cleveland skipper, made a point to mention that Jim and fellow prospect Dick Stigman were the two youngsters who stood out to him in their first bullpen workouts of camp. The reward was an opportunity to pitch in some early "B" games, which usually included reserve players and young prospects who were just getting a taste of the big league atmosphere.

By mid-March, however, when most of the other prospect types were being shipped off to Cleveland's minor league camp in Daytona Beach, Florida, Jim's performance was demanding special treatment. Instead of being sent to Florida's Atlantic Coast, he remained in the desert, pitching in "A" spring games with the bulk of Cleveland's regular lineup of veterans.

One of those veterans was starting right fielder and cleanup hitter Rocky Colavito, who quickly took a liking to the young rookie. "I liked him from Day One," said Colavito. "I didn't think he was cocky. I thought he was a gentleman. He was just trying his best to make a good impression like any young guy would."

Colavito's roommate was starting pitcher Herb Score. The two had been close friends since coming up together in the minors. Score also took a liking to the aggressive young rookie, as the two often ran together in the outfield during the pitchers conditioning program. When Jim had an opportunity to join them for dinner he was concerned about the optics of a rookie cozying up to the two veteran team leaders. "If anybody gives you a hard time, you tell 'em we invited you," Colavito reassuringly told the rookie.

As March wound down, Jim continued to stick around. The young righthander's talent could not be denied. "He had a good fastball, but it was a different kind of fastball," explained Colavito. Herbie (Score) was blazing fast, but Perry was sneaky fast. He had this effortless windup and then all of a sudden the ball was on you."

Team beat writer Jim Schlemmer stated, "Winding up the last full week of training camp (manager Joe) Gordon pointed to (Gene) Leek, (Ray) Webster, (Woodie) Held, Carroll Hardy and Jim Perry as the bright discoveries thus far."[125]

Sold

Jim's Cinderella Spring Story culminated with an April 2 start against the Cubs that many observers considered to be the best performance of the spring by a Cleveland pitcher. It was the team's final game before they would break camp and begin barnstorming their way toward their April 10 season opener in Kansas City. Jim wrapped up his stunning Arizona spring in what reporter Carl Porter of the *Tucson Citizen* termed "a thrilling pitcher's duel with Cub bonus ace Moe Drabowski."[126] The unflappable rookie limited Chicago to three hits and two walks while striking out five over six shutout innings.

"That sold me on Perry," admitted Cleveland manager Joe Gordon. "I don't think too many American Leaguers are going to like him."[127]

Perry's outing, the longest of the exhibition season by a Cleveland starter, left him with a sparkling 2.35 ERA and only 16 hits allowed over 23 spring innings. One of Cleveland's local newspapers, the *Akron Beacon Journal*, ran the headline, "Indians Are 'Wild About Perry'" the following day.

"I hadn't even heard of him before he came to camp," remarked Gordon.[128] "He's just one of the fellows we brought in to pitch batting practice until our regulars got their arms in shape... Now here he is, showing up the others as the best of the lot."[129]

Beat writer Jim Schlemmer, present for a firsthand view throughout the spring, detailed the exploits that brought

> *I hadn't even heard of him before he came to camp. Now here he is showing up the others as the best in the lot.*
>
> — Manager Joe Gordon on rookie Jim Perry

Perry to this point. "Working in 93 degree heat, the 6-4, 185-pound sinker-ball artist pitched with the poise of a seasoned old-timer and was in complete charge although nursing only a 1-0 lead ... He is thin as a rail; all arms and legs and motion. He is deceptively fast. He has fine control... and he has a kind of confidence which includes tones of arrogance and bitterness. He doesn't go around talking about it but if one asks, he'll say he is a good pitcher, ready and willing at all times to prove it, and he has no intentions of pitching for any club other than the Indians."[130]

"Gordon keeps saying it's impossible for a 22-year old with only three pro years behind him to be as good as Perry appears to be," wrote Schlemmer.[131]

"He has looked so good it must be an optical illusion," the Tribe manager half-jokingly exclaimed.[132]

Hit the Books

Cleveland general manager Frank Lane provided an insightful illustration of Jim's studious determination. "He was always so serious," said Lane. "We brought him to Tucson that spring just to pitch batting practice. I saw him in the hotel lobby writing in a little black book. I asked him what he was doing and he said he was figuring out how to pitch to (Royals cleanup hitter) Bob Cerv in the first game of the season in Kansas City.

"He wasn't even on the roster. I asked Joe Gordon, 'Is he going to pitch your first game?' Gordon said, 'No—what do you mean?' I said, 'He's pitching the first game right now over there.' I never saw a more serious-minded kid. He pitched his way right onto the ball club that year."[133]

The information in that little black book dated back years before that first spring training. Jim began taking notes on big league hitters when he saw his first game on television. He continued to build his strategic inventory whenever he got the chance.

"I studied hard," Jim explained. "When I wasn't pitching, I stayed in the dugout and took notes on the other team. I did anything that would help me get a guy out."[134]

Hop on the Bus

On April 3, the Cleveland Indians broke camp, boarding a bus that would take them to Phoenix for the windup to their Arizona exhibition schedule with a game against the San Francisco Giants. From there, they would start the long haul east with exhibition stops in Salt Lake City (UT), Denver (CO), Topeka (KS), Des Moines (IA), and Omaha (NE) before beginning the regular season on April 10 in Kansas City, Missouri. Jim Perry was on the bus.

Not only was Jim an official member of the Opening Day roster, but manager Joe Gordon had reportedly begun to toy with the idea of starting Perry on Opening Day in Kansas City. Three days before the opener, Gordon told reporters that he had narrowed his choice of Opening Day starter to Gary Bell or Perry, but he was hesitant to tip his hand, primarily in order to avoid overwhelming his confident rookie.

"If I should decide to go with Perry," cautioned the manager, "I wouldn't want him to know or suspect until right up to game time."[135]

4-4 = 0

As Jim Perry looked back on his decision-making process of which major league team to sign with three springs prior, his mathematics arithmetic exercise had proven amazingly prescient. Just as he surmised when he decided to go with Cleveland, the four standout veteran pitchers who had carried the Cleveland staff through much of the 1950s were now gone.

Bob Feller retired following the 1956 season and Bob Lemon did the same midway through 1959 spring training. Early Wynn, now 39, had moved on to the Chicago White Sox. The final member of the foursome was 35-year old Mike Garcia, who had suffered through a miserable spring. As they maneuvered to set their 1959 Opening Day roster, the Indians announced Garcia would open the year on the disabled list due to a pulled thigh muscle. Amazingly enough, that transaction would open the roster spot that would be filled by young Jim Perry.

Debut a Hit

Gordon ultimately decided to go with the second-year veteran Bell for the Opening Day nod, allowing his prized rookie to soak in the atmosphere of his first official MLB game from the comfort of the bench. Jim waited patiently to make his major league debut as the team came out of the gates red hot. The Indians won their first six games and eight of their first nine as off days and strong starting pitching limited the opportunities for mound work. Six of those first nine games featured complete games by Cleveland starting pitchers.

On Thursday, April 23, Cleveland was set to wrap up a three-game series in Detroit. The Tigers had stumbled out of the gates by losing eight of their first nine, including the first two against the Indians by a combined score of 24-2. Joe Gordon had been looking to get his rookie phenom's feet wet "and this is as good a place as any," stated the Cleveland manager.[136]

After Cleveland went down 1-2-3 in the top of the first, Jim took the mound for his major league debut. Despite his confidence, the 23-year old rookie had to be battling some nerves as he issued a walk to Tigers leadoff man Eddie Yost. Perry quickly recovered, however, coaxing a tailor-made 6-4-3 double play grounder off the bat of Rocky Bridges. The next batter, Harvey Kuenn, picked up a single before Perry retired cleanup hitter Gail Harris on a pop fly into the glove of first baseman Vic Power.

In the top of the second inning, Cleveland got two runners of their own on with two outs, bringing up eight-hole hitter Billy Martin. Knowing a green rookie pitcher making his big league debut was on deck, veteran Ray Narleski, on the mound for the Tigers, pitched around Martin, eventually walking him to load up the bases. Narleski was about to find out that Jim Perry was no ordinary rookie pitcher.

The switch-hitting Perry was batting from the left side against the right-handed Narleski. Jim worked the count full. He then proceeded to foul off four consecutive pitches. Finally, on the tenth pitch of the at bat, Perry got a pitch he could handle, smacking a hard grounder back up the middle for a single into center field. The hit scored the first two runs of the game and gave the Indians a lead they would never relinquish.

Jim retired Detroit in order in the bottom of the second, enticing three routine ground outs. In the third inning, he recorded his first major league strikeout, ringing up Tigers leadoff man Eddie Yost to avenge the first-inning walk. A third inning Cleveland rally had given Jim a seven run cushion before he allowed his first run on a single by Frank Bolling that scored Gail Harris.

Unfortunately, even as he entered the fifth inning with an 8-1 lead, Jim's lack of work during the season's first two weeks caught up with him. Uncharacteristically, he served up back-to-back one out walks, followed by two straight singles. After Jim got Harris to pop to third for the second out, Al Kaline singled to load the bases. Concerned that his rookie was tiring and not wanting him to lose confidence after four strong opening innings, manager Gordon went to the bullpen, leaving Jim one out short of qualifying for the win in his big league debut.

Bullpen Bounce Back

While he didn't get the win in his first start, Jim still did nothing to lose the faith of his manager, who went right back to the rookie in both ends of a double-header against the Chicago White Sox three days later. Jim fired a shutout inning in each game, striking out a pair and allowing no hits. The successful relief work convinced Gordon to give Jim another start on April 29 against Boston only to have the game rained out.

Reduced once again to biding his time in the bullpen while the veteran starters stayed on their normal rest, Jim came on in relief May 6 with two perfect innings in a one-run loss to Baltimore. Jim notched his first major league victory the following night. Unfortunately, it doesn't show up in his statistics because it came in an exhibition game held, ironically enough, in Minnesota's Metropolitan Stadium.

Built in 1956, "the Met" was a product of the Minneapolis Chamber of Commerce in hopes of luring a major league team to the Minneapolis-St. Paul metropolis. It was built to MLB specifications and became the home of the American Association's Minneapolis Millers as local politicians campaigned for an MLB team.

Before Cleveland kicked off a 13-day 12-game road trip beginning in Chicago, they took a detour to Minneapolis where they met up with the cross-state rival Cincinnati Reds, who were beginning an

18-game road swing of their own. With 10,101 fans in attendance for the mid-season exhibition game, Jim tossed a pair of shutout innings while Cleveland overcame a 3-2 deficit, making Perry the winning pitcher in the 4-3 final over the Reds.

The Boy With Guts

Following a four-game series in Chicago, the Indians stopped off in the Big Apple on May 12 for a quick two-game set with the New York Yankees. Leave it to the brash rookie to save his coming out party for the game's biggest stage. Though it was the first time he had ever seen Yankee Stadium, not to mention the largest crowd (34,671) he had ever pitched in front of, the young farm boy was unfazed. A UPI reporter summarized Jim's exploits in a story that was carried in several newspapers around the country the following day.

"Rookie hurler Jim Perry put the New York Yankees on notice today—'Don't make me mad.' The 22-year old North Carolina farm boy came out of the Cleveland Indians bullpen Tuesday night and struck out four of the seven batters he faced in the eighth and ninth innings to save a 7-6 victory for the Tribe.

"After striking out Enos Slaughter and Andy Carey to end the eighth, Perry was greeted with a double by Tony Kubek in the final frame. Perry was irked at the blemish, slapped his glove, reared back and struck out Mickey Mantle on three pitches.

"Yogi Berra popped out to Billy Martin and the still angry young fastballer then proceeded to strike out Elston Howard (on three straight pitches) to erase any doubts about who was in command."[137]

During his post-game meeting with the press, which was always intense when visiting the major media market of New York, Cleveland manager Joe Gordon was challenged by a writer who stated, "You had a lot of guts sticking in that kid."[138]

"The boy had the guts," Gordon countered.[139] "What Perry did was the greatest thing that has happened to our club since the season began."[140]

"Once in a while, you make a pitcher by calling a kid into a spot like that," Gordon continued. This could mean the difference to us of 10-15 games if he does that kind of a job for the rest of the season."[141]

In light of Perry's lockdown performance, Gordon dismissed

further thoughts of moving the youngster into the rotation. "He'll stay right where he is," stated the manager. "He has as good control as anybody on the club. He goofed off in Detroit (failing to get out of the 5th) and Chicago (3 BB, 1 H, 4 R while getting only one out), when he tried to be a cutie (by 'throwing curves'). I told him to forget that and fire the ball. When he does that, he's not as much of a gamble as you might think."[142]

Jim explained his thought process following the leadoff double by Kubek and the heart of the lineup (3-4-5 hitters) coming up for the Yankees. All three hitters–Mantle, Berra, and Howard–had homered earlier in the game off of Cleveland ace Cal McLish, but Jim paid no mind. "I started to think about those tough hitters, and then I said to myself, 'Heck with that thinking, man. Just fire that ball over the plate.'"[143] And that he did.

"He's as fast as anyone I ever saw," Mantle conceded.[144]

"I certainly did not expect to see an unknown kid walk out there and thumb his nose at Mickey Mantle," marveled legendary New York Yankees manager Casey Stengel.[145]

"That young fellow is for real," Stengel added. "He's as good as I've seen this year."[146]

More Where That Came From

Three nights later, young Perry was back at it, this time on May 15 in Boston, coming on with little margin for error and securing a big win for the Tribe. Associated Press reporter Bob Hoobing recounted the encore performance.

"For the second time in four nights, Perry strolled in from the bullpen to save a one-run victory for the Indians Friday night. His efforts kept Cleveland half a game ahead of fast-closing Chicago by means of a 4-3 verdict over Boston... The 23-year old North Carolinian's secret—self-confidence and control... It's his cockiness that explains Perry's jump from Class A ball to the majors in a few short months.

"Perry was invited to the Tucson, Arizona spring training camp as a temporary batting practice pitcher. Upon his arrival Jim told manager Joe Gordon and the Indians' brass he was going to make the club. He did."[147]

Following his second straight save, the burgeoning fireman provided some interesting insight into the difference between the two game-saving outings.

"When I came in Mr. Gordon told me: 'Keep it low and get 'em out,'" Jim explained to post-game reporters in Fenway Park's visiting clubhouse. "I wasn't as fast as I was in New York, but I had a plan here. I worked for control, knowing a walk, followed by a hit, could lose it. I threw fastballs and sliders—no curves.

"In New York it was hot and I felt like pitching," Jim continued. "Here it was cold and I went out just to get the ball over."[148]

By the end of the month, Jim had notched two more saves in tight situations and established himself as manager Gordon's most trusted reliever. Unfortunately, just as Perry became the go-to guy at the back end of the bullpen, first-place Cleveland entered a cold streak that saw them lose 11 of their next 13 games. Despite pitching in six games, four of which he finished, it wasn't until June 13—a full 2½ weeks after his fourth save—that Jim would enter a game eligible for another one.

Of course, "save" situations in 1959 were nothing like the typical one-inning (or less) events they would later become. At that time, top relievers may be called on at any time during the final three innings, asked to get out of a tough situation and then often counted on to go the rest of the way, whether that be one, two, or even more innings of high-leverage work.

On June 13, 1959 at Washington, Jim was called on to start the seventh inning with the Indians nursing a slim 7-6 lead. The ball was flying out of the park on this night and not even Jim's tough sinker was immune. After striking out the first batter he faced, Jim saw future teammate Bob Allison pull a home run deep into the left field stands. It was the sixth home run of the night between the two teams and knotted up the game at seven, costing Jim any chance at his fifth save.

Undaunted, the resilient rookie went right back to work, retiring five of the next six hitters and sending the game to the ninth inning still deadlocked. With one out in the top of the ninth, eight-hole hitter Ray Webster laced a triple, bringing up Jim's spot in the order. Manager Joe Gordon summoned veteran Jim Piersall to pinch-hit for his young relief ace. Piersall came through with a sacrifice fly, which not only put Cleveland back on top, but made Jim now the pitcher of record. When fellow reliever Dick Brodowski retired the Senators in order in the bottom of the ninth, Jim had finally earned his first (official) major league victory.

Doing Double Duty

The win set off a stretch in which Jim pitched splendidly. He would notch five more wins over his next 12 outings, while posting a sparkling 1.49 ERA. On Sunday, July 12, Cleveland starter Al Cicotte was getting cuffed around by the visiting Tigers early in the second game of a doubleheader. When a third-inning double put the Indians down four, manager Gordon called for his trusty rookie in hopes of putting out the fire before the game got out of hand. With runners on second and third, Jim coaxed a routine groundout to get out of the jam.

He would proceed to fire six more scoreless innings, scattering four singles and walking no one while racking up five strikeouts. In the meantime, Cleveland hitters were busy erupting for eight runs, giving them a big 8-4 come-from-behind win, which allowed them to avoid what would have been a demoralizing double-header sweep. The fact that Jim earned the win for his yeoman's work is not surprising. What is remarkable is that it was the young hurler's second win of the day!

The previous night's 8 p.m. game was interrupted by rain for a 58 minute delay. What beat writer Jim Schlemmer described as a "riotous affair" was halted three other times for heated arguments with umpires. When the two teams were playing, it was a back-and-forth slugfest that featured five home runs between the two teams. Jim was called on with two on and only one out in the eighth inning and the Indians trailing by a run. The trusty youngster promptly retired Detroit's number two and three hitters, Harvey Kuenn and Charlie Maxwell, on back-to-back foul pops to extinguish the fire.

By the time Cleveland rallied one final time in the ninth inning for an 8-7 comeback win, the clock had already struck midnight, giving Jim his first of what would be two wins on that Sunday. As previously highlighted back in chapter two, of course, it would not be the last time the durable workhorse won two games on the same day in his big league career.

Despite Perry's reliable durability that was becoming quite apparent, manager Joe Gordon fought the urge to insert him into the starting rotation. Following the game, the Tribe skipper explained to reporters that he planned to stick with Perry and Gary Bell as his top relief hurlers. A significant event would soon change his mind.

Big Game Perry

Little more than a week after Perry's double-win effort helped to keep Cleveland in first place in the American League, the mighty New York Yankees came into town July 21 for a three game series. After splitting the first two games, the Yankees pulled out to a quick 4-0 advantage early in the rubber match, prompting manager Gordon to again turn to his trusty rookie. Though it was only the third inning, Gordon knew that losing this game and the series to the Yankees could be devastating.

Young Jim Perry proceeded to shut down the Yankees with four shutout innings of work, limiting them to only a meager single. The Indians offense, meanwhile, came storming back with a seven-run sixth inning, capped off by a Minnie Minoso grand slam. After Cleveland had closed out an 8-5 win in front of a capacity crowd of over fifty thousand fans on Postal Employees Night, Gordon called it "the biggest victory of the season."[149]

The outing must have made an impression on his manager, because three days later, on July 26, Gordon tabbed Perry to start the first game of a doubleheader against the Washington Senators. Jim responded by firing a two-hit shutout in just his second major league start. The only hits he allowed were a fourth inning infield single that bounded over the mound and then a bases-empty double in the ninth. The outstanding effort left his skipper elated.

"He made it look easy out there," Gordon gushed after the game. "That was a masterful show."[150]

A widely circulated UPI news service story provided an analysis of the rookie's pitching approach: "Perry serves batters a steady diet of fastballs, curves and sliders. He's not afraid to come in with a change-of-pace in a tight spot, but his fast deliveries are his bread-and-butter pitches."[151]

Jack Hand of Associated Press echoed Gordon's sentiment. "Perry has all the earmarks of a real find for the Indians," Hand observed.[152] "When he comes in from the bullpen, Perry usually fires hard, doesn't worry about pacing himself. He did the same Sunday and tamed the Senators in one hour and 57 minutes."[153]

Yes, that is an accurate account of the fact that Jim polished off Washington in less than two hours, as he faced only 29 batters—just two over the minimum. It would not be the last time that the quick-working strike-thrower would come in under the two-hour mark for a complete game effort. Perry even helped his own cause with a bases-loaded RBI single that contributed to Cleveland's nine-run offensive attack.

Following the big game, the rookie provided insight that proved him wise beyond his years. Even without the benefit of videotape to study, Jim explained how concentration and focus on the manner in which Cleveland's staff ace Cal McLish went about his business helped Perry ready himself for this opportunity.

"I've followed all of the games Cal pitches carefully," the youngster explained. "You'd be surprised how much you can learn that way."[154]

Jim also credited Cleveland pitching coach Mel Harder for the development of his second pitch. "Mel has worked a lot with me on the curve. It breaks sharp now and is just as good as my fastball."[155]

Gordon made his rookie hurler a regular member of the starting rotation the rest of the way. Beginning with that game, Jim would post an excellent 2.39 ERA over his final 16 appearances, including six more complete game efforts.

Big Four

On August 6, Cleveland manager Joe Gordon announced that he had settled on a "Big Four" starting rotation for the remainder of the season in hopes that the Tribe could capture the American League pennant. According to beat writer Jim Schlemmer, the Big Four were "Jim Perry, Cal McLish, Jim Grant, and Gary Bell—in that order."[156] Cleveland trailed the first place Chicago White Sox by just a game and a half at the time, but stood a full nine games ahead of third place Baltimore, setting up a two-team race for the stretch run.

Jim notched his second shutout on August 23, but he almost didn't even get the win. Pitching the first game of a doubleheader against Boston, Jim found himself locked in a scoreless duel with Red Sox starter Tom Brewer. Manager Joe Gordon let Perry hit for himself in the bottom of the eighth (Jim singled, but was left stranded on base) and Jim followed with a shutout ninth, setting the stage for a walk-off win. The Indians finally broke through when Tito Francona took Brewer deep for a game-winning home run leading off the bottom of the ninth, giving Jim his ninth win of the year. It was the second walk-off homer by Francona of the season and his fourth game-winning blast in the team's final at-bat. A doubleheader sweep pulled the Indians back to within a game-and-a-half of Chicago, but they were having trouble keeping pace.

Although now a full-fledged member of the Tribe starting rotation, Perry was still the answer for manager Joe Gordon when Gary Bell ran into trouble in the eighth inning against the Yankees three days later on August 26. Bell had just allowed a two-run, game-tying double to Elston Howard and Gordon was unwilling to press his luck further with the tiring starter. Although he had just two days of rest since his complete game shutout over the Red Sox, Perry was called on to put out the fire. He promptly got Hector Lopez to ground out, shutting down the New York rally.

After Rocky Colavito took flame-throwing Ryne Duren deep in the bottom of the eighth, Gordon sent Perry back out to finish it. Pinch-hitter Enos Slaughter began the ninth by slicing a double down the left field line, but he got no further as Perry retired the next three Yankees in order.

"I sure got a thrill out of Perry's work in the ninth," beamed Cleveland GM Frank Lane. "He showed me a lot of stomach."[157]

Fans and Family

Following the pair's heroics, it would not have been a surprise to see Jim Perry and Rocky Colavito in the parking lot after the game signing autographs until every remaining fan went away happy. They would not be surrounded by a swarming throng, however.

"These kids would come waving their pens at you, and that ink could stain your clothes," Colavito explained. "I didn't want that, so

I told the kids to get in a straight line—and no cutting!

"Jim caught on real quick," Colavito continued, "and we would have two lines of fans stretched out sometimes as far as the eye could see."

"After a Saturday afternoon game, the two of us might sign autographs together in the parking lot for an hour and a half," Jim proudly recalled.

Indeed, Jim Perry was far from the cocky, aloof celebrity that might be expected in a young, rising star. Indians traveling secretary Harold "Spud" Goldstein, who got to witness Perry daily behind the scenes, provided insight that belied the outward braggadocio that was associated with his rookie year.

"He's a very quiet young man," revealed Goldstein. "Sometimes his family and friends—about a dozen people—come to visit him when we're in Washington. Jim carries a walletful of pictures of his family. When the folks come to Washington, he introduces them, individually and formally. I'd say he's just a conscientious athlete, a perfectionist, in fact. And he takes pride in his hitting."[158]

Goldstein shared one other nugget of information that revealed his appreciation for having Perry on the team. "His mother makes excellent cookies and I'm always happy to eat them when she sends some to him."[159]

Close but No Cigar

The big win pulled the Tribe to within one game of the lead with the first-place White Sox coming to town for a huge four-game showdown. Unfortunately, that was the closest the Indians would get to first place the rest of the season. Chicago swept the four-game series, delivering a resounding blow from which the Indians never recovered. Jim gave the Tribe their best shot at a win in the critical series, with a complete game effort in the second game. He allowed only one earned run, but Cleveland's offense could offer no support, as Chicago's Dick Donovan hurled a 2-0 shutout.

The "Go-Go" White Sox went on to win their first American League pennant in forty years, leaving Cleveland with a solid, yet disappointing second place finish, five games behind the champs. With the end result decided midway through the season's last week, Jim was excused from attending the team's final series. Manager Gordon allowed him to return early to North Carolina in order to prepare for a six-month military commitment set to begin on October 4.

It had been a great rookie year for the slender righthander. He finished with a 12-10 record and a team leading 2.65 ERA. His fine rookie season prompted the birth of an official "Jim Perry Fan Club," headed up by club president Mary Alice Hall. According to a notice that made it into the *Akron Beacon Journal*, "Membership is only 25 cents and all members will receive an autographed picture of Jim plus a membership card."[160]

Soon after the season's conclusion, Jim was named to the MLB All-Rookie Team by *The Sporting News*, universally considered the premier baseball publication of the day, as well as *Topps*, the iconic baseball card company.

In the official American League Rookie of the Year voting, Jim finished second to future teammate Bob Allison, then of the Washington Senators. Allison blasted thirty home runs as the Senators' everyday center fielder, making him a worthy winner of the award.

His outstanding pitching was not the only thing Jim had to be proud of. The switch-hitter also posted an excellent .300 batting average, which ranked third best in all of MLB for pitchers with at least 50 at-bats.

In addition to the official recognition, plaudits came in from around the league following the 22-year-old rookie's fantastic debut season.

"He pitches with the savvy of a 30-year-old veteran," his manager Joe Gordon marveled.[161]

Opposition managers chimed in with accolades, as well. Baltimore Orioles skipper Paul Richards was asked what he thought of the young rookie. "(He's) great. I'm not surprised at his success," Richards revealed. "I knew he had it the first time I saw him."[162]

"That kid's really something," exclaimed veteran all-star Roy Sievers. "It's hard to follow his pitches. The ball is on top of you before you realize it."[163]

"Part of his deception comes through his flapping-arm delivery," explained Hal Lebovitz, writing for The Sporting News. "He crosses his long arms in front of his body before releasing the ball and this makes it difficult for the batter to pick it up. And then there's the fact that Perry has better-than-average speed. He is wise enough to keep his fastball low and he has excellent control.

"This is a combination hard to beat. But, never satisfied, the industrious pitcher labored mightily under Mel Harder's tutelage to improve his curve and slider as well as practice a let-up pitch.

"'I've worked hard for everything I've come by,' declares Perry. 'It's been that way all my life. You don't get anything if you don't work.'"[164]

The overwhelming self-confidence that accompanied Jim's arrival was perfectly summed up by Lebovitz in *The Sporting News*. "Perry's teammates soon discovered that he backed up his words with performance and he really wasn't trying to be boastful. They found him to be a 'nice guy' who didn't mean to give a know-it-all impression. He became one of the most popular players on the squad. He is quiet and somewhat of an introvert off the field, rather than a pop-off."[165]

Another explanation for Jim's quick success was observed by Nate Dolin, who was not only the team's vice-president, but also a part owner of the Cleveland franchise. "This kid Jim Perry would make a fine story," Dolin gushed following the 1959 season. "When he pitches, he writes everything of note into a book as soon as he returns to the bench. He puts down what he pitched to each batter and what happened. He studies these entries. I have seen studious pitchers, but this young man is in a class by himself insofar as that is concerned."[166]

For a kid who was invited to his first spring training camp just to serve as an extra batting practice pitcher, the summer of '59 could hardly have gone any better.

> *I have seen studious pitchers, but (Perry) is in a class by himself.*
>
> — Nate Dolin
> CLEVELAND INDIANS V.P.

8
Settling In

In early October of 1959, Jim reported to Fort Knox, just south of Louisville, Kentucky, for the Army's basic training. While it was tough, Jim's innate ability helped him to stand out. He played basketball for the Army team, which came with some privileges.

"The players on the basketball team were able to get out of camping outside when it snowed," Jim recalled. "We got to stay back for the game and then go out to meet the rest of the platoon the next morning."

Jim's experience shooting varmints on the farm growing up also proved quite useful. He was an expert marksman even before any "official" Army training. "We were shooting 850 yards with an M-1 and one of the guys couldn't shoot at all," he explained. "Sarge just wanted to get us through this training. I was the best shot, so he told me to go back out and shoot for him!"

As Jim was fulfilling his patriotic duties in service for his country, back in Cleveland the Indians were busy preparing for the 1960 season. Much to Jim's chagrin, however, manager Joe Gordon was intent on keeping him confined to the bullpen as his ace reliever, despite the strong finish to his rookie season in a starting role. The Tribe skipper shared his rationale during an off-season banquet in Canton, Ohio.

"Which would you prefer?" Gordon asked rhetorically; "to see

Perry starting every fourth or fifth day, or see him in the bullpen every day; ready, willing and able to come in with his hummer for two or three innings… He is the greatest competitor I have ever seen in a 23-year old."[167]

> *He is the greatest competitor I have ever seen in a 23-year old.*
>
> — Joe Gordon
> Cleveland Manager

Despite what was scheduled to be a six-month military commitment, putting his preparedness for Opening Day in doubt, Dependable Perry found a way to come through. His hard work and dutiful training earned him an honorable discharge a month early. As a result, Jim was able to fly to Tucson, Arizona in time for the first official workout with other Indians pitchers and catchers.

Upon learning of his "ace reliever" status, Jim was not pleased, though pouting was not a consideration. He calmly explained that he felt fully confident in his ability to be a 20-game winner. Of course, Dependable Perry would do whatever the team needed, whatever his manager asked of him. "But I'll tell you this," Jim clarified." "I want to be a regular starter and I'm going to work as hard to win a starting role as I worked last year to make the team."[168]

The manager remained steadfast. "A good reliever is equal to a 20-game winner," Gordon countered to reporters. "Who on our staff would you rather see coming in to pitch in a tight situation? Why Perry, of course. I'll bet you that every last man on our squad would say the same."[169]

A Star(ter) is Born

Gordon's commitment to keeping his young ace confined to the bullpen did not last long. Only two days after Cleveland general manager Frank Lane arrived in camp, Gordon suddenly announced that he agreed with his boss that Perry should be a starting pitcher.

Lane explained how he got Gordon to come around. "(Perry) looks like he could be our best pitcher. If we had four real good starters, then I wouldn't mind seeing him relieve. But it doesn't look as though we do."[170]

Jim started Cleveland's second game of the 1960 season, working into the ninth inning, but he was tagged for three home runs in a

6-4 defeat at Detroit. Among the three hitters to take him deep was former teammate and friend Rocky Colavito. In a trade that many still consider the worst in Cleveland history, Colavito had been traded for Harvey Kuenn just before the start of the season. The trade marked the only time in MLB history that the reigning home run king (Colavito, 42 in '59) was traded for the reigning batting champ (Kuenn, .353).

Norm Cash and Al Kaline—both far from slouches—hit the other two dingers. Though all three homers were hit by formidable sluggers, manager Joe Gordon took the blows as an opportunity to re-implement his original plan. Following the game, Gordon announced that Perry would be dropped from the rotation and pushed back to the bullpen for the next week.

"Maybe it'll shake him up," declared the skipper. "When he relieves he goes out there and fires, but when he starts he tries to get cute and mix 'em up. He didn't use his fastball enough against the Tigers."[171]

Whether he was "shaken up" or not, Jim came out of the pen four days later to secure a save, striking out two of the four batters he faced as he sealed up Cleveland's second win of the young season. Two games—and three days—later, Jim received another start and he responded with a complete game effort over Kansas City. Most importantly from the manager's perspective, Jim retired nine of the last eleven Royals batters, scattering just a pair of inconsequential singles over the final three innings of the one-run decision.

"I can't afford to keep Perry in the bullpen," Gordon admitted after the game. "I need him as a starting pitcher. He did a good job tonight and finished strong."[172]

Even in the wake of his vow, however, Gordon continued to flip-flop his sophomore star between starting and relief. By May 18, a month into the 1960 season, Jim had appeared in nine of Cleveland's first 25 games, starting five and relieving four. His numbers reflected his inconsistent usage, as he had all of one win, a pair of losses, and a save to go along with a mediocre 4.14 ERA.

Kicking it Into Gear

On May 21, Jim was given another start and he responded with eight innings of four-hit, one-run pitching in a 6-1 win over the Boston Red Sox. He would proceed to win six straight starts, posting a sterling

1.48 ERA in 49 innings of work. The masterful stretch included a phenomenal start against Washington on May 25.

Locked in a scoreless duel with Senators starter Bill Fischer, Jim found his strong night suddenly in jeopardy. Beat writer Jim Schlemmer detailed the situation: "Perry broke a blister on a control finger while pitching to Jim Lemon in the seventh inning.

"Gordon ordered the bullpen into action while trainer Wally Bock was treating the injury—which loomed more serious then than it does in print.

"Lemon singled on Perry's next pitch and the bullpen tempo increased.

"But Harmon Killebrew, Julio Becquer and Earl Battey all stuck out swinging as Perry proved it would take more than a blister to beat him."[173]

Amazingly Jim fired four more scoreless innings, even as another blister developed, before Cleveland finally pieced together three singles to pull out the 1-0 win in the bottom of the eleventh. It is interesting to note that Jim led off the bottom of the 11th, grounding out to shortstop, so manager Joe Gordon was most certainly prepared to leave Perry in to pitch longer, blisters and all.

"My breaking stuff got better around the sixth inning," Jim explained. "I tried to pace myself and wasn't too tired. I might have been able to go a couple more innings."[174]

According to game reports, Jim finished with an astronomical 166 pitches–107 strikes against only 59 balls. His manager proclaimed it to be Jim's "best performance ever"[175] while Schlemmer in his write-up for the *Akron Beacon Journal* dubbed the game "one of the great pitching duels of modern times."[176]

> *I tried to pace myself and wasn't too tired. I might have been able to go a couple more innings.*
>
> — Jim Perry
> Following 166-pitch,
> 11-inning shutout

By June 15, Jim was 7-2 and had lowered his ERA to a sterling 2.63. He would retain a regular spot in the rotation for the remainder of the season. Another hot streak beginning in late July saw Perry go 5-1 with four complete games and a 2.12 ERA over a six start stretch.

Even as Jim continued his winning ways, however, the team fell on hard times. Cleveland lost nineteen of 28 games following the mid-July

All-Star break. Of the team's nine wins in that span, Jim earned the win in six of them. Tribe general manager Frank Lane bemoaned the failure of the starting rotation to keep the club afloat, particularly Gary Bell and Mudcat Grant, who were both in the midst of disappointing seasons.

"We depended a lot on both of them and they haven't come through," Lane sighed. "Luckily, Jim Perry has. It's so bad now that when Perry doesn't win, it becomes a catastrophe."[177]

Things got so bad for the rest of the team that the Indians made the first "trade" of managers in MLB history. On August 2, Cleveland GM Frank Lane swapped Joe Gordon to Detroit for Tigers manager Jimmy Dykes.

The bold move failed to turn the tide for the struggling club as Cleveland finished with a losing record, fourth in the American League. Despite the losing atmosphere, Jim capped off a fine sophomore season by firing a five-hit shutout over the White Sox on the final day of the season, giving him his eighteenth win of the year. He struck out a season-high nine opposing batters, while walking only two. Only one Chicago base runner managed to get as far as third base.

Undisputed Leader

Overall, Jim finished the 1960 season with an 18-10 record. No other Cleveland pitcher managed to top the ten-win mark. Jim's 18 wins tied for the American League high with Baltimore's Chuck Estrada, who had notched his 18th win the day before Perry matched him. Jim's 261 innings were also over one hundred more than any other Tribe hurler. Mudcat Grant, one of two nine-game winners on the club, ranked second with only 160 innings. Jim's ten complete games and four shutouts were also easily team bests. The four shutouts tied for the A.L. high, as well. By season's end, Jim Perry was the undisputed leader of the pitching staff. Not bad for a guy who had to fight his way into the starting rotation to begin the year.

Jim Perry received votes on two Most Valuable Player ballots cast by writers following his fine 1960 season, yet he curiously did not receive a single vote for the Cy Young award. In fact, every vote cast for the award honoring baseball's best pitcher went to National League hurlers. While separate A.L. and N.L. honors were awarded for both

Most Valuable Player and Rookie of the Year, inexplicably only one award was given for MLB's best pitcher. Many voters lamented their inability to vote for a winner in each league with several suggesting they would have leaned Perry's way for a separate A.L. prize. It would not be until 1967 that this puzzling aberration would be corrected.

Amongst all of his achievements in 1960, Jim did set one dubious mark, as well. Of his league high 35 home runs allowed, 15 were hit by the New York Yankees. That number eclipsed the all-time MLB mark for home runs by a team off of one pitcher. Jim was in fine company, however, as hall-of-famer Warren Spahn was among the three pitchers to have previously held the distinction. Spahn allowed 13 round-trippers to the Chicago Cubs just two years prior.

Manager Jimmy Dykes, who was unable to right the Cleveland ship after taking charge, lamented the fact that he was not blessed with more pitchers like his new ace. "Thank heaven for Jim Perry," the new manager exclaimed at one point. "Wish we had more like him. The Commodore makes managing easy. He knows what he's doing out there. He has good control and he's thinking on every pitch."[178]

Veteran catcher Red Wilson, who came over to Cleveland in a trade with Detroit just a few weeks prior to the manager swap, got the opportunity both to face Perry at bat, as well as catch his pitches from behind the plate. "He fools you," Wilson explained about Jim's success. "From the dugout he doesn't look overpowering. And the ball doesn't blaze into the catcher's mitt. But he throws a surprisingly large number of pitches past the hitters. The ball is on top of them before they know it."[179]

Wilson also detailed what it was like to work behind the plate with Jim on the mound. "He throws what I call," the catcher explained. "But he has his own idea where the ball should go. He throws for spots and his control is excellent. And he knows how to mix up his speeds. The batter never knows what to expect."[180]

Tigers outfielder Charlie Maxwell said it was a frustrating experience to bat against Perry. His "flapping wings (make it difficult for the hitter to) pick up the pitch," Maxwell explained. "He's herky-jerky. Those arms flop around, hiding the ball. Suddenly it's coming at you."[181]

Put a Ring On It

As he served another Army stint in late October of '60, this time at Fort Hayes near the downtown region of Columbus, Ohio, Jim received news of several awards for his fine 1960 campaign. First, he was named Sophomore of the Year by the Associated Press. Then he was selected as "Man of the Year" by the Cleveland chapter of the Baseball Writers' Association of America.

The best news, however, was bigger than any award, as detailed in *The Sporting News*: "The past week was a big one for Jim Perry. First, the Indians' pitcher announced his engagement, or rather his fiancé did the proclaiming... Right now, Jim is most excited about his impending marriage. Attractive Daphne Snell of Raleigh, N.C. becomes his bride next month. The two have been dating for some time."[182]

Daphne, of course, had been dating—and *waiting*—for some time. Though the pair became serious very quickly, Jim told her he wanted to wait for marriage. "He had seen how hard it was for players and their families during the years in the minors," Daphne explained. "So he wanted to play at least two seasons with a major league club before getting married. I must say that I did not agree. Marriage was what I wanted, but he insisted, so I had to go along with him."

After completing her studies at Campbell in the spring of 1960, Daphne had taken a job in Raleigh, NC at King Drug Company while she waited for Jim to finish up his fine sophomore season. Most importantly, she was counting down the days until Jim would qualify—in his own mind—for marriage. "He never really formally asked me," Daphne later recalled. "We had just both agreed that we would do it after his second year and once he got home, it was time. We got the church, got the family together, and got it done."

Indeed, the best pitch Jim Perry ever made was to seal the deal with his college sweetheart. An AP story announcing the December 3 ceremony highlighted a couple of Daphne's many talents. As the story stated, "Miss Snell, 20, is a talented singer and musician."[183]

One of the tough parts about being a professional ballplayer is that down time is tough to come by, even when the grind of the season comes to an end. The season generally concludes in late September or early October. Before you know it, Thanksgiving is just around the corner, ushering in the holiday season. Then, it's Christmas, the calendar flips to a new year, and it's suddenly time to start getting in shape for spring training.

For young Jim, who had vowed to wait for marriage until he was firmly established in the major leagues and could support his wife, he had to move quickly if he and Daphne were going to get this done. That left little time between the official post-season engagement and the early December 3 wedding. In fact, their honeymoon lasted almost as long as the engagement!

Daphne accompanied Jim to the annual Ribs and Roast show at Cleveland's Hotel Hollenden on January 23, 1961. That is where Jim was honored by the Cleveland Baseball Writers as "Man of the Year" for 1960 in front of 600 fans and local dignitaries. For the young pitching ace and "the girl from back home," this was an extra special trip.

"We spent a few days in Virginia after the wedding," Jim explained, "but decided to make the trip to Cleveland our real honeymoon."[184]

For a young woman who had finally seen her dreams of marriage come true, Daphne was quickly learning that her life would never be the same. "Did I say I wanted marriage?" she would later ask facetiously as a speaker for Christian Women's Club. "What changes! What a lot to get used to. Married life, being away from my home and family. Then there was baseball. How could a little ball rule my life? Tell me when to eat, when to sleep, the separation by long road trips. What a schedule!" Daphne would regularly make it a priority to accompany her husband whenever possible, which was undoubtedly a key to their long, strong marriage.

Giving Thanks

Though normally a man of few words, Jim shared his heartfelt appreciation with the Ribs and Roast crowd that evening for those who had played a part in his success. Tribe beat writer Jim Schlemmer was on hand and related the speech:

"Thanking the crowd and the writers for the honors paid him, the always serious Perry was even more so," Schlemmer explained, as he summarized the early words of Jim's speech. "(Jim) reached this new high point in his career through determination, and a lot of hard work—and much helpful advice, he told them.

"'I owe a lot to my Dad, who was a good ball player but never got beyond the minors because of the war. He wanted me to have every opportunity and he saw that I got it,' Jim said. He said no one ever helped him more than Clyde McCullough, his manager at Reading in 1958.

"'I also owe a lot to a couple great guys sitting out there tonight: Mike Garcia and Bob Feller. And there's another fine fellow who was traded away, Rocky Colavito. Nothing ever got Rocky down, and I can never forget how he was always first, along with Herb Score, to help me to get back up after I had been floored.'"[185]

Going Gets Tough

Jim unsurprisingly got the Opening Day nod as the 1961 season got underway, twirling a complete game win in Detroit. He would win again two starts later in Baltimore, but would go more than a month before notching his third win of the year. Perry was not pitching poorly so much as having some tough luck. A prime example came in a home start on May 14 against Baltimore.

Although he fired eight shutout innings, Jim had nothing to show for it when he was lifted for a pinch-hitter. Frank Funk would proceed to follow with seven scoreless innings of his own, which allowed the duo to enter the record books when the Tribe finally scratched across an unearned run to win the marathon in the 15th inning. Only eight 1-0 games had ever gone further than 15 innings in MLB history before being decided.

A four-game winning streak in June boosted Jim's record to 6-4 with a 3.41 ERA, but a five-hit 2-1 complete game win against the Orioles on June 18 would mark the high point for both Jim and the team in an up-and-down campaign. Cleveland stood at 40 wins and just 23 losses following that game, just a half-game out of first place, but a seven-game losing skid immediately followed and the Indians were never higher than third the rest of the way.

Cleveland would finish the 1961 season in fifth place with a record of 78-83. Jim was not immune to the team's struggles. Even so, the multi-talented athlete managed to showcase his all-around skills, with Baltimore once again the victim. On September 2, Jim was a one-man wrecking crew, as he not only hurled a masterful four-hit shutout, but showed off his hitting skills, as well. Batting left-handed against righthander Hal Brown, Jim laced an RBI-single to get the Cleveland scoring going in the second inning. Runners were on first and second his next time up and Perry socked a drive high off the right field wall, narrowly missing a three run homer. The RBI-double gave the Indians a two-run lead and that was all the lanky righthander would need, as he cruised to an eventual 6-0 win.

Unfortunately, the rest of the season would not be nearly as fruitful. Jim lost his last four starts, finishing with a disappointing 10-17 record to go with an inflated 4.71 earned run average that would be the worst full season of his career. Some said that he had changed his delivery, leading to a loss of the deception that made him so difficult to face. As writer Hal Lebovitz of *The Sporting News* explained, "Perry was a raw, rough pitcher: He had moved up to the majors rapidly, employing an unusual 'floppity' motion. He flapped his arms during his windup and, before the hitter knew it, the ball had been released."[186]

"He hid the ball and you couldn't pick it up," explained an unnamed opposing hitter of facing Perry his first couple years in the league. "It was something like a magician, going abra-kadabra with his arms and suddenly a ball was coming at you."[187]

"Then, last season, Perry, who is a student of pitching, acquired polish," Lebovitz continued. "Unconsciously, perhaps, he had copied the deliveries of the established hurlers, such as Early Wynn. Wynn is a picture book pitcher, with fine form. There is nothing herky-jerky about him. In a word he's sm-o-o-th. Last season Perry, too, was sm-o-o-th. But with un-Wynn-like results."[188]

"You could follow the ball all the way," remarked another opposing batter. "Perry isn't fast enough to throw the ball past you, he doesn't really have a curve and so he became easy to hit. He's got to come up with another pitch or he's dead."[189]

Even as he suffered the loss in his final start on September 27 at Minnesota, however, Jim had reason to be joyful. Back home in Edenton, North Carolina, wife Daphne was giving birth to their first child, son James Christopher (Chris). Being away during the final days of Daphne's pregnancy, Jim understandably had mixed emotions as Cleveland played out the string in a lost season.

Still, Jim had remained a steadfast member of Cleveland's rotation, starting all 35 games in which he pitched. As he looked forward to bouncing back in 1962, Jim faced a couple hurdles in addition to issues with his repertoire and delivery. Not only would he be playing for another new manager—his third in four major league seasons, but the Tribe had a new general manager, as well.

Back to Square One

With rookie manager Mel McGaha at the helm in the dugout and former Cincinnati Reds and Houston Colt .45s general manager Gabe Paul now overseeing Cleveland's baseball operations, Jim faced the prospect of making a new "first impression."

The one constant that remained was longtime Cleveland pitching coach Mel Harder, who made returning Perry to his 1960 ace form a top priority as 1962 spring drills got under way.

"We want to get him to improve his curveball and develop a pitch like a screwball," Harder explained. "Something that'll go away from lefthanders."[190]

Whether it was experimenting with his delivery, working on a new pitch, or simply putting pressure on himself to impress his new bosses, Jim struggled to get results throughout spring training. The rest of the team fared no better. Back in 1962, results mattered just as much as getting prepared for the regular season, and a team spring training record of 9-20, which marked their poorest spring record in thirty years, sent the new braintrust into a state of panic. When he was tagged for six straight hits on April 4, not only was Perry pulled from his final spring training start before he could get an out, but he was also bumped from his role as the presumptive Opening Day starter.

As the 1962 regular season got under way, Jim found himself right where he began his great 1960 campaign—relegated to the bullpen, wishing he could start. Just as he did in 1960, however, Jim quickly demonstrated that he was too good to be confined to relief work. Four splendid relief appearances without allowing an earned run finally convinced skipper McGaha to insert the resilient right-hander back into the starting rotation.

Perry responded with back-to-back outstanding efforts. On May 5 after Cleveland had been bombed by Kansas City 18-6 in the first game of a doubleheader, Jim took a shutout into the ninth inning of the nightcap before the Athletics scratched across a pair of unearned runs in a 5-2 Indians win. Five days later, he went the distance in a 9-4 win at Minnesota. Aside from a handful of intermittent relief appearances, Jim would remain in the starting rotation for the rest of the year.

While he was not as consistently outstanding as he had been during his sophomore 1960 season, Jim had some spectacular moments. The first performance that made his new skipper stand up and take notice came on June 1 in Detroit, when Jim carried a perfect game into the sixth inning before an infield single broke it up. Though he would give up two more singles, plus a solo home run by Norm Cash with two outs in the ninth, Jim was in control the entire night.

Not only did Detroit have difficulty getting the ball out of the infield, they could hardly get it by the slick-fielding pitcher. Jim used his power sinker to induce a ridiculous six comebackers, converting every one of them into outs. Detroit hitters admitted they were also flummoxed by a puzzling new pitch of Perry's that "breaks away from a lefthanded hitter."[191]

Perry also contributed two hits of his own for good measure, coming around to score both times in a dominant 7-1 complete game performance.

"I didn't see Jim Perry in 1960," McGaha marveled to reporters after the game, "but Mel Harder tells me that's the way he used to pitch. It's certainly the best game he's pitched since I've seen him."[192]

McGaha also felt that Perry had effectively increased his endurance thanks to an adjustment in his preparation. "Between starts, he pitches in batting practice and he has become stronger," stated the manager.[193]

Jim hurled five more complete games from that point, three of which were shutouts. A ten-inning complete game against Detroit in the first game of a Fourth of July doubleheader especially stands out because the effort was classic Perry. He scattered a walk and five harmless singles while allowing only one runner to get as far as second base. After ten dominant shutout innings, Perry must have still looked like he had plenty left in the tank, because manager Mel McGaha elected to let the pitcher hit for himself to lead off the bottom of the tenth inning.

The sweet-swinging switch-hitter, batting right-handed versus southpaw Hank Aguirre, lined a base hit to open the inning. Even then, McGaha saw no reason to pinch-run for the athletic Perry. Instead, he had leadoff man Willie Tasby sacrifice Jim to second base. Tito Francona tapped a slow roller that he beat out to move Jim to third, before pinch-hitter Gene Green singled Perry home to score his own walk-off winning run, sealing the 1-0 masterpiece.

In mid-September, Jim would hurl another shutout, this time defeating the Washington Senators, 3-0. Again, he allowed only singles (six) and walked just two. Although he retired the side in order just three times, Perry once again allowed only one opposition runner as far as second base. Beat writer Joe Durbin called it "one of the best games of his career."[194]

Gems like those were too few and far between, however, as Cleveland suffered through another second half slump that saw them again fall out of the American League pennant race. When the dust had settled on the 1962 season, Jim sat with an even 12-12 record to go with a 4.14 ERA.

Same Old Song

Another year, another new manager for Jim Perry and the Cleveland Indians. 1963 saw seven-year veteran Birdie Tebbetts replace Mel McGaha, who was shown the door following a disappointing rookie season at the helm. Once again, Jim faced the prospect of re-proving himself despite the positive signs he had shown in the latter half of the prior season, not to mention throughout four years with the club.

As before, however, the new manager elected to go with other pitchers in the starting rotation, relegating Jim to bullpen work as the season got under way. Despite a couple good early outings, Jim suddenly found himself a forgotten man on the Tribe staff hierarchy. As the 1963 calendar flipped to May, it had been ten days since Jim Perry had appeared in a game. He was about to be liberated in a move that would change his career and his life.

9

9,999 More Lakes

Though frustrated by his lack of action, Jim continued to work and stay ready. On Wednesday, May 1, he pitched three innings of mop-up work during an 11-3 loss to the Athletics that saw the Indians drop into ninth place, thanks to a dismal 5-9 record. As he got ready for the game the following evening, Jim could tell something was up.

"I was on the field at Kansas City playing pepper," he explained. "Manager Birdie Tebbetts called me to the clubhouse. Birdie started by saying, 'We need a left-handed pitcher.' Immediately, I knew I was gone. The way the Indians are going, I knew something was going to happen."[195]

Jim Perry was going from a Great Lake (Erie) to The Land of 10,000 Lakes. The Minnesota Twins had begun the season with a four-man starting rotation that featured three lefties—Jim Kaat, Dick Stigman, and Jack Kralick—and only Camilo Pascual throwing from the right side. The surplus led to the Twins giving up what they considered to be surplus in Kralick to buy low on a 27-year old righthander who had displayed flashes of brilliance previously in his young career.

"It balances our staff," explained Twins manager Sam Mele, "particularly in our park and against right-handed power clubs like Boston at Fenway Park."[196] Jim was already establishing himself as a Boston killer, posting a 10-5 record against the Red Sox over his first four seasons. He would finish his career with far more wins against Boston (34) than any other team. (25 vs. Texas ranked second.)

For his part, Jim was thrilled with the new opportunity, and especially with the opportunity to immediately rejoin a starting rotation. "I'm glad to join a team that wants me," he explained. "I think every pitcher prefers to start. I had my best year as a full-time starter in 1960. Working as an every fourth-or-fifth day starter, you can better regulate your throwing between assignments. Lately I've been going between relief and starting. Some arms take to it, but warming up virtually every day and then sitting down isn't the best way to pitch."[197]

Jim then let his fierce competitiveness show through. "I like to be boss on the mound," he stated to reporters. "I'll give my best to win for the Twins, just like I did at Cleveland. I hate to lose, but win or lose, I'm the same guy. Right now, I need some work."[198]

When asked if perhaps he did too much tinkering after winning 18 games in 1960 as basically a two-pitch pitcher (sinking fastball and slider), Jim took offense at the suggestion.

"I don't experiment on the mound," he protested. "When I go out to pitch a ball game, I'm all business. I use the best stuff I have at my command.

"However, I won't say that I haven't tried to improve myself. The fastball and slider are my best pitches. Lately, I've been working on a change of speeds and, for the past year, a bigger curve. I think I've finally got the bigger breaking curveball where I can use it in a game."

"You can't sit still in this game," the unusually loquacious hurler continued. "While it's true a pitcher learns the hitters, the hitters also learn something about the pitcher. And you'd better keep improving on your repertoire or the hitters will go right by you."[199]

As Jim returned to Cleveland for some clean laundry and to help wife Daphne plan her transition with their 18-month old son, Jim's new teammates shared their excitement about the acquisition.

"Jim Perry is an intelligent pitcher," related Vic Power, who spent three years with Jim in Cleveland. "He'll help us. He won 18 one year, then had an off year. You'll find very few players who don't have an off year now and then."[200]

Minnesota bullpen coach Hal Naragon, who had been the

Cleveland starting catcher in Jim's 1959 major league debut, was ecstatic. "I'm sure Perry can help us," stated Naragon. "He could always throw hard and had good control. All he needs is work and he will become a winner."[201]

At least one famous fan was broken hearted to hear news of the trade. Sandusky, Ohio native Jacqueline Mayer, the reigning Miss America, said that Jim Perry was her favorite player, but now she would need to switch.[202]

While Jim was pleased with his new pitching prospects, he was even more excited about the new opportunity for his young family. His first call was to his wife, who was back in Cleveland with their now 18-month old son. "I remember (Daphne) was upset," Jim later revealed. "She had a lot of good friends in Cleveland and didn't want to move."[203] She would quickly come around.

"When he called me with news of the trade," Daphne recalled, "Jim said of all the places we could possibly be traded, this was the best. The people in the Twin Cities are so nice, and the area is beautiful. We were very excited and hopeful to be making this transition at this stage in our lives."

Finding A Home

The Minnesota Twins had been "born" just a little more than two years before Jim's arrival. Prior to the 1961 season, the Washington Senators had been successfully recruited to pack up and become tenants of the same Metropolitan Stadium in which Jim had collected his first (unofficial) major league victory back in 1959. The Senators had a long history of losing prior to making the move, so the hope of owner and team president Calvin Griffith was that the change would help to inject new life into the franchise.

Sure enough, after a seventh place finish (out of ten American League teams) in their first season, the Twins jumped up to a strong second place showing in '62, just five games back of the pennant-winning Yankees. Needless to say, hopes were high heading into 1963, yet Minnesota had struggled out of the gate, dropping nine of their first 13 games and languishing near the bottom of the American League standings after almost a month of play.

Jim was determined to help his new club get back in the race and to capitalize on another opportunity to work as a starter. "I'll report Friday, ready to pitch," he declared to reporters on (Thursday) the day of the trade.[204]

Slow Start

Although he did not get to pitch until the following Tuesday, May 7 in Los Angeles, Jim did not lie about being ready. Despite being limited to only ten innings of work over the previous month, Perry hurled a complete game three-hitter and issued only one walk as he needed just 96 pitches to work eight innings. Unfortunately, Jim had little help behind him, as he suffered a hard-luck 2-0 loss against the Angels. The only runs of the game came across in the first inning, aided by a pair of mental miscues by Twins fielders. Especially encouraging was the way the new Minnesota starter finished. Once he found his groove, Jim retired the final 17 batters he faced. Despite the loss, the Twins were thrilled with their acquisition.

Battery mate Earl Battey, who caught Jim's Twins debut, told manager Sam Mele that the new guy was every bit as good as he looked. "Perry knows how to set up batters," Battey explained. "And his control is very good. He pitches to a batter's weak spots when he wants to."[205]

Battey further explained how Jim relies mainly on his fastball and slider, mixing in a slow curve only occasionally, just to "show" the hitter, but keeping it out of the hitting zone. Battey noted that "a pitcher must have exceptional control to keep a batter off stride with only the fastball and slider."[206]

Jim shed further light on his recipe for success. "I've been working on some kind of off-speed pitch (the slow 'show me' curve) and it worked well for me," he explained. "But the main thing I was firing the ball as hard as I could."[207]

Mele was particularly impressed with Jim's dutiful work ethic, pointing out to reporters that Jim "kept himself sharp by working on the sidelines between assignments."[208]

"I didn't think I'd be able to go the route," Jim confessed. "But the fact I ran a lot every day kept me in real good shape."[209]

The excellent debut gave Mele a glimpse of not only Jim's potential to help the team with his performance, but also with the example he could set for other pitchers on the staff. "If he can pitch this well often, he will win a lot of games for us," declared the Minnesota skipper. "I was very, very pleased. That is the way a pitcher should work when he is behind by two runs—hold them close. He could have had a shutout and certainly should have gotten out of the first inning giving up only one run. If we were behind only 1-0, I could have bunted when we got the three hits and a lot of things might have changed."[210]

Another tough-luck 2-1 loss against Kansas City in his second start failed to dampen Jim's excitement about his new club. "That black cat has to get out of my path one of these days," he sighed.[211] "I've got to win some ball games pitching like I did today. I felt real strong—the best I've felt in a long time. I'm surprised that I'm throwing as well as I am with no more work than I'd had before coming over here. I'm surprised I'm getting the ball over the plate as well as I am."[212]

Jim made a point to not lay blame at the feat of his teammates. "I can't fault the ball club. These guys still pull for each other. That's a good sign on a baseball club."[213]

"What's happening now is that everyone is quiet at the same time," Jim continued, referring to the lack of offensive support. "On a good club like this, that is rare. But I know this club will break loose and start hitting. The only thing I can do is go out and work harder. The runs will come."[214]

Coming on Strong

It would prove to be a prophetic statement, as Jim prepared for an emotional return to Cleveland five days later to face his former team. With the Twins on a four-game losing streak that saw them plummet to last place in the American League, the offense suddenly erupted for five home runs, including three by right fielder Bob Allison, en route to an 11-4 drubbing of the Indians. Jim might have gone the distance again if he hadn't been forced out of the game by a muscle spasm in his back in the seventh inning.

Ironically, the hitting explosion came against Gary Bell, who the Twins had reportedly been targeting in trade talks with Cleveland before they pivoted to Perry. Never one to gloat, Jim put the spotlight on his new teammates. "I knew we'd get some runs one of these days," he stated matter-of-factly.[215]

In typical Perry fashion, Jim was more focused on shaking off his injury and looking ahead. "Nothing serious," he clarified to reporters. "I'll be okay in a day or two. It tightened up on me in the last game I pitched (against Kansas City). I'll be ready for my next turn."[216]

After working so hard and waiting for another chance to be a member of a starting rotation, Jim wasn't going to let an injury sideline him if he could help it. Sure enough, the slender workhorse was right back out there four days later on May 21, hurling a complete game 8-2 win in Boston.

A sportswriter for the local *Minneapolis Star* made a prescient observation of the new Twins starter: "Pitcher Jim Perry is no more overly excited after two straight victories than he was dejected after two defeats on well-pitched games. 'You have good nights and bad nights,' said Perry. 'I knew this team would start hitting.'"[217]

Almost as good as his pitching for his new club was Perry's hitting. In the win over the Red Sox, Jim came through with a clutch two-run single that blew the game open. That followed a two-hit game in his prior start at Cleveland. He also coaxed a walk in both games. After four games with the Twins, Jim sported a .400 batting average and a .500 on-base percentage. Things were definitely looking up.

With a couple wins under his belt and full of confidence, Jim proceeded to reel off six more wins over his next eight starts. Included in that stretch was a masterful four-hit shutout in Kansas City on June 4. Jim finished off a fantastic month of June by hurling a complete game victory over Detroit, which left him with a 5-2 record for the month and a fine 2.80 ERA over a massive 45 innings of work. Most importantly, the win pulled Minnesota to within three games of the first-place New York Yankees.

Reversal of Fortune

The Twins had been on a roll since shortly after Jim's arrival. They had compiled a splendid 33-12 record since Jim captured his first Twins win, and they were on the verge of completing a run from last (tenth) place to the top of the American League standings. Unfortunately, the good tide was about to turn. The Twins swept a double-header in Washington on June 28 while the Yankees were losing to Boston, which pulled Minnesota to within a game and a half of first. The Twins and Senators were rained out the next day, however, while New York was exacting revenge on the Red Sox. Minnesota would never get that close again in 1963.

On July 3, Jim lost a matchup with Jim Bunning in Detroit that started a fall in which the Twins lost nine of ten, dropping to 8½ games out of first place. It also began a stretch in which Perry went seven starts without a win.

Jim finally stopped his personal slide on August 9 when he fired a four-hitter in a 5-3 win over Boston. The only damage came via a pair of home runs, one by Dick Stuart and the other by Carl Yastrzemski. Twins manager Sam Mele had an interesting observation about the lithe righthander's performance.

"Perry pitched hard tonight," stated Mele to reporters after the game. "That's what he has to do to win. We've noticed that when Jim lets up—throws a softie up there every now and then—he gets into trouble. Tonight he stayed fast."[218]

For Jim's part, he did not necessarily disagree, but he felt the key was location as much as it was pure velocity. "Stuart hit a hanging curve, Yaz hit a fastball," he explained. "Most of the time, I was low and quick. I went high on both the home run pitches . . . high and out of the park."[219]

Jim was even better his next time out, limiting Baltimore to only one run over seven innings, but it took the Twins offense until the thirteenth inning before they could score their second—and winning—run, leaving Perry with a frustrating no-decision.

Though he seemed to be coming around, a couple rough starts to close out August saw Perry quietly bumped from the starting rotation. He made only two short starts while appearing five times in relief during the season's final month as the Twins played out the string, finishing a distant third in the American League.

Even as he dealt with the disappointment of being bumped from the starting rotation, Jim was already standing out as an exemplary citizen of the Twin Cities. A story in the *Minneapolis Star* highlighted his giving nature.

"Donald Kilian Jr., a 12-year-old St. Louis Park Little Leaguer who lost his leg to cancer, will start school next week at Michael Dowling School in Minneapolis. A station wagon will pick him up at his home every day.

"'Please thank all the people who sent me cards and models.' said Donald. Also a special thanks to Jim Perry, Minnesota Twins pitcher, who came out to visit him."[220]

Déjà Vu II

As Jim and Daphne, along with their toddler Chris, enjoyed their first off-season in The Land of 10,000 Lakes, they were happy with their new hometown. Jim had taken an off-season job with Hansord Pontiac and they were quickly becoming part of the fabric of the Minneapolis community. At the same time, however, Jim's status with his new team was disconcerting. Not only had his name been bandied about in various trade rumors throughout the winter, but with the start of Spring Training on the horizon, Jim's name was conspicuously absent from discussions of the 1964 starting rotation.

In addition to Pascual, Kaat, and Stigman, who were Jim's rotation mates upon his arrival the year prior, two new names had gained manager Sam Mele's attention. 27-year old Lee Stange, who had finished the '63 season by winning nine of his last twelve starts, was a lock for the number four starter spot, and young Jim Roland, a 21-year old hard-throwing lefty with shaky control who had been given a $50,000 signing bonus out of high school, was widely expected to be the fifth starter.

On top of that, the same pundits who had lauded his initial starts in a Twins uniform were now discussing how Cleveland had gotten the better end of the trade that brought Perry to the Twins. Lefthander Jack Kralick, who Minnesota gave up, had proceeded to post a 13-9 record with a fine 2.92 ERA as a member of the Indians rotation after the trade. This was in contrast to Perry's more middling 9-9, 3.74 Minnesota marks. Heading into the 1964 season, Kralick was considered a key member of the Cleveland pitching staff while Perry had suddenly slipped into something of an afterthought.

As the spring exhibition season commenced, the "flexibility" of the Twins pitching staff was considered to be one of the team's underappreciated strengths. Much to his chagrin, of course, Jim had quietly established himself as one of the most versatile and durable pitchers in the game. Despite a strong camp, he was set to open the year in a long-reliever/spot-starter "swingman" role. As he always did, regardless of his disappointment, dutiful Jim Perry put his head down and got to work.

The Twins opened in Cleveland and when starter Camilo Pascual got knocked out early, Perry was ready to do his part. He pitched a shutout inning of relief and was the winning pitcher when Minnesota battled back, but it was something of an empty victory for a pitcher used to being a workhorse. And so it went for the next 161 games.

For an established major league pitcher in the prime of his career at 28 years old, the 1964 season was arguably the most difficult and frustrating of Jim Perry's career. Every time he started to gain some momentum with a string of good outings, it seemed a rough one would sink his stats. For a reliever, it takes longer to correct a subpar stat line due to the shorter pitching opportunities in comparison to starters.

Overall, Perry appeared in 42 games for the '64 Twins, all but one out of the bullpen. He pitched both short relief (13 appearances in which he worked less than one full inning) and long (seven appearances of three innings or longer). He finished with a 6-3 record and a very respectable 3.44 ERA. Perhaps most significantly, even as the team faded out of the pennant race in the second half, Jim seemed to get better as the season went on. Over his last 15 appearances, Perry posted an excellent 1.90 ERA. This final stretch included a splendid outing in New York when he pitched four and two-thirds scoreless innings, allowing just one hit and one walk while striking out four to beat the eventual pennant-winning Yankees.

Shake It Up

1964 marked the fifth straight year and the ninth time in ten that the Yankees won the American League pennant and advanced to the World Series. (The post-season "playoff" system would not be implemented until 1969.) Frustrated by his team's miserable sixth place finish, twenty games behind the Yankees, Twins owner Calvin Griffith did not blame the manager, Sam Mele, but decided that a new mix of coaches was in order. Included in the reshaping of the coaching staff were two new faces that would positively impact both the Twins and specifically Jim Perry.

A new pitching coach was the move that would be of immediate importance to Jim's fortunes. Johnny Sain, who was already building a reputation as an outstanding pitching guru, was hired to replace Gordie Maltzberger. A four-time twenty game winner with the Boston Braves, Sain had been pitching coach for the mighty Yankees for three years until he quit over a contract dispute following the 1963 season. Griffith successfully coaxed Sain out of "retirement" and a position with an automobile agency he had procured back home in Arkansas.

The other new coach who would meaningfully impact both Jim and the organization was Billy Martin. Of course, Martin would go on to become a legendary manager, but at this point, he was simply a former player who had just wrapped up an 11-year playing career, spent mostly with the New York Yankees. During his career as a player, Billy was known as both a fiery player and a drinking buddy of Mickey Mantle. Martin had spent the bulk of his final season in 1961 playing for the Twins and retired to become a scout with the team during 1962 spring training. Though he had helped out as an extra coach in 1964 spring training, Calvin Griffith felt that putting Martin in uniform full-time was just what the team needed to increase its intensity on offense, as well as in the field.

"We were too lackadaisical at times (in 1964)," the owner explained in announcing the promotion of Martin to the big league staff. Griffith stated that he wanted a more aggressive team and said that with Martin "we are going to put a bomb under everyone."[221]

Sportswriter Max Nichols, who covered the Twins for *The Sporting News*, provided some insight into the hire. "Martin has long been noted among American Leaguers for needling players verbally into hustling more," wrote the scribe. "And he is outspoken about what it takes to make up a winning team."[222]

Martin claimed any complaints about his antics were simply due to misunderstanding. "When you are on a winner and you needle the other players, they call you a sparkplug," he explained. "And when you are on a loser, they call you a clubhouse lawyer. On the Yankee clubs I played for, everyone needled everyone else. We kept each other awake.

"It wasn't until I played for a loser that I even knew what a clubhouse lawyer was."[223]

"Billy won't hesitate to put plenty of 'heat' on the Twins," wrote

Charles Johnson in reporting the hire for the *Minneapolis Star*. "Unless he goes too far, he could be the pepperpot the club has needed."[224]

Just a couple months later, Martin was a guest speaker for a pre-season banquet at the St. Paul Hotel, and he didn't hesitate to make what many felt was a far-fetched prediction. "The Twins have the personnel to beat New York," proclaimed Minnesota's new third base coach. "The only advantage the Yankees have is that they play as a team. We aim to eliminate mental mistakes and win this year."[225]

Little did banquet attendees realize how prophetic the team's newest coach would turn out to be.

Odd Man Out

As 1965 spring camp opened, Jim once again seemed to be something of an afterthought to his manager and many pundits. There was one observer, however, who remained optimistic about his ability to contribute and it was a notable one at that. Twins owner and president Calvin Griffith made some interesting comments to the press.

"Jim Perry could be a real pitching bonus for us this year," stated Griffith. "He seems to pitch good ball in the early innings and then lets up in the eighth or ninth. He has the stuff to be a winner for us."[226]

Now, the evidence does not seem to quite back up the specifics of Griffith's critique, but the most important aspect of this quote is the sentiment that Jim Perry was still destined to be a big part of the Minnesota Twins. Perhaps Griffith had an inkling that new pitching coach Johnny Sain would be a key to making this happen.

As the start of the regular season approached, however, it was basically the same story as '64, albeit with a few of the names changed. The Twins had traded for yet another Cleveland starting pitcher, getting Jim "Mudcat" Grant, who was poised to join incumbents Camilo Pascual, Jim Kaat, and (former Indian) Dick Stigman. Even for the fifth spot/swingman role, Jim Perry's name seemed to be conspicuously absent from the discussion. Rookie Dave Boswell had an excellent camp and quickly emerged as the favorite.

Even more disconcerting, not only was Perry missing from discussion of the starting rotation, it seems his name was alarmingly close to being absent from discussion of the Twins opening day roster. On Friday, April 2, just ten days before the start of the 1965 season, the Twins made the last big cut of their spring training roster, reassigning 11 players to their top farm team in Denver. This left 30 players remaining for 28 roster spots. An ominous story appeared in the *Minneapolis Tribune* the following morning.

While there were no quotes in the story and no byline other than "By Staff Writer," the story appeared on the front page of the Sports section and appeared to be written with insider's knowledge of the thought process of the Twins brass. "The plan (for getting down to the maximum 28-man roster limit)," said the story, "is that pitcher Jim Perry will be sold outright to another club, or traded."[227]

Four days later in an exhibition game against the Cincinnati Reds in Tampa, Perry was knocked around for five hits and three runs in two innings of work. The rough outing appeared to be another nail in the proverbial coffin of his Twins career. When it came time to make a decision on the final cuts, however, a surprising vote of confidence emerged from one of the newest members of the Twins braintrust.

"I like what I've seen of Perry this spring," stated new pitching coach Johnny Sain. "No man has worked harder to improve than Jim. He's making progress."[228]

On April 8, the day after Jim's rocky performance against the Reds, the Twins announced that a pair of youngsters who appeared to be locks for the Opening Day roster would instead be reassigned to minor league camp. Outfielder Andy Kosco and shortstop Bill Bethea were both sent out, which trimmed the roster to the Opening Day limit.

Though Jim survived the final cut, that was just the first hurdle. His goal, of course, was much greater than to simply make the team. Even as the season began, rumors continued to swirl regarding his future in Minnesota.

Work the Way Back

To begin the 1965 season, new pitching coach Johnny Sain had designed a plan that would keep Opening Day starter Jim Kaat and number two starter Camilo Pascual pitching every fourth day whenever possible. This was regardless of how much work any other pitcher on the Twins staff may have received of late. Between rainouts and off days, this structure left very few innings available for the rest of the

Twins pitching staff. Not surprisingly, the supposed last man on the staff coming out of spring camp was affected the most.

Making matters worse (for hurlers seeking pitching opportunities), Kaat and Pascual combined with number three starter Mudcat Grant to throw eight complete games over the course of Minnesota's first twenty. Perry pitched only once during the first month of the season. It was no surprise that he was rusty in that lone outing, walking three of the eight batters he faced over two innings of work.

It would be another twenty days before Jim appeared in his second game, the 25th of the season for the Twins. In the first six weeks of the 1965 season, Perry received only three and two-thirds innings of work for the Twins. According to beat writer Max Nichols, "there even were reports that he had been waived out of the league."[229] He truly was a forgotten man.

A lesser man might have thrown a tantrum or sat and sulked, but when the going got tough, Jim Perry got to work. Despite the fact he was not appearing in games, the veteran prepared relentlessly, confident that his time would come again.

"I've worked hard, almost every day, in the bullpen, to stay ready," Jim would explain. "It's not that I haven't worked hard before. I've always worked. But I worked even harder this year.

"We have a second baby on the way. That will mean another mouth to feed. The major leagues are the only place to pitch. I want to stay," pointedly stated the seven-year veteran.[230]

Each day, Jim would gauge how the flow of the game was going. If it looked like he was not going to pitch, he would warm up anyway, executing his pitches just as if he was doing a regular bullpen workout. This allowed him to not only stay sharp, but also provided opportunity to continue refining a new curve that Jim was working to develop under the tutelage of Johnny Sain.

"I think it's best for a relief pitcher to work a little bit every day instead of working hard one day and not the next," Jim explained.[231]

Sain was in awe of Jim's work ethic. "You have to pull for a guy who has tried as hard as Perry has this year," remarked his new pitching coach.[232] "I've never seen a man work so hard on his own.[233]

> I've never seen a man work so hard on his own. He refuses to be discouraged.
> — Johnny Sain
> TWINS PITCHING COACH

"He has gambled a little, throwing so often, but when he got his chances, he was ready."[234]

On May 26 in Boston during Minnesota's 36th game of the 1965 season, the first real chance came. Camilo Pascual got knocked out in the second inning and Jim came in to put out the fire. He pitched three and two-thirds innings, matching his season total to date, while allowing only one unearned run. While Perry was quieting the Red Sox bats, Minnesota's were coming alive. The Twins rallied back for a 9-7 win and Jim was the winning pitcher as Minnesota moved into a tie for first-place with the Chicago White Sox.

Three days later, manager Sam Mele turned to Perry once again, and again Perry was the winning pitcher, retiring the only two batters he faced during an 11-8 slugfest with the Washington Senators. The opportunities quickly picked up from there, with Jim being called upon often, normally for multi-inning long-relief work.

"You have to have a pitcher to stop them cold when your starter has a bad night," Mele explained. "That is what Sain had been preaching. Relievers for those middle three or four innings sometimes are as important as the finishers.

"Perry did a good job as a middle-inning man last year. I think he is throwing the ball a lot harder now than he was this spring. I have no intention of starting him. I need him for the middle relief job."[235]

And so it went, Dependable Perry was there, as usual, ready to do what needed to be done. With a home now in the Minneapolis suburb of Edina and a nice off-season job at the local automobile dealership, Jim was asked if he had been worried about all of that being in jeopardy due to his shaky job security in the spring.

"My wife and friends do all the worrying," he reassuringly stated. "All I can do is stay in shape and be ready when I'm called upon."[236]

Double Dips Mean Double Time

While Mele may have had "no intention of starting Perry," the early spring rainouts soon forced his hand. As the calendar turned to July, all of the games lost to Mother Nature in April were now showing up on the schedule on top of the regularly scheduled games. With the ballclub facing a grueling onslaught of six double-headers in a 23-day July stretch, Twins manager Sam Mele worried for how his relief corps would hold up.

"We've got to get a complete game somewhere," the manager pleaded. "Every man in my bullpen is overworked."[237]

On Monday, July 5 the team had just returned home from a three game sweep of the Kansas City Athletics, but the starters had been knocked out early in each of the last two wins. To compound Mele's dilemma, his top two (every fourth-day) starters were dealing with health concerns. Jim Kaat was battling a slightly strained forearm and number two starter Camilo Pascual was sidelined with a nagging back injury.

With an unusual morning-night doubleheader against the Boston Red Sox pending, ominous clouds appeared to be forming above the now tied-for-first-place Twins. Rookie Dave Boswell was set to start the 11 a.m. game, but manager Sam Mele still had to come up with a plan for the 8 p.m. nightcap. Naturally, the skipper turned to the always reliable port in the storm—Dependable Perry. The decision did not come lightly, however.

When Mele informed coach Hal Naragon that he settled on Jim as the game two starter, it was assumed that they would want him rested for the night game.

"Do you want Perry to go home then and not suit up for this morning?" Naragon questioned the skipper.

Mele briefly pondered the day ahead of him. "No," the manager decided. "We have to win the first one first. Maybe I might need him.'"[238]

Fortunately, Boswell was able to give the team a solid start in the morning game, leaving Jim ready to come back for the nightcap, and boy was he ready. Making just his second start in almost two years, Perry hurled a complete game shutout. He scattered seven hits and three walks, allowing only one opposing runner to advance as far as third base. In complete control throughout the night, Jim struck out eight Boston hitters. Even when he gave up a pair of singles in the ninth inning, putting runners on first and second with one out in a tight two-run game, Mele didn't flinch. He allowed Perry to retire the final two batters and finish off the 2-0 whitewash.

The manager was visibly relieved after the game. "This gives our pitching staff a real lift," he sighed.[239]

Beat writer Max Nichols described the scene as he conducted his postgame interview with the star of the day.

"Perry was so tired he could scarcely smile," the writer observed. "He sat on the chair in front of his locker, head bowed, and answered reporters' questions sincerely. His serious nature wouldn't allow him to dance or sing or go through any of the other antics normally associated with victorious joy."[240]

"The only way I know how to pitch is to work hard every inning," Jim explained to reporters.[241]

"I never gave up on myself," he continued. "I always felt I would get another chance to start if I kept working.

"Sain helped me more than I can explain. I threw that curve right much tonight," Jim said of his ability to incorporate his newest offering. He explained that throwing his slower breaking curve away from hitters allowed him to pound his running two-seam fastball inside to great effect. "I broke about four bats with my fastball inside," said the satisfied pitcher.[242]

Five days later, on July 10, Jim got another chance to start during a doubleheader, this time in the first game, and this time against the New York Yankees. Going up against Yankees ace Whitey Ford, Perry matched him pitch for pitch until the fifth inning. Minnesota left fielder Jimmy Hall led off with a single and center fielder Joe Nossek followed with a double, putting runners on second and third with nobody out. Ford then reached back and struck out Twins second baseman Jerry Kindall for the first out. With the pitcher's spot coming up, it looked like Minnesota's chance to take the lead might be in jeopardy, but of course this was no ordinary pitcher.

Between a litany of signs and even a couple conferences with third base coach Billy Martin, Jim worked the count to two balls and a strike. As Ford delivered the next pitch plateward, Hall took off down the third base line. Perry squared around and executed a perfect suicide squeeze bunt to the left side of the infield, forcing Ford to take the out at first as the Twins plated the game's first run.

Perhaps a bit rattled, Ford then served up a home run to leadoff man Zoilo Versalles. That would be more than enough for the lanky righthander as Minnesota cruised to a 4-1 win. Perry worked eight innings, giving up just an unearned run on four hits and a walk. The only thing keeping Perry from a second straight complete game was a pulled groin suffered while making a pitch in the eighth inning. That led the manager to take him out for precautionary purposes.

"I shouldn't have told Sam (Mele) I pulled a muscle over-striding," Jim lamented. "But I'll be okay. It's nothing serious."[243]

After the game, reporters made a beeline not for the pitching star, but rather for his new mentor, Johnny Sain. They wanted to know the recipe for the "magic potion" Sain had used to revitalize Jim Perry and turn him back into the budding star he appeared to be when he broke in with the Indians. To his credit, Sain deflected the praise onto his latest prize pupil.

"Listen," said the soft-spoken, tobacco-chewing coach. "Every ounce of credit for what Perry has done belongs to Jim himself. He's the guy who was willing to work; he's the fellow who is doing the job out on the mound, and I might say it's a pretty good job he's doing."[244]

"We thought all Perry needed was a little more rotation on the ball," the pitching guru continued. "Perry has picked it up, along with control. He's added a quick-breaking curve to go with his fastball and slider. He has confidence in his pitches and his control."[245]

Yankees hitters Bobby Richardson and Clete Boyer explained their frustration. "Perry looked pretty much the same except his control was sharp. He was pitching to spots, low and away, right about where he wanted the ball. We didn't see many good pitches to hit, mostly sliders and fastballs."[246]

Jim emphasized that he mixed in his newest pitch effectively, as well. "I struck out pinch-hitter Mickey Mantle on a low 3-2 curve," he explained.[247]

Simply put, Jim's confidence was sky high, likely as good as it had ever been since he reached the major leagues. "I think I'm pitching as sharp now as I did in 1960 when I won 18, perhaps with a little more knowledge and coaching to help me," he explained.[248]

Jim was going so good so suddenly that manager Sam Mele, who had left him buried on the bench just a couple months ago, was now campaigning for Perry to be named a batting practice pitcher for the American League in the All-Star Game that was coming to the Met.

Back in the Saddle

Following the 1965 all-star break, Jim was a fixture in the Twins rotation, starting 16 times, pitching into the eighth inning in ten of them as Minnesota cruised to the pennant. The double-header sweep back on July 5 in which Perry had given the team "a real lift" pushed the Twins out into first place and they never looked back.

On September 19 in a start against Washington, Jim scattered eight singles and a double en route to an 8-1 complete game victory. The win was Minnesota's ninth in a ten game span and reduced their magic number for clinching the American League title to three with a full two weeks remaining in the regular season.

On September 26, the Twins completed a weekend sweep of the Senators, clinching the American League pennant, ironically on the very field the franchise had called home before packing up and moving to the Twin Cities in 1961. The Twins were headed to the World Series for the first time since their move, which sent the team into a raucous post-game celebration. The accolades were flying among a team that genuinely played like a team.

"It was one of the greatest team efforts I've ever experienced in my 19 years in baseball," manager Sam Mele exclaimed. "It was not a one-man, or two-man show. It was a total effort from every person connected with the ball club."[249]

"It wasn't one pitcher or one player," pitching coach Johnny Sain chimed in. "Even the Yankees never had such a concerted team effort to win a pennant."[250]

The players were effusive in their praise of each other. Mudcat Grant summed up the feeling amidst the post-game locker room celebration.

"Credit Zoilo Versalles, Don Mincher and Jim Perry, who all picked us up when we needed help, and Al Worthington in relief," said Grant. "This is the best team I've ever played on for harmony and spirit."[251]

The festive mood led even normally low-keyed Jim Perry to let loose a bit. "There is nothing like being on a winner," he stated. "Coach John Sain even went so far as to call me a rowdy today in the celebration. But that's the way I feel. I'm proud to be with this club and I was glad I got the opportunity to redeem myself and help out. It took a lot of hard work. Twenty-five players did it."[252]

Give (Birth) and Go

There was another person celebrating the championship and looking forward to the World Series. Daphne Perry, wife of Jim, could see it coming and was busy making preparations. Atop the most important tasks on her "to do" list was giving birth to the couple's second child, and she darned well did not want to have to do it while her husband was away on a road trip.

"With the big lead we had as my due date approached, I just knew that we were headed to the World Series, Daphne explained. "I told my doctor, 'Listen, I had my first child by myself (back in North Carolina while Jim was playing). Can't you help me have this baby while Jim is at home? Oh, and by the way, I've got to go to the World Series…

"So labor was induced a few days ahead of my due date and our daughter, Pamela, was born (on September 12) in time for me to share the thrill of our first Series."

It was a prudent move. Despite Jim's long, illustrious career, the 1965 World Series would turn out to be the only one Daphne and her husband would get to take part in.

During the final week of the regular season, Minnesota had the luxury of getting some players much needed rest and others tuned up for the World Series. While all-star Tony Oliva sat out the last five games, slugger Harmon Killebrew was playing every day in an effort to shake off the rust from being sidelined with an elbow injury for almost two months. Manager Sam Mele, meanwhile, looked to get his rotation set for the Series where the Twins would be facing the red-hot Los Angeles Dodgers.

The Dodgers had finished the 1965 season with a flurry, winning 13 straight and 15 of their final 16 games to overcome a four-and-a-half game deficit to their arch-rivals, the San Francisco Giants. (The same Giants for which Gaylord Perry was pitching, meaning the sports world just barely missed out on a Perry brothers World Series showdown.) Los Angeles was led by the one-two pitching combo of Sandy Koufax (26-8 in 1965) and Don Drysdale (23-12), plus steady number three starter Claude Osteen (15-15). With two off-days scheduled for travel in the 2-3-2 best-of-seven series, Los Angeles manager Walter Alston announced that he would use only these three starters, who had combined to start 123 of the Dodgers 162 regular season games.

Mele planned to counter with Mudcat Grant (21-7) in game one, followed by Jim Kaat (18-11). The question facing the Minnesota skipper was what to do in game three. Should he go with Jim Perry, who had saved the staff and been a stalwart down the stretch or should he go with Camilo Pascual, who had been the team's ace dating back to before the move from Washington? The issue was further muddied by the fact that the season's second half had been something of a struggle for Pascual. Besides missing more than a month following surgery to remove a tumor in his back, he had scuffled to a 4.06 ERA over his final nine starts.

Surprising Series

Pundits considered the Dodgers prohibitive favorites to win the World Series, thanks to their dominant starting pitching. They had swept the New York Yankees in the Series just two years earlier, with Koufax winning twice and Drysdale once. Dodgers vice president Buzzie Bavasi reportedly predicted a similar result against Minnesota, but Twins third base coach and resident pot-stirrer Billy Martin had a different view, based on his experience as part of several Yankees World Series winners in his days as a player.

"The Yankees were playing in their umpteenth World Series," stated Martin. "It might have been new to Bavasi and the Dodgers, but it was old hat to the Yankees... The Dodgers will see something else in the Twins—a club making its first World Series appearance. The Twins will be charged up and ready to lick a cage of tigers, not to mention Dodgers."[253]

Just as Martin predicted, Minnesota was ready, knocking out Drysdale in the third inning of game one on the way to a stunning 8-2 win at Metropolitan Stadium. Don Mincher and American League MVP Zoilo Versalles each blasted home runs while Mudcat Grant went the distance.

The second game was a pitcher's duel between Koufax and Kaat until an LA error, followed by key hits from Tony Oliva and Harmon Killebrew gave Minnesota the game's first two runs in the bottom of the sixth inning. The Twins plated three more after Koufax was lifted for a pinch-hitter in the seventh inning and Kaat finished off a 5-1 complete game victory, giving the Twins a 2-0 advantage as the series moved to Los Angeles.

With a two-game series lead, Mele gave the game three start to Pascual, but the veteran was tagged for eight hits and three runs over five innings. Mele called on lefty Jim Merritt for two innings, followed by Johnny Klippstein to pitch the eighth. The Twins offense was held in check by Claude Osteen, who finished with a five-hit shutout in a 4-0 Dodgers victory. The win gave Los Angeles new life just when Minnesota seemed on the verge of a shocking four-game sweep.

Game four saw another matchup between Grant and Drysdale. The game was tight with the Dodgers holding a 3-2 lead into the sixth inning. When Grant gave up a walk and a single to open the bottom of the sixth, Mele went to his closer, Al Worthington in hopes of keeping it a one-run game. Unfortunately, Worthington could not get the job done, as he gave up hits to the first two batters he faced, allowing three runs to score in the inning. With a comfortable cushion, Drysdale settled in, cruising the rest of the way to a 7-2 complete game victory. Not only had Minnesota squandered their 2-0 series lead, but the Twins had not yet used one of their best pitchers from the regular season. Part of it was circumstance, but part may also have been a grave miscalculation on the part of Mele.

With momentum now on their side, Los Angeles came out swinging in game five. They scored two off Jim Kaat in the first and twice more in the third before Mele went to the bullpen. In what would seem to be a perfect spot for Perry, however, the manager instead went with 20-year old rookie Dave Boswell. Perhaps at this point he was saving Jim to start a potential must-win game six in place of Pascual? That proved not to be the case, either.

Boswell pitched through the fifth inning, holding the Dodgers to just one more run, but the Minnesota offense was being overpowered by Sandy Koufax, who had faced the minimum 18 batters through six innings. The only hit had been a measly single by Harmon Killebrew, who was immediately erased by a double-play ball off the bat of Earl Battey.

After Boswell was pinch-hit for with the Twins trailing 5-0 in the sixth, Mele surprisingly decided to call on Perry for his World Series debut in what essentially amounted to mop up work. Jim pitched the final three innings, giving up a pair of runs while Koufax completed his four-hit shutout. The most puzzling aspect of this three-inning usage was not only that there was little Perry could do at that point to help win this critical game, but it also left him unavailable as a starting option for game six.

With the Twins returning to Minnesota down three games to two and Mele now in full panic mode, the skipper made the decision to go back to Mudcat Grant on just two days rest. Pitching on short rest and battling a heavy cold, Grant came through with an outstanding effort, limiting the Dodgers to five uneventful singles and a solo home run. He even blasted a three-run homer of his own as Minnesota won 5-1, sending the series to a decisive seventh game.

While Grant had been the hero in his incredible complete game effort, it left him unavailable for game seven. Mele decided to test his luck again, going with another starter on short rest. Jim Kaat, however, had not been nearly as sharp as Grant in the series or the regular season. Los Angeles manager Walter Alston followed a similar line of thinking, going back to his ace Sandy Koufax on two days rest, as well.

When Kaat gave up three straight hits and two runs to open the fourth inning, Mele must have thought better of his gambit, electing to lift his starter and go back to bullpen ace Worthington. After two shutout innings from Worthington, Klippstein and Merritt followed, each holding the line before Perry finally got his second appearance of the series, again with Minnesota trailing, but this time only by two.

After pitching a shutout inning in the top of the ninth, Jim would have been the pitcher of record if the Twins could somehow find a way to break through against Koufax in the ninth. A one-out single by Killebrew was all they could muster, however, as Earl Battey and Bob Allison both went down swinging. The strikeout of Allison was the tenth of the night for Koufax who completed an iconic performance with the series-clinching three-hit shutout.

While it was a disappointing end to 1965 for both the Twins and for Jim Perry, it had been an excellent season, overall. Especially for Perry, it had been a season of redemption. As he joined several teammates on the Twins winter caravan covering a hundred cities across Minnesota, Iowa, the Dakotas, Nebraska and Wisconsin, Jim had high hopes for 1966.

10

Déjà Vu
All Over Again

As the Minnesota Twins 1966 spring training got under way, the starting rotation was in a state of flux. Mudcat Grant was mired in a holdout, as he attempted to leverage his 21-win 1965 season for a greater salary in '66. Grant's absence was magnified when Jim Kaat suffered a back injury in the first exhibition game. That left longtime staff ace Camilo Pascual and Jim Perry, along with a pair of youngsters, Dave Boswell and Jim Merritt, who had both emerged as key contributors down the stretch for the pennant-winning '65 club.

"Those four most likely will start the first week of the season," stated Twins President Calvin Griffith in a meeting with reporters two weeks before Opening Day. "We aren't worried about our starting pitching."[254]

Within a week, however, Grant, who had finally reported, was looking ready to go and Kaat was steadily progressing. Manager Sam Mele raved about Minnesota's 1966 pitching prospects.

"This is the best staff we've taken north since I've been manager," stated the skipper. "We have six capable starting pitchers in Jim Grant, Camilo Pascual, Dave Boswell, Jim Perry, Jim Kaat, and Jim Merritt ... Our staff is as strong as any I saw in Florida this spring."[255]

Mudcat Grant got the Opening Day call and he proved ready, hurling a masterful six-hit complete game 2-1 win over Kansas City.

Pascual started the second game, going eight innings before Johnny Klippstein finished up for the save in a 5-3 Minnesota victory. Kaat got the ball for the season's third game and showed no lingering effects from the spring training back issue, as he struck out ten A's hitters while pitching into the ninth inning before lefty Jim Merritt came on to record the final out and lock down a 4-2 Twins win.

Dave Boswell started the fourth game and got knocked out in the sixth inning leading to a trio of relievers, none of which was Perry. As opening day starter Grant prepared to return for the fifth game, not only was it apparent that Jim Perry was not one of the four starters, he was perilously close to once again being an afterthought for manager Mele.

Jim finally made his first appearance on April 22 in the team's seventh game of the season. He pitched the final two shutout innings of a 2-1 loss in California against the Angels. Despite four and a third innings of spotless work, Perry only appeared in three of the team's first eighteen games. Mother Nature didn't help Jim's quest for work, as the team saw five consecutive games rained out during their first road trip.

Twice during the season's opening weeks, Twins manager Sam Mele mentioned Perry as a potential spot starter, but both times he elected to stick with the youngster Boswell instead. Finally, with the showers of April bringing flowers—and better weather—of May, that also meant more games and a long-awaited opportunity for Perry.

On Monday, May 9, in the Twins 19th game of the 1966 season, Jim faced off against the New York Yankees. Despite being only his second game action in two full weeks, Dependable Perry was ready. He pitched seven strong innings, giving up only solo home runs to sluggers Mickey Mantle and Roger Maris before leaving for a pinch-hitter. Though Minnesota lost it on another solo home run, this one by Joe Pepitone off reliever Al Worthington in the ninth, Mele was effusive in the praise of his security blanket pitcher.

"Jim Perry pitched marvelously well," stated the Minnesota skipper. "His control (no walks) was excellent. There's just not too much more you could ask of the guy."[256]

While Jim felt good about his performance, he lamented the pair of long balls and expressed his desire for the opportunity to make amends. "I made a couple of bad pitches and that was that," he groused to reporters after the game. "I hope I get another chance to start."[257]

Even Yankees manager Ralph Houk was impressed by Perry's performance, taking exception to the Minnesota righthander's self-degradation.

"I thought Perry was real sharp," observed the New York field general. "He kept the ball down real well and Mantle hit a good pitch. It was real low and Mantle lifted it as only he can."[258]

Rotation Encore

Just as he hoped, Jim's performance earned him another start. "We're going to give Jim Perry a chance to start Sunday against Washington," Twins manager Sam Mele explained to the press a few days later. "This means Dave Boswell won't start. Perry deserves a chance because of his fine work this spring and in the game against the Yankees the other day."[259]

Mele's faith was rewarded as Jim tossed a five-hitter, beating the Senators 6-2. He even persevered through a 45-minute mid-game rain delay in the complete game effort. In addition to his masterful pitching, Jim contributed two of 11 Twins hits, including a line drive single immediately upon the resumption of play that scored a critical insurance run.

"He's a remarkable man," said the Twins skipper. "I know he's ready when I need him. He was last year. He is this year. And he's ready because he makes himself ready."[260]

"Being ready is a part of baseball," Jim explained. "Like last year. It was my duty to be in shape, if Sam wanted me. I got the chance—and I'm grateful—and I helped the team.

> *He's a remarkable man. I know he's ready when I need him. And he's ready because he makes himself ready.*
> — Sam Mele
> TWINS MANAGER

"You must satisfy yourself, first of all," Jim continued. "It's a matter of conscience, really. Then you know you've done your share."[261]

"He refuses to be discouraged," marveled pitching coach and mentor Johnny Sain.[262]

Beat writer John Wiebusch asked Jim how he is able to prod

> *Being ready is a part of baseball. You must satisfy yourself, first of all. It's a matter of conscience, really. Then you know you've done your share.*
>
> — Jim Perry

himself daily into a disciplined running and throwing regimen.

"A pitcher's most important assets are his legs," Jim answered. "Running and a regular schedule of throwing can't do anything but help. You know it's really tough pitching relief. You might pitch the equivalent of two-three-four straight days out there (in the bullpen) and never get used."[263]

Bullpen coach Hal Naragon, who had an up-close view of Jim's never-ending bullpen work ethic, revealed that the secret to his success was more than just physical. "Jim keeps himself mentally ready," Naragon explained. I think one big reason is that Johnny Sain has leveled with him—told him he might not get to work for a while, but that the time would come. Jim never lost his confidence."[264]

"My wife worries about me more than I do," Jim confided to beat writer Max Nichols.[265]

Daphne, who Nichols accurately described as Jim's "pretty wife," concurred. "He's right," she confessed. "He doesn't worry near as much as I do. Other baseball wives and friends ask me how he takes it. I tell them he keeps saying everything will be all right."[266]

Wartime Pitcher

Jim's perpetual optimism was tested following his next start, as he found himself the casualty of a bean ball war. With Minnesota riding a four-game winning streak that began with Jim's complete game victory over Washington, the Twins faced off against the Chicago White Sox in the final game of a two-week 13-game homestand. Minnesota had won all four games between the neighboring state rivals at this point in the young 1966 season, and the Sox had begun to take out their frustrations on Twins hitters during this three-game series.

In the first game on Tuesday night, May 17, the Twins jumped out to an early lead when Tony Oliva blasted a three-run homer in the bottom of the first inning. After Zoilo Versalles followed with a solo homer in the next inning, Chicago pitcher Joel Horlen sent the next Minnesota batter, Cesar Tovar, sprawling with a fastball high and inside. Minnesota would proceed to bang out four home runs among eleven hits, including another long ball off the bat of Oliva en route to an easy 8-3 win.

The next night, the Minnesota bats stayed hot, rolling to a 7-1 victory, but White Sox pitcher Gary Peters followed up Horlen's "purpose pitch" with one of his own, firing one "under the collar" of hot-hitting Oliva. While neither Chicago pitcher had hit a Twins batter, Minnesota had certainly taken exception to the unmistakable pitch location to a pair of their top hitters. This set the stage for the final game of the series when Jim took the mound for a Thursday afternoon matinee against veteran righthander John Buzhardt.

After White Sox catcher J.C. Martin cracked a two-run homer off Perry to get the scoring started in the second inning, Jim promptly drilled the next batter square in the back with his next pitch. While the timing may have appeared intentional, the fact that it was light-hitting eight-hole hitter Al Weis would suggest otherwise. When Jim came to the plate for his first at-bat an inning later, however, there was no question about the intentions of the man on the mound.

Leading off the bottom of the third inning, Perry found himself dodging a barrage of fastballs, all unmistakably in the vicinity of the occupied batter's box. The first pitch was in the dirt, with Jim easily skipping out of the way. The second sailed over his head, but not by so much that the catcher, Martin, could not snag it. The third pitch broke in high and tight, causing Jim to bow his back but not enough to send him sprawling. Though he was able to elude the first three, Perry was unable to escape a fourth consecutive heat-seeking missile.

"You finally got him, didn't you, you (blankety-blankety-blank)," Twins manager Sam Mele shouted as he angrily stomped in front of the home dugout.[267]

Worst of all, the switch-hitter was naturally batting from the left side against his right-handed counterpart. That left Jim's pitching elbow exposed, which is precisely where the purpose pitch got him. Though the durable hurler refused to go down, Perry was left doubled over in pain as a welt the size of a softball quickly emerged just above his right elbow.

Jim Kaat entered to pinch-run as Jim headed off to a nearby clinic for X-rays. At this point, home plate umpire Nestor Chylak finally decided it was time to put a stop to the plainly evident bean-ball war. "Both managers were warned," Chylak explained. "Any more knockdowns and it will be a $50 fine on the pitcher."[268]

After the game, which the Twins came back to win on a walkoff double by Oliva to pull within three games of first place, tempers were flaring in both clubhouses.

"(Buzhardt) threw at Perry," Twins manager Sam Mele heatedly charged. "And he was under orders to do it. I know his control is a lot better than that and he keeps the ball down. Those pitches were all up around Jim's head."[269]

When confronted by reporters in the visitor clubhouse, White Sox skipper Eddie Stanky not only failed to make a denial, but he offered a thinly veiled admission.

"I never have ordered a pitcher to throw at a batter before a game," stated the Chicago manager, speaking in a soft voice, carefully enunciating each word for emphasis. "But during a game things change. I'm a retaliation manager. Perry hit Al Weis on his uniform number (six) the preceding inning. Do you know what that means? Do you know the significance of that?"[270]

Though Stanky seemed to be implying that Jim's hitting Weis was clearly intentional, the Minnesota hurler explained otherwise. "Why would I want to put a .111 hitter on base?" Perry queried as he iced his thankfully bruised-not-broken elbow.[271]

Upset at allowing the home run to Martin, Jim admitted that he might have let his emotions get the best of him. "I tried to throw my next pitch extra hard," he explained. "It was a sliding fastball—and it tailed in on him."[272]

As for the retaliation, Jim was assertive in characterizing Buzhardt's intention. "He certainly was trying to hit me," Jim countered. "He tried for three pitches, and on the fourth he succeeded."[273]

Buzhardt countered with a rather unconvincing defense, although one cleverly shrouded in truth. "I wasn't throwing at him. I pitch Perry inside because he's a good hitter."[274]

Home plate umpire Nestor Chylak, who was later elected to the Hall of Fame, detailed after the game why he waited to step in despite the sudden "wildness" from a pair of veteran pitchers both known for their control.

"Perry's pitch that hit Weis put me in a bad position, coming after a home run like that," stated the widely respected arbiter. "But I didn't think it was intentional. Buzhardt's first pitch to Perry was in the dirt. His second was far enough over Perry's head it might have been wild. The third one was a breaking pitch—I don't think he would try to hit a guy with a breaking pitch. The fourth one hit him. After that, I warned both managers that the next guy who throws at anyone gets chased."[275]

Postlude: It is interesting to note that during Jim's final season while playing for the Oakland A's, sports writer Ed Levitt of the *Oakland Tribune* did a story on "purpose pitches" in which he interviewed several A's players. One of those interviewed was Jim Perry, who offered up a tacit confession some ten years after the fact.

"I've had managers tell me to knock down certain hitters," admitted the veteran hurler. "I have enough control of my pitches that if I want to hit a batter I can hit him. I've hit four, five this (1975) season. I don't hit guys on the head. I throw at their sides."[276] Of course, that is precisely where Jim hit Weis back on that May afternoon in 1966—square in his back-side.

Getting Back on Track

While the injury thankfully proved not to be serious, it effectively derailed Jim's 1966 season just as he was beginning to get on a roll. The Twins announced Perry would miss at least one start, but he was not placed on the disabled list. Sure enough, the reliable workhorse declared himself ready to go just five days later, coming out of the bullpen to help save the staff when starter Camilo Pascual could not get out of the second inning in Boston. However, Jim was limited to just two more bullpen appearances over the next three weeks. When he finally got another start in Kansas City on June 13, Perry fired a six-hit complete game, striking out eight and walking just one in a 6-1 Twins win.

Though he tossed another complete game two weeks later in Detroit, this one a masterful three-hitter in a 7-1 Minnesota victory, Perry continued to be frustrated by an inconsistent role. The team was also plagued by an inconsistent offense as it struggled to stay in the pennant race. As the Twins slipped into the bottom half of the

American League standings, more than a dozen games off the pace of league-leading Baltimore, manager Sam Mele complimented the resiliency of his key pitchers.

"These pitchers have put up with a lot—working without runs all the time, and they really have showed me something" the skipper asserted. "Jim Kaat, Jim Grant, and Jim Perry all volunteered to work with two days' rest when we ran into four double-headers in two straight weekends. They have never given in."[277]

Mele's inclusion of Perry's short-rest contribution was an understatement. Jim gave both the team and his personal season a big lift when he volunteered to take the ball on extremely short rest. Not only was his arm short on rest, but his entire body was going on little sleep when he pitched what he considered possibly the best game of his life.

Fighting the Schedule

Following the 1966 All-Star break, Minnesota opened the second half with an unusual six-game homestand. A conventional three-game set with Washington Thursday through Saturday was followed by the Yankees coming in for a quick three games in 24 hours. Thanks to an early-season rain-out, the two teams played a 1:30 p.m. Sunday afternoon doubleheader followed by a Monday matinee, also starting at 1:30. After that quick set, which was swept by New York, the Twins were due in Washington D.C. for a twi-night doubleheader with the Senators on Tuesday, while the Yankees needed to get back to New York for a Tuesday home game with Kansas City. Complicating the travel for both teams was a strike by airline workers that was impacting five major air carriers.

Because of the strike, the only charter the Twins were able to arrange was with Overseas National Airways, an airline that, as the name implies, specialized in international travel. In addition, because of the nationwide nature of the strike, MLB and its teams were forced to be creative in coming up with solutions for cross-country travel. In this case, the fix called for both the Twins and Yankees, plus the umpires from the just completed series to all share the same charter flight to the east coast. An addition to this traveling trio were several Twins wives, who were accompanying the team on this flight. This included Jim's wife Daphne, plus their two young children, four year old Chris and little Pam, a baby of just ten months.

This unusual traveling contingent waited together in the Minneapolis Airport for the scheduled 9:30 p.m. charter. It was rare to mix opponents like this so soon after playing. The Yankees, weary but feeling good about the three-game sweep, were forced to join the Twins, who were not only disappointed about just getting swept at home, but were also dreading the late-night travel that would be immediately followed by not one but two road games the following day. Against this backdrop, the large group prepared for the East Coast flight.

Some mingled in the airport lounge, some at the bar, and others at small tables. Most sipped drinks, talking baseball as they waited. And waited. The Overseas National plane being used for this charter was coming in from Norway, and it was significantly delayed.

By the time the charter finally arrived, it was well after midnight and the drinks had been flowing for some since the mid-afternoon conclusion of the game. While the group boarded without incident, the steward had trouble with several boisterous passengers who refused to be properly seated as the plane began to taxi toward the runway. Among the offenders were a pair of Yankees players, plus Twins coach—and former Yankee—Billy Martin.

Twins traveling secretary Howard Fox, who was also accompanied by his wife, did not take kindly to the loud and sometimes profane language being used by the rollicking threesome, not to mention the group's refusal to follow the instructions of the steward. When Fox suggested to Martin that he get the Yankees players under control, Martin retorted that it was not his job to be "mother hen" to the Yankees.

New York manager Ralph Houk finally interceded with his Yankees players, letting them know in no uncertain terms that further belligerence would not be tolerated. That left Martin with no one to carry on. Hard feelings between Martin and Fox, which had been simmering since soon after Billy arrived in town more than a year ago, were now bubbling dangerously close to the boiling point.

When the plane finally arrived at Washington's Dulles Airport, the Twins deplaned with the Yankees remaining aboard to continue on to New York. On the Twins' charter bus from the airport to the team hotel, more words were exchanged between Martin and Fox. By the time Fox was handing out room keys to the tired players and staff in the lobby of the Statler-Hilton hotel, it was almost five o'clock in the morning. Beat writer Tom Briere of the *Minneapolis Tribune* described the scene:

"Fox tossed Billy's room key to him after most of the other players had dispersed to their rooms. Martin remained at the desk and continued the harangue. Catcher Earl Battey attempted to pacify Martin, with little success.

"Finally Martin said to Fox, 'I'll deck you,' and Fox presented himself and said: 'Okay deck me.'

"Punches were thrown. (Bob) Allison finally grabbed Martin with a necktie hold. Harmon Killebrew and Jim Perry were other Twin players on the scene as peacemakers."[278]

Of course, Jim was not only there as "peacemaker," but he was also standing by in order to secure a single room from Fox for his family. When the fracas broke out with the entire Perry clan looking on, Noreene Mee, wife of Twins P.R. man Tom Mee, quickly grabbed young Chris Perry's hand to make sure he was safe from the commotion, while Daphne protectively shielded baby Pam.

It wasn't until after 6 a.m. (7 a.m. central time) that Jim finally got settled into bed with wife Daphne, the kids tucked safely asleep. It was a short slumber. After less than five hours of shuteye, Jim was up and headed back to the airport with his family before noon so that Daphne and the kids could continue on, catching a midday flight to visit her parents back in North Carolina.

Jim Kaat, who had pitched Friday's game, started the first game of the evening, pitching on his normal three days rest. Kaat scattered 13 hits en route to a 5-4 complete game victory. Jim Perry then took the mound for the nightcap of the Tuesday twin-bill, with only one day off since he had started the second game of Sunday's doubleheader with the Yankees.

From the outset, it was clear that Perry was on his game. He retired 11 of the first 12 Senators he faced, with the only baserunner coming via an error by second baseman Cesar Tovar. With two outs in the fourth inning, Washington cleanup hitter Frank Howard hit a one-hop smash back up the middle to Perry's backhand side. Jim lunged for it, but was unable to glove it, with the ball deflecting off his glove toward third base. The pitcher quickly recovered the bouncing ball, but his rushed throw was wide, pulling first baseman Don Mincher off the bag. The play was ruled a hit by the home scorekeeper. It was the only hit Perry would allow until the ninth inning.

In the meantime, Jim was at work pacing the offense. In the top of the fifth inning, he lined an RBI-single into center field, plating Tovar with the game's first run. He came to bat again in the seventh inning with one out and runners on first and third. Again, Perry came through, this time lofting a fly ball to deep center field that easily scored Andy Kosco from third base with a big insurance run.

Entering the bottom of the ninth inning, the Twins held a 4-0 lead, with Perry working on a one-hitter, the lone hit being of dubious quality. Washington leadoff man Don Blasingame led off the bottom of the ninth by pulling a drag bunt to the right side, beating first baseman Mincher to the bag for a clean, albeit quite unmanly hit. Though it too failed to escape the infield, the clean base hit took the official scorer off the hook from having to debate the merits of reversing the decision on the first hit, thus giving Jim Perry a no-hitter.

Unfazed by the loss of any chance at a potential no-hitter, Perry immediately got back to work finishing off the Senators. He retired the next hitter on a sacrifice bunt, leading one to question if the overmatched Washington club felt it would be a moral "victory" to even manufacture a single run against the dominant Perry on this night. After three-hole hitter Fred Valentine walked, Jim got Frank Howard to ground into a 6-4-3 game-ending double play.

Following the game, Perry was elated about his two-hit shutout, calling it "the best game I've ever pitched. (Especially) under the circumstances, considering the short sleeping time," he added. "I thought I had great command tonight. I had a good sinker and a good hard slider."[279]

Asked if losing the no-hitter because of the fourth inning scoring decision weighed on his mind as the game progressed, the humble hurler denied any regard. "I was only concerned with winning, the no-hitter was secondary," he clarified.[280]

From that point, Jim got on a roll, posting an 8-3 record with a 2.03 ERA over his final 15 starts, including five complete games. His success helped lead the team to a 46-25 record over their final 71 games.

Sweet Swing

In an 8-1 complete game win over the California Angels on August 16, Jim racked up a season-high ten strikeouts while firing a three-hitter, but headlines in the morning paper were raving about "sweet swinging" Jim Perry's bat. In a rare feat, the all-around athlete contributed as many hits at the plate as he allowed on the mound.

"We've got the best hitting staff of pitchers in the league," manager Sam Mele gushed after watching Jim rap out a single and two doubles.[281] The Twins skipper then explained to reporters how he might even consider using his sweet-swinging pitchers as pinch-hitters.

"Kaat is very good against right-handed pitchers," the skipper explained. "I think Camilo (Pascual) would be best against left-handers. Perry is a switch-hitter, so that gives us versatility."[282]

Beat writer Max Nichols elaborated on the manager's assessment: "Jim Merritt and Jim Grant are considered capable hitters, too. Perry takes an even swing—always makes contact. Kaat takes the biggest swing and leads the pitchers in home runs..."[283]

"I always wanted to pinch-hit," confirmed Perry when told of the manager's plotting. "The year (1959) I hit .300, I got on deck one time for Cleveland. But I never got up to bat. That's one thing I hope to do one day."[284] It is one of the few goals that Jim Perry would never achieve.

Setting the Stage

Jim wrapped up the 1966 campaign with a pair of outstanding starts, beating Cleveland, 5-1 with another three-hitter and then finishing with seven and two-thirds innings of shutout work in the final game of the season to beat the eventual World Series champion Baltimore Orioles, 1-0. He even drove in the only run of the game with an eighth-inning base hit to cap off a great finish to a fine season.

The win over Baltimore was especially satisfying, as it secured a second place regular season finish for the Twins, one game ahead of Detroit. This meant a World Series share bonus of $2,235 for players on the second place team, as opposed to $1,500 for third place. The $735 difference was no small thing in this era before free agency when the minimum player salary was $6,000 and the overall average was only $19,000.

"Remember, I won the game that earned all of us a lot more money for Christmas," Jim would later point out with pride.[285]

On an 89-win team that ended up finishing second, Perry's 184 innings pitched ranked third. It was quite an accomplishment, considering he had to fight his way into the starting rotation at the beginning of the year and then work his way back into it again following the bean-ball casualty. Best of all, Jim's sparkling 2.54 earned run average ranked fourth among all American League pitchers.

The stars seemed to be aligned for Jim Perry to open the 1967 season finally as a full-fledged workhorse member of the starting rotation. As explained in the book's opening chapter, however, he was once again the victim of his own amazingly durable versatility.

More Than a Friend

There were other forces at work in conspiring against Jim's chances of becoming a full-fledged member of the '67 Minnesota starting rotation. Pitching coach Johnny Sain, who had been a major factor in jump-starting Jim's career in 1965, left the Twins to join the Detroit Tigers shortly after the conclusion of the 1966 season. A long-running feud between Sain and manager Sam Mele finally came to a head when Mele asked team president Calvin Griffith for permission to replace Sain and coach Hal Naragon, both of whom Mele felt were disloyal.

Sain made no bones about the fact he had been at odds with the manager. One week before the end of the 1966 season, he made a comment that seemed to echo Jim Perry's ongoing frustration.

"It has been no pleasure working for number 14 (Mele)," stated the pitching coach. "I have no say-so about who is going to start, how many starters we use, who goes to the bullpen, anything."[286]

Sain must not have been alone in his assessment. Hal Naragon, another Jim Perry advocate, was released from his contract, as well, due to the fact that he strongly supported Sain over the manager.

Jim Kaat, a 25-game winner in 1966 who was named American League Pitcher of the Year by *The Sporting News*, likely felt most empowered among the players to speak out.

"From a front-office standpoint, I'm not qualified to give reasons for what I'm afraid will come to be known as a 'great mistake,'" stated the miffed Twins ace just days after news of the coaching change broke. "I'm sure there were complications involving the two coaches and Mr. Mele. (But) from a player's standpoint I am qualified to say that this is the worst thing that could happen to our club at this time."[287]

You've Got Mail

Kaat was so upset about the loss of Sain, in fact, that he penned a lengthy "open letter" to Twins fans that was published in the October 6 edition of the *Minneapolis Tribune*.

"Some 2,600,000 fans poured into Met Stadium to see our team play championship baseball and do our best to win the pennant in 1965 and 1966," the letter began. "We had the finest pitching coach money can buy and now, suddenly, he's gone. I think the fans should know what a huge void we have to fill.

"When you dress and undress with 25 men in the same room, eat, sleep and rub elbows with them for the better part of seven months, you find out a great deal how men feel about each other—who they respect and who they don't; who they listen to and who they don't; whose opinions are in the best interest of the team and whose are just idle chatter.

"I have based my opinions on John Sain and Hal Naragon from that seven-month tour of duty with 24 other members of the Minnesota Twins... Please allow me to say this: Every move John Sain and Hal Naragon talked about, or attempted to do, was in the best interest of the Minnesota Twins baseball club and to attempt to improve our position. To me that is not disloyalty.

"Two years ago the Minnesota Twins were known as a club with fine hitters (which we still have) but not much pitching strength. Now we have a surplus of starting pitchers and some very capable relievers, largely because of a man named John Sain. Allowing him to leave our ball club is like the Green Bay Packers allowing Vince Lombardi to leave them." (Which ironically is precisely what would transpire in Green Bay little more than a year after this cryptically prophetic warning by Kaat.)

"If I were asked to name two coaches who have done more for the Twins and have helped me the most since I have been with them," Kaat's letter continued, "it would be Sain and Naragon. Hal Naragon was the last instrument of communication between Mr. Mele and the players. Now there is a complete division.

"John Sain had more mechanical knowledge about baseball (not just pitching), leadership qualities, and knew how to convey this knowledge to the players better than any man I ever have known...
"Believe me, he molded our staff. He stood up for Jim Perry when Jim appeared to be on his way out of the majors. Now (Perry) is one of our best."[288]

Kaat's letter continued for several more paragraphs, including one that stated "John Sain is in a league by himself when it comes to pitching knowledge... John is one of those rare individuals you get the opportunity to work with once in a lifetime."[288]

Needless to say, losing Sain would be a blow for several members of the Twins pitching staff as they prepared for the '67 season. If he was going to take his game to the next level as he desired, Jim Perry would need to do it without one of his biggest boosters and mentors in his corner fighting for him. In an interesting twist, Sain's replacement would be Early Wynn, who was one of the Cleveland starters Jim had correctly predicted would soon be gone when he decided upon signing with the Indians to begin his pro career.

Another shoe dropped in early December when the Twins traded for 1964 Cy Young award winner Dean Chance during the Baseball Winter Meetings. Even after 1965 staff ace Camilo Pascual was shipped out in another deal, that left six capable starters in Minnesota as the players prepared for 1967 spring training. In addition to Chance, returning 25-game winner Jim Kaat was a given in the rotation, leaving Perry to battle with Mudcat Grant (just one year removed from winning 21 games), Dave Boswell, and Jim Merritt.

"I've done everything the club has asked me to do," stated Perry. "I think I've got a chance to be a regular starter coming to me."[289]

Jim was not wrong in his assessment, but as had become the pattern, the chance he thought he had coming would take time to come to fruition.

Same Ship, Different Skipper

It was the same old story as the 1967 season got under way, with Jim Perry something of a forgotten man. As the "number five" starter on a team with a four-man rotation, Perry was limited primarily to occasional middle relief stints. He made just one start through the season's first two months. On the afternoon of Friday, June 9, with Minnesota languishing in sixth place and one of the team's best pitchers rotting on the bullpen bench, a ray of hope appeared. Manager Sam Mele was suddenly fired just prior to the start of a weekend series with the defending World Series champion Orioles. Mele was replaced by Cal Ermer, who was promoted from the same post with the Twins' triple-A Denver affiliate.

Ermer arrived with a reputation as a fiery competitor and a straight shooter. He was charged with injecting new life into the Twins team and propelling them back into the pennant race. Looking for some new life, himself, Jim wasted no time in appealing to his new boss for an opportunity. "I went right to him," Perry explained. "I told him I just needed work—any kind of work. I needed to pitch."[290]

Nothing changed initially, as far as Perry's usage was concerned. He remained limited to periodic relief appearances. On July 4, after going 11 days without pitching, Perry finally received his first start under Ermer. Facing their second doubleheader in a three-day span, Ermer had little choice but to turn to sore-legged Mudcat Grant and little-used Perry for a big twin-bill with the New York Yankees. After Mudcat went the distance in an 8-3 win in game one, Jim pitched into the sixth inning in the second game, limiting New York to only one earned run while driving in a pair at the plate. His big two-run base hit helped the Twins to an eventual 7-6 win and a big doubleheader sweep.

"I'm just sorry I couldn't go farther," Jim confessed after the game. "But I was tiring. We've all got to do what we can to help."[291]

Thrilled with the big doubleheader sweep, manager Ermer gave plaudits to the work of his starters. "We got quite a lift from Grant and Perry," Ermer explained. "Perry kept us in the second game. It's tough for them to keep sharp when they aren't getting to pitch very much."[292]

Despite his success and the words of affirmation from his manager, it was right back to the bench for Perry. It would be another 12 days before he would see the mound again. Over the next three weeks, Jim made just two relief appearances, covering a total of three scoreless innings. Finally in late July, with doubleheaders piling up in the heat of summer, the new Twins skipper turned to the same solution regularly employed by his predecessor—adding Dependable Perry to the rotation.

Though he again tired in the sixth inning on July 26 in New York, Perry kept the Twins in the game, limiting the Yankees to three runs on four hits in his second start under Ermer. With the rust now effectively knocked off, Jim was ready when he got the ball again for the nightcap of a doubleheader in Boston just three days later.

Pitching on short rest, Jim scattered nine hits while walking only one on the way to a 10-3 complete game victory. The win was notable in that Perry reinforced his reputation as a Red Sox killer. The victory marked the 21st of 93 career wins by Perry that had come against Boston.

"That was a game we had to have," stated an elated Ermer. "Jim did a terrific job. And he was pitching with only two days rest."[293]

Just over a week later, with the team now in the thick of the pennant race, they blew a 7-0 lead against Washington. The Senators erupted for seven runs in the seventh inning and the two teams would proceed to trade zeroes for the next 12 innings. Minnesota eventually lost 9-7 in 20 innings, a potential back-breaker that stretched into the wee hours of the morning. Worst of all, the loss cost Minnesota two places in the standings, dropping them back into fourth place.

Faced with a quick turnaround for a Businessman's Special matinee the day after the devastating defeat, Ermer turned to who else but Dependable Perry. Jim was ready. He struck out eight Senators while hurling a masterful five-hit shutout. The manager detailed the significance of this key performance.

"Boy, that was a big one for us to win," Ermer explained. "That's a point where a club can fold. That 20-inning loss really was hard to take. We had a day game the next day after playing until 1:45 a.m. If we had lost the next one, it might have been bad. But Perry really picked us up—when we needed him most."[294]

Five days later in Anaheim, Jim was even better, working out of an early jam and shutting out the California Angels. Faced with a one-out, bases loaded situation in the first inning, Perry reached back and punched out back-to-back Angels to escape unscathed. He would proceed to rack up ten strikeouts in all on the night, as he extended his personal scoreless inning streak to 19-and-two-thirds. After the dominant performance, Twins catcher Jerry Zimmerman raved about the explosive movement on Perry's fastball.

> *Perry really picked us up—when we needed him most.*
> — Cal Ermer
> TWINS MANAGER

"It's alive when he throws it high, and it sinks when he throws it low," Zimmerman explained. "He always has liked to pitch down around the low, outside corner to right handed hitters. But it's best to pitch high to certain batters. And I think he should."[295]

Twins pitching coach Early Wynn was also enthused about Jim's heater. "We've been pushing Perry," stated Wynn. "We've been trying to get him to cut loose and throw hard. Boy, he sure has done a job of it."[296]

"We're definitely going to stay with a five-man rotation the rest of the way," an excited Cal Ermer announced. "(And Perry's) in the rotation as long as he does the job."[297]

It turned out to be an empty promise. On September 11, less than a month after Jim's shutout of the Angels, the Twins sat in first place, a half-game up on the second-place Boston Red Sox. Cal Ermer was not satisfied with the slim lead, however, and with 18 games remaining in the regular season, he decided to change his managerial approach.

Ermer explained that he was going to gamble for the big inning, shuttling players in and out as needed, both for defense and to play for the win at virtually any time he saw the chance. The result might mean more pinch-hitting and thus more turnover of pitchers. In preparation for this pitching lineup volatility, the manager announced he was returning to a four-man rotation of Dean Chance, Jim Merritt, Jim Kaat, and Dave Boswell. Ermer's ace in the hole, his dutiful on-call utility pitcher would be, of course, Dependable Perry.

"I told the manager that I was willing to help any way I could," the dejected yet always team-oriented Perry explained after being told of the plan. "To me a relief pitcher is as important as a starter. He's like a pinch-hitter. He's given a job and is expected to do it. And if I pick up a victory or two that way, fine."[298]

Jim proceeded to go right out and do precisely that. Only hours after Perry's meeting with Ermer, Twins starting pitcher Dean Chance gave up five first-inning runs to the Washington Senators. True to his word, Ermer pinch-hit for Chance in the top of the fourth inning as Minnesota erupted for a seven-run inning. Enter Dependable Perry, who pitched six brilliant shutout innings to finish up the victory and earn his eighth win of the season.

Bad Dream

Jim continued to work out of the bullpen for the remainder of the campaign as the team engaged in a thrilling four-way battle for the pennant with Boston, Detroit, and Chicago that came down to the final weekend. The White Sox, who had been swept in a doubleheader at Kansas City on Wednesday, lost again at home to Washington on Friday night, knocking them out with two days remaining. The Twins headed to Boston with a one-game lead over both the Red Sox and Tigers.

The atmosphere in Boston was electric as the Red Sox attempted to complete an "impossible dream" season. Many felt 1967 would be a rebuilding year for the Red Sox after they had finished ninth in the ten-team American League the previous season. Because of rainouts, Detroit, who was tied with Minnesota at 69 losses but had two fewer wins, was hosting the California Angels for back-to-back doubleheaders. If the Tigers could pull off a pair of doubleheader sweeps, they could win the pennant or at least force a playoff with Minnesota. Such a feat is rare in baseball, however, meaning the Twins were in prime position to clinch the American League pennant and another trip to the World Series if they could win at least one of the two games with the Red Sox.

While some expected that Ermer might turn to Red Sox-killer Perry to start one of the final two games, the Minnesota manager elected to go with Opening Day starter Jim Kaat for the first matchup on Saturday. Kaat started strong but felt something pop in his forearm while delivering a pitch in the third inning. At that point, Ermer turned to his middle relief ace, who had delivered a sterling 0.66 ERA over 14 innings in this role down the stretch.

Perry was flawless for two innings, nursing an early 1-0 lead, but luck began to go Boston's way in the fifth. Reggie Smith started the inning with a fly ball that made it into the left-center field gap for a double. Boston manager Dick Williams then sent up Dalton Jones, a left-handed hitter, to pinch-hit for catcher and eight-hole hitter Russ Gibson. Jim induced a weak grounder to the right side of the infield, but the ball took a bad hop on second baseman Rod Carew, allowing Jones to reach safely. With runners on the corners and nobody out, Jim bowed his back and notched back-to-back strikeouts, whiffing pitcher Jose Santiago and leadoff man Mike Andrews.

Unfortunately, more bad luck struck for Perry and the Twins as the next hitter, Jerry Adair popped up Jim's first offering into shallow right center. As Carew broke on what appeared to be a catchable pop fly, he slipped and lost his footing. By the time he recovered, the ball had dropped in for a run-scoring single. Eventual American League MVP Carl Yastrzemski, who would go 7-for-8 on the weekend, then grounded a 3-2 pitch past first baseman Harmon Killebrew. Carew fielded it on the outfield grass, but had no play, allowing a second run to score for Boston. Jim retired the next batter, Ken Harrelson, with a pop out to third to end the inning, but the damage was done. As seemed to be the case all too often for Jim Perry, a couple breaks going against him conspired to keep him from being the hero, though he certainly was no goat.

Minnesota battled right back in the next inning, tying the game, which prompted manager Cal Ermer to pinch-hit for his middle relief ace. With two on and two outs, Perry's replacement at the plate, Frank Kostro, drew a walk to load the bases, but leadoff man Zoilo Versalles popped out to end the rally. A home run by George Scott leading off the next inning against reliever Ron Kline gave Boston a 3-2 lead, and a three-run blast by Yastrzemski an inning later off of Jim Merritt put the Twins in a deep 6-2 hole. Killebrew cracked a two-run homer with two outs in the ninth inning, but it was not enough, as Minnesota came up short in a disappointing 6-4 defeat.

Up in Detroit, the Tigers split their first doubleheader with the Angels, leaving all three teams with 70 losses and Detroit only a win behind heading into the final day. The Minnesota-Boston game featured 20-game winner Dean Chance for the Twins against 21-game winner Jim Lonborg of the Red Sox. Detroit would win the first game of their Sunday doubleheader, creating a brief three-way tie but, for the second day in a row, lost the nightcap, meaning the Minnesota-Boston game was for all the marbles.

Again, Boston overcame an early Twins lead and hung on for a 5-3 win. It was a devastating end to a fine season for the Twins and particularly disappointing for Jim Perry, who had sacrificed his desired role for the good of the team, only for them to come up short.

Airport Save

Jim would begin 1968 the way he did every year since he had joined the Twins. "I'll go to spring training looking for a starting job," Jim explained. "I think every pitcher wants to start, working every four days and getting regular rest. A reliever never knows when he'll get in there. The worst job on a ball club is long relief or working as the middle man. At least the short man in the bullpen knows that when he's called upon, it will be only for the last inning or two. The long man never knows."[299]

Jim Perry's willingness to do whatever it took to help the team was not limited to his contributions on the field. In the midst of what was a trying summer personally, Perry would play a key role in helping to save a teammate's career.

In the summer of 1968, 22-year old Rod Carew was juggling two commitments during his second year in the big leagues. Not only was he the all-star second baseman for the Minnesota Twins, but Carew was also tasked with serving a commitment to the Marine Reserves that required him to be away from the team periodically.

While the Panama native was not a U.S. citizen, he was a permanent resident, which, in the mid-1960s, with America's involvement in Vietnam escalating, required him to fulfill a military obligation. Carew had joined the U.S. Marine Corps following his first minor league season back in 1964, an obligation that would run through 1969. In addition to periodic weekend commitments that caused him to be away from the team, Carew was required to leave the Twins to participate in an annual "war games" exercise for two weeks every summer.

Following a June 7 doubleheader in Washington D.C., Carew departed for his 1968 "war games" training, heading across the country to Hawthorne, Nevada. The Twins lost their first six games without Carew in the lineup, but bounced back with a six-game winning streak. He returned to the club on June 23 on the heels of back-to-back Twins losses, but was not immediately reinserted into the lineup. Utilityman Frank Quilici, who was filling in at second base in Carew's stead, was in the midst of a nine-game hitting streak and manager Cal Ermer figured he could give his young all-star a few games to get his baseball rhythm back.

With Carew looking on from the bench, Minnesota reeled off four consecutive wins. On June 29, Carew was finally reinserted into the lineup. He was hitless in four at-bats as the Twins lost, 5-1 to the Orioles. They lost again the next day with another oh-fer for Carew before the team traveled from Baltimore to Cleveland. On Monday, July 1, the Twins lost a third straight game, being three-hit by Sam McDowell and Stan Williams. Although Carew had one of the three Minnesota hits in the 4-1 defeat, the youngster was reportedly despondent over his inability to help the team get a win, as they dropped to fourth place, ten games in back of first-place Detroit.

When the Twins arrived back at the team hotel, the Holenden House, in downtown Cleveland, Carew warned his roommate, Tony Oliva, that he was considering leaving the club and returning to his off-season home in Brooklyn, New York.

"Are you crazy?" Oliva asked incredulously. "You can't do this. Call your dad and talk to him. He will tell you the same thing."[300]

The next day, Carew failed to appear at a noon luncheon, despite the fact he was a scheduled speaker. A hotel desk clerk reported that Carew had checked out at 6:45 a.m., but his roommate, Oliva, told Ermer that he had not left and, in fact, was back in their room sleeping.

"That's fine," replied Ermer. "Tell him he's due at the ballpark at

5:30."[301]

At 3:45, however, Carew was spotted by Dwayne Netland of the *Minneapolis Tribune* piling his luggage into a taxicab in front of the hotel. Netland queried the young all-star about what was going on.

"I don't have to talk to you or to the manager or to the owner," stated Carew. "And that's all I'm going to say."[302]

Coach John Goryl, who had taken it upon himself to conduct a first-hand investigation, heard a rumor that Carew had headed out for the airport. When he got no response at Carew and Oliva's room, Goryl began to panic. He called Jim Perry's room and explained what was going on.

"Jim you pitched last night (in relief to two batters)," the coach told Perry, "so we won't be using you early tonight. I need you to get to the airport and see if you can find Rodney. You can't let him leave!"

So Jim set off in search of his distraught teammate. Sure enough, Jim tracked him down.

"I feel guilty," the youngster confessed to his veteran teammate. "The club hasn't won since I started playing again."

"Look Rod," Jim pleaded, "the team needs you. It's not your fault. We lost all three in Chicago when you were gone for the weekend prior to this, and then we lost the first six when you left this time. You have to come back and help us work through this rough patch together."

With no cell phones or other means of communication, Jim had no way of letting his bosses know that he had tracked down the future hall-of-famer and talked him out of quitting.

With the news of Perry's successful intervention yet to make its way back to the team, Goryl told the manager that Carew had likely boarded a plane for Chicago. Ermer was left with no choice but to scratch the second baseman from the lineup.

"I'm confounded," a bewildered Ermer confessed. "In all my time in baseball I've never come across anything like this."[303]

At 5 p.m., word got back to the Twins clubhouse that Carew had returned to the team hotel. He showed up in the visiting clubhouse at 5:50 p.m., an hour and forty minutes before gametime, but twenty minutes past the manager's reporting deadline. Carew did not participate in pre-game batting practice or infield drills.

"I took him out of the lineup for those other 24 guys out there," said the manager. "I'm playing the men who want to play."[304]

In a raucous visitor's clubhouse after a 6-0 Minnesota win that night, Carew sat quietly at his locker and again declined to explain where he had been or his reasons for temporarily leaving the team. Asked if he was going to play in the All-Star game to which he had been selected a starter the following week in Houston, Carew replied, "Maybe. And maybe not."[305]

"The boy is obviously confused," explained Ermer. He's had a rough time of it, having to take off for weekend reserve meetings and then serving that two-week stretch of training. He's back on the club and we're happy to have him. We want to get him into shape to play baseball."[306]

"He's just a mixed-up boy," added Twins traveling secretary Howard Fox. He just got out of the service and feels he's not in shape and isn't helping the club."[307]

After two more games on the bench, Carew was reinserted in the lineup, where he remained for the rest of the season. "As far as I'm concerned, the air has been cleared," stated Ermer, effectively putting the matter to rest.[308]

Rod Carew not only played in the 1968 All-Star Game, but he went on to play in 16 more after that. He would win the first of seven batting crowns the following season and was selected American League Most Valuable Player when he batted an amazing .388 in 1977. In 1991, he was inducted into the Baseball Hall of Fame. None of that might ever have come to pass if not for the most important, yet little known "save" of Jim Perry's career.

Best Yet To Come

On the field, 1968 would be one of Jim Perry's best professional seasons in many respects of his ten-year career to that point. An unremarkable 8-6 record belied a sparkling 2.27 ERA. As detailed in chapter one, however, it was also one of his most frustrating years, as both Mother Nature and misfortune conspired to keep him from his quest to become a regular starter.

His persistence would finally pay off in 1969, of course, as Jim made 36 starts (along with ten relief appearances) en route to reaching the exclusive 20-win plateau. It was an immensely satisfying season and one that earned him many well-deserved plaudits. Little did onlookers realize, however, that the best was yet to come.

11
Good to Great

After winning the new American League West division by nine games over Oakland in 1969, the three-game playoff series sweep at the hands of the Baltimore Orioles stunned the Twins. Some fans even showered the team with boos during the lopsided loss in the final game of the series. A week later, players and fans were stunned again as Twins manager Billy Martin was suddenly fired. "Lack of communication" was given as the reason but many felt a mid-season altercation between Martin, pitcher Dave Boswell, and outfielder Bob Allison involving fisticuffs outside a Detroit bar also played a role.

Twins President Calvin Griffith addressed Martin's popularity, both among the players and the fans in announcing the dismissal. "Martin is popular to a certain degree," Griffith admitted. "And he could charm the hell out of a crowd. But every organization has to have a policy. I asked him to come and see me several times, and he didn't do it. He didn't like me talking about his players. But they are as much my players as his. I have to sign them."[309]

Regardless of the reasons, as he prepared for the 1970 season, Jim Perry was faced with playing for yet another new manager, the eighth in his twelve-year career. Most importantly, Perry lost one of his biggest supporters in Martin, who had given him the opportunity to top 30 starts for only the third time in his career and the first since 1961. For a pitcher who took great pride in not only starting, but in finishing what he started, the new manager was especially a concern.

Bill Rigney had been an MLB manager since 1956, with five years managing the Giants of New York and then San Francisco, followed by nine seasons at the helm of the California Angels. Rigney was known to have a quick hook when it came to starting pitchers. His "hook" was so quick, in fact, that many pitchers privately referred to Rigney as "Captain Hook." Upon being introduced to members of the Minnesota press corps, Rigney explained his philosophy:

"I don't believe in warming up a pitcher in the bullpen and then not using him. If he's warm, I'll get him in there. But everything depends on how I feel at the moment. If I know the man in the bullpen can get the batter out better than the man on the mound, then I'll use the reliever.

"I don't know if starters use (the complete game) statistic to argue salary or not," the new skipper continued. "But the big thing is winning, not who wins or completes games."[310]

Most recently under Rigney's leadership, the California Angels had seen their starters complete only 19 games in 1967 and 29 in 1968. As pundits pointed out, however, Rigney had likely never managed a starting rotation the likes of what he was inheriting in the Twin Cities.

In addition to longtime rotation anchor Jim Kaat, both Jim Perry and Dave Boswell had become first-time 20-game winners in 1969. A new face had replaced Dean Chance, who was only able to contribute 88 innings during an injury-marred 1969 season. Chance had been shipped to Cleveland in a winter trade that netted the Twins 29-year old righthander Luis Tiant. A twenty-one game winner in 1968 who led the American League with a 1.60 ERA, Tiant had surprisingly slumped to losing twenty games in a disappointing 1969 season.

No Rest

As Jim reported to training camp for the 1970 season, he was not resting on the laurels of his long-sought 20-win season. Columnist Dick Cullum of the *Minneapolis Tribune* explained:

"Jim Perry, a winner of 20 games for the Twins last year, is, by reports, his usual spring training self. This means he never has arm problems and is always in condition to pitch when he reaches camp. The Twins call him one of the best batting practice pitchers in baseball. They say, 'He knows what each player wants and he puts the ball there. Some of these kids are trying to strike you out but Jim just lets us take our swing.'"[311]

When the spring games got underway, Jim was as sharp as ever. He certainly wasn't letting opposing hitters "take their swing" when he fired three perfect innings against the Tigers to open the exhibition slate. As Perry proceeded to have an outstanding spring training, however, the rest of the team struggled. The Twins lost 14 of their first 15 spring training games, which is disconcerting even for games that theoretically don't matter. The defending division champs are expected to perform better than that, even if they are just playing their way into shape.

On March 24, with less than two weeks remaining in the spring schedule, Perry combined with Tom Hall on a 4-0 shutout of the Cincinnati Reds. It was the second straight victory for the Twins and just their third in 17 games. Despite the fact the games did not yet count for the record books, new manager Bill Rigney had been feeling the heat of the team's poor spring performance.

"I've been waiting a long time for that shutout," the new skipper sighed after the game.[312]

Perry, who was the staff leader with 25 spring exhibition innings pitched, also became the first to pitch seven innings in an outing, as he scattered eight hits and two walks while preventing any Reds player from crossing home plate.

"I could have worked more innings today," Jim related afterward. "But I don't think I'm quite ready to go nine innings yet."[313] (In *spring training!*)

"I threw about the average number of pitches for me for seven innings, about 80," Perry continued. "I had a good sinker and the slider is starting to come along. Most of their hits were off the label or the end of the bat. The best thing was that I was able to keep the ball below the belt most of the time. A couple times I got the ball up. But like Pete Rose told me after the game, 'You weren't giving us anything to hit.'"[314]

While other Twins pitchers had issued 81 walks in 120 spring innings (almost six per game, an awful mark), Perry had issued just four free passes in his 25 innings of work. While he also had only four strikeouts, he explained why the failure to miss bats did not impede his effectiveness.

"I'm not a strikeout pitcher like Boswell or Kaat," the veteran pointed out. "I can't try to throw the ball past a guy because when I try to do that I throw the ball high. I try to make the batter hit my pitch."[315]

Two days later, Rigney announced that Jim Perry would be the 1970 Opening Day starter for the Minnesota Twins. It was the first time Jim received the honor since 1961 in Cleveland when he was coming off his 18-win 1960 season.

Four days after his seven-inning spring outing, Jim pitched eight innings before leaving with a 4-2 lead against Houston. Unfortunately, reliever Stan Williams, who had been acquired with Tiant in the Dean Chance trade to help Ron Perranoski at the back end of games, gave up a three-run pinch-hit game-winning homer, leaving the Twins with yet another exhibition defeat. While an exasperated Rigney was beside himself about Williams' continued awful spring, he "ran out of adjectives praising Perry," according to Sid Hartman of the *Minneapolis Tribune*.

"He's our Opening Day pitcher for sure," exclaimed the Minnesota skipper. "Perry had all the pitches and I'm sure he could have gone another inning and won the game for us."[316]

Full of confidence and peaking at just the right time of spring, Perry considered the outing his best of the exhibition season.

"I had control of all of my pitches and was able to throw them just where I wanted to," he explained. "I threw only 95 pitches in the eight innings I worked, which is good for me."[317]

As the Twins wrapped up a horrible exhibition season with a record of seven wins and 20 losses, just about the only bright spot of the spring had been Jim Perry's efficient work. Jim Kaat and Dave Boswell were both dealing with nagging injuries and Luis Tiant had been struggling with his control throughout camp. In an ironic twist, the man who had worked so hard for so long just to become a regular member of the starting rotation was suddenly considered the unquestioned staff ace as the 1970 regular season got underway.

Burst From the Gates

As Jim Perry prepared for his first Opening Day as a member of the Minnesota Twins starting rotation, not to mention his first MLB Opening Day start in nine years, he reflected on the difference from past seasons.

"This year I came to spring training knowing I was going to be used as a starting pitcher," explained the pleased veteran. "Knowing that, I worked hard to stay in shape during the winter, getting up at 6 in the morning to work out before going to work. I won 20 games last year because the guys played well behind me and I'm sure it will continue this year. You don't win 20 games without your teammates. We've got the personnel here, the personnel to show people we can win it again."[318]

It was as if he had a crystal ball, because the next day in Chicago, Tuesday, April 7, Jim's teammates gave him all the runs he would need before he ever took the mound. The Twins scored three runs in the top of the first, three more in the fifth, and then exploded for six runs in the seventh inning. It turned out he only needed one. The big righthander hurled a six-hit shutout in a 12-0 win over the White Sox, but his biggest challenge was adjusting to the bountiful offensive support.

"Your arm starts to stiffen up on you when you sit that long," Jim explained after the game. "In one inning (the seventh, after the Twins had scored six runs) I threw four straight balls to a batter before I started to get loose. I started to talk to myself out there, telling myself to get the ball down and over the plate."[319]

The first inning presented the first of those difficulties, which brought the new trigger-happy manager out to the mound only ten pitches into Jim's first start. Thankfully, the trip was not for a call to the bullpen, but simply to give his ace starter a quick pep talk. After Minnesota scored three runs to begin the game, Jim walked the first two White Sox batters in the bottom of the first inning. Despite pitching himself into a quick jam, the veteran was not flustered.

"When I'm wild low like I was early in the game, I don't worry," Jim explained. "When I'm wild high, there is reason for concern."[320]

Directly in line with his sage self-diagnosis, Perry's control was spot-on the rest of the day. His only other walks came in that seventh inning when he had trouble getting loose after the long inning by the offense (which included a contribution from Perry, not surprisingly, as he brought a run home with a sacrifice fly).

After the awful exhibition season, the new Twins manager was obviously relieved by the dominant Opening Day showing by his club. "I've never wanted to win a game more than this one," said Rigney. "We looked horrible this spring. I felt a victory would get us off to the right start."[321]

Considering all he had been through to get to this point, Perry was rightfully proud.

"It was an honor to be selected as the opening day pitcher," he said after the win. "In a way it's just another game, but it still means something. It's always a lot easier to pitch when you've got all those runs, but I still wanted to get that shutout."[322]

Twins catcher George Mitterwald, working his first career opening day behind the plate, had a prime view of Perry's focus and tenacity. "Jim didn't let down today, even when he had that big lead," the catcher remarked. "A lot of times a guy will just start laying the ball in there, trying to let the batters hit it. But Jim pitched like he was only leading 1-0."[323]

The fantastic Opening Day effort was so impressive that it prompted sports columnist Dick Cullum to share some insightful observations in the *Minneapolis Tribune*. His thoughts would prove amazingly prescient.

"The story of Jim Perry is an odd one," Cullum wrote. "Over his six years of service with the Minnesota Twins he has been the most helpful and reliable pitcher on the staff. Yet it remained for Bill Rigney, in Perry's seventh season, to find it out and put him in the starting rotation from opening day.

"In each of his first six years with the Twins, Perry had to wait until something happened to another member of the staff before he was recognized. Another pitcher was hurt, or pitched badly in several turns. Then, reluctantly, or so it seemed, the manager called Perry to fill the void. And Perry invariably filled it.

"Perry falls into that category of pitchers who '*know how to pitch.*' We've spoken before of pitchers who have no sparkling amount of stuff on the ball but who know what to do with what they have.

Another pitcher, with infinitely more stuff, wastes it. He doesn't have the cunning which is the important element in a pitcher's equipment.

"Perry has cunning, control and a good slider but, otherwise, is no better equipped than some of the league's average pitchers. Rigney has given Perry his first early-season start. Give him freedom from injury and the support of a few runs, and he is likely to have his best season. This would call for his winning more than 20 games."[324]

Between rain and snow, Jim did not get his second start for more than a week, despite being only the team's fourth game of the season. In fact, the Twins' five-game opening homestand was limited to just one game with the A's due to the typical freezing, wet early spring Minnesota weather. Jim was forced to wait until the club was once again on the road before he could make his second start. Neither travel nor time off would force the ace off stride.

On Wednesday, April 15 in Anaheim, Perry was on his game once again, facing a hot-hitting California Angels team. He finally gave up his first run of the season when the Angels scratched across one in the fourth inning, but California's starter Andy Messersmith was just as tough on Minnesota's hitters. In fact, only Jim Perry, serving a soft liner up the middle in the third, had been able to collect a hit off Messersmith through the first five innings. In the sixth inning, the Minnesota offense finally came alive, exploding for an eight-run outburst that featured three home runs, including a grand slam by left fielder Brant Alyea. Perry took it from there, cruising through the last four innings by retiring 12 of the last 14 hitters of the game, including the last nine in a row.

"I didn't have great stuff," the modest Perry admitted after a second straight complete game victory. "But when I had to have it, I was able to throw the ball where I wanted. It was cool (for Southern California—60 degrees), but anytime your guys get you seven or eight runs it makes you warmer."[325]

With four consecutive wins out of the gate, half of them led by Jim Perry's pitching, the Twins were quickly in the division lead and all memories of their awful spring exhibition record had quickly been forgotten. They would lose their first regular season game the next day before traveling to Oakland for a big early-season weekend series with the team many picked to unseat the Twins as A.L. West

Division champs. The teams split the first two games before Jim took the mound for the Sunday afternoon rubber match.

Once again, Perry was hot from the start, retiring nine of the first ten hitters he faced. In fact, the only baserunner he allowed through the first three innings came when he walked shortstop Roberto Pena with two outs in the first inning. And Jim promptly picked Pena off first base to end the inning.

The offense built up another lead while Jim held the A's at bay until a seventh inning home run by Reggie Jackson cut the Twins lead to 6-3. Manager Bill Rigney finally went to the bullpen for the first time in a Jim Perry start after Rick Monday singled to begin the eighth inning. Ron Perranoski finished up with two scoreless innings and Jim was already 3-0 just eight games into the 1970 season.

After the game, he was asked what it was like to be considered the ace of the pitching staff after fighting for so long just to be a regular member of the rotation.

"It used to be that I was the one being pushed back in the rotation if there was a rainout or something," Jim explained. "That's baseball. Number 18 (manager Bill Rigney) says who moves back."[326]

"A lot of people could not understand how I kept up my spirits all these years," Perry continued. "My theory was to stay ready and when a break came I would be able to fill in. That should be true of every player who doesn't play every day. Now, whenever I pitch, I just think I'm the best pitcher out there that particular day."[327]

First Bumps

Finally making his first home start of the year on Friday, April 24, Jim encountered his first difficulties, lasting only three innings against the hottest team in the American League—the East division leading Detroit Tigers. When Dick McAuliffe pulled a home run into the right field bleachers on Perry's second pitch of the night, that might have served as a clue he would not be as sharp. However, some bad luck made the night worse than it otherwise might have been.

After giving up three consecutive singles to begin the third inning with the game tied at two, Jim reared back and struck out Willie Horton. He then induced a tailor-made inning-ending double-play grounder off the bat of Jim Northrup. Unfortunately, Cesar Tovar, pressed into playing second base in place of injured Rod Carew, threw the ball into left field. Four runs would score in the inning, costing Perry a chance at a fourth straight win.

Jim finally suffered his first loss on April 28, losing to the Cleveland Indians, 3-1, despite pitching a complete game and allowing only one earned run. Back-to-back wins to open May pushed Jim's record to 5-1 with a fine 2.50 ERA. He lost his second game in a tough 5-4 defeat against the Orioles, but on May 17, Jim pitched another complete game in a 6-1 win in Milwaukee that pushed the Twins back into first place. They would not relinquish the division lead for the remainder of the season.

Double Duty

As May turned to June, Perry suffered three straight losses, though he was hardly pitching poorly. After a 5-1 defeat at Boston on June 2, Jim's record stood at 6-5 with an even 3.00 ERA. They were very respectable numbers, albeit a bit disappointing in the wake of his hot start. Perry's line was perhaps even more impressive given the context of the labor strife brewing under the surface of MLB's 1970 season.

Marvin Miller had become the representative of the MLB Players Association and he was handling increasingly contentious negotiations with the owners. As the Twins player representative, Jim was heavily involved in communicating between Miller and the rest of the team's players. Several times during the 1970 season, Jim was charged with taking team votes on proposals from the owners. With the players strongly considering a one-day strike, Jim was forced to handle the pressure of that responsibility plus keeping focus on what had started out as a great season.

In mid-May, Twins President Calvin Griffith returned from a meeting with fellow owners noticeably agitated. Television was driving an increase in revenue for MLB thanks to an additional round of postseason play produced by the new division format and the players wanted their share.

"The owners have the investment and the players want the profits," Griffith complained. "Make a composite box score on 24 major league clubs last year on profit and loss and it would come out in red ink. Let the players strike and they'll find out how good they have it when they go without a paycheck."[328]

As the team's player representative, Jim was caught in the middle, trying to do what was right for the players while at the same time trying to maintain what had long been a good relationship with the man who signed his paycheck, Calvin Griffith.

"I have not heard of any strike or boycott," Perry cautioned, "because the players would have to approve that, too."[329]

"I don't think Miller is prepared to recommend a strike or moratorium by the players," Griffith stated.[330] He would be proven right in the short-term, but as time would tell, the storm clouds were only beginning to form.

Against that backdrop, Perry amazingly went on a roll. On June 6 in Washington, he hurled a six-hit complete game in a 4-2 Twins victory. He won again six days later, working six innings in a 5-2 win over the Red Sox. A pair of off days between the two starts left Jim complaining that he was not getting frequent enough work to stay sharp.

On June 16, four days later, back on his preferred three days rest, Jim was as sharp as ever. In a classic Jim Perry performance, he hurled a six-hitter in a 7-3 complete game victory over the Washington Senators. It was Perry's sixth complete game of the season, while the rest of the pitching staff combined had only four. Not only did he limit Washington to six hits, but Jim aided his own cause with three base hits, raising his season average to a sparkling .361 mark. Twins catcher George Mitterwald hit a two-run homer to lead the offensive attack, but after the game all he wanted to talk about was how enjoyable it is to catch the Twins ace.

"Perry is almost a perfect spot pitcher," Mitterwald gushed. "He throws a sinker and slider and seldom misses the area he's throwing at. He nibbles at the corners. Jim has the best control of any of the Twins starters, and I'd place only relief pitcher Ron Perranoski ahead of him for hitting spots. You can catch Perry in a rocking chair."[331]

Mitterwald estimated that only about five of the approximate 125 pitches Perry threw on the night were not where he wanted them. Senators third baseman Aurelio Rodriguez drove in two of Washington's three runs with a second inning double on a low fastball and ninth inning home run on a fastball that sailed up high. "Maybe

Perry would take those two back," said his catcher. "Otherwise, Perry was near perfect."[332]

> *Perry is almost a perfect spot pitcher. He seldom misses the area he's throwing at... You can catch Perry in a rocking chair.*
> — George Mitterwald
> TWINS CATCHER

Star-Studded Reunion

By the all-star break, Jim had a phenomenal 13 wins against only seven losses. He notched his 13th win on July 8 in Oakland. Amazingly, little brother Gaylord won his 13th game of the season earlier that same day pitching for the National League's San Francisco Giants at Atlanta. As the MLB All-Star Game approached, there was much talk about the prospect of the great Perry brothers facing each other. Some even discussed the possibility of a Perry brothers showdown, facing off as opposing All-Star Game starters.

Not surprisingly, Minnesota manager Bill Rigney cared more about winning games for the Twins than who pitched against who in the All-Star Game. With that perspective, Rigney kept Jim on his normal turn, which had him starting Minnesota's final game before the all-star break. With the All-Star Game coming just two days later, this timing effectively eliminated Jim from consideration of starting the game. Curiously, the Giants did the same thing with Gaylord, starting him on Sunday, July 12, likewise taking him out of contention for the start.

Even with only one day of rest, however, American League All-Star manager Earl Weaver of the Baltimore Orioles stated he was not going to pass up the opportunity to make use of Jim Perry's talent. Weaver announced that he planned to start his own Jim Palmer, followed by Sam McDowell of Cleveland, but would then look to go with Perry as his third man, likely in the late, crucial innings of the game.

National League manager Gil Hodges was playing his pitching plans closer to the vest, refusing to hint at who might follow starter Tom Seaver of his New York Mets for the N.L. squad. Still, as the players gathered in Cincinnati's brand new Riverfront Stadium for a workout on Monday, the day prior to the All-Star Game, hope remained that the brothers would get a chance to square off. Jim confirmed to manager Earl Weaver at the workout that he was, indeed, ready to go. Since he usually threw a light bullpen on the second day after a start, pitching a couple innings in the All-Star Game would be quite feasible, Jim reasoned. Fellow workhorse Gaylord, who had led the National League by pitching 325 innings the prior season, no doubt shared a similar sentiment.

It is important to bear in mind that the All-Star Game of this era was not yet the frivolous exhibition it later became where managers were less concerned with winning than with getting every player in the game. In 1970, there was great honor at stake among the players selected to represent their respective leagues, accompanied by pressure to show their league's superiority in this mid-season matchup. Players and managers took great pride in representing their league and in playing to win. When Earl Weaver stated that he wanted three pitchers to pitch three innings each and he wanted Jim Perry to finish up a hopeful win, that is really a compliment of the highest degree. Especially considering the National League had won seven consecutive All-Star Games and led the all-time series with a record of 22-17-1 over 40 previous All-Star matchups.

Of course, this game would go down in history as the All-Star Game in which Pete Rose famously scored the winning run in the 12th inning in a violent home plate collision with catcher Ray Fosse. Long forgotten is the fact that the game should never have even reached that point.

The game got underway with Seaver and Palmer trading zeroes for three innings. N.L. skipper Hodges turned to former Twin, now Cincinnati Red, Jim Merritt for the fourth and fifth innings, while Earl Weaver brought on McDowell for the middle three, just as he stated he would. With the game still scoreless through five, the first Perry got his chance, as Hodges lifted Merritt after just two innings of work.

The American League immediately scratched across the first run of the game against Gaylord with a Ray Fosse single, a sacrifice bunt by the pitcher, McDowell, followed by an RBI-single off the bat of Carl Yastrzemski. McDowell then pitched his third inning, working around a pair of walks to keep the game at 1-0. In the top of the seventh, the American League hitters were right back at it against Gaylord, loading up the bases with one out. Fosse lined a sacrifice fly to deep center field, plating the second American League run, but Gaylord was able to escape further damage. The stage was now set for Perry vs. Perry and Weaver, again, was true to his word, bringing on Jim in relief of McDowell.

Much like his little brother, Jim quickly found himself in a jam. Switch-hitter Bud Harrelson pulled a grounder that squeaked just under the glove of first baseman Yastrzemski. Jim then walked Cito Gaston before a wayward fastball sailed up and in, clipping pinch-hitter Denis Menke in the shoulder. With the bases loaded and nobody out, Gaylord was due up to bat. Against his big bro. In Major League Baseball's All-Star Game.

It would have been a matchup for the ages, with the pitcher on the mound holding a decisive advantage over the pitcher at the plate, of course. Playing for the win, however, National League skipper Gil Hodges eschewed poetic theater, instead sending up future hall-of-famer and reigning N.L. home run king Willie McCovey to pinch-hit. Jim was undaunted by his perilous plight. The unflappable veteran bowed his back and induced a bouncer that shortstop Luis Aparicio converted into a double play, allowing Harrelson to score from third. Perry then struck out slugger Dick Allen, to avoid further damage, escaping with only one run allowed and maintaining the A.L lead at 2-1.

The American League stormed right back in the eighth against Bob Gibson when Yastrzemski and Willie Horton hit back-to-back singles before Brooks Robinson plated them both with a triple. Jim came back out for the bottom of the eighth inning to face the heart (3-4-5) of the National League lineup. He proceeded to mow them down. Perry sandwiched strike outs of Pete Rose and Jim Hickman around a can-of-corn fly to left by Billy Grabarkewitz, putting the A.L. in prime position for their first All-Star Game win in eight years.

As the game headed to the ninth inning with the American League on top 4-1 and Jim in line for the save, A.L. manager Earl Weaver suddenly changed course. Though he had pledged to pitch Palmer, McDowell, and Perry for three innings apiece, Weaver turned to Catfish Hunter as the bottom of the ninth got under way. It would not be the last pitching change of the night for Weaver, as the switch seemed to breathe new life into the National League bats.

Catcher Dick Dietz, who had replaced Johnny Bench in the seventh inning, greeted Hunter with a home run that ignited a stunning comeback rally. Two more pitchers and two more runs later, the N.L. had tied it up, sending the game to extra innings. Jim Hickman finally ended it in the bottom of the 12th, lacing a single up the middle off Clyde Wright that sent Pete Rose flying around third base and into his iconic collision with A.L. catcher Ray Fosse, just as the throw from center fielder Amos Otis arrived. Rose was safe with the winning National League run, sending the home fans into a frenzy.

After the game, a dejected Weaver called lifting Jim Perry in the last of the ninth with a 4-1 lead the toughest thing he ever had to do.

"Remember that Perry pitched Sunday," Weaver explained, "and when he had to throw so many pitches in the seventh, I felt he might be tired."[333]

"If this was a September pennant race, I would have left him in," Weaver continued. "Don't get me wrong though, Perry didn't beg off. It was my decision."[334] Gone unsaid, of course, was the appearance that the game was well in hand.

"Naturally, you like to stay in the game," Jim confessed, "but Weaver felt I was tired after pitching Sunday."[335]

It was a disappointing ending for Jim Perry and the American League, but still a fun and unique event as the Perry brothers took advantage of the rare opportunity to showcase their farm-bred talents on the national stage. Though Jim missed out on the chance for the save, Gaylord avoided being the losing pitcher when the N.L. rallied to send the game into extra innings.

No Beat Skipped

As the second half of the season got under way, Jim picked up right where he had left off. He notched a win in Baltimore four days after the All-Star Game, and then he won again on July 18 at home against Detroit. In the win over the Tigers, Jim began by retiring the first 15 Detroit batters until Don Wert finally broke it up with a single leading off the sixth inning.

When Elliott Maddox drove in the first Detroit run with an eighth inning sacrifice fly, manager Bill Rigney called on Ron Perranoski to finish up. Perranoski retired all four hitters he faced to preserve Jim's American League leading 15th win. Following the game, Jim gave a tip of the cap to his trusty teammate.

"You can't imagine the feeling a Perranoski in the bullpen gives a starting pitcher," said Perry. "He gives the starter a mental rest. If he has to leave a short lead late in the game, Perranoski is like money in the bank. I can't remember how many he's saved of my 15 this year, but I take my cap off to him."[336]

Of Perranoski's league-leading 24 saves at that point, nine had come finishing off Jim Perry wins. Not surprisingly, in each of Perry's other 15 victories, he had finished them off himself with complete game efforts.

Death by 1,000 Paper Cuts

Jim was stuck with losses in each of his next two outings despite quality starts in each one. A July 26 defeat at home against the Orioles provided a prime example of how the box score often disguised Jim Perry's greatness. Although his final line showed 12 hits and three runs allowed over six innings of work in an eventual 11-1 Minnesota blowout loss, a closer look reveals another excellent effort.

Not only did Perry keep every hit to a single, but he also avoided adding fuel to the fire by the issuance of walks. Despite those accomplishments, Jim was victimized by a defensive Achilles' heel that Orioles hall-of-fame manager Earl Weaver managed to expose.

"It's a shame we don't bunt on (third baseman Harmon) Killebrew more," Weaver mused aloud earlier in the weekend series.[337]

After watching Perry work around four singles through four shutout innings, Weaver decided to put his plan into action. Baltimore batters laid down three bunts over the next two innings, twice for hits, as they capitalized on the 34-year old slugger's limited mobility. While the Orioles managed to manufacture three runs, Jim avoided further damage by stranding five baserunners.

"We were going to wait until the playoffs (to bunt on Killebrew)," Weaver confided after the game, "but Perry was pitching awfully good."[338]

Although the bullpen let the game get away late, before he left, Jim kept it close by accounting for Minnesota's lone run of the day.

Batting right-handed against lefty Dave McNally, Jim pulled what was reported as a 370-foot home run into the left field pavilion. It was Perry's fifth career home run, and the second time he had victimized McNally. Jim's first career home run back in 1966 had also come off the Baltimore southpaw, and the Orioles ace knew it.

"That's the second home run I remember Perry hitting off me," McNally sighed. "I must be pitching him wrong."[339]

Dog Day Grind

As the season entered the "dog days of August," Jim got back into the win column with a masterful effort on August 3 against the Brewers, but it was not without concern. While Jim held Milwaukee to one run on just five hits through eight innings, it took Minnesota until the bottom of the eighth inning until they could plate their second run off Brewers starter Marty Pattin. With his first lead of the night, Jim was suddenly pulled from the game for lefty Tom Hall, who struck out the side in the ninth for his third save. Hall was brought on instead of Perranoski, who had blown a pair of saves while pitching each of the previous three days, but the bigger concern surrounded Minnesota's starter, who it was learned had come out of the game because of "a slight muscle grab" in his right (push-off) leg.

"It's not serious," Jim assuringly explained following the game. "I didn't want to take a chance of hurting myself more and missing any starts."[340]

His leg must have been fine, because Jim was more concerned about his ERA being up a quarter of a run over the same time the previous year. Despite notching his sixteenth win, which tied him for the MLB lead with Cleveland's Sam McDowell and Tom Seaver of the New York Mets, Jim was perturbed that his 3.25 ERA was up from 3.00 at the same time a year ago when he won twenty games for the first time.

"I may have pitched a little better last year," Perry admitted. "I think I had only two bad ball games all year."[341]

Then, however, Jim went on a surprising rant about more lively baseballs that seemed to have quietly been put in play for the 1970 MLB season.

"I think the ball is a little hotter and it goes a little farther than it did last year. Some balls are woven real close at the seams. Others are looser and larger. If a ball feels large it has real wide seams. The ball that is woven real tight is the one that is going to sail out of the park much quicker than the other ball."[342]

Four days later at home against the A's, Jim demonstrated his leg was, indeed, fine, while also briefly amplifying his concerns about the live baseball. Oakland leadoff hitter Bert Campaneris drilled Jim's first pitch of the night into the left field seats for a home run. The shot was particularly alarming in light of Jim's post-game comments earlier in the week. It would be the last hard contact of the night off Perry by A's hitters, however, and it was a long night.

Tied 1-1 after nine innings, Jim was still going strong. He must have been, because "Captain Hook" stuck with his ace. Perry gave up a harmless one out single in the tenth, but quickly retired the next two hitters. In the bottom of the tenth the Twins loaded the bases with nobody out, but Harmon Killebrew grounded into a home-to-first double play before Rick Renick grounded out to kill the threat.

Perry went right back to work, retiring the side in methodical 1-2-3 fashion. Finally, Jim Holt hit a home run leading off the bottom of the eleventh inning to make Jim Perry the first 17-game winner in the majors. The fact that "Captain Hook" Rigney would allow a starter to pitch an 11-inning complete game is a testament to Perry's stamina, allowing him to maintain his stuff as the game progressed into extra frames. Indeed, Perry confirmed as much speaking with reporters after the game.

"I believe I could have gone at least one more inning without any trouble," stated the workhorse. "I was very comfortable and felt good throughout. Every pitch I used tonight moved well."[343]

Perry's workmanlike effort was just the second time in his last 903 games as manager that Rigney allowed his starter to pitch 11 innings. Asked if he had his sights on repeating as a 20-game winner, Jim maintained his typical feet-planted-in-the-moment, team-oriented focus.

"The only thing I'm thinking about now is number 18," insisted Perry. "I'm very proud to know I'm the first major league pitcher to win 17 games, but the main thing is that we won."[344]

His next two starts, a no-decision against the Senators and a loss in Boston, were more a reflection of poor run support Jim had been receiving than any sort of slump on his end. On August 19, Perry fired his second shutout of the season, downing the Yankees, 3-0. It was a masterful four-hitter that was completed in an absurd one hour and forty eight minutes.

Perry's only free pass of the night was to Horace Clarke, the Yankees leadoff man, who walked on four pitches to begin the game. From that point on, Perry was almost flawless, allowing just two runners to get past first base the entire night. After the game, Minnesota manager Bill Rigney raved about his ace.

"It was the best I've ever seen him," gushed the Twins skipper.[345]

"When he walked that first man on four pitches, I almost went out to the mound," Rigney admitted. "He didn't look like he got anything on any of those pitches. After that he was just super."[346]

Jim provided insight into his lightning quick pace. "That's the way I like them—fast," stated the smooth-working veteran. "At that rate, I might have been able to go all night."[347]

> I don't see much point in standing around out there thinking about what to throw. Lots of times you get yourself in trouble by thinking too much.
> — Jim Perry

"I don't see much point in standing around out there thinking about what to throw," he continued. "Lots of times you get yourself in trouble by thinking too much."[348]

20 x 2 = Perry

With brother Gaylord just one behind Jim at 17 wins, the topic of becoming the first brothers to reach the 20-win plateau came up after the game.

"I've been reminded of that all year," stated Jim. "He's pulling as hard for me as I am for him. We're not trying to outdo each other. We just try to go out every time and do the best we can."[349]

After a rough outing against Washington on August 23 that resulted in his eleventh loss, Jim went on a run that would cement his status as the American League's top 1970 hurler. He pitched a complete game in a 5-2 win over Boston on August 27 and followed that up by winning his twentieth game in spectacular fashion. Jim hurled a five-hit shutout over Milwaukee on September 1 that featured no walks and nine strikeouts. He allowed only two Brewers to get past first base, one doing so on an error.

Perry was the first Minnesota pitcher to win 20 games in back-to-back seasons since Camilo Pascual achieved the feat in 1962-63. Perhaps most significantly, Jim became the first 20-game winner to ever reach that plateau under "Captain Hook" Rigney in his fifteen years as an MLB manager—quite a feat. After the milestone game, Jim made a point to give credit to former manager Billy Martin.

"I owe Martin a lot," Jim stated. "He gave me a chance to prove what I could do. I'm grateful for that."[350]

"He gave me the opportunity to pitch regularly," Jim continued. "A pitcher always has to keep himself ready because he never knows when he's needed. Martin gave me a chance and convinced me to believe in myself. He knew how to handle each man individually."[351]

"I would have liked to have been a full-time starter before I was 32 years old," Jim admitted. "Maybe I could have won 20 before 1969. Two twenty-victory seasons give me a lot of satisfaction. I don't hold any grudges though. But maybe during the last two years, I opened some eyes of managers who had me before."[352]

Wins against the California Angels and Oakland A's followed, giving Perry a 22-11 record with three weeks still to play. In capturing his 22nd win on September 9 against Oakland, Jim displayed his all-around baseball skill, as well as his outstanding game awareness. Not only did he limit the A's to one run on five hits over eight innings of work, but he knocked in his own game-winning run with the bat. Coming to the plate with the game tied in the bottom of the seventh, two outs and runners on first and third, Jim looked over the defense and stepped to the plate with a plan. Batting from the left side against A's right-handed starter Chuck Dobson, Jim detailed his thought process.

"I was trying to hit the ball up the middle or even to left field. (A's third baseman Sal) Bando was playing in on the grass and I thought I might be able to drive the ball past him."[353]

Perry promptly hit a bouncer up the middle that got past the pitcher Dobson and scooted into center field, scoring Jim Holt from third base and giving Minnesota a 2-1 lead. They would tack on an insurance run in the eighth and Stan Williams, the right-handed complement to lefty closer Ron Perranoski, finished up for his twelfth save.

Record Breaking Brothers

The next day, September 10, Gaylord tossed a four-hit shutout over Houston to join Jim as a 20-game winner, making the duo the first brothers to reach the milestone in the same season. Though both had previously accomplished the feat (Gaylord in '66 and Jim the prior year), Gaylord had been determined to join his brother in that same 1970 season.

Pitching in San Francisco on September 1, just over a week earlier, Gaylord had allowed the Cincinnati Reds to tie the game in the seventh inning when teammates pointed to a message on the scoreboard that Jim had just won his 20th game. Gaylord retired the final eight hitters of the game as the Giants rallied for his 18th win of the season. That inspiration began a remarkable streak in which Gaylord fired four straight shutouts. After the second of those, in which he captured his twentieth victory, Gaylord revealed how following in the footsteps of his big brother had long provided inspiration.

"Jim's a hard man to keep up with," his little brother admitted. "I've been watching his progress closely. We always knew he'd be an outstanding pitcher."[354]

Asked if they dreamed about this accomplishment when they were growing up, starring together on high school and semi-pro teams back in Williamston, North Carolina, Gaylord laughed.

"When we were youngsters," the younger Perry recalled, "we never thought about winning games in the majors—we were just hoping we'd have a chance to get there."[355]

While the media celebrated the achievement, the workmanlike brothers took it in stride as both simply doing their job. "It seemed everyone talked about it, but we didn't discuss it much," Jim revealed. "He called me after I won my 20th and I called him after he won his."[356]

Not only were Jim and Gaylord both leading their respective leagues in wins, but both were among the leaders in innings pitched, as well. Jim attributed much of the credit to their upbringing.

"Gaylord is always high in innings pitched in the National League, too," Jim explained. "We both like to work; I guess it comes from growing up on the farm. We learned you don't get anything unless you work for it. We learned that hard work is the best teacher."[357]

The man who instilled that work ethic was not the least bit surprised by their success. "There was never any doubt in my mind that the boys were going to make it," Evan Perry stated matter-of-factly back on his farm in Williamston,

> We learned you don't get anything unless you work for it. We learned that hard work is the best teacher.
> — Jim Perry
> on growing up on the farm

North Carolina. "The three of us used to play and pitch for the same semi-pro team. They'd go to work (on the farm) at 6 A.M. and for 10 hours we'd do a thing that's called priming. Then we'd drive to Elizabeth City for a game.

"You should have seen them the year Williamston High won the state championship. Jim and Gaylord took turns pitching and playing third. Gaylord was only a freshman then, tall, shinny and wild, and when he'd get in trouble Jim, who's almost two years older, would switch with him, get him out of the jam and then switch back."[358]

Great "Spot" Pitcher

In a story for *The Sporting News* contrasting the styles of the 20-game-winning brothers, sportswriter Bob Fowler broke down Jim's approach. While Gaylord was known for a good fastball and his "super sinker," which many accused him of aiding with moisture, Jim was known for his impeccably precise location.

"Hi, everyone," Fowler began, feigning a play-by-play announcer. "We're ready for the start of today's game as Jim Perry prepares to face the leadoff man. Here's the first pitch . . . it just nipped the outside corner for strike one. Now Perry winds and delivers . . . strike two, it was low, but it just caught the knees on the inside corner. Perry winds again . . . oh, that pitch was two inches from the batter's chin. He picks himself up, dusts himself off and steps in as Perry delivers . . . it's a breaking pitch over the outside corner that is popped up.

"Control, friends, is how Jim Perry became one of the winningest pitchers in baseball," Fowler continued. "He is one of the game's great 'spot' pitchers."[359]

Jim attributed his pinpoint accuracy from all of his practice playing with brother Gaylord and father Evan in the pasture by the tobacco fields with their homemade ball.

"Because of the way the ball was made, you had to pitch to spots if you wanted to get anyone out," he explained. "You could make it curve or drop a little bit, but it hurt your arm (to do it, so the best strategy was to focus on precise location.)"[360]

Brothers Jim and Gaylord were both country-strong, farm-bred 6-foot-4 right-handers, each in the 205-pound-range in their prime. The pair learned the game together, playing with the same homemade ball in the same pasture adjoining the tobacco fields.

"But our styles are different," Jim explained. "Gaylord throws hard; he always had a great arm, even when we were kids. I have to rely on control. He had a no-hitter in 1968 against the Cardinals, but I'll never throw one. I'm not a no-hit pitcher. I just try to hit my spots with something on the ball. It's not an overpowering style. You don't get many strikeouts that way."[361]

Finish Strong

On September 17, Jim picked up his 23rd win of the season in a home matchup with the Angels. He pitched shutout ball through six innings, limiting California to just three singles and a walk. They began to get to him in the seventh, however, and manager Rigney turned again to Stan Williams for the final five outs.

Four days later, Jim took the mound in Oakland, not only shooting for his 24th win, but also with a chance to clinch the pennant against the arch-rival A's. Unfortunately, this night belonged to his opponent. Making just his eighth start in the big leagues, A's lefty Vida Blue fired a no-hitter. Blue was so dominant, in fact, that only a fourth-inning walk to Harmon Killebrew prevented a perfect game. It would not be the last time Jim had the misfortune of being on the other side of a no-hitter, but he also realized that's just the nature of the game.

Ever the gentleman and good sport, Perry made a congratulatory phone call to Blue over in the Oakland clubhouse. Manager Bill Rigney had the clubbie send over one of the unused bottles of "victory" champagne that was on standby for Twins pennant-clinching celebration that would have to wait for one more night.

After the Twins bounced back the next night with a 5-3 division-clinching win, manager Bill Rigney wasted no time in naming Jim Perry as the starter for their first playoff game, set for October 3 in Minneapolis. Jim took the mound on September 25 in Kansas City preparing to show the skipper he was ready.

As he loosened up, however, Jim had an eerie feeling. He felt especially good warming up in the bullpen. "When that happens, you usually go out and get shellacked," he later explained. "It's funny, sometimes you feel bad warming up and get everybody out."[362]

On this night, however, Jim's pregame feeling was not so prescient. He was also almost proven wrong about his assertion that he was not a "no-hit pitcher," if not for Royals second baseman Cookie Rojas. Jim retired the first 15 batters of the game with ease, but a grounder by Rojas to begin the sixth inning snuck through the right side of the infield for Kansas City's first hit. Jim then retired eight in a row until Rojas came up again in the eighth and picked up another single, this time pulling the ball into left field.

Jim calmly proceeded to retire the next four batters to finish off a masterful two-hit shutout for his 24th win of the year. The fact that he did it with no margin for error in a 1-0 Twins victory only reinforced his unquestioned ace-of-the-staff status. He walked nobody and struck out seven Royals in a game that manager Bill Rigney called "the best game I've ever seen Perry pitch."[363] The gem took only one hour and fifty five minutes to complete.

Following the masterpiece, the Twins ace stood firm in his self-analysis. "I maintain I'm not a no-hit pitcher," Perry protested. Rojas broke the no-hitter on what I thought was a good pitch. He hit a slider low and away to right field for a single. On his second hit, in the eighth inning, he got it on a fastball inside. But I'm not worried about no-hitters, I'll take the wins. I'd like to make it a 25-victory season by winning my last start. I felt strong in the cool weather tonight and had good stuff."[364]

Perry explained how the 59-degree Kansas City weather aided his superb outing. "When it's cooler, you stay stronger all through the game."[365]

Back at home once again on September 29, Jim took the mound to face the Royals in his final start of a fantastic season. The righthander knew that he would need to count on more help from his teammates than he normally required. Manager Bill Rigney planned to limit the workload of his ace prior to starting game one of the playoffs.

"If Perry's going to win his 25th, he'll have to be ahead by the fifth," the skipper announced before the game. "That's all he's pitching."[366]

Even with the arbitrary restrictions in place, things looked bright early. Jim pitched around a Kansas City hit in each of the first three innings as the offense staked him to a 5-0 lead. After retiring the first batter in the fourth inning, however, the Royals suddenly piled up a ridiculous six consecutive singles to tie the game up at five.

Disgusted after watching ball after ball find its way to the outfield grass, Jim finally took matters into his own hands, picking Pat Kelly off first base to squelch the rally. The Twins took the lead back in the bottom of the fourth and then Jim pitched a 1-2-3 top of the fifth. True to his word, manager Bill Rigney sent up Bob Allison to pinch-hit for Perry leading off the bottom of the fifth. Allison reached and eventually scored, as the Twins took a 9-5 lead with Perry officially out of the game, but comfortably in line for his 25th win.

Stan Williams, finishing up the best season of his 14-year career, pitched three shutout innings, bringing the game to the ninth inning with Minnesota still holding the comfortable four-run advantage and Jim on the verge of capturing win number 25. Similar to Rigney's handling of Perry, the skipper did not want to push Williams, who had become his most reliable bullpen arm down the stretch. So Rigney called on Ron Perranoski, who was the leading American League fireman with 33 saves. Unfortunately the lefty closer, who had been so clutch through the first two thirds of the season and saved several of Jim's early wins, was showing the effects of his heavy usage. Perranoski had blown six of his last 14 save chances while posting a 4.14 ERA over his previous 23 games.

Four of the five Kansas City hitters to face the Twins closer got to him for singles. With the tying run suddenly on first base, Rigney yanked Perranoski and brought on Bill Zepp, a rookie who had made twenty starts before recently being bumped from the rotation. Zepp retired the first batter he faced on a fielder's choice, putting

Minnesota one out away from the win, but Lady Luck played Perry yet another tough hand.

Utilityman Cesar Tovar, who appeared in all but one of Minnesota's 1970 games and played all but ten of them in the outfield, was making just his fourth start of the season at third base. There is a long-held baseball adage that the ball has a way of finding the player playing out of position or who is otherwise ill prepared. Sure enough, Zepp induced a potential game-ending grounder by Lou Piniella, but Tovar misplayed it for an error. The next batter, Ed Kirkpatrick, whistled a double into the right-center field gap, vaulting Kansas City into the lead and erasing Jim's chance at a 25th win.

Tovar would fumble away another grounder before the inning was over to cost Minnesota one more run. Incredibly enough, the Twins tied it up with two runs in the bottom of the ninth, and the teams traded two-spots in the 11th. Kansas City finally won the game, 14-13, in twelve innings. The Twins, who committed a total of four errors on the day, set a major league record by using 27 players.

Lady Luck Loads Dice

The American League Championship Series rematch between the Minnesota Twins and defending World Series champion Baltimore Orioles was set to begin with a matchup of 24-game winners in game one. Backed by the highest scoring offense in the American League, the Orioles boasted two pitchers who had matched Jim Perry's 24 wins. Mike Cuellar, who would oppose Jim in game one, posted a record of 24-8, while teammate Dave McNally went 24-9.

Following a workout at Metropolitan Stadium the day before the series began, Baltimore slugger and future hall-of-famer Frank Robinson voiced his respect for the Twins game one starter.

"Perry is always tough, because he is not going to beat himself," explained Robinson. "If you are going to beat Perry you will have to hit him to win. He is not going to walk himself into trouble. He will be around the plate all the time."[367]

Saturday, October 3 brought blustery winds blowing across the plains of the Upper Midwest. With northwest gusts consistently topping 30 miles per hour straight out toward the outfield, what was originally expected to be a pitcher's duel suddenly loomed as a slugfest. Adding to the disconcerting pitching conditions, MLB umpires went on strike that morning, leaving scrambled crews of replacements to umpire both the American League and National League playoffs.

"The wind could decide this," Perry ominously observed as he headed out of the dugout to warm up.[368] In addition to the strong winds blowing out, the game time temperature was a crisp 52 degrees for the late afternoon start. Both starters who had each been outstanding throughout the summer would have a difficult time dealing with the unusual playing conditions.

"The elements made it hard to get a grip on the ball," explained Orioles manager Earl Weaver after the game.[369]

Baltimore's game two starter Dave McNally confirmed the brutal conditions. "I don't care if it's hot or cold, but I don't like it gusty" McNally explained. "The wind does things to any pitches—fastballs run too much and curves hang or break too much."[370] Both starting pitchers on this day would deal with similar aggravation.

On top of all those hurdles, the Twins gameday staff was surprisingly unorganized, leading to a delayed start to the game. For the meticulous and routine-oriented Minnesota starter, the delay threw him off of his routine.

"Why was the game at least six or seven minutes late starting?" Perry queried aloud after the game. "I always allow myself 16 minutes before games at home to get ready–15 to warm up and another one to catch my breath before walking to the mound. But today it was cold and it didn't help me. I don't want to blame that, but when they schedule a game to start at 3 o'clock, they should start it at 3 o'clock. Some pitchers like to go by the clock, and I'm one of them."[371]

Whether it was the delay, the weather, adjusting to an unfamiliar umpire's strike zone, or even just nerves of starting the Championship Series opener, Jim promptly issued a four-pitch walk to Baltimore leadoff man Don Buford to begin the game. After a routine fly out by the next batter, Paul Blair, the Twins ace induced a double play bouncer off the bat of Boog Powell.

Cesar Tovar singled to get things going for Minnesota and Leo Cardenas sacrificed him to second, bringing up the engine that made the Twins offense go, Harmon Killebrew. A base hit into center field by Killebrew scored Tovar, and the Twins were off to a good start.

In the second inning, Jim once again faced early trouble. Elrod Hendricks and Brooks Robinson knocked back-to-back one-out singles before Jim plunked Davey Johnson to load the bases. Unfazed, Perry induced a routine double-play grounder to shortstop Leo Cardenas off the bat of eight-hole hitter Mark Belanger. Cardenas flipped to rookie Danny Thompson for the first out, but Thompson's relay to first baseman Rich Reese skipped in the dirt wide of Reese's outstretched glove. Not only did Hendricks come in from third, but Robinson scampered all the way around from second to score a second run on the miscue.

Perry struck out opposing pitcher Mike Cuellar to avoid further damage, but not before third baseman Harmon Killebrew dropped a tricky foul pop by Cuellar for the second Twins error of the inning. This misplay did not impact the scoring, but the wind-induced gaffe provided an eerie clue of what was to come.

In the bottom of the second, Jim used his bat to help his own cause, pushing a one-out grounder at first baseman Boog Powell that brought home George Mitterwald from third to tie the game at two. Perry retired the top of the Baltimore lineup in order with three groundouts in the top of the third, but he was still fighting the inconsistency brought on by the elements.

"I'd have good stuff for only an inning and then I wouldn't," he lamented after the game. "Then it would come back again."[372]

When Cuellar followed by working around a two-out double by Tony Oliva in the bottom of the third, it looked like perhaps the two aces might settle in and defeat the wind after all. Mother Nature, however, would not be denied.

An Ill Wind Blows

Frank Robinson and Elrod Hendricks began the fourth inning with back-to-back singles off Perry, putting runners on first and third for Brooks Robinson. Jim pitched him tough, but Robinson lofted a fly ball to right field that traveled far enough for Frank Robinson to tag up at third base and score the go-ahead run. After the game, Brooks shared his surprise at the result of the play.

"That sacrifice fly I hit in the fourth was on a pitch jammed in on me. I barely hit it, but it ended up on the warning track in front of the fence."[373]

Davey Johnson followed with a single to center that moved Hendricks up to second, bringing up eight-hole hitter Mark Belanger in a key situation once again. Despite being just a .218 hitter during the regular season, Belanger was normally able to get the bat on the ball. His potential double play grounder the first time up, of course, enabled two runs to score.

This time up, Belanger hit a hard come-backer. It was another potential double play ball, but alas, Perry was unable to field it cleanly. The ball deflected off his glove to Leo Cardenas at shortstop, but Cardenas had no play. Belanger reached, all hands were safe on the single, and Jim Perry and the Twins faced a bases-loaded jam for the second time under the very trying conditions.

"I was just trying to stop that ball any way I could coming through," Perry would say after the game of Belanger's hit. "It wasn't an easy chance, but if I handle that ball cleanly, the double play ends the inning with only one run scored and Cuellar never bats."[374]

Unfortunately, opposing pitcher Mike Cuellar did bat, resulting in one of the most improbable moments in baseball history. Just as he did with Brooks Robinson, Perry put his 1-0 fastball exactly where he wanted, jamming it inside on Cuellar, who pulled a high pop fly toward the stands down the first base line. Perry didn't even bother to glance at the flight of the ball, thinking it was certainly a foul ball out of play to even the count at 1-1.

"The pitch I threw to Cuellar was up and in, where I wanted it," Jim would later explain.[375]

Cuellar's reaction was the same as Perry's. "I didn't bother to run when I hit it," he confessed after the game. "It was three feet foul. Then the wind got it."[376]

Twins catcher George Mitterwald was even more confident on the success of the pitch. "Cuellar hit a fastball up and in. It was eight feet foul. Then the wind got it and you could see the wind push it fair."[377]

With perhaps the best view of all, home plate umpire John Stevens insisted there was initially no doubt. "It was 20 feet foul when Cuellar hit it. But the wind…"[378]

Bob Maisel, Sports Editor of the *Baltimore Sun*, described the scene: "It became obvious to the Orioles in pre-game practice that a stiff and erratic wind would probably have a definite bearing on the game. They decided then that they wouldn't give up on any ball hit in the air no matter how foul it might look at first, and that nine men would challenge every fly ball with the hopes that one would catch it.

"The strategy eventually paid dividends. They ran together on a couple of pop flies but surrounded them for putouts. When (Cuellar) hit his high fly toward the right field corner with the bases loaded in the fourth, it not only looked at least 15 feet foul, but didn't seem to have a chance of reaching the seats. The wind not only blew it fair, but gave it the necessary distance to fall into the second row of the bleachers just inside the foul pole.

"Right fielder Tony Oliva played it as though he considered it a foul ball almost all the way. He sort of drifted over into the corner, and just reached the spot as the ball got there. Had he made it in time to set himself for a leap, I thought he might have had a chance to catch it. Instead, he reached over the fence without jumping, and the Orioles were in front to stay."[379]

Mark Belanger, who was on first at the time, said he had never seen anything like it. "It must have been 25 feet foul when it went by me," stated the veteran shortstop. "I took a couple of steps toward second, then returned to the bag to tag up. The wind didn't sweep it fair, it sort of pushed it over all at once and it dropped straight down."[380]

Hal Bock of Associated Press had a slightly different perspective on Oliva's approach to the swirling fly. "Right fielder Tony Oliva angled over and seemed to be deciding whether to catch the ball, risking a sacrifice fly, or to let it drop in foul territory," wrote Bock. "Finally it dropped, but it was fair and just over the wall for a grand slam."[381]

For his part, Oliva was just as stunned. "It was eight feet foul at the start," estimated the Twins right fielder, "that's why I slowed down. I started running again and jumped, but it landed in the third or fourth row."[382] (Video replay showed the ball hit the back of a seat in the first row, clearly catchable, but also showed Oliva drifting toward the spot, out of position to make any kind of skillful play on the ball.)

Stunned by the game-changing fluke, Perry gave up another home run to the next hitter, leadoff man Don Buford, and his day was suddenly over. Bill Zepp came on in relief, serving up a third Baltimore home run in the inning, a 400-plus foot bomb by Boog Powell, and the previously tied game was now 9-2 in favor of the Orioles with the game not even to the halfway point. Minnesota battled back, chasing Cuellar during a three-run fifth, but that was all they could muster, as the Orioles won by a final score of 10-6.

After the game, Cuellar spoke of how the elements prevented his bread-and-butter pitch—the screwball—from having its normal effectiveness and caused his curve to hang far too often. "Some kind of weather," sighed the Cuban native. "Everything I throw high—couldn't keep ball down. Wind pretty bad but I can't blame wind. I not hit that ball good, but I hit it high. I know it foul, but the wind bring it fair—first grand slam I ever hit."[383]

"It was a fastball, high and inside, and my catcher (Mitterwald) said it was at least 15 feet foul and blew back," a dejected Perry lamented afterward.[384]

No Recovery

In their final game at home the following day, the Twins were unable to even the series, as Baltimore again knocked out the Minnesota starter in the fourth inning. Twins southpaw Tom Hall was the victim in this game, but Minnesota stayed within a run at 4-3 through eight innings. Baltimore broke it open in the ninth inning with seven runs, including five off of closer Ron Perranoski.

Down 2-0 in the best-of-five series, the Twins had their backs to the wall against the powerful Orioles for the second year in a row. Making matters worse, this was in the era before days off for travel, which might have given Minnesota a reprieve as they tried to recover from the two disappointing defeats. After a Sunday afternoon 3 p.m. central time start, the series moved to Baltimore—for a 1 p.m. eastern time Monday matinee.

As might be expected, the Orioles rode their momentum, cruising to a 6-1 win over the weary Twins. Baltimore got a complete game effort from Jim Palmer, who pitched what he considered to be one of his two best games all year. Jim Kaat started game three for Minnesota and was hit hard, failing to register an out in the third inning before he was replaced by rookie Bert Blyleven. The Twins pitching, which had been considered a strength, posted a 7.62 ERA in the series. The hitters also underperformed and the Minnesota defense made two errors in each game to go with several mental miscues. It was a disappointing end to what had been an otherwise great season, as Minnesota was swept by Baltimore for the second year in a row. For Jim Perry, however, any bitter taste left in his mouth would soon be washed away.

Cy of Relief

On Thursday, November 5, Jim Perry was announced as the winner of the 1970 American League Cy Young Award, given to the league's best pitcher. In a close vote, Perry edged out Dave McNally and Mike Cuellar, both also 24-game winners with the World Champion Orioles, and Cleveland's Sam McDowell, who won 20 games while racking up a league-leading 304 strikeouts. For Perry, it was the ultimate validation after almost a decade of fighting for the chance to show what he could do in a consistent starting role.

"I was just hoping. I had my fingers crossed," admitted the wily veteran who had learned never to take anything for granted. "I'm really nervous now. A thing like this shakes you up. I'm usually calm and collected in a game. It's quite an honor—some players work so hard and don't get such an honor in a lifetime. I can't express it in words."[385]

"It's like winning two games in a World Series," Jim continued as he searched for a way to describe his elation. "I waited so long hoping something like this would happen. It's great to have your family and friends and business people behind you. And it's a great feeling to have something like this happen to you here. Last year I worked so hard . . . then this year."[386]

"I think Jim was more excited (about receiving this award) than when he won 20 games," wife Daphne chimed in.[387]

Of his years of frustration being bounced back-and-forth between the bullpen and the starting rotation, Jim said "people wondered about me. But you keep faith and keep your head up high and things will work out in the end."[388]

Gotta Have Faith

Max Nichols, sports editor for the *Minneapolis Star*, penned a column detailing Jim Perry's faith. The column is so good and so revealing of Jim Perry, the man, much of it bears repeating here. Nichols shared a brief conversation he had with Jim as the pitcher was boarding an elevator back in April of '65. Perry had just passed through waivers unclaimed by any other MLB team and was perilously close to getting cut by the Twins.

"'I'm working hard,' said Jim. 'I am throwing every day. And when I get my chance, I'll be ready. That's all I can say.' The elevator closed. I remember having little hope for him," Nichols recalled.

"With Jim it was a matter of faith in himself. That was how he proved his courage. 'It's a matter of conscience after all,' he once told me. 'A man knows whether he is doing his best. I did my best to stay ready.'

"Daphne, his pretty wife, told me years ago that Jim never got down on himself even at home in his darkest days. She said the same thing again Thursday night, when Jim was celebrating his Cy Young Award.

"'I used to worry and tell Jim I wish they would trade him so he would get a better chance,' Daphne said. 'But he never let it worry him as much as it did me. He kept saying everything would be okay.'"[389]

"He's so strong about all things," said Daphne admiringly.[390]

"It sounds kind of corny, this faith business," Nichols continued. "Athletes all talk about it. But most of them wait for someone to have faith in them–wait for the opportunity. Jim lives the faith he talks about. And he attracts individuals who feel the same way.

"Thursday night at Jim's house there was only one player—Dick Woodson, a man Jim would like to see get ready for his opportunity. The rest were Jim's friends, some of them business associates.

"'They were our friends before—when things weren't so good,' said Daphne. 'They would be here no matter what.'

"One of them, Wayne Konga, explained it this way: '(Jim) has a

Christian mind. I can name six men here who are attracted to Jim for the same reason. Of these six, any one can ask anything of any of the others—and it will be done. Jim is the same.'

"Jim could have quit—back in the 1960s when the Twins were looking every year for someone to take his place. He could have complained about working as a reliever, about being wasted in his prime years, about not getting to start. He could have asked to be traded. He never did.

"And now that he is on top, he could have the last laugh, lord it over those who held him back. He won't do that either. Al Worthington wrote a letter saying that if Sam Mele had let Jim pitch, Sam might still be managing. But Jim had no unkind words for Mele at his celebration.

"Perry is 34. He had to wait until most athletes are past their prime to enjoy his peak of success. He had it coming. That elevator back in 1965, by the way, was going up."[391]

Perry = Class

For anyone who has been blessed with the pleasure of knowing James Evan Perry, it comes as no surprise that the theme of the stories about his greatest pitching honor focused more on the man than the baseball player. The November 28, 1970 edition of *The Sporting News* that highlighted Jim's Cy Young award included a feature titled "In Twin Cities, Perry Synonym for Class."

Writer Bob Fowler described Jim as follows: "There are some in baseball you just can't believe. They're too good to be true... Like Jim Perry. He speaks honestly, so sincerely, so nicely, you think at first it is a put-on and your first reaction is to put him down. But when you know him well, you know he is no actor... Perry proved that nice guys can finish first by winning the 1970 Cy Young Award for the American League. It climaxed a remarkable season and a remarkable comeback."[392]

Jim's brother, Gaylord, who finished the season with 23 wins ranked second in National League Cy Young Award balloting behind Bob Gibson of the St. Louis Cardinals. "This has been quite a season for the Perrys," Jim commented.[393] Quite a year, indeed, and it was about to get even better.

Perryston

North Carolina Governor Robert Scott proclaimed Tuesday, November 10, 1970 "Perry Brothers Day." More than 1,000 people gathered in Jim and Gaylord's hometown of Williamston, NC, including sports figures, politicians, celebrities, family and friends to honor the famous brothers for their great year. Ceremonies were scheduled to open with a motorcade parade during the afternoon followed by a banquet in the packed Williamston High School gymnasium. Though rainy weather forced cancellation of the parade, it did nothing to dampen the enthusiasm for the town's famous duo.

According to an account of the festivities, "the two hurling aces were showered with glowing tributes, standing ovations, trophies, plaques, gifts, the Governor's proclamation of "Perry Brothers Day" and even congratulatory telegrams from such National figures as President Richard Nixon and Ronald Reagan, governor of California."[394]

Williamston Mayor N.C. Green opened the festivities by lauding the region's famous sons. "Two of Martin County's native sons have brought honor and distinction to not only themselves but to Williamston, Martin County and North Carolina," stated the mayor.[395]

Principal Ed Farnell announced that Williamston High School would retire the high school uniform numbers of Jim (16) and Gaylord (18). Jerseys with these numbers would be placed in the school's athletic trophy case along with plaques commemorating their record achievements.

The featured speaker, representing Major League Baseball Commissioner Bowie Kuhn, was former New York Yankees great Bobby Richardson, currently head baseball coach at the University of South Carolina. After stating that the Perrys' contributions to the sport will never be forgotten, Richardson, who was a regular for the Yankees during the first eight years of Jim's career, spoke of the pleasure it was to compete against the oldest of the Perry brothers. Not surprisingly, however, Richardson's comments quickly turned to the character of the man.

"This is a sports-oriented society," Richardson asserted, "and the American athlete is the greatest exponent of the Christian witness because he knows only to win. He experiences the pain and perspiration for one purpose—to give his greatest performance and effort every time he goes out on the field.

"I am enthused about Christian athletes across the country," Richardson continued. "And I know the Perry brothers, like myself, would want all the kids here to become a man's man. This is a man who dares to stand for a principle when the world stands against him. This is a man who has the courage to be an individual in this materialistic and secular society. He is not governed by the stupid philosophy: 'Everybody's doing it.' He has strength in will, not mind, and knows it's what is in the heart and not the head that counts. A man's man has the ability to finish what he starts and sees things through."[396]

There could be no better description of the Perry brothers— the ability to finish what he starts and see things through. Jim and Gaylord wrapped up the gala affair by thanking the throng that descended upon the small high school gymnasium in the town of approximately 8,000 people.

"At a time like this, you are short of words," Jim assured. "But for myself and my family, it is just beautiful that you have thought of us so well.

"My baseball career has brought me some terrific times but I have worked hard and this is where I started. I started at the bottom. And, seeing the turnout here tonight makes me proud to come from a city like Williamston."[397]

Jim concluded his remarks with insight into his faith: "In the Christian life I try to run, I feel the Guy above is with me all the time. A baseball team is only allowed nine men on the field but I always feel I have ten on my side."[398]

Gaylord paid tribute to the boys' proud parents, Evan and Ruby, both in attendance. "I learned from my mother and father that if you cannot give a good effort every time out, you do not deserve to be out there."[399]

Finally, Gaylord sent everyone off happy with his concluding sentence, "Just remember, happiness is a baseball game."[400]

12

Veteran Leader

Between his new off-season business venture in the mobile homes industry and working the Upper Midwest "rubber chicken circuit," Jim had to make an effort to find time for his normal pre-season training routine. Suddenly a hot ticket as the certified top pitcher in the American League, more than once Perry was forced to turn down an invite to be some group's guest of honor.

"I'm having a hard time accepting all of the invitations I've received to award banquets," the reigning A.L. Cy Young winner sighed. "I'm going to make a few, but it's impossible to go every place and still get ready for the baseball season."[401]

Award banquets were not the only ones seeking the time of the newest local celebrity. In late November, Jim and Gaylord were named Honorary State Chairmen for the Salvation Army Christmas Cheer Program. Gaylord traveled to Minnesota in order to join Jim in serving as ambassadors for the great cause.

To get an idea of Jim's hectic off-season following his award-winning 1970 campaign, on Monday, January 18, he was guest of honor for the annual Mid-Winter Baseball Banquet at the historic Leamington Hotel in downtown Minneapolis. With several of baseball's greatest stars on hand, including Henry Aaron, Willie Mays, Harmon Killebrew, and several other Twins players, baseball commissioner Bowie Kuhn formally presented Jim with the 1970 American League Cy Young Award. The next morning, Jim jumped on a plane and traveled to Washington D.C., where the local chapter of the Baseball Writers' Association of America presented Perry with its Walter Johnson Award, given each year to the chapter's choice as A.L. pitcher of the year.

Perry was in such demand, in fact, that he had a hard time avoiding being double-booked! On one occasion he missed the Old-Timers' Hot Stove League dinner just across the river in St. Paul even though he was the scheduled featured speaker. Apparently they forgot to tell Jim that he was the headliner and he was back in his home state of North Carolina speaking at another event.

Fight for What's Right

Another challenging aspect of every off-season was the annual negotiation of a new contract for the upcoming season. In the pre-free agency era of the early 1970's, the leverage in such negotiations strongly favored the team over the player. Contracts for the upcoming season would be mailed out in mid-January with a salary offer based primarily on the player's performance the previous season, plus some factor of his service time and general standing on the team.

With those factors in mind, it is not unexpected that an 11-year MLB veteran who had just won the Cy Young Award in his eighth year with the Twins might be expecting a healthy raise from his $50,000 1970 salary. Especially considering that National League Cy Young winner Bob Gibson was reportedly making in the neighborhood of $150,000, Jim Perry certainly felt that being paid at least half that much would not be an exorbitant request. It is not hard to imagine his disappointment when he received a contract in the mail calling for a 1971 salary of only $58,000.

"When I got my contract, my first thought was that Mr. Griffith made a mistake and sent me somebody else's contract," Jim exclaimed. "We're a long ways apart, but Mr. Griffith has always been right with me and we'll have to talk it out."[402]

While it may be difficult to fathom in today's era of ever increasing salaries just for hanging around, it was not uncommon for a player coming off a subpar season to expect a salary cut, regardless of stature or service time. The fact that Twins President Calvin Griffith was offering pay cuts to established veterans like Jim Kaat, Dave Boswell, Luis Tiant and Rich Reese no doubt helped him rationalize that offering Perry a 16-percent raise was being "fair."

About two weeks after the contracts were sent out, Griffith was asked by Dan Stoneking of the *Minneapolis Star* if he had received an inquiry from Perry regarding being sent the wrong player's contract. "I haven't received any letter from Jim yet," the Twins president replied. "But when I send a man a contract for $60,000, I know whom I'm sending it to."[403]

Still being pulled this way and that, the star pitcher did not have much time for contract negotiations. Jim began February by attending several banquets in New York City before joining Gaylord for a southern swing that included affairs in Atlanta, Georgia and Raleigh, North Carolina. Before reporting for spring training and the grueling marathon of the 1971 season, Jim and wife Daphne finally snuck off to the Bahamas for a little R & R.

Minnesota Twins pitchers and catchers reported for spring training on Wednesday, February 17, but the staff ace and reigning American League Cy Young Award winner was not among them. He was not the only one missing. Closer Ron Perranoski, who had led the American League with 34 saves in 1970 also failed to report. At a time before agents became prominent to handle the haggling and with no mechanism to go on the open market, holding out was the only leverage in a player's arsenal when it came to the annual contract negotiation.

Ever since Marvin Miller had become the first full-time head of the MLB Players Association in 1966, he had been encouraging the players to stand up for themselves and holdouts were becoming more widespread. Both Dave McNally and Mike Cuellar, who joined Perry as 24-game winners in 1970, similarly joined him in holding out at the start of training camp in the spring of '71.

"It could be rough," admitted Griffith of his negotiations with Perry, "because Jim won't tell me what he wants. He just wants me to keep upping the offer.

"It's just the current trend," the Twins President continued, in reference to both Perry and another imminent holdout, star outfielder

Tony Oliva. "I don't like it but there's nothing I can do about it. But I am not going to be that kind of a nice guy and pay the kind of money a lot of players are asking. I think pro basketball started it. I just don't see how they can pay the kind of salaries they claim."[404]

The day after Minnesota pitchers and catchers held their first workout, Calvin Griffith told members of the press that Jim Perry had informed the Twins he would stay in the Bahamas until he received a suitable contract offer. (You gotta hand it to Jim, he picked a great spot to "holdout" with his pretty wife!) "I wished Jim a pleasant summer in the Bahamas," Griffith added in announcing that the high-stakes game of "Chicken" was officially ON.[405]

Two days later, Griffith said that Jim had telephoned him and said he and Daphne were done sitting around in the Bahamas and they were headed back home to Minneapolis. Jim informed Griffith, however, that he planned to make a stop at the Twins spring training facility in Orlando on his way back home.

"Perry is due in tonight," Griffith told the press the following day. "I expect to see him tomorrow morning. But we are still a long way apart. I'm not hopeful."[406]

After meeting for about an hour the morning of February 23, Griffith claimed "we are still far apart," but added that Jim intended to stay in Orlando for a couple days in hopes they could come to an agreement.[407]

On February 24, Minnesota infielders and outfielders joined in for the Twins first "full-squad" workout. In addition to Perry and Perranoski, outfielders Tony Oliva and Cesar Tovar, along with infielder Frank Quilici were also now officially holding out, not to mention pitcher Bill Zepp who was threatening to quit baseball if he didn't get traded to Detroit in order for his wife to be close to her family.

Manager Bill Rigney was matter-of-fact about the situation. "Both are veterans," the skipper said of his pair of pitching aces, "and know what they must do to get themselves ready to pitch."[408]

As a very team-oriented player, Jim obviously wanted to be in uniform working out with his teammates. As an extremely principled man, however, he had to balance that with the need to fight for what he deserved based on his performance. On top of that, Jim's position as a long-standing player representative encouraged support for the union cause that had top players across the game fighting to raise the industry salary structure for all players.

Three days later, Griffith announced that he had reached agreement with Perry on a contract. "We compromised," stated the team president. "I went up a little and Perry came down from his original request for $85,000. Jim is a sensible man and he realized he was hurting both himself and the ball club by staying out any longer."[409]

While player salaries were not publicly announced at that time, newspapers the following day referred to Jim's reported $65,000 salary for the 1971 season among the day's "big-money" signings. Of course, few could see how close the game's oppressive salary structure was to being totally blown up. Less than five years later, Jim "Catfish" Hunter would sign a five-year contract for a guaranteed $3.75 million as baseball's first official free agent.

Veteran Mentor

As the Twins prepared for the 1971 season, Jim Perry was comfortably entrenched as the unquestioned ace of the starting rotation for the first time in his major league career. With no need to fight for his own opportunity, he was free to serve as a mentor to other players still trying to find their way. One such player was 26-year old pitcher Dick Woodson. Miffed at being cut from the team in spring training the year before, Jim tried to explain that nothing is a given. You must work to earn your chance and to be ready when the opportunity arises.

"I came to camp (last year) taking for granted that I was going to stay with the club," Woodson admitted. "Most of the time I felt awfully tired. I'd work out and then go play golf or something, and the next morning I'd feel pooped. It affected my pitching.

"This spring I came to camp with the idea I was going to work. Right now if they told me to take 20 hard wind sprints, I'd take them. Perry told me last winter that when you hurt during a workout, do some more work. I found that things are getting easier instead of harder. I've told myself to keep my mouth shut this year and keep cool. I think it's made the difference of night and day in my pitching."[410]

When Jim finally got on the mound for his delayed first action of the spring exhibition season, the veteran quickly showed the late start would not be a factor. He gave up a line drive single to the first hitter he faced, but then retired nine batters in a row to polish off three crisp innings of work. He would finish the spring exhibition schedule with a sparkling 1.00 ERA.

As Opening Day drew near, however, Twins manager Bill Rigney was having a difficult time trying to line up enough starters to go after his ace. Bert Blyleven, who had impressed as a rookie in 1970, was slated to pitch the second game, followed by lefty Tom Hall after that. Erstwhile rotation anchor Jim Kaat, who had averaged 36 starts and 251 innings for the last seven years had somehow fallen out of favor with Rigney. Dave Boswell and Luis Tiant, both viewed as key cogs in the rotation just one year ago, were each released by the Twins as spring training concluded.

Long a team strength, Minnesota pitching was suddenly so thin the Twins braintrust publicly contemplated pitching Perry every third game. In fact, a March 29 story in the *Minneapolis Star* ran under the headline "Griffith names 'Rain' as fourth pitcher." Regardless of the schedule or Mother Nature, Rigney asserted that Perry would pitch every four days and that others would work around him. It was truly a remarkable position for Jim Perry to find himself, considering how he struggled for so long just to get a consistent opportunity.

True to his word, Rigney started Perry on Opening Day and then brought him back four days later to start Minnesota's fourth game. Tightness in his pitching elbow that Jim had been dealing with throughout the spring led the manager to skip his ace the next time around, but Jim came back strong after the rest.

On April 16 against California, Jim carried a no-hitter into the seventh inning, but a flare into right field by 1970 American League batting leader Alex Johnson broke it up. Still nursing a 1-0 lead in the eighth, Sandy Alomar hit a wind-blown fly ball that flicked off the outstretched glove of Tony Oliva for a two-run triple and the Angels came back for a 3-1 win.

Minnesota manager Bill Rigney was beside himself over Jim getting stuck with the loss on a day he dominated for over two-thirds of the game. "I've never seen Jim Perry pitch better than he did today—and he comes up empty," sighed the Twins skipper following the team's sixth loss in their first ten games.[411]

Jim did not necessarily agree. "I've pitched better than I did today, but not this year," he asserted after the game. "That's the way it is when you're losing. Some days you can't make a nickel. Normally Tony Oliva catches Alomar's ball and we're out of the inning. That's the difference between winning and losing. At least I had a better idea about my pitching, my control was better and even the pitch that Alomar hit was where I wanted it—a fastball up and in."[412]

Following his game-winning hit, Alomar was thankful a confrontation with the game's premier "spot" pitcher went his way for once. "Perry is just about the smartest pitcher I've seen," said the Angels leadoff hitter. "He doesn't give you anything to hit. I don't think I have two hits off Perry the last two seasons."[413]

By the end of April, the Twins were still languishing below .500, but Perry was rolling. On April 20, he dominated Kansas City for eight innings before tiring in the ninth and getting help from Ron Perranoski to close it out. Despite his success, however, Jim's arm was still not feeling one hundred percent.

"I thought I pitched to spots today as well or better than I did against California last week," Perry assessed of the outing in comparison to his prior six-plus no-hit-inning effort. "But my arm stiffened a little in the ninth today."[414]

His next time out, Jim went the distance in a 7-2 complete game win over Washington. As he pitched his arm into shape, Jim had to be feeling good going into his next outing. It was a Saturday afternoon game in Boston that would be nationally televised as the Game of the Week. This would allow Jim's parents, Evan and Ruby, a rare chance to watch their oldest son pitch. Unfortunately, the game did not start off well.

The first two hitters Jim faced, Luis Aparicio and Reggie Smith, hit home runs. After a single by Carl Yastrzemski, Jim uncharacteristically served up back-to-back walks, loading the bases with nobody out.

"I know my mother was watching the game on television and I'll bet she was covering her eyes" Jim recounted after the game. "I knew that if the next hitter got on I was out of the game."[415]

Inspired by his desire to stick around for the folks back home,

Perry bowed his back and battled back. He induced a 6-4-3 double play grounder by the next batter, Duane Josephson. A third run scored on the play, but it would be the last run of the game for the Red Sox. In fact, he would not allow a runner past second base the rest of the afternoon as Minnesota stormed back for a 7-3 win.

In addition to his stellar job on the mound, Jim led the offense, scoring three of the team's seven runs on the strength of a big three-hit day. In his first at-bat leading off the third inning, Jim laced a single into left field. He would proceed to work his way around the bases and score Minnesota's first run. The next inning, Jim singled again—another solid line drive—and eventually came home with the tying run. In the fifth, Perry came up with his third hit in three innings, knocking opposing starter Gary Peters out of the game while driving in a big insurance run to give himself and the Twins a 5-3 lead before coming around to score for the third time.

"I think those hits of mine might have helped the other guys," the sweet-swinging hurler assessed after the game. "They see me getting hits and they say, 'Hey, let's get some ourselves.' As far as the pitching goes, you're going to have innings like I did. Sometimes it's in the eighth inning, or the fifth. Today, I had mine in the first."[416]

Thinking Man's Pitcher

That enlightened and level-headed philosophical approach to the game is part of the reputation Jim Perry cultivated as he became one of the most respected pitchers of his era.

Minneapolis Tribune reporter Tom Briere broke down Perry's meticulous pitching technique, calling it a "study in concentration and practiced control." Briere stated that Perry "relies mainly on his knowledge of hitters, mixing fastball, slider and change of speeds." The writer then used the pitcher's late-April win over Kansas City to illustrate the sage veteran's approach in action.

"The 34-year old right-hander threads his pitches on the outside corner of the plate, preferably low. Then occasionally, Perry gets mean with a fastball inside.

"'You go in and out all day to set up the batters,' Perry said. The strong batters try to pull Perry's outside pitches–and it's either a ground ball to the shortstop for a double play (by Bob Oliver in the first inning) or a pop fly (by Ed Kirkpatrick to center field in the third).

"Of course, there's the Perry 'purpose pitch,' too. He won't admit to trimming a batter's sideburns with a fastball, but he dusted off the Royals' Lou Piniella with a fastball in the fourth inning. On the next pitch, Piniella flied out meekly to center field.

"Perry brushed back Cookie Rojas with a tight fastball in the eighth inning. Rojas then was looking for a pitch away but Perry threw tight with a fastball and Rojas hit a pop out to shortstop.

"There is one more lesson to learn from Perry's style of pitching. Perry learned it when he came to bat in the eighth inning. After Kansas City saw Jim brush back Piniella and Rojas earlier with inside fast balls, right-hander Jim York gave Perry the same treatment. He threw two 'purpose pitches,' but finally walked him.

"'That's part of the game,' Perry said with a smile after he pocketed the victory."[417]

Pitching With Purpose

Jim explained his thoughtful approach to pitching inside. "I never would throw at a batter's head," he explained. "I don't believe that's what the game is about. If you throw near a batter's waist or legs, he gets hit only in the hip or thigh if he freezes and can't get out of the way.

"I think a pitcher must protect himself on the mound," Perry continued. "Say a batter has had a couple of hits and the third time he really digs in. He has to be reminded that you're still in control of the situation. An inside pitch can help you then because it keeps everyone loose. You have to throw batters off-balance. That's the secret to good hitting and good timing."[418]

Kansas City shortstop Freddie Patek was in his fourth year in the big leagues and his first in the American League when he encountered the "Perry purpose pitch." After collecting hits each of his first three trips to the plate, Perry's first pitch in the next at-bat came in high and tight to singe the bill on the cap of the 5-foot-4 Patek.

"Yah, I think Perry had something in mind on that first fast ball," said Patek. "I think he wanted to loosen me up. But I don't blame Perry for throwing it. In fact, I admire him. He's a tough competitor and that's part of the game you have to expect."[419]

> I don't blame Perry for throwing it (a high-and-tight brushback pitch). In fact, I admire him. He's a tough competitor and that's part of the game you have to expect.
> — Freddie Patek
> 3-TIME ALL-STAR SS

Pitch location was not the only nuance of the game where Jim excelled. Tommy Harper, considered one of the game's best baserunners of the era, explained. "I know which (pitchers) like to throw to first," said Harper. "Which ones have a good move there. And which ones have a quick release to the plate. Some—like Jim Perry—have both a good move to first and quick release. They are hard to steal on."[420]

A June 26 game against the Milwaukee Brewers exemplified Jim's ability to control the running game. After Harper had reached on a fielder's choice, he looked to get a good lead with two outs in the inning. Most pitchers will not throw over to first more than a couple times, mainly because they don't want to make a mistake and give the runner a free base with an errant throw. On this occasion, Perry made six consecutive pickoff throws, finally nailing Harper with the last one.

From his purposeful approach to attacking hitters to his mindful approach to controlling the running game, Perry was always working to hone his craft. Prior to Opening Day, as the Twins headed north at the conclusion of spring training, they had stopped in Houston to wrap up their exhibition schedule with two days of action in the renowned Astrodome.

On Friday, April 1, Minnesota took part in a novel three-way tripleheader with the Astros and the New York Yankees. The event entailed each team playing two separate five-inning games in a round-robin format. With Jim scheduled for his final spring tune-up the following night, he could have easily begged off at least a portion of the 15-inning marathon. Instead, the wise veteran dutifully sat through four-plus hours of exhibition action, focused on studying the New York and Houston hitters.

"I'd like to think that I'm a pretty good student of the game," said Perry. "And you never know what you might be able to learn about one of the hitters. I think that if you take care of yourself and study what happens and what other pitchers do, you can help yourself," he explained. "That and hard work."[421]

"When I first came up with the Indians, I started keeping a little black book on the hitters," the wily veteran revealed. "I don't keep one anymore. I remember about hitters. I know just about every batter now. I still have that black book, though.

"Maybe I'll publish it someday," he added with a sly grin.[422]

Consistently Inconsistent

By the end of June, Perry was 12-6, one win ahead of his 1970 Cy Young-winning pace, but something still wasn't right, both for the pitcher and the team. For one thing, Jim's ERA sat at 4.03, which would be his highest in a Minnesota uniform if he were to finish that way. The chief culprit had been his control—the kiss of death for the game's preeminent "spot" pitcher.

Following a five-hit complete game 3-1 win over Detroit on June 1, Jim detailed his battle. "I've walked 25 men in my previous six games, and it's been beating me. Tonight I decided I'd keep the ball in play and my control was better. It was the best stuff I've had all year. I walked Aurelio Rodriguez twice and one was semi-intentional. It cost me a run, but that was the only run."[423]

The team was similarly performing short of hopes and expectations. Co-closers Ron Perranoski and Stan Williams were both struggling and the offense was not hitting as expected. Waging a season-long battle to stay above .500, the Twins ended June in third place in the division, but a distant 12.5 games behind Oakland. Earlier that month, Minnesota had dropped seven of their last eight, including their last four in a row when manager Bill Rigney became desperate. So frustrated with his team's lethargy, on the afternoon of Saturday, June 12, Rigney decided to do everything "backwards."

Reliever Stan Williams started the game, followed by fellow co-closer Ron Perranoski. Before the game, the Twins starters took batting practice before the reserves, the reverse of custom. Rigney himself even hit pre-game infield practice—very unusual for a big league manager. To top it all off, when Minnesota came from behind to take a 5-4 lead in the ninth, Rigney called on his *ace starter* to come in for the *save!*

Perry, who had started two days prior in Baltimore and was due to start two days later in Cleveland, had already thrown before the game as part of his normal routine. He was sitting comfortably on the bench with his fellow rotation mates when Minnesota was one pitch away from their fifth straight loss. With two outs and nobody on, Danny Thompson lined a single into left field. After Steve Braun coaxed a walk, Cesar Tovar and Rich Reese delivered back-to-back RBI base hits, giving Minnesota their first lead of the night. Suddenly, Rigney hollered for Perry to warm up. Jim had to scramble back into the clubhouse and grab his glove out of his locker before he raced down to the bullpen.

"I thought maybe I couldn't get loose when I warmed up in the ninth," Jim admitted. "But the hot weather (87 degrees at gametime) helps."[424] Whether it was the adrenaline from his scrambling glove recovery or from making his only relief appearance of the year, the big right-hander quickly got to work. Perry retired pinch-hitter Gates Brown on a groundout, got leadoff man Dick McAuliffe to pop to short, and then struck out .320-hitting Al Kaline to polish off his first save in three years.

Back on Track

Taking his regular turn on the mound two nights later, Perry was no worse for the wear, and frankly, about as good as ever. Perhaps inspired by his appearance as a fire-balling closer two days earlier, Jim spent the night firing high, hard ones as he struck out a career-high 11 batters en route to a six-hit, complete game 3-1 win over his old club in Cleveland.

"I had good stuff tonight, maybe the best of the season," said Perry as he tried to downplay his success.[425] "I'm no strikeout pitcher. Sometimes you strike out ten a game and the next time you don't get any. My fastball—I had good control of it early in the game and I hit some pretty good spots. This is the best game for all nine innings this year."[426]

Backup catcher, Paul Ratliff, behind the plate that night, expanded on the recipe for his battery mate's success. "His fastball was his big pitch. We threw 85 percent fastballs, Ratliff estimated. "Jim had a good one tonight, the best I've seen this season. With that early lead (from a first inning Tony Oliva three-run homer) we kept throwing fastballs and Jim kept getting them out."[427]

"(Perry) called a great game," Ratliff continued. "He's a very deceptive guy."[428]

The Twins skipper was especially encouraged. "Jim has been getting better each of his last four or five starts," said Rigney. "He is throwing like last season."[429]

The slender ace was back on a roll, winning his next two starts to run his record to 11-5. In a 4-3 win over the White Sox on June 18, Jim brought home the tying run with a perfectly executed suicide squeeze bunt.

In his next outing on June 22 at home against the first-place Oakland A's, Perry was brilliant, carrying a no-hitter into the sixth inning. He finished with a three-hitter, going the distance in a 10-1 Minnesota win. Perry faced just one batter over the minimum through five innings and was comfortably in control, inducing weak contact throughout the night.

"Jim's not afraid to rear back and throw the ball now," explained starting catcher George Mitterwald. "He's been getting ahead of the hitters and his control has been better. He mentioned early in the year that his elbow was stiff and maybe he was scared to cut loose for fear he might hurt himself."[430]

Not surprisingly, the durable workhorse denied any physical concerns. "You can't think about that when you go out to pitch," said Perry. "You've got to go hard all the time. But early we had some cold weather and on days when I threw to get loose I couldn't because the cold kept the stiffness in my arm. My arm never really bothered me, but it was just a little stiff."[431]

Frustrating Stretch

While it seemed the defending Cy Young Award winner was well on his way to a third consecutive 20-win season, Jim Perry was about to enter possibly the most frustrating starting stretch of his career. Another win over Oakland on June 30 brought him to 12-6, but it would be the last game he would win for almost two months.

On July 7, with his record still at 12-7 and his ERA temporarily below 4.00, Jim was named to the A.L. All-Star team for the second straight year. With Jim's peripheral numbers not quite as strong as the previous year, however, and with Gaylord failing to make the National League squad, the excitement was not quite the same for the July 13 game in Detroit. Jim spent the eighth and ninth innings warming in the bullpen, but did not see action as the American League pulled out their first victory in nine years.

In his first start out of the break, Jim picked up right where he left off, retiring the first 15 hitters he faced at Boston. After nine innings, Jim had a four-hit shutout going, but in an ironic twist, Twins hitters were likewise being stymied by the same Luis Tiant Minnesota had cut at the end of spring training. After a scoreless tenth, Perry finally conceded fatigue and was lifted for a reliever. Amazingly, it was his legs that were more tired than his arm, as Perry spent most of the night on the move. He was either running to cover first base or fielding a ground ball on a ridiculous 12 of the 30 outs he pitched.

"I seemed to be running toward first base most of the night," Perry commented in characterizing the game as one of his most complete outings as a professional.[432]

Manager Bill Rigney concurred. "I think that's the best I've seen Perry pitch since I've been here," the skipper observed. "But we must have the worst record in the game as far as scoring runs in Fenway Park."[433]

Minnesota's bats came up empty for another three innings after Perry's departure. In the bottom of the 13th inning, Stan Williams issued back-to-back two-out walks before Rico Petrocelli took him deep for a game-winning three-run homer over the Green Monster in left field.

And so it went as Jim suffered through a winless month-and-a-half. In six July starts, his offense scored a total of ten runs while Perry was charged with five losses to go with the no-decision in Boston. In addition to his lack of run support, a lack of luck was a culprit, as well.

On July 24, Jim was shutting out the Red Sox for the second time in ten days, this time working on a three-hitter through seven innings. "He had the second best stuff he's had all year," observed manager Bill Rigney. "I was almost going to have a chuckle on the bench because we finally had scored some runs for him. We hadn't scored a run for him in his two starts since the All-Star break, had we?"[434]

Rigney must have choked on his chuckle when slap-hitting leadoff batter John Kennedy pulled a fly ball that carried just over the left field fence for a game-tying home run with two outs in the eighth inning.

"Perry usually pitches me away and once in awhile will throw a fastball inside," Kennedy explained. "I don't think he got the pitch where he wanted. I didn't think the ball was going out, but I thought it might hit the wall. They tell me it made it to the first row of the bleachers. Well, that's about as far as I can hit 'em."[435]

After Reggie Smith led off the ninth inning with a double," Perry was lifted only to see his bad luck get even worse. Ron Perranoski, who had teamed up with Jim on so many good moments the year before, allowed Jim's run to score plus two of his own, as the Twins lost, 6-3.

Jim's rough stretch continued into August. The offense finally got him some runs (five), but he was tagged for seven of his own in six innings of work and suffered his 12th loss of the year. Perry gave up nine hits, including a pair of home runs, and walked three, but a pair of double play balls the defense failed to convert permitted five of the seven runs to score.

"It seems to be just one of those years when everything happens against you," an exasperated Perry sighed.[436]

"If I or the guys behind me make a mistake, it costs me," he continued. "People look at my big earned-run average (4.15) and home runs (24 in four months after only 20 in his entire Cy Young season). But they fail to see what has happened in some games."[437]

Manager Bill Rigney agreed that it was "one of those years" for the entire team. "What we get, 15 hits? All singles?" the manager queried disbelievingly. "Last year we would have had a couple of homers in between and we'd have had nine or ten runs."[438]

"I'm pitching defensively," assessed Perry. "I don't have my good control and I'm falling behind the hitters. Then I have to come in with a good pitch, one they can hit, and they do. I've got to start thinking more offensively and getting ahead of guys."[439]

A good chance for a win against Baltimore on August 11 turned into a no-decision when Jim was pulled with a 5-2 lead and reliever Jim Strickland promptly gave up a game-tying home run to Boog Powell. An eighth straight loss followed that, dropping Perry's record to 12-14.

Puppy Love

On August 20 in Baltimore, Jim had a feeling that he might finally get off the schneid. "Before the game I got a telegram from Roy Carr and my dog Stoke," he laughed. "Roy trains my dog and the telegram said they knew I could do it. I've been leading kind of a dog's life recently."[440]

Jim tried to change things up by getting to the park early but that didn't seem to help his control, as he walked five Orioles batters in the first two innings. Only one of them led to runs, but Frank Robinson touched up Perry for a pair of two-run homers. After the second Robinson homer gave Baltimore a 5-0 lead in the bottom of the fifth, Twins manager Bill Rigney made a trip to the mound. He had the intention of going to the pen, but "Captain Hook" made the surprising decision to stick with his ace starter.

Asked why he changed his mind, Rigney replied, "I just thought I'd try something different. I had to tell him to go with what he's always thrown, and if it's not good enough, the heck with it."[441]

Inspired by the surprising vote of confidence from his boss, Perry bore down and retired the next eight hitters. When he was finally removed from the game in the eighth inning, however, the Twins were still trailing 5-1 and Jim appeared headed for his 15th loss. "After (Rigney) pinch-hit for me, I just went back to the clubhouse," said Perry. "I just sat there and listened to the radio."[442]

The exasperated pitcher could hardly believe his ears when the offense suddenly sprang to life, erupting for five runs in a rally that Leo Cardenas capped off with a three-run homer to give Minnesota a 6-5 lead. Not only was Jim off the hook for a 15th loss, but he suddenly was the pitcher of record for the win! The Twins tacked on a pair of insurance runs in the ninth while Stan Williams polished off the Orioles with two shutout innings for the save and Jim Perry captured his first win in 51 days while sitting in the clubhouse.

"I think this will take some of the pressure off (Perry) now, and he'll be all right," Rigney predicted.[443]

"I'm relieved it's over," Perry sighed. "I don't care how we won."[444]

Jim explained the frustration of trying to make adjustments during the losing streak, but nothing seemed to work. "I tried warming up longer before a start and throwing more on the sidelines between starts. I didn't want to change my style completely. After all, I've pitched this way all my life."[445]

Back in the Saddle

With the hard-luck losing streak finally behind him, Jim had his sights set firmly on moving forward, as he took the mound for his next start in Detroit. He allowed three baserunners, including an Al Kaline solo home run in the first inning, but avoided further trouble by getting Jim Northrup to ground into an inning-ending double play. Perry would allow only two more baserunners the rest of the night, as he cruised to a 3-1 complete game victory that evened his record at 14-14. Most importantly, he walked only one batter.

"You can't live on last year. Last year's past," philosophized the sage veteran, as he rubbed an ice bag on his pitching elbow in the post-game locker room. "You've got to just go out there and try your hardest always."[446]

"I've become an offensive pitcher again instead of a defensive one," Jim asserted. "I made up my mind to try to get batters to hit the ball and not walk anyone."[447]

"Getting it over the plate did it for me," Perry continued. "When you don't have your control you are on the defensive because you are behind the batter. When you are getting it over you are ahead of the batter and can attack him. I was attacking tonight."[448]

Jim kept the streak going with another road win his next time out in Cleveland on August 29. He had to work around 12 hits in the 6-5 win and needed rookie Hal Haydel to come on for the final out after a two-run ninth inning homer by Vada Pinson, but Perry did not issue a single free pass.

Another win at home against division-leading Oakland on September 3 pushed Jim's record to 16-14 and with the team sitting in a distant fifth place already eliminated from the race, personal goals became the focus of the manager.

"We're going to give Perry every chance to win 20 games, said Bill Rigney. "If it means pitching him out of turn, and he wants to, we'll give him the opportunity."[449]

Limp to the Finish

Unfortunately, Jim's control issues resurfaced in his next start at Chicago. He walked three batters, all of which came around to score, as the Twins lost to the White Sox, 8-7. Perry rebounded in his next start, another duel in Oakland with Vida Blue, who was going for his 24th win. When George Mitterwald took Blue deep for a three-run homer with two outs in the top of the eighth, giving Perry and the Twins a 5-1 lead, it looked like Jim was primed to pick up his 17th win.

A Reggie Jackson home run leading off the bottom of the eighth made it 5-2. Jim retired the next two hitters, but a two-out walk, followed by a single prompted Rigney to go to the bullpen. Rookie reliever Jim Strickland gave up a hit to Gene Tenace, allowing one of Jim's runners to score and then Bob Gebhard, another rookie reliever, allowed the other one to come in on a hit by Mike Hegan.

Perry was still in line for the win, but Reggie Jackson blasted his second homer of the night, taking yet another rookie reliever, Ray Corbin deep with one out in the bottom of the ninth to send the game to extra innings. Minnesota won it with two runs in the tenth and Corbin backed into the win after blowing the save of Perry's win. Not only was Jim's good pitching line muddied by ineffective relief in his final inning, but the no-decision all but eliminated any shot at a third straight 20-win season for Perry.

Five days later at home against the Royals, a Leo Cardenas solo home run was the only offense the Twins could muster, leaving Jim a hard-luck 2-1 loser. On September 21, Perry carried a one-hitter into the seventh inning against Milwaukee, but Brewers cleanup hitter John Briggs got to him for a solo home run in the seventh inning and then again in the ninth. Added together with a pair of unearned runs in the eighth and Perry was handed a hard-luck 4-2 complete game loss, dropping his record to 16-17.

Sunday, September 26, Jim made his final start of the 1971 season in the first game of a doubleheader in Kansas City. It was a classic Jim Perry outing as he limited the Royals to just five hits and walked none over eight innings before Tom Hall finished up the 6-2 win. One of the hits off Perry was a solo home run, which tied the franchise record of 39 homers allowed set by Pedro Ramos during the team's first season in Minnesota.

"I'm not after those negative records," Perry quipped when told of the dubious accomplishment. "But I'm glad to get even."[450]

Taking Stock

It was quite an accomplishment, indeed, to finish with an even 17-17 record. Especially on a disappointing team that finished in fifth place, 12 games under .500. In fact, while the Baltimore Orioles starting rotation made the headlines with three 20-game winners (Cuellar, Palmer, Pat Dobson) and one 21-game winner (McNally) in the same season on a 101-win team, Jim made the point that he may have meant more to his club.

"I won only three fewer," he explained, "and none of the four had as many decisions as I did."[451]

Beat writer Tom Briere of the *Minneapolis Tribune* summed it up with an enlightened perspective: "Truthfully, Perry was in virtually every game he pitched until the late innings and then the relief pitchers were seldom able to help him."[452]

If Stan Williams (4.15 ERA, 4 saves) and Ron Perranoski (6.75 ERA, 5 saves) had pitched anywhere close to the way they had in 1970, Rigney would not have been forced to turn to unproven rookies in hopes of holding onto a lead. It is near certain that Dependable Perry would have been a 20-game winner for a third consecutive season, ranking him among the game's elite.

There was another record achieved by Jim Perry in 1971 that did not make the news of his "negative" record. He set a new team mark by fielding 61 defensive chances (17 putouts and 44 assists) without an error. Despite his flawless work in the field, the American League Gold Glove Award for Pitcher inexplicably went to teammate Jim Kaat (1 error in 54 chances) for the tenth consecutive season. (For those who aren't familiar, the very subjective Gold Glove voting tends to coincide with reputation more than any solid analysis of the evidence. From this analyst's perspective, it's just one more instance of the understated greatness of Jim Perry.)

Winds of Change

A shocking development in regard to the famous pitching Perry brothers occurred at the Baseball Winter Meetings following the 1971 season. On November 29, amidst a flurry of trades by MLB teams, San Francisco traded Gaylord, who had been with the Giants organization since signing with them out of high school 14 years earlier. Along with minor league shortstop Frank Duffy, Perry was dealt to the Cleveland Indians in exchange for enigmatic flame-throwing lefty Sam McDowell.

It was a stunning trade after Gaylord had just started two playoff games for San Francisco less than two months prior. "Naturally, it was a shock," said his wife, Blanche. "But Gaylord took it like the man that he is. It wouldn't have hurt so much if Gaylord had been traded for somebody other than a pitcher. They did get a lefthander, but I don't think that makes much difference."[453]

Twins manager Bill Rigney, who had firsthand knowledge of the Perry competitive instinct, concurred. "Perry knows how to pitch, and he's a winner," stated the Minnesota skipper of Gaylord. "I think it's a good deal for the Indians."[454]

Giants manager Charlie Fox had been infatuated with McDowell ever since scouting him in high school ten years earlier. In explaining how he could part with his workhorse who had just started the first game of the playoffs, Fox stated, "We badly needed a left-handed starting pitcher who can strike somebody out, and we got him." Fox also pointed out that Gaylord was 33 years old while McDowell was only 29, "so the age factor was in our favor."[455]

McDowell had led the American League in strikeouts five times in the previous seven seasons, including 304 in 1970. He also led the A.L. in walks issued five times during that same span, including an absurd 153 free passes over 215 innings in the just completed 1971 season. McDowell would strike out only 294 more batters and win just 19 more games in his career, which, ironically, was over before he turned 33 (Gaylord's age at the time of the deal). Gaylord, of course, went on to pitch for 12 more seasons, winning 180 games after the swap. Needless to say it turned out to be a disastrous deal for San Francisco.

From Jim's perspective, Gaylord's move from the National to the

American League presented for the first time other than their All-Star Game matchup the possibility that the two brothers might face off against each other. When Jim called his younger brother upon hearing news of the deal, he had a feeling that the move was going to be good for Gaylord.

"Jim told me," Gaylord recalled, "'You're going to have one of the finest catchers in the game in (Ray) Fosse. You're going to like him a lot.'" Gaylord was on the verge of the best season of his 22-year career, prompting him to later say, "(Jim) sure was right."[456]

Jump Start

Anxious to get off to a good start in '72, Jim wanted to avoid the protracted contract negotiations that caused him to begin training camp late the previous spring. Considering the massive transformation that would soon take place in the salary environment for star athletes, it is remarkable to consider that after pitching 270 innings and winning 17 games, many believed Perry would be forced to take a pay *cut!*

On January 13, however, both Twins veteran pitching Jims—Perry and Kaat—emerged from a meeting with team owner Calvin Griffith smiling. Although no contract terms were announced, a team spokesman confirmed they "definitely didn't get cuts." (Later reports were that Perry received a $5,000 raise to $70,000.) What Perry would confirm is that he wanted to sign "as fast as I could" in order to get down to Orlando and begin preparation for the season.[457]

The strategy paid dividends as Jim, who reported to camp early, was in mid-season form when exhibition play got under way. Most encouraging for the renowned control artist was that he only issued one walk through his first 12 spring innings. Five shutout innings against the Yankees on March 15 that required only 64 pitches were indicative of Perry's strong spring "spot" pitching.

"Everybody has been saying I've been getting too cute," said Perry. "Now all I'm trying to do is make guys hit the ball."[458]

Another positive development was that Jim's longtime roommate, Al Worthington, had been coaxed out retirement for a second time. Now 41 years old, however, Worthington was not returning to pitch. This time, the former closer was coming back to the Twins to serve as pitching coach. Perhaps the best part of all, as far as Perry was concerned, is that Worthington considered himself to be a pitching coach in the same mold of Johnny Sain, the man credited with reviving Jim's career.

"I believe Johnny Sain is the best pitching coach in baseball," said Worthington. "He gets along with the pitchers and they respect him. We have similar thoughts. He is a positive thinker who instills confidence into pitchers. I believe, too, confidence is a big part of winning; of course, winning helps build confidence, too."[459]

Things were definitely looking up for Jim Perry as the start of the 1972 season approached.

Well Earned Break

Even as he took his preparation quite seriously, Jim always understood the importance of time away from the game. Mike Lamey of the *Minneapolis Star* provided insight into the star pitcher's recreational escapes.

"Perry continues to be one of the Twins' hardest workers yet he still finds time to enjoy himself," Lamey wrote. "Before exhibition games started the 35-year-old was always out fishing or golfing after the morning workouts. Monday he and Dick Woodson and a Minneapolis business associate, Elmore Gooddale, flew to the Bahamas for some tuna and barracuda fishing.

"'It is more fun in spring training because you have time to spend with your family,' said Perry. "You've got to relax. But I'm here to get ready for baseball first and then I enjoy myself. That's what I'm getting paid for.'"[460]

13

Tower of Strength

Preparing himself to pitch in the spring of '72 was not the only concern for the veteran team leader. As the long-standing Twins' player union representative, Jim was responsible for coordinating and communicating issues related to what was becoming an increasingly contentious labor situation.

Marvin Miller, executive director of the Major League Players Association, had been pushing the players to fight for more rights and a greater share of what he could see was the owners' growing financial pie. In early 1972, the issue was an increase in pension funding from the growing revenue produced by World Series and All-Star Game television broadcasts. A frustrated Miller contended the owners refused to bargain in good faith and he was advising the players that a player strike on March 31 (the expiration date for the existing three-year labor agreement) would be necessary if the issue was not settled. The owners questioned whether the players had the guts or cohesion to go on a full-scale walkout. At most, owners believed the Players Association would limit the strike to a few select early season TV games of the week, a tactic that had been rumored during previous negotiations.

As the Twins player rep, Perry was charged with serving as the communication conduit between Marvin Miller and the Minnesota players. On Sunday, March 12, Miller held a two hour meeting with all of the Twins players, explaining the issues and answering questions about the players association negotiation strategy. Following the meeting, the players voted unanimously to reject the latest proposal from the owners, raising the prospect of a strike, though Jim clarified that nothing had been decided in that regard.

"We voted down the owners' offer on the pension," Perry cautioned. "We didn't vote to strike."[461]

On March 31, Jim traveled to Dallas, Texas along with alternate player rep Phil Roof where Marvin Miller met with player reps from every team for a vote on whether to strike. Before he left for the meeting, Jim was asked what he planned to do.

"I'm going to listen to all of the facts and then decide on how to vote," responded Perry. "I was in favor of the owners meeting with the players. But the owners refuse."[462]

On the evening of Friday, March 31, the Twins were in the Astrodome in Houston, Texas preparing for an exhibition game against the Astros. Around 7 p.m., word reached the Astrodome that the players' representatives had, indeed, voted to strike at midnight.

At 7:30 p.m., the Astros took the field, but the Minnesota dugout was empty. Only starting pitcher Dick Woodson, warming up in the bullpen, was anywhere near the field of play. Much to Jim's dismay when he found out, the rest of the players were holed up in a clubhouse meeting discussing repercussions of the strike vote with Twins president Calvin Griffith and team vice president Howard Fox.

Fifteen minutes later, as the delayed game finally got underway, there seemed to be confusion among Twins players. According to Griffith, although the union announced they had voted to strike, the players in the team meeting denied being a part of any such vote. "Our players just told us in the clubhouse that they didn't vote to authorize a strike," announced the Twins president to members of the media in the Astrodome press box.[463]

Perry and Roof rejoined the team during the game and met with the rest of the players afterward for almost an hour, explaining what had transpired at the meeting with Marvin Miller.

"I repeat what I said earlier," said Perry, "that we never took a strike vote among the Twins. When we got into the meeting today in Dallas, Marvin Miller, our Players' Association director, assured us that we had the right to vote for a strike without going back to our team. He's our leader and that's the way we voted."[464]

Mother Perry

It was the first leaguewide strike in the 102-year history of organized professional baseball. It was the first organized strike in the history of major American professional sports leagues, for that matter, and nobody really knew what happened next. When the players woke up in Houston the following morning, April 1st, the announcement by Calvin Griffith that the team had terminated their daily meal allowance of $18.50 was no April Fools' joke. Perry and Roof called a players meeting in which they discussed what to do next.

While he was not pleased with the stance of the players, Griffith said that any players who wished to return to Minnesota were still welcome on the team's charter plane, which was scheduled to fly back to Minneapolis on Sunday if the impasse was not resolved by then. Because nobody knew how long the strike might last, some of the players wondered if they should head back to their off-season homes.

Hopeful of a quick resolution and subsequent start to the regular season, 21 of 26 Twins players returned on the team plane, though many had no place to go once they arrived back in the Twin Cities. Perry and Roof immediately got to work organizing carpools, house pools, and equipment pools as they scrambled to make sure no man was left behind in dealing with the unusual crisis.

"We're all trying to help each other," Perry explained. "Those players with homes here are taking in some of the others. Rod Carew has Danny Monzon, Rick Dempsey, and Cesar Tovar staying with him. Dick Woodson is with me. Phil Roof is at Jim Kaat's house. Ralph Rowe is renting Billy Martin's house in Richfield and has Eric Soderholm and Tom Norton.

"Today we have a practice set at St. Olaf College and we'll have a carpool, especially for those not used to driving in the snow. Maybe we should all go skiing instead," he added, only half kidding.[465]

An early spring cold snap through the Upper Midwest had

sent Twin Cities temperatures plummeting down into the 30s, complicating the impromptu workout logistics. To no one's surprise, it was the affable Perry who was able to come up with a plan. Because of his friendship with St. Olaf baseball coach Jim Dimick, Perry was able to arrange for use of the indoor fieldhouse at St. Olaf College in Northfield, about 40 miles south of Metropolitan Stadium. The indoor facility included not only batting cages, but a practice area, as well, so it was an ideal solution.

"Some of the older players, such as Kaat, Carew, Killebrew and myself will be in charge," Perry confirmed. "We'll see everybody gets his work. We can't wear any of the team uniforms, but we have our own gloves and shoes."[466]

Marvin Miller cited Jim's leadership as a prime example of players who stepped up to play a key role in the process. "Perry had grown up in a farm community in North Carolina. He had no experience with unions, and yet overnight he became an efficient, dedicated leader. He was the first to organize the housing of younger players with veterans, and he rented a school bus to transport players back and forth to a local gym which he had arranged to use for workouts. He telephoned me each day for reports on the negotiations and even put together a public address system in the gym so that I could report directly to all of the Twins working out there."[467]

Perry had the players pool money together to handle any shared expenses as they held out hope that an agreement could still be reached in time to save Opening Day. The Twins were scheduled to open the regular season at home on Thursday, April 6 against the California Angels. With Jim doing so much to see that everyone had all they needed to get by, several of his teammates had taken to calling him "Mother Perry."

"Everybody wants to know what is going on," sighed a beleaguered Perry. "You have to keep repeating it, but it is something that takes longer than two minutes to explain."[468]

"You almost have to be a lawyer and have a degree," Jim's wife Daphne chimed in. "After this he might go into a pension committee."[469]

As the mother of three young children, Daphne was cognizant of the constant demands being placed on her husband and the toll it was taking on their family. She said it had been a hectic week, especially the almost non-stop phone calls.

"I thought Sunday, because it was Easter, things might let up, but they didn't. Even our oldest boy (Chris, now 10) is being asked in school about when they are going to play.

"It is difficult," Daphne continued. "And I hate the idea of people thinking Jim is against Mr. Griffith and Mr. Griffith is against Jim. They have been good to us, and it is not that way at all."[470]

In a prophetic sign of things to come later in his professional career, Jim determined a more efficient way to make use of the telephone. In order to answer some of the more complex questions about the negotiations, he arranged an open-line telephone hookup—a conference call, which was a relatively novel idea at the time. This enabled Marvin Miller to provide an in-depth update all at once to the Twins players, as well as members of the local press corps.

"It took me more than an hour and a half just to call all the press people up to tell them where to come," Jim explained. "Then I had to get the players. And finally, I had to see that there was some donuts, coffee, and orange juice there for everyone."[471]

Mother Perry, indeed.

Forging a Deal

At the Wednesday, April 5 "Welcome Twin Luncheon," which went on as originally scheduled the day prior to the now-postponed Opening Day, Perry took offense when he was referred to as "the Twins negotiator. "Marvin Miller is my negotiator," Jim clarified. "I'm just the player representative. What the players tell me they want, they get. This is just not a Jim Perry thing. It is a team thing and I'm getting a lot of help. I happen to enjoy the job (despite the fact there is no extra pay—only extra headaches) and am interested in what is going on in baseball."[472]

As the strike dragged on into its second week, the workouts at St. Olaf continued. Pitcher Bert Blyleven explained that he felt the team had grown closer through the experience of living together at players' homes, plus the informal workouts. "Driving over here (to St. Olaf) makes you know the guys better, too," said Blyleven. He also explained how they hold a team meeting before each workout so that "Jim Perry, our player representative, can give us a report every morning on the strike."[473]

With baseball's opening weekend canceled and some players beginning to get restless, Marvin Miller called for a Tuesday, April 11 meeting with all of the player reps in his New York City office to discuss the stalemate. Expecting this to be nothing more than an in-person update on the negotiations, Jim headed East that morning, expecting to return home later that same evening. Miller, however, had a more pressing reason for calling the player reps together.

With the bargaining heating up on both sides, Miller wanted the ability to discuss aspects of counter-offers from the owners and to quickly vote on any potential agreement. Miller had secured a hotel ballroom where the player reps soon found themselves hunkered down in discussions that at times became animated. The Tuesday meeting went late into the evening, and then picked up again early Wednesday morning, followed by a similar schedule the next day.

"The meetings were long and intense," Jim recalled. "We hardly had time to eat, and we certainly didn't have time to go shopping. I had to wear the same clothes for three days!"

Another issue was the New York media contingent, desperately seeking information as to when the baseball season might get under way. The owners had moved their base of negotiating operations to Chicago in an effort to avoid the New York press, leaving the contingent of players as the most accessible source of information. Writers, reporters, and television cameras were set up in the hotel lobby and regularly camped out in the hallway just outside the ballroom. At one point, legendary sports broadcaster Howard Cosell made his way into the ballroom where the players were meeting and attempted to get his cameraman set up for a live shot.

"The other players knew I got along well with Howard and urged me to intervene," Jim recalled. "I said, 'Howard, you can't be in here. You have to wait outside with everyone else and we will give you a statement when we have something to report, but right now we have to work in here.'

"After that, the players knew we needed to maintain a united front in dealing with the press," Jim continued. "Brooks Robinson,

Tom Seaver, and I were chosen to speak to the media on behalf of the other players."

Finally, on the third day of meetings and back-and-forth conference calls with the owners, news began to leak out that an agreement was imminent and that players should have their bags packed and be on "standby." With the Twins opening homestand now completely wiped out, the team had a Northwest Airlines charter waiting to take them westward once the expected agreement became official where they would open the season in Oakland.

When the dust settled, neither side was happy. "We offered the owners the same settlement last Sunday," Perry grumbled upon rejoining the team. "I don't know whether they wanted to cost us more money in penalty or what.

"We're not satisfied; we're not happy, but what can you do?" Perry continued. "Everyone loses. I don't know whether there will be any hard feelings held over."[474]

Local businessman Bob Short, who was the current owner of the Texas Rangers, shared a similar sentiment. "It cost us $6 million to give the players $500,000 of their own (pension) money," said Short.[475]

Later estimates showing the owners lost approximately $5.2 million in revenue (not to mention how much in goodwill), while players lost about $600,000 (nine days pay) backed up Short's analysis. In the wake of the settlement, rumors circulated that many teams would cut their player reps during the course of the summer as punishment for leading the players' strike against management.

"I doubt that," Perry commented. "The representatives were only speaking for the players after consulting with them. They'd have to drop all the players, not just one. We were united in the strike."[476]

One curious aspect of the agreement was that no canceled games would be made up. Because each team lost a different number of games depending on their specific schedule, it was determined that pennant winners would be determined solely on a percentage basis. The Twins, who saw eight games canceled, including their entire seven-game opening homestand, were left with an official 154-game schedule for the 1972 season. In addition, that truncated schedule would include six more road games than home games for the Twins.

Back to Baseball

While the Twins may have grown closer during their informal workouts, they also suffered some physical setbacks. Pitching off the unfamiliar indoor mounds in unusual conditions, Jim Kaat developed a sore shoulder. Jim Perry also dealt with multiple issues that would fly under the radar. Not only was his training routine interrupted by his myriad duties during the strike, but he also twisted his knee working out. It was an ailment that he would deal with throughout the summer.

With both Jims not up to full speed for Opening Day, Bert Blyleven started the opener, followed by Dick Woodson in the second game. Jim Perry finally made his 1972 debut in the team's third game on April 18 at California. Perry was facing off against Nolan Ryan, who was making his first start for the Angels after being acquired from the New York Mets. Jim pitched well, limiting California to only one earned run, but he appeared to tire in the sixth and manager Bill Rigney went to the bullpen. Ryan, meanwhile, was electric in his American League debut as he carved up the Minnesota offense with ten strikeouts en route to a four-hit shutout.

When cold, rainy weather helped push Perry's next start back to a full week later at home against Boston, the veteran was rested and ready, cruising to a four-hit shutout. Scheduled to throw approximately six innings or 100 pitches, according to manager Bill Rigney, Perry needed only 102 pitches to go the distance, as he consistently worked ahead in the count throughout the afternoon.

"I feel when I go to camp in spring training I've got to do my job," the grizzled veteran explained of his ability to go the full nine in just his second outing. "Just let me go about my business and I'll be ready when the bell rings. Of course, as you get a little older you need a little more time to get in shape."[477]

Perry retired the last seven Boston hitters of the game and confirmed that he still had more in the tank at the end. "I felt I was throwing the ball in there just as well in the ninth inning as I was in the first," he said.[478]

It was Jim's 168th career win, making him the winningest active right-handed pitcher in the American League. The shutout was number 26 in his career. The victory also ran his career record to

27-13 against the Red Sox. The 27 wins were the most against Boston by any active pitcher, as well.

"I don't think about all those figures when I go out to pitch a ball game," said Perry when told of his accomplishment. "And I don't feel that old, either, to be the winningest right-hander.

"And how can I explain that record against Boston?" Jim continued, addressing the final "figure" offered up after his great day. "It's hard to pinpoint because Boston has a good hitting club today and has always been a good hitting club, particularly at Fenway. But I'll take 12 runs whenever the Twins want to give them to me."[479]

Cunning Craftsman

Jim beat the Red Sox again (for the 28th time) a week and a half later in Boston and on May 10 he combined with Wayne Granger on a 2-0 shutout of the New York Yankees. Gaylord won games for Cleveland on both those same days, prompting reporters to crowd around Jim's locker for his thoughts on the possibility of the first Perry brother matchup with his younger brother playing in the same league for the first time.

"I like that when the Perry brothers win together," said Jim, "and I hope Gaylord and I can face each other in our series this summer."[480]

"I don't think the managers would shuffle the pitching rotation to get us against each other," Jim cautioned. "But I think it would be good for both of us and good for baseball, especially if both of us pitched a good game."[481]

Some considered Jim's third win of the season to be among his craftiest performances. The Yankees led off each of the first four innings with singles but failed to score. In fact, Perry's lone 1-2-3 inning of the night came during his final inning of work.

"A lot of young pitchers get upset when they're in a jam and try to throw that much harder," explained the battle-hardened hurler. "After you've been around awhile you learn to go with your best stuff. If that's not good enough, let someone else take over. You don't have to throw the bullet (fastball) all the time. You have to keep a cool head out there and make the batter hit the pitch you want him to hit. A lot of times a hitter will be looking for a fastball. You can't be afraid to throw a change-up or curve."[482]

Manager Bill Rigney could appreciate having wise veterans like Perry and Jim Kaat on his staff. "Experience has to help them out on nights like these," said the Minnesota skipper. "Both can change speeds on their pitches, making their fastballs seem quicker than they might be.

"Each knows his own strengths and stays with it. In this game, with a runner on third base with just one out in the sixth inning, Perry changed speeds on Rich McKinney and got him to hit a line drive to shortstop. It was a soft liner, and he got out of the inning."[483]

During his final inning of work, Jim aggravated the right knee issue that he had been dealing with since he wrenched it during the pre-season workouts at St. Olaf. "It is nothing serious," he reassured all concerned after the game, "but I didn't want to take any chances on getting hurt or blowing the game."[484]

Dry Patch

Whether it was the injury or just misfortune, both Perry and the team were about to enter a tough stretch beginning the very next day. On Friday, May 12, the Twins and Milwaukee Brewers played 21 innings before their game was halted by the 1 a.m. American League curfew rule. When they picked up the action the next afternoon, the two teams only needed one inning before the Brewers won it, but they proceeded to play 15 more innings in Saturday's regularly scheduled game before Minnesota finally pulled it out. The pair of games lasting a combined 37 innings was a new American League record and perhaps the grueling weekend took something out of the Twins. Though they managed to win again on Sunday over Milwaukee, they lost six of their next seven to begin a 10-15 stretch that saw Minnesota fall from leading the division by a game-and-a-half to third place, six games back of first-place Oakland.

That dry patch for the team was just as difficult for Perry. He made six starts, posting a 1-4 record with an unsightly 6.14 ERA. Even during this frustrating time, however, Jim managed to mix in some fun. With brother Gaylord now in the American League, accusations of him throwing a spitball were causing much consternation among opposing players and managers. One manager who had been particularly outspoken was Jim's good friend and former boss, Billy Martin, now at the helm of the Tigers.

Just Add Water

On Saturday, June 3, before his start in Detroit, Jim engaged in some friendly gamesmanship with his old skipper. Twins beat writer Jon Roe provided an account of the high jinks:

"Perry, brother of Cleveland's Gaylord Perry, had greeted Tigers manager Billy Martin with a friendly handshake. But Perry had coated his right hand with grease to chide Martin about accusations that brother Gaylord threw some sort of grease, vaseline, or hair-cream pitch. Martin and Perry had both enjoyed the joke and when Perry faced the Tigers' leadoff batter, Dick McAuliffe, he went through several exaggerated motions suggesting he was 'loading' his pitches—adjusting his cap and putting his right hand to the back of his head."[485]

Jim retired McAuliffe on a pop out, but Aurelio Rodriguez followed with a single before Gates Brown hit a two-run homer. McAuliffe got revenge his next time up, pounding a three-run home run, putting Jim and the Twins in an early 5-2 hole. Perry would retire 13 of the next 14, allowing only a walk, but the damage was done. He had retired 12 straight hitters when Rigney pinch-hit for him in the sixth inning, but Minnesota could only muster one more run and Jim absorbed the loss, dropping his record to 4-4.

The following weekend, the Twins traveled to Cleveland where Jim did not pitch, but brother Gaylord hurled a complete game 7-1 win over Minnesota, striking out 11 Twins in the process. While Gaylord was dominating the Twins, Jim's name was starting to come up in trade rumors. Minnesota was looking for a bat to offset the absence of all-star outfielder Tony Oliva who had yet to play in 1972 due to a right knee injury. While teams in the pennant race valued Jim's veteran experience, the Twins, who were quickly falling off the pace in the A.L. West, were debating the need to start rebuilding with youth. It was not surprising that Billy Martin, who had his Detroit Tigers in first place in the American League East division, might have interest in acquiring his former ace starter before the June 15 trade deadline.

On Monday, June 12, Billy Martin and the Tigers arrived in Minnesota for a three-game series. Reporters naturally went immediately to Martin for comment on the rumors.

"I have a lot of respect for Perry," said Martin. "After all, Perry won 20 games for me in 1969—the first time he had ever won 20. But Perry is 35 years old. We're going to get a pitcher but it won't be Perry."[486]

The following night, Martin got to see firsthand that the 35-year old Perry still had plenty to offer, as Jim limited Detroit to one run in a rain-shortened 3-1 Minnesota win. Despite gusty winds and heavy rain causing a 40-minute delay in the fourth inning, the sage veteran returned to the mound, throwing two more shutout innings before the rain returned. After a 12-minute delay, the tarp came off a second time, but Perry could only make one pitch to begin the seventh inning before the skies opened up yet again, this time with no sign of letting up. The game was called 30 minutes later and Jim had himself a complete game win—the only shortened complete game of his career.

Twins president Calvin Griffith, who said he would be watching Perry closely as he considered potential trades, was pleased with what he saw from the veteran. "I thought he looked real good once he got going," said Griffith.[487]

Perry agreed with the assessment. "I felt a lot better tonight. A guy can get into a rut sometimes and he can't get out of it. It can happen to a pitcher or it can happen to a hitter, like with some of our guys right now. The batter is told to hit the ball up the middle and he tries as hard as he can. But it always looks like he's trying to pull the ball. The same with the pitcher. He's told to challenge the hitters and he gives it his best. But maybe to some people it doesn't look like he is. I felt like I started to get out of that rut tonight.

"As far as talk about trades," Perry continued, "I don't pay any attention to that stuff. I know what kind of a pitcher I am and I've been around long enough to know not to listen to any of that talk."[488]

The Professional

As the clock ticked down on the midnight, June 15 trade deadline, Jim was not home pacing back-and-forth nervously waiting for the phone to ring with news of a trade. Rather, he was using a rare off-day to give back to the community. With the whole family in tow, Jim was at the Crossroads Mall J.C. Penney's in St. Cloud,

Minnesota, about an hour-and-a-half northwest of Minneapolis, signing autographs for fans. As the evening wore on with fans of all ages flocking to the corner of the store for a picture autographed by the Twins' star, J.C. Penney officials could hardly believe their eyes.

"Boy, he really must be tired," one worker said to another standing nearby. "He's been at it two hours now, and he hasn't quit or slowed up yet."[489]

Finally, the crowd dissipated and Jim was preparing to depart with wife Daphne and their three kids when he shared the underappreciated difficulty of his profession with sportswriter John Jackle of the *St. Cloud Times*.

"The real hardship of any professional sport is that it takes you away from your family half the time, and I don't like being away. Like, I checked my son's (Chris) Little League schedule, and I won't be able to see him play at all during August—not even a practice. That's a common problem, though," Perry shrugged. "Harmon (Killebrew) has two boys playin' ball, and he feels bad about bein' away so much.

"To play in the majors you need a great wife that understands," Jim emphasized, putting his arm around Daphne. "My wife is a wonderful mother, AND father. She has to be when I'm away."[490]

With another day's work pleasing his fans complete, Jim Perry finally made his escape to enjoy a little of that precious family time. On his way out, Jackle made an observation as he watched the distinguished star player and family man.

"One thing stands out," wrote Jackle, "seeing his two tiny blonde daughters (Pam and Michelle) tugging at the very sleeve-ends of the lanky 6-4 pitcher's natty maroon sport coat. Those patent leather white boots of his.

"Naw, ol' Jim hasn't slowed-up any. The only hint of 14 major league seasons on the road is some gray around the temples. But even that adds to the overall atmosphere of class—the professional."[491]

Still Standing

As the trade deadline passed with the Twins standing pat, Perry The Professional went on a roll. Including his shortened complete game win over

> *Even some gray around the temples adds to Perry's overall atmosphere of class— the professional.*
>
> — John Jackle
> SPORTSWRITER

the Tigers, Jim posted a 7-4 mark over a 13-start stretch in which he compiled a sterling 2.11 ERA. With any luck, however, the hot streak could have been even better.

Following a 5-0 loss June 23 in Kansas City, Tony Oliva hung his head as he slowly peeled the tape from his aching and swollen right knee. "I feel bad tonight because I lost the game for Jim Perry," groaned the Twins' star right fielder.[492]

Perry was locked in a scoreless pitcher's duel with Paul Splittorff when Oliva bobbled a sixth-inning single, allowing an extra base and eventually Kansas City's first run. Then with two outs in the eighth inning, Oliva could only limp toward a base hit that fell toward the foul line, allowing Lou Piniella to stretch the hit into a double. That opened the floodgates to a quick four-run inning that culminated with a John Mayberry three-run homer.

"No excuse for that first error, knee or not," Oliva moaned. "I just dropped the ball when I was going to throw it. On Piniella's hit, I throw him out by 50 feet at second if I can run and get the ball."[493]

The final line that showed five runs allowed served to conceal what many considered to be the best game Perry had pitched all season. "That's the best stuff I've caught all year," marveled Twins catcher George Mitterwald after the game.[494]

Oliva, who singled twice, lifting his batting average to .321, was dejected about his inability to be an all-around contributor. In these days before the "designated hitter" gimmick, Oliva was asked if he felt he should be playing on his aching knee.

"I don't know, Oliva replied. "I want to help but tonight I lose the game. The knee hurts me more fielding and running bases than hitting, but it's weak and I can't pull the ball much."[495]

Jim would not fault his beloved teammate. Three days later it was announced that Oliva would undergo yet another operation and his 1972 season was over after only 28 at-bats.

On July 1, Jim limited the White Sox to one run over seven innings before being lifted for a pinch-hitter in the eighth inning of a 1-1 tie. Chicago proceeded to score four runs off of Dave LaRoche, Wayne Granger, and Jim Strickland, Minnesota's top three relievers, as they fell 5-1.

His next start, four days later in Boston, Jim duplicated the feat.

He again pitched seven innings while allowing just one run and even that run would not have scored if right fielder Cesar Tovar did not misplay a Carlton Fisk looping liner into a double. Opposing pitcher Marty Pattin of the Red Sox pitched a five-hit shutout as the Twins offense continued to struggle without key cog Oliva.

"Our pitchers are starving for runs," complained manager Bill Rigney.[496]

Two of the five Minnesota hits came off the bat of Jim Perry, who might have pitched a complete game if manager Bill Rigney did not feel compelled to pinch-run for his pitcher after Jim beat out an infield hit with two-outs in the eighth inning.

The next day, July 6, the Twins fired Rigney and named Jim's longtime teammate Frank Quilici to replace him. Though the bats heated up for a bit, the move did not help Minnesota's results on the field.

In all, Jim's 13-start hot streak from mid-June to early August could have easily seen Perry go 9-3 if luck would have swung his way. Perhaps he was lucky, however, considering the events of Jim's July 10 win over Milwaukee. The offense finally provided some support, scoring four runs in each of the first two innings. Jim was cruising with a six-hitter and an 8-1 lead in the eighth inning when pinch-hitter Brock Davis hit a low liner that caught Perry flush on his right thigh.

Jim was removed from the game immediately and taken to the hospital for precautionary x-rays. Though x-rays were negative and he did not miss a turn in the rotation, it is likely not a coincidence that the only two subpar starts of this mid-season hot streak came in his two outings immediately following the scare.

Great Groove

As the bruise on his thigh subsided, Jim kicked it into high gear, dominating the opposition over four consecutive starts from July 23 to August 7. He went 4-0 with a microscopic 0.26 ERA, allowing just a single run over 34⅓ innings of work. Perry allowed only 15 hits while walking just four. In the only game in which he was scored upon, a 9-1 win at Texas on August 3, Jim took a one-hitter into the ninth inning. The only hit he had allowed came on a sixth-inning bunt single by Dave Nelson.

The Rangers plated their lone run in the ninth on a pair of singles and a sac fly as Perry completed the three-hitter. After the game, Jim was far from bitter about Nelson breaking up the no-hitter with a bunt. In fact, as a fellow competitor, he tipped his cap.

"It was a good idea and a perfect bunt. If that had been the only hit I wouldn't have had any gripes coming. It was a perfect bunt just a couple of feet off the third base line. No way you'll get him out on a bunt like that. I'm not about to let losing a no-hitter bother me too much. Sure I'd like to pitch one, but all I'm concerned about is winning."[497]

Perry came back with an even better outing four days later, once again against the Rangers, this time at home. He hurled a two-hit shutout that was only overshadowed by a rare fielding feat he pulled off—an unassisted double play.

With another no-hitter going, the Rangers finally got to Perry, managing back-to-back singles to open the fifth inning. With runners at first and second and nobody out, Bill Fahey hit a soft popup between the pitcher's mound and third base. Perry let the ball drop, thinking he might be able to turn two. With his momentum carrying him toward third base, the pitcher fielded the ball off the bounce and continued in that direction. Unbeknownst to either Perry or Rich Billings, the runner on second, the umpires had called "infield fly," meaning the batter was automatically out and the runners could advance at their own risk, though they were not required to do so.

"I didn't hear the infield fly call," admitted Perry. "When I ran to third and stepped on the base for what I thought was the forceout on Billings, I got no signal of any kind from third base umpire Marty Springstead. I asked him and got no reply, so I figured something was up."[498]

"Everybody was yelling throw the ball to first base or throw it to second," Perry continued. "Someone even said throw it home. I knew I had to do something so I tagged Billings" (who, thinking he had been forced out, had wandered off third base toward the dugout and was now officially out on the tag).[499]

What Perry did do after that was throw across the infield to first base where the last remaining runner was camped out. The throw sailed high for an error, but Perry proceeded to retire the next 13 batters in order to finish off the two-hit shutout masterpiece.

"I've pitched some two-hitters before, but there aren't any of them easy," asserted a satisfied Perry.[500]

After a month-long slump, Perry was suddenly back in Cy Young form. The secret? He was finally healthy.

"I run a lot because I believe a pitcher must have strong legs," stated Perry. "I wasn't able to run during the first part of the season. During the strike, while we were practicing at St. Olaf College, I injured my right knee and couldn't run a lot between starts."[501]

"I didn't think it was serious, but I wasn't able to do my normal day-to-day running. I didn't say much about it and I continued to start in rotation every fourth day. Now my knee is sound again, I'm able to run and I'm pitching like I know I can."[502]

No Night Owl

Anyone who knows Jim Perry knows he is an early-to-bed-early-to-rise kinda guy. It dates back to growing up on the farm where "you gotta make hay while the sun's shinin.'" Sportswriter Bob Fowler characterized Perry's nightlife in a story for *The Sporting News*:

"He doesn't drink or smoke. His idea of a good time is to watch television. A night on the town means he goes to a restaurant and perhaps, a movie. For him, the 'Late Show' is the 10 o'clock news."[503]

Of course, choosing a profession with the hours of a professional baseball player certainly put such a regimen to the test. "There is so much travel in baseball and so many late nights due to the games," said Perry, "it's important for all players to take care of themselves. The ones who do last."[504]

Jim was no speed demon, either. "I don't even go fast on a snowmobile," he confessed. "(Minnesota Vikings running back) Dave Osborn loves to go fast, so when we're out together, I make sure he's ahead of me. I don't want to take any chances with him behind me."[505]

Taking care of himself meant not only being able to run, but having a healthy routine. That might explain Perry's success in day games. Following his masterful mid-summer stretch, Jim's record stood at eleven wins and nine losses. Of those 11 wins, ten had come in day games, while eight of his nine defeats had come at night.

"I get up early every day," Perry explained. When I'm pitching a day game, I can eat eggs and a small tenderloin for breakfast and go to the park to pitch. But when I'm pitching at night, I have to wait around all day and eat another meal around 3 p.m. before going to the park."[506]

Subdued Finish

Just as quickly as he got on a roll to get his record to 11-9, Jim suddenly found himself stuck in another rut, as he lost four straight starts from August 11 to August 29, all night games. When he finally took the mound for a day game on September 3 at home against Cleveland, it was under heavy clouds. Unfortunately, the Twins defense played like they were under a black cloud, committing six errors while mustering only four hits in a 4-1 defeat. Though Jim absorbed a fifth straight loss, there were subtle signs of hope.

"Perry was sharper today than he has been in three weeks," stated manager Frank Quilici. "We just didn't execute."[507]

"He had good stuff and I'm sorry to say we didn't give him much help," added catcher Glenn Borgmann, who was charged with three of the team's defensive miscues.[508]

Perry likewise was encouraged. "I think I broke five bats today," he said, noting that Cleveland's hits were all singles and each of the four runs scored via errors or outs.[509]

Sure enough, Jim stopped his personal five-game losing streak his next time out, limiting Texas to just three hits over seven shutout innings. He beat the Rangers one more time for his final win of the season on September 20 in Texas. It was also the 180th victory of his career, making Perry the winningest active pitcher in the American League. It was a bittersweet accomplishment, however, as the man he passed was teammate Jim Kaat, who had been out of action since breaking a bone in his pitching hand on July 2.

"I don't believe that makes me feel any older," said Perry of the achievement that requires the passage of time as much as it does successful performance. "I guess it means that I've stayed healthy for 14 major league seasons, and I'm not ready to retire on that. I never would have caught Kaat in victories this season. I wish we wouldn't have lost Jim and Tony Oliva to injuries—we might still be in the pennant race."[510]

Minnesota finished third in the A.L. West division with an even .500 record of 77-77, a distant 15.5 games behind the eventual World Series champion Oakland A's. The team's fade was part of the reason Jim could only manage a 2-3 September record even as he finished with a strong 2.05 ERA over the final month. His 13-16 final record masked not only his strong close to the season but also his outstanding mid-season stretch to go with a solid full-season 3.35 ERA over 218 innings.

In late October, brother Gaylord, who had won 24 games with Cleveland, was announced as winner of the 1972 American League Cy Young award, making the Perrys the first brothers to accomplish the feat. "Not even Dizzy and Paul Dean did it," said Gaylord. "I'm real thrilled."[511]

"Nobody worked any harder than Gaylord did so he deserved the honor," said his proud big brother. "He had a lot of good support behind him just like I did when I won it in 1970. It was funny. He phoned to tell me the news. But I knew all about it before he called. The entire Perry family is pretty excited."[512]

Key Player

Despite his status as a rotation anchor coming off another solid season, plus his well-earned reputation as a great teammate and clubhouse leader, Jim was once again the subject of trade rumors following the 1972 season. The Twins had suffered their lowest attendance since moving the franchise from Washington D.C. in 1961, and had reportedly lost $942,000. Following reported losses of $418,000 in 1971, owner Calvin Griffith was looking to pare payroll. With an, ahem, "astronomical" salary of $65,000, plus his age (turning 37 during the off-season), Perry was a prime candidate to be shopped. He was also a prime target for teams with legitimate pennant aspirations, due to his track record of consistent success.

While Jim's name appeared repeatedly in connection with various other teams, the Baseball Winter Meetings, where many deals often go down, came and went without any major Twins deals. As spring training approached, in fact, Jim was preparing as usual to be a key member of the Minnesota rotation. However, one thing he definitely was not doing was reporting early to training camp.

The Twins were scheduled to start spring training in Orlando, Florida on February 19, but Marvin Miller, executive director of the Players' Association, had been continuing his push for the players to gain more rights. With everything from free agency, to trade veto rights for veterans, to better pension benefits, Miller was taking a hard-line stance. Desperate to avoid another strike that could jeopardize 1973 Opening Day just as it had in '72, the owners decided to lock the players out of training camp until an agreement had been reached. As the Twins player representative, this put Jim front and center once again.

A week before training camp was scheduled to open, Twins president Calvin Griffith sent a letter to each player advising them not to report for spring training until there was an agreement. With players still at their respective off-season homes, scattered all over the country by and large, this made informal group workouts like they did the prior spring impossible. Every player was on his own to begin getting in shape. This left player rep Jim Perry the freedom to devote more time and energy to helping to forge an agreement, and he would need it, because he was set to play a major role.

Hoping to avoid the inevitable confusion brought on by having 24 player reps and their alternates all in the same room, Marvin Miller had come up with a new four-man leadership group. Along with Brooks Robinson of the Orioles, Tom Seaver of the New York Mets, and Milt Pappas of the Chicago Cubs, Jim Perry was on the owner-player negotiating committee.

"We are all anxious to go to spring training and no one is talking strike," Perry said reassuringly. "I imagine I'm going to have to go to New York sometime this week."[513]

Though he may have been reassuring about the chances of avoiding a strike, Jim was quite pessimistic about the prospect of starting spring training on time.

"When we finally get a proposal we are going to have to get a vote from all the players," he said. "That is going to take some effort. We can't get it done in a couple of days."[514]

In the days before electronic communication, tracking down and communicating with each player at various distant locations was, of course, a much more convoluted process than it is today.

"We (the four-player negotiating committee) will have lengthy discussions on the offers," Perry explained. "But the entire membership (all 900+ major league players) will have to vote on acceptance or not. This can not be done by telephone. It may call for meetings of players with (Marvin) Miller wherever most of them now are. And I would guess that means Florida and Arizona where many players will be."[515]

"Once we see how things stand, we'll poll all the players to get their vote," Perry continued. "That could take up to two or three weeks. We're all anxious to get the thing settled, and report for spring training. But I see no way we'll be training in February."[516]

Jim detailed the rule that required teams to allow a minimum of ten days of conditioning before the first exhibition game can be played, which would put games currently scheduled for the first week in March in jeopardy.

"I suppose they'll have to cancel the early exhibition games, if it comes to that," Perry concluded. "You can see that this thing could go around and around."[517]

Needless to say, Jim was helping to lead major league baseball players through uncharted territory in their fight for more rights and a greater share of MLB's growing revenues. The negotiations were intense and tight-lipped as representatives met in New York the weekend of February 17-18. In exclusive negotiating sessions with the two league presidents, Joe Cronin of the American and Chub Feeney of the National, Miller chose two player representatives to accompany him—Joe Torre of the St. Louis Cardinals, representing the National League and Jim Perry of the Twins representing the A.L.

Following the four-hour session, Torre quipped, "The only thing the owners and the players agreed on is that we won't say anything (in regard to areas of disagreement)."[518]

Upon Jim's return to his Edina, Minnesota home following the weekend of haggling, he provided a little more insight behind the news blackout. "There was so much name-calling and insinuations made last week that both sides have agreed not to say anything until this is settled," he explained. "I can't discuss what we talked about, but we did plenty of talking. I may have to return to New York this week."[519]

Perry went on to explain that Marvin Miller planned to hold a series of seven regional meetings across the country. "They are to advise the players of what is being done and to allow them to vote on the proposals made to date by the owners."[520]

By Wednesday, February 21 Jim was back in New York taking part in meetings once again, a cautiously optimistic sign that progress was being made. After more back-and-forth negotiations lasting into the subsequent weekend, on Sunday, February 25 an agreement was finally announced. It was a major agreement that contained gains heretofore only dreamed of by the players.

The players gained the right to salary arbitration—a mechanism that would play a central role in the astronomical rise in player salaries in future years. The players gained a hefty boost in benefits and in the pension plan. They gained an immediate 11-percent increase in the minimum salary (from $13,500 to $15,000) plus another ten percent rise (to $16,500) two years later. The players gained more meal money, more restrictions on teams in regard to sending veterans to the minor leagues, and the right for a player with ten years of service, the last five with the same club, to not be traded without his consent.

Present in the critical final negotiation sessions of the groundbreaking agreement were both league presidents, the owners' chief negotiator, John Gaherin, an actuary, and several attorneys from the owners' side. Representing the players were Marvin Miller, Dick Moss, counsel for the players' association, and one player—Jim Perry.

Marvin Miller credited Perry for playing a key role in bringing an end to the impasse.

"Jim Perry was a tower of strength down to the wire and all through the negotiations," said the executive director of the Players Association. "During the negotiations it's important to have on hand a knowledgeable veteran player—who knows the conditions and knows player reaction so you can check your own perception. Perry was with me the most crucial times—the last four meetings—Wednesday, Thursday, Saturday and Sunday."[521]

"I'm glad the thing is settled," said a relieved Perry. "There was a lot of work and a lot of hassling, but things worked out well. We have another meeting in Miami Wednesday morning to review and ratify the settlement. It was good to see both sides shake hands and be happy when an agreement was reached in New York City.[522]

Eight years later, during the momentous mid-season player strike of 1981, superstar Reggie Jackson paid tribute to Jim and those who fought for players' rights during these critical early days. "If it wasn't for free agency, and guys like Brooks Robinson, Jim Perry, Flood, McNally, Messersmith, and all the guys who caught hell before me," said Jackson, "I wouldn't be making the money I'm making today."[523]

> *He had no experience with unions, and yet overnight he became an efficient, dedicated leader ... Jim Perry was a tower of strength down to the wire and all through the negotiations.*
> — Marvin Miller
> EXECUTIVE DIRECTOR, MLBPA

Back to Work

With his focus on the greater good of all players, Jim had not been able to give proper attention to his own cause. "I've spent so much time on this that I haven't had a chance to get together with Calvin and talk about my own contract," he remarked.[524]

Once the agreement was unanimously approved by the 24 player reps, Jim had finally completed his immediate duties and was able to check into camp on February 28. Like many other stars, Jim had held off any individual contract negotiations until parameters of the new basic agreement were in place. Battle hardened from the just completed negotiations, Jim was now prepared to stand firm for what he felt he was worth.

"If we come to an agreement, I'll just stay here and go to work," Perry commented following an initial meeting with Twins president Calvin Griffith. "Otherwise, I'll go back to Minnesota."[525]

He was not alone. As the training camps scrambled to open, the Twins were tied with Kansas City for the most players holding out. In addition to Perry, virtually all of Minnesota's stars were slow to agree to 1973 contract terms, including Harmon Killebrew, Rod Carew, Jim Kaat, Bert Blyleven, and Danny Thompson. While three-time batting champ Tony Oliva did sign quickly, he was not happy about it.

"I need no agent," said Oliva when asked if he could have used help in his negotiations. "I talk for myself. As far as the signing,

I almost had to do it now. I need the work down here. If I don't sign while I'm here, then I go back home and it's another three or four weeks until I sign. They (the Twins) know that, and they used that."[526]

Griffith stated that he would stand firm in demanding pay cuts for several of the higher paid players. "I didn't see any of the players return any of the 35 percent to 48 percent raises when they had bad years," said the Twins president. "I'm not going to let these guys put me out of business. I've made fair offers to all of them and that's going to be it."[527]

Jim finally agreed to terms a couple days later, reportedly for close to his same 1972 salary. While the main reason for any pay cut was likely Calvin Griffith's insistence on cost-cutting as his approach to regaining profitability, another factor might have been the sudden decrease in Jim's talent utility. No longer would his above-average ability as a hitter from the pitcher's position be a useful part of his game.

Lost amid the rancor and headlines of another labor impasse was the fact that American League owners quietly voted 8-4 for the trial of a gimmick called a "designated hitter." This would allow a position player who was not starting at a defensive position to be designated to hit for the pitcher every time the pitcher's spot comes up in the order. Needless to say, this immediately lessened the value of great all-around baseball players like Jim Perry and teammate Jim Kaat who could pitch skillfully and also handle the bat. Of course, this scourge on the game is not only still with us today, but encouraged the implementation of other gimmicks that continue to subtly degrade the MLB version of America's pastime.

14

The Heist

On March 27, 1973, in a move that sent shockwaves throughout baseball, the Detroit Tigers acquired former Cy Young Award winner Jim Perry in exchange for a little known prospect named Dan Fife. The fact that Perry was traded by the belt-tightening Calvin Griffith was not unexpected, but the fact that the Twins got so little in return stunned both pundits and fans alike. Tigers manager Billy Martin, who had, of course, first put Perry in the rotation full-time four years earlier, had been urging Detroit general manager Jim Campbell to do everything possible to acquire his former ace.

Martin was ecstatic upon learning that Campbell had pulled off the deal, especially without giving up anything that would impact Detroit's immediate outlook. "Earl Weaver (Baltimore Orioles manager and chief competition in the A.L. East) will be sick when he hears about this," cackled Martin. "I think Perry is capable of winning 15 games for us this year without any problem at all."[528]

"For the first time since I've been here, I have four starters," Martin beamed. "We got the non-cheating Perry. We've been scouting him—we think he can help us win the pennant."[529]

"We're not thinking ahead to next year," Campbell emphasized. "We're trying to win this year. And we think Perry can help us. We hated to give up Fife, but he just didn't figure in our plans."[530]

Sportswriter Jim Hawkins of the *Detroit Free Press* wrote, "It's already obvious that the Perry deal ranks as one of Jim Campbell's best."[531]

Twins president Calvin Griffith denied that the trade was made for cost-cutting measures or because of any animosity related to Jim being the team's player rep and playing an instrumental role in the latest contentious negotiations. In fact, Griffith claimed that the deal was made out of necessity.

"We've got several good young pitchers in our organization," stated Griffith. "We had too many starting pitchers with Perry on the roster."[532]

When asked why the Twins could not get more in return for an established veteran like Perry than an unproven minor leaguer, Griffith had an interesting explanation. He cited the new "ten-and-five" rule that Jim himself had been instrumental in procuring for the players in the latest collective bargaining agreement just negotiated with the owners.

"It wasn't easy to make a deal for Jim, because as a ten-year major league man (with at least the last five with the current team) he can refuse to report to another club. That rule has the owners strapped. I'm sure the Tigers used that knowledge in making the deal, but what could we do? Jim agreed to play with Detroit, so we went ahead with it."[533]

After Jim was told of the trade by Griffith, he spoke on the phone with Billy Martin and then walked to the clubhouse at Tinker Field to clean out his locker. He shook hands with every man on the team and wished them all well. Then he hopped in his car and drove from the Twins training complex in Orlando over to Lakeland, Florida, where the Tigers train.

"I can't say that I'm surprised," Perry confessed. "I knew that either Jim Kaat, Bill Hands or myself would go this spring. I could see it coming. Our ball club has too many starting pitchers. I know that Billy Martin was after me, and I'm happy to be traded to a pennant contender. I'll be one of the four regular starters for the Tigers.

"I had ten great years in Minnesota. The Twins were good to me, and I believe I contributed something to them. Despite all those labor negotiations, and the part I had in them, I had a fine relationship with Calvin Griffith. Calvin assured me there were no hard feelings, and I feel the same way. It's baseball. You don't stay in one place forever."[534]

Looking ahead to joining Detroit, Jim was enthused. "I know I'm going to a great ball club, and Billy obviously has faith in me. Billy is looking for a guy who can win in double figures and I don't plan on letting him down."[535]

Ready for Action

Jim got his first exhibition game action for the Tigers on Friday, March 31, tossing six innings of one-run ball against the Braves. He wanted to throw seven innings, but manager Billy Martin took him out after six so that he could give other pitchers some action. In order to get his work in, Perry went straight to the bullpen and threw the equivalent of another inning on his own just to make sure he was building up his arm strength to his expectations.

"I could have gone eight innings if Billy had wanted me to," stated the Tigers' newest workhorse.[536]

Enthused about his performance in his first outing wearing a new uniform, Jim brimmed with optimism. "I'm even happier about the trade now," he gushed. "I know most of the Detroit players and they've accepted me. I felt real good pitching today against the Braves. In fact, I've given up just a couple of runs in my last three starts down here."[537]

Martin was confident in his ability to get Perry's best out of him. "Jim Perry's trouble in the past has been his inability at times to challenge the hitter," stated Martin. "That's the one thing I was able to convince him of in 1969 when he won 20 games for the first time. This is one thing I'll remind him about here, too."[538]

Back in Orlando at the Twins camp, some of the young pitchers were lamenting the loss of a role model and mentor. "Perry helped the younger players tremendously," explained rising star Bert Blyleven. "He is a great competitor and was sort of a master of our staff."[539]

On MLB's 1973 Opening Day, Jim may have been in a different

uniform, but his thoughts were still with his former teammates and the organization in which he became a star. He sent a wire, addressed to president Calvin Griffith that said, "Wishing you and the Minnesota Twins a successful season. Best Wishes –Jim Perry."[540]

Due to off days and weather, Jim did not make his Detroit debut until the team's sixth game on Saturday, April 14 as the season entered its second week. Despite the layoff, the veteran was ready, scattering four harmless singles over the first eight innings and carrying a shutout into the ninth. With the Tigers holding an eight-run advantage, manager Billy Martin kept Perry in to finish even as he was tiring. Three ninth inning hits leading to a pair of Cleveland runs spoiled the shutout, but still left Jim with a fine complete game win in the first outing with his new club.

Though it had been two weeks since Jim had seen game action in his final spring training start, his manager was not surprised by his effectiveness. "I know what Jim Perry can do," said Martin, beaming. "I had him when I managed Minnesota, remember? He knows how to keep himself sharp along the sidelines and he knows how to warm up."[541]

"He's one of the few pitchers who can lay off such a long time and do such a good job," Martin continued. "And he didn't complain because of the layoff."[542]

A satisfied Perry explained his preparation. "I threw 25 minutes of batting practice Wednesday (three days prior) and that helped me get ready. Tomorrow and the next day I'll workout hard, mostly running. A good sweat will help. Some pitchers like a day off after they pitch, but I don't."[543]

Not only in the same league as his little brother, but now even playing in the same A.L. East division, the odds of a Perry brothers matchup were higher than ever, but they missed by one day this time. Gaylord pitched a gem of his own the day after Jim's masterpiece, shutting out the Tigers with a two-hitter on April 15.

Before his team faced off against Gaylord, Billy Martin bemoaned the prospect of going up against the purported spitball specialist. "I told my players to bring along their raincoats," Martin quipped. "I just don't understand how one boy (Jim) can turn out so well while another (Gaylord) from the same mother cheats."[544]

In Jim's next start, four days later in Boston, it was more of the same. Once again, he carried a shutout into the ninth inning before giving up a meaningless run in a 7-1 complete game victory. The Red Sox could manage only five singles the entire night and did not even get a runner past first base until the final frame. Tigers manager Billy Martin was ecstatic.

"If Perry keeps pitching the way he is right now, he's going to have a banner year," raved the Detroit skipper. "He's challenging hitters now, the way he pitched for me in Minnesota. Last year he had a tendency to pitch away from guys but now he's going after them again. I'll tell you this, Jim Perry is a lot more of a competitor than most people give him credit for being."[545]

"It sure helps to have all those hits behind you," said Perry. "When you've got a big lead and you go out there in the late innings, all you want to do then is get the ball over the plate with something on it. You don't have to pick your spot the way you do in a tight game."[546]

> I'll tell you this, Jim Perry is a lot more of a competitor than most people give him credit for being.
> — Billy Martin
> LEGENDARY MANAGER

"It's not an easy ballclub to pitch against," Perry explained after running his lifetime record against the Red Sox to 29-15, the best mark of any active pitcher. "You just try to keep them off balance, to keep them off-stride so they can't pull the ball."[547]

"This is a different ball club than the Boston I used to beat," Perry continued. "This is a tougher ball club with much tougher hitters than the Red Sox used to have."[548]

No-Lucker

Jim finally suffered his first loss of the season, a 5-3 decision, on April 22 in Baltimore, but it was his second defeat on April 27 at home against Kansas City that was particularly difficult to stomach. While Jim came within one out of his third complete game, Steve Busby of the Royals no-hit the Tigers in a 3-0 loss. It was the first no-hitter in the American League since Oakland's Vida Blue handcuffed the Twins September 21, 1970. Of course, Jim Perry was the hard-luck pitcher on the other side of that one, as well.

Ever the gentleman, just as he had done following Blue's

masterpiece, Jim phoned over to the visiting clubhouse to offer congratulations to his opponent. "You pitched a great game," Jim told Busby.

"I wish I had the control you had," Busby replied, referring to his six walks compared to Perry's two.

"You had the wildness to get the job done," Perry countered.

"I had to call him," Jim explained. "It isn't every day a pitcher throws a no-hitter. I had to congratulate him."[549]

"Perry pitched well enough to win," stated a frustrated Billy Martin. "We've had good pitching, we're just not hitting right now."[550]

Close Shave

Jim bounced back with a win in his next start and then got his revenge in a rematch with Busby in Kansas City on May 9. The Tigers got to Busby early, knocking him out of the game after three innings, while Perry allowed only a solo home run to John Mayberry over eight innings of work. John Hiller finished up for the save in a 3-1 Detroit win.

The game was marred by a bench-clearing incident that involved Perry and Kansas City left fielder Lou Piniella. In the seventh inning with Piniella at the plate, Perry brushed him back with a good fastball that rode up and in. On the next pitch, Piniella swung and missed, with his bat flying through the air in the general direction of the pitcher's mound. Both teams spilled out onto the field, but cooler heads prevailed, although not before Detroit utilityman Ike Brown had confiscated Piniella's bat and busted it against the artificial turf.

"I don't think a guy should get away with throwing his bat at the pitcher," explained Brown. "Everybody knows (Piniella) did it on purpose. If you've got any guts, go on out there to the mound and get the man but don't throw the bat."[551]

Detroit manager Billy Martin admitted that Perry's chin music was tight, but stated that is part of the game. "The ball was close," Martin admitted, "and he probably threw the bat. Moving a guy back is part of the game. When the ball's not thrown at your head, you have no argument."[552]

As for the principal culprits in the ordeal, Jim provided more insight into what took place. "When Piniella grounded to first in the fourth inning and I ran over to cover the bag, he yelled at me, 'I don't like your brother, and I don't like you either.' So when he came up to bat the next time, I dusted him."

Piniella, who was known for losing his bat during his swing, must have known that he started the events leading to the fracas, because he quickly moved to put an end to it. ""Let's just leave it on the field," he said. "It's all forgotten."[553]

Best Start Ever

On May 17, Jim hooked up with John Curtis of the Red Sox in a pitcher's duel that remained scoreless into the bottom of the eighth inning. Detroit's 37-year old second baseman Tony Taylor finally broke the deadlock with an opposite field home run to give the Tigers a 1-0 lead. Perry then finished off Boston in the ninth, working around an error and a walk to notch his third complete game of the season and the 28th shutout of his career. Perry, who had skipped his normal between-starts bullpen after manager Billy Martin moved his start up a day, felt strong throughout the night.

"I threw the ball harder in the last inning than the first," Perry claimed after running his career record against Boston to 30-15.[554]

Because of a doubleheader on May 20 and manager Billy Martin's desire to stick with his four-man rotation of Mickey Lolich, Joe Coleman, Woodie Fryman and Perry, he brought Jim back after his complete game shutout to start the second game of the twin bill on only two days rest. Jim gave his usual yeoman's effort, bouncing back after a three-run first to throw five scoreless innings against Milwaukee before John Hiller finished up the 5-3 Detroit win.

Thankfully, an off day in the schedule enabled Jim to get four days off before he would make his next start on May 25 at home against the A's. The rest would come in handy as Perry faced off against Oakland ace Catfish Hunter. The two traded goose eggs for nine innings in a fantastic pitcher's duel. When Detroit's Mickey Stanley and Gates Brown got to Hunter for back-to-back singles leading off the bottom of the ninth, A's manager Dick Williams went to the bullpen. Darold Knowles struck out Duke Sims and then Rollie Fingers whiffed both Tony Taylor and Dick McAuliffe to send the game into extra innings.

Detroit manager Billy Martin kept his faith in Perry, who rewarded him with another scoreless frame, leading to another great opportunity for a Tigers victory in the bottom of the tenth. Ed Brinkman doubled with two outs, but was subsequently called out on a head-first slide at home trying to score on a single by Mickey Stanley. Brinkman jumped to his feet, screaming in protest, but was quickly overtaken by a beet-red Martin, who came flying out of the Detroit dugout, furiously going after home plate umpire Larry McCoy. Martin appeared to bump McCoy repeatedly as the two went nose-to-nose before second base umpire Nestor Chylak could wrangle Martin into a bear hug and wrestle him off the field.

Perry worked one more scoreless frame, giving him 11 innings of sensational five-hit, one-walk shutout work before John Hiller finally took over in the 12th. The Tigers finally pulled out the win in 13 innings, but after the game all Billy Martin wanted to talk about was the call at home plate.

"The umpire took a win away from Jim Perry right there," said the Tigers skipper, still steaming. "He flat took it away. That was an out-and-out screwed up call. It was one of the worst calls I've ever seen in this game. This is the winning run. Anything close like that goes to the runner."[555]

Even after being stuck with a no decision despite 11 brilliant shutout innings, Jim Perry was off to the best start of his 15-year major league career. He had a 6-2 record with a sensational 1.82 ERA while pitching eight or more innings in six of his first ten starts. That heavy workload was about to catch up with him.

Heavy Load

Jim lost three of his next four starts, twice failing to make it out of the first inning. Even after his longest outing during this cold spell, Jim could feel that something wasn't right. He pitched into the seventh inning in a 4-0 loss at Oakland, but was still flummoxed.

"I'm not pitching like I want to," the veteran admitted. "I know some people are saying I'm not challenging the hitters, or I'm not doing this, or I'm not doing that, but that's just not true. This was just one of those games. When things go wrong they all seem to go wrong. You're going to have games like that. There's not much you can do about it.

"I'm not trying to alibi, but something's just not there. I don't know what it is. It's just something I've got to work out. I didn't pitch all that badly. I made only one bad pitch all day. But that doesn't make much difference now, does it?"[556]

Perry righted the ship on June 18 at Cleveland. He was locked in as he hurled a four-hit complete game in a 5-1 Detroit win.

"I was keeping the ball down and had good control," Jim explained. "I threw a variety of pitches, but I had a good sinker and kept ahead of the hitters."[557]

Again Jim barely missed matching up with Gaylord, who had pitched the day before and was suffering through a streak of six straight starts without a win. Asked if he had any advice for his younger brother, Jim said, "When I see him after the game we probably won't even talk baseball."[558]

Catch A Train

Jim's next start was scheduled for June 22 in New York against the Yankees. Early that morning, however, a steady rain began in New York City and continued throughout the day with no signs of stopping. If there was anyone who knew how to play this, it was former longtime Yankee player and current Detroit manager Billy Martin. Convinced the field would be too wet to play even in the unlikely event the rain were to let up, Martin concocted an ingenious plan. By moving the team bus back from 5 p.m. to 6 p.m., that would give the Yankees more time to announce the inevitable postponement and thus prevent the need for the Tigers to waste time and energy traveling to and from Yankee Stadium.

Shortly after five o'clock, however, a funny thing happened. The rain suddenly subsided, the skies cleared, and the sun shined down on the rain-soaked streets of midtown Manhattan where the Tigers were staying. The Yankees announced that the field was playable and it was all systems go for what now projected to be a beautiful summer evening. So, with only 90 minutes remaining before the scheduled 7:30 p.m. first pitch, the Tigers began their seven-mile trek over to the Bronx.

As nice as the evening was now shaping up to be, however, the daylong rain showers had left the Friday evening New York City rush hour traffic even more of a snarled mess than usual. Into the fray the Tigers bus began inching its way down Madison Avenue through five lanes of bumper-to-bumper traffic, block by block. After about 45 minutes had passed (the time it normally takes a team bus to make the trip), they were less than halfway there.

With the realization that he would have limited time to warm up, Jim Perry, that night's starting pitcher, began pacing up and down the narrow aisle of the bus in order "to get loose" while Martin took increasingly nervous glances at his watch. With Yankee Stadium still more than two miles away and the bus stuck at a standstill near 134th street, manager Billy Martin suddenly stood up, loosened his tie, slung his coat over his shoulder, plopped an unlit cigar into his mouth, and ordered the starting lineup off the bus. They would beat the traffic jam by taking the subway, Martin announced. Though nobody knew where the nearest subway station was nor which train would take them to the stadium once they found it, anything was better than being stuck on that bus, as far as their fearless leader was concerned.

If they asked a dozen people along the way how to get to Yankee Stadium, they must have got a half-dozen different answers. The group finally found a station and boarded the White Plains Road Line, though nobody was convinced that was the right train. They soon realized it wasn't, so they got off and changed to a train that would successfully get them to the 161st Street station.

The Martin-led platoon finally arrived at 7:40 p.m., sprinting from the subway station to Yankee Stadium, only to find the team bus had arrived ten minutes earlier. When the television broadcast began back in Detroit, viewers were surprised to see a substitute from *Sports Illustrated* filling in for the familiar voices of George Kell and Larry Osterman, who had also taken alternate routes to the ballpark. Osterman had tagged along with Martin's subway brigade, while Kell reported that he took a taxi cab part way, before he finally got out and ran the rest of the way. The game finally got underway at 8:05, a full 35 minutes late.

For starting pitchers who are so used to a set pre-game routine, the chaotic scene presented quite a hurdle. As usual, however, Perry rose to the occasion. He had allowed only two second-inning runs before Thurman Munson hit a solo home run to start the bottom of the seventh. With a 4-3 lead, Martin went to the bullpen leaving Jim in line for the win, but Fred Scherman promptly gave up two runs and the Tigers went down to a 5-4 defeat.

Short Rest Showdown

Jim's next outing came on Monday, June 25 in Boston before a national television audience in primetime with the inimitable Howard Cosell calling the action. Amazingly, Jim was starting on only two days rest for the third time, in part because Joe Coleman and Mickey Lolich had pitched in a doubleheader the day before and Billy Martin continued to stick exclusively with his four-man rotation. In fact, Perry's last start on short rest had been his complete game win over Cleveland, which also happened to mark Detroit's last win. With the team in the midst of its worst stretch of the season, Martin hoped Perry could put an end to a losing streak that had reached seven games.

While Dependable Perry would always do his best to answer the call, he had another reason for getting keyed up to pitch on this night. Brother Gaylord was pitching this same night against the Yankees. With the Tigers set to meet the Indians for a four-game series the following week, a start by Jim on this night would make the odds of the long-awaited Perry brothers showdown better than ever.

"He wanted it, revealed Martin. "He figured about when Gaylord would pitch, and I went along with him."[559]

Even on short rest, Jim was on his game, matching Boston lefty Bill Lee in a pitcher's duel. Unfortunately, the sputtering Tigers offense could muster only an Al Kaline solo home run. Boston tied it in the sixth with a Rick Miller RBI single and then Carlton Fisk broke a 1-1 deadlock with a one-out homer off Perry in the bottom of the eighth. That blow proved to be the difference in a hard-luck 2-1 loss. Jim finished off the inning to register his fifth complete game, but the Red Sox were able to sneak out with the win against their long-time nemesis.

"Any time you get a run off Jim Perry it's like money in the bank," remarked Fisk. "I hit a good slider."[560]

The loss marked the fifth consecutive one-run defeat for the reeling Tigers, who had quickly fallen seven games behind the first-place New York Yankees in the American League East.

Battle of Brothers

The event that had been anticipated for years finally came to fruition on July 3, 1973, as the Perry brothers faced off in a major league regular season game. One local paper billed the matchup as "Good vs. Evil," while Detroit manager Billy Martin was telling everyone it was "the honest one against the cheat."

In the wake of his 1972 Cy Young award winning season, Gaylord found himself under the microscope more than ever as his reputation had preceded his arrival to the American League. After his great first year in the A.L., players and managers alike were voicing complaints about not only Gaylord, but other pitchers accused of "loading up" the baseball.

The uproar had become so pronounced, in fact, that in Gaylord's previous start, June 29 in New York, the Yankees had reportedly set up a "special closed-circuit camera" that would "be equipped with slow-motion and stop-action." The camera was trained on Gaylord throughout the game so that "experts" could study his every move in order "to determine once and for all, whether he uses a foreign substance on the ball, and if he does, to see if we can put a stop to it."[561]

While Jim took great pains to avoid getting in the middle of his brother's spitball shenanigans, the looming marquee matchup forced him to finally weigh in.

"What he throws is a forkball," said Jim, alluding to the similar drop. "We've talked about it. If you make what he throws illegal, why not make the knuckleball illegal? It moves just as much."[562]

Gaylord was not the only pitcher accused of doing something to the baseball and throwing an illegal pitch, but he famously went through a series of gyrations on the mound before each delivery, rubbing his fingers behind his ear, wiping his brow, then the back of his neck, under his cap, under his arm, etc. It was this routine followed by a devastating pitch that really aggravated opponents. They contended he was gathering a clear medicinal jelly hidden at various places around his body. The ensuing complaints were about a "grease ball" more than anything involving actual saliva. It was not uncommon, in fact, for opponents to beg the umpire to make Gaylord wipe himself off with a towel on the mound in the middle of an inning.

Asked what he thought about all the fuss made by others around the league, not the least of which was his own manager, Jim replied with a smile. "It's great. Look at all the publicity (Gaylord) gets. Maybe I should start doing all that stuff."[563]

Jim added that all the commotion caused by the controversy "could throw someone off, make him upset. But I don't think it really bothers my brother. Nothing aggravates him."[564]

If Jim felt that way, he certainly didn't prevent his manager from trying. Of all Gaylord's aggravated opponents, Detroit manager Billy Martin was among the most vocal. The day prior to the matchup, Martin said he was "trying to get a German shepherd dog, and so is Jim. We told Gaylord I had one trained to sniff out that greasy stuff he's supposed to use."[565]

As Martin chuckled at his prank, a diabolical twist occurred to him. "Hey, wouldn't it be something if the dog bit Jim, and I found out he was using the stuff, too?"[566]

The gag was enough to make an impression on Gaylord, apparently. When word began to circulate the day of the game that Martin, indeed, had a German shepherd chained in the umpires quarters that was specially trained to sniff out grease on a person's body, a Cleveland official called down to the Tigers staff in the visiting clubhouse to emphasize that animals were not permitted in the stadium.

And so it went, with the first regular-season matchup of brothers in the 73-year history of the American League providing a light-hearted oasis in the midst of the marathon grind of the long season more than it elicited any kind of high-tension drama. Before the teams squared off the day before, Jim and Gaylord clowned around for the benefit of reporters during a pre-game photo op. Gaylord even demonstrated his "forkball" grip for the cameras, and Jim lifted Gaylord's cap off his head purportedly looking "to find where he hides it," but both promised it would be all business when they took the mound.

"I'm going to try to beat him and he's going to try to beat me," stated Jim. "I hope we both pitch good games. I hope I win."[567]

"It's a different feeling," Jim admitted. "We pitched against each other once in spring training, but that's different. That was in 1961 or 1962 when I was with Cleveland and he was with San Francisco. I think I won, 4-3."[568]

Historic Rivalry

Indeed, the two did face off in 1962, when the Indians hosted the Giants in Tucson, Arizona on March 10. Both Jim and Gaylord entered as relievers in the fourth inning. Jim worked three shutout innings, allowing only one hit, while Gaylord was tagged for four runs on five hits in two innings of work. The Tribe held on for a 5-4 victory and Jim was awarded the win while Gaylord suffered the loss.

However, Jim was likely thinking of a much more high profile showdown that occurred between the two brothers in the following spring of '63. Cactus League play in Arizona had wrapped up and the Giants were beginning a barnstorming tour with the Cleveland Indians up the coast of California for their final week of exhibition play. The first game was scheduled for March 31, a Saturday night under the lights at Westgate Park in San Diego, home of the minor league Padres. The game was also being televised back to the Giants local audience up the coast in San Francisco, so for being only an exhibition game, it was kind of a big deal.

The local promoter in San Diego thought it would really be great for ticket sales if he could sell a matchup of the Perry brothers. Young Gaylord was still a longshot to crack the San Francisco rotation after making seven starts as a rookie in 1962, and Jim was already battling his back-and-forth battle between the bullpen and the rotation. Both pitchers were ticketed to begin the 1963 season in bullpen roles, but both clubs surprisingly agreed to the exhibition matchup.

After Cleveland scored a run in the top of the first off Gaylord, Willie McCovey stepped up and launched a towering home run off of Jim to tie it at one. It was a prodigious blast down the right field line that cleared a high bank beyond the outfield fence and was estimated by some to be a 480-foot shot. That brought cleanup hitter Willie Mays to the plate.

Jim's first pitch was a hard fastball up and in that sent Mays diving into the dirt. San Francisco manager Alvin Dark immediately began yakking at home plate umpire Chris Pelekoudas.

"That's it," yelled Dark sarcastically in a voice loud enough to be heard clearly up in the press box. "Wait for somebody to get hurt."[569]

Pelekoudas turned to the Giants bench and waved his hand high, indicating that the pitch was not quite as close as the extreme evasive action by Mays made it appear.

"I always throw Mays high and tight," Jim would later declare. "He doesn't like the ball there. He always goes down at anything close. Everybody knows that."[570]

"Well, Alvin didn't know that," said Gaylord. "He began pacing up and down like a steam boiler itching to blow. He kept looking at me, but he said nothing. His usual response to that situation was, 'You know what to do.' Or, 'Take care of that.' That meant knock 'em down. As I went to the mound, he mumbled something."[571]

Jim retired Mays without any further issue to end the inning, but Jim's catcher, John Romano, was the first batter up in the top of the second. When Gaylord promptly beaned Romano in the shoulder, Pelekoudas yelled, "Hold everything!" and called for both managers.

"Dark wouldn't budge out of the Giants dugout until (Cleveland manager) Birdie Tebbetts started out of Cleveland's," according to Giants beat writer Harry Jupiter. "Alvin and Birdie and the four umps conferred, with Pelekoudas doing most of the talking. They finally broke up with Alvin tossing a 'who started it?' rejoinder over his shoulder on the way back to the bench."[572]

Upon Dark's return to the San Francisco dugout, "Alvin smiled at me," Gaylord recalled. "Later in a team meeting, he said, 'I could never ask a brother to hit a brother. But I knew you'd take care of it, Gaylord. I appreciate what you did out there.'"[573]

As Harry Jupiter documented, "The boys behaved themselves after that, giving the 5,894 fans in Westgate Park a tight, interesting contest."[574]

Woodie Held belted a home run one batter later, giving Cleveland a 3-1 lead. Jim would give up a couple more long homers, one by Giants catcher Tom Haller in the bottom of the second and another off the bat of McCovey in the third, but he settled in after that. With the game tied at four in the top of the fourth, Jim laid down a key bunt that led to Cleveland's fifth and final run. "Neither Perry looked long for this game," according to Jupiter, "but both settled down after that for some brilliant hurling."[575]

The Giants threatened in the fifth when McCovey singled and immediately caught catcher Romano off guard with a surprising steal of second base. Jim responded by striking out the middle of the Giants order—Mays, Orlando Cepeda, and Felipe Alou, 1-2-3.

The final play of the night was an unusual 3-6-1 double play with Jim expertly covering first to take the game-ending relay from shortstop Tony Martinez. Jupiter called it "a whale of a play" and it secured a 5-4 win for Jim and the Indians over brother Gaylord and the Giants.

Both brothers went the distance, pitching nine-inning complete games—in spring training! A half century later, with incessant counting of pitches having taken control of the game, it is a feat that is difficult to imagine, and certainly one that is unlikely to ever be matched.

Decade-Long Wait

Finally, ten years later, the two were about to meet for the first time in the regular season. A lot had changed since the brothers last faced off.

"When we were in different leagues we used to pitch on the same day a lot," Jim continued, alluding to the feeling that this matchup might be imminent at some point. "But last year it didn't work out that way."[576]

"We talk, but we've been all over the country," Jim explained in regard to discussions over the years about a potential showdown. "Sometimes the time difference makes it tough. We did kid about it when we got in the same league.

"I used to tell him I was going to pitch close to him and he used to tell me the same thing. Now we don't hit anymore (due to the designated hitter gimmick)."[577]

Tigers manager Billy Martin summed up the situation. "It'll be a good game. They're both good competitors."[578]

Jim's final summation was a bit more ominous. "He's family, but he's on the other side of the fence."[579]

Gametime

Considering the buildup, the game itself was a bit anticlimactic. Not only was neither brother in Cy Young form, but the scourge that is the DH removed the pitcher-batter showdown that would have inevitably evoked memories of facing off back on the farm under Daddy's watchful eye.

The Tigers immediately jumped on Gaylord, as Norm Cash blasted a two-run homer in the top of the first inning, quickly dashing hopes of the anticipated brotherly pitching duel. Jim held up his end of the bargain early, retiring the first eight batters he faced before nine-hole hitter Leo Cardenas finally broke the string with a harmless two-out single to center in the bottom of the third. Still holding the 2-0 lead in the fourth inning, Jim encountered his first trouble of the night and controversy ensued.

John Lowenstein looped a single to open the inning and then cleanup hitter John Ellis worked a one out walk, bringing Cleveland's designated hitter Charlie Spikes to the plate. Jim snapped off a slider that the right-handed hitting Spikes managed to slice out toward the right field foul pole. As the looping liner crossed over the fence, first base umpire Merle Anthony signaled that the ball hit the foul pole, making it a fair ball and a three-run home run.

The players in the Tigers bullpen, located just a few feet away went berserk, with several later insisting the ball was foul by at least a foot. Anthony's opinion was the only one that mattered, of course, and Jim and the Tigers were suddenly down a run.

After a shutout fifth inning, Jim was touched up for another home run, this one unquestioned off the bat of Oscar Gamble. When George Hendrick followed with an opposite field double two outs later, Martin pulled the plug on the historic confrontation, replacing Jim with Ed Farmer, who got out of the inning.

Now staked to a 4-2 lead, Gaylord was unable to capitalize. Norm Cash, leading off the top of the seventh, took Gaylord deep for the second time, sparking a three-run rally that not only knocked Gaylord out of the game, but made him the losing pitcher and gave Jim a no-decision in the 5-4 final—the same score and team result, amazingly enough, as both their 1962 and 1963 exhibition matchups.

"I just couldn't handle Cash tonight," lamented Gaylord. "He hit two of my forkballs."[580]

"I should have won that game. That ball was definitely foul" said Jim, clearly frustrated over what he felt was a blown call on the Spikes home run.[581]

Despite their respective disappointment, the brothers were grudgingly complimentary towards each other.

"Jim pitched good until Spikes' homer," said Gaylord, though even he later conceded the Spikes home run was foul.[582]

"Gaylord pitched pretty good, but he got some bad breaks," said Jim. "That bad pitch to Cash and that wild pitch and passed ball in the seventh."[583]

Asked about any pre-game interaction between brothers, Gaylord said, "We wished each other luck before the game and that was that."[584]

Gaylord said he hoped it was not the last time they would get to face off. "I'd like to pitch against him again. Both of us will have to do a better job, though. Maybe if we pitched against each other again it would do us some good."[585]

Bad Luck or No Luck

With the "Battle of Brothers" in the rear view mirror, it was back to the regular season grind. The Tigers were fighting to get back into the pennant race and Jim was nursing a 2-1 sixth inning lead in Kansas City on July 7 when the Royals generated a rally that seemed to typify Jim's luck when it turned bad.

Royals catcher and number nine hitter Fran Healy chopped a slow bouncer toward third and beat the throw for a one-out hit. Then Jim broke the bat of leadoff man Freddie Patek, but the looping liner dropped into center field, taking a high bounce off the Royals Stadium artificial turf and over the head of center fielder Mickey Stanley. This put runners on second and third. Jim induced a ground ball to the left side by the next hitter, Cookie Rojas, but it squirted into left field for a single, scoring both runs. Jim was suddenly trailing 3-2 in an inning that could have just as easily gone 1-2-3.

A two-run homer by Amos Otis in the eighth inning finished off the scoring, but the fact that his manager allowed him to pick up his sixth complete game of the season was more of a reflection on Jim's pitching than the 5-2 final. The Detroit offense, which was limited to four hits and ranked third from the bottom in the American League with a .245 team batting average was the more concerning culprit.

Father-Son-Daughter?!!

One of the highlights for any MLB player's son is getting the chance to take the field and play against Dad in the annual "Father-Son" exhibition game many teams often held before one of their regular season games. On July 10 of the 1973 season, the Tigers held their ninth annual "Father and Son" game prior to their game with the Texas Rangers. However, this year's game was marked by good-natured controversy.

Prior to the festivities, eleven daughters of Tigers players, including Jim Perry's two girls, Pam (7) and Michelle (4), staged a protest on the field. The girls marched with signs, including one that read "Remember Ypsi," demanding the right to join the boys in the game. The reference was in regard to a controversy earlier in the spring of '73 in nearby Ypsilanti, Michigan that captured nationwide attention as a girl tried out for the local Little League team.

Though national Little League official rules prevented girls from competing, the local chapter had allowed Carolyn King, a 12-year old with a strong arm to try out. When she made the team, Little League International threatened to pull the Ypsilanti charter. When local league officials grudgingly relented, the Ypsilanti City Council responded by saying that if King was not permitted to play, they would not allow the league to use the city's fields. This forced the local league to again reverse course and when King took the field with her team for their first game on May 10, the stands were packed with fans as television crews filmed one of the biggest events in the city's history. When Little League International followed through with revoking the Ypsilanti Little League's charter, it set off a landmark sexual discrimination lawsuit.

Against this backdrop, it was only natural that the daughters of Detroit players be considered for the first time in this family-oriented event. As honorary "commissioner" of the event, Ed Browalski of the *Polish Daily News*, who also served as the Tigers' official scorer, ruled that yes, the girls could play! So eleven daughters joined 14 sons and the kids went on to pummel Tigers pitcher Woodie Fryman for 25 runs on 25 hits. It became apparent early on that the Dads were in trouble, as the umpires, Sonny Elliot and Oopsy the Clown overwhelmingly sided with the kids on virtually all calls, both close and otherwise.

Seven-year old Pam Perry, sporting a fresh chaw of Bazooka bubble gum, whacked a double with her oversized Fat Albert bat to key the early scoring. Eleven-year old Chris Perry, the eventual winning pitcher, raised some eyebrows as well as the suspicions of Dads manager Norm Cash when he took the mound carrying a metal pail labeled "Unk Gaylord's Gunk." When Cash pleaded with home plate umpire Sonny Elliot to do something, Elliot gave young Chris the once-over, carefully inspecting behind his ears and around his cap. Similar to his MLB umpiring brethren, however, Elliot could find nothing incriminating, and allowed Chris to go back to work on what would be a stunning shutout of the Dads.

When father Jim stepped up to bat, he prepared for the first offering from his son. Chris peered in for the sign, then reached down into the metal bucket, went into his windup, and fired across the plate one big, red tomato. Daddy Jim swung and–*splat!*–sent pieces of tomato spraying everywhere. With no evidence of a "hit," Jim was naturally called out and Chris continued with his shutout. Unsurprisingly, under the guidance of big Frank Howard, father of six, the Boys (and Girls) cruised to a 25-0 win over their famous fathers with many laughs and great fun had by all.

Three Times No-No

The family fun seemed to loosen up the Tigers hitters, as they immediately went on a rampage, scoring 34 runs over the next four games, all of them wins. Jim was the beneficiary of a 14-run explosion on July 11 that included eight RBIs by leadoff man Jim Northrup. Although Perry had retired the last seven hitters he faced and could easily have gone the distance in the 14-2 blowout, he gave way to reliever Ed Farmer for the final two innings. Manager Billy Martin had mentioned the day before that he was going to make a concerted effort to decrease the stress he was placing on his starting pitchers, including the possible use of a fifth starter. The move here was likely related to that intention.

Detroit's five-game win streak and sudden hitting prowess all came to a screeching halt on Sunday, July 15, as Jim was hit with more tough luck. For the second time in the 1973 season and the third time within three years, Jim had the misfortune of being on the opposing side of a no-hitter. This time it was Nolan Ryan of the California Angels, who carved up the Detroit offense with 17 strikeouts. For Ryan, who was on his way to setting the modern day MLB single-season strikeout record, it was his second no-hitter of the season, coming two months to the day after his first in Kansas City.

Even as Ryan was dominating Detroit, Jim was giving his team every chance, holding the Angels to one run on just four hits through seven innings. Just as in Jim's prior start, Martin elected to go to the bullpen in the eighth. This time, the move opened the floodgates, as the Angels tacked on five runs, giving Ryan plenty of cushion to finish off the no-no.

Second-Half Roller Coaster

The All-Star break came at a good time for the Tigers, who limped to the end of the first half, dropping six of their last seven games. Standing 49-48 in fourth place, six games out of first, things were looking bleak for a team filled with aging veterans. The three day break provided a much needed respite, however, and Detroit came storming out to begin the second half. The Tigers won eight in a row and 17 of their first 21 second half games. Jim Perry was a big part of the surge, going 2-0 with a 2.42 ERA as the Tigers rocketed into first place, a game-and-a-half ahead of second-place Baltimore.

On August 12, Jim won the sixteenth game of that hot streak—his second in a row—with a complete game effort in a 6-2 win over the White Sox. Though he had a shutout going until giving up two meaningless ninth inning runs, Jim was not satisfied with giving up eleven hits.

"I've pitched better . . . I'm still not satisfied," he said softly as he packed his bag for the pending 13-game, two-week, four-city road trip.

"I know what I'm doing wrong—it's just a question of getting myself straightened out," Perry continued. "At least this time the umpire (Jerry Neudecker) gave me the corner pitches—and that's something I haven't been getting. I'm not asking for anything extra—I just think strikes should be called strikes. I'm not a 'down the middle of the plate' pitcher. That's just not me. And if the umpires won't call the pitches on the corners strikes, I'm in trouble.

"It makes a difference when you get a few runs to work with," Perry added, in deference to the pair his offense provided on this day in each of the first, third, and fourth innings. "When you go out there and you're two or three runs behind right away, you're pitching on the defense all the time. But when you're ahead the whole time, it makes a big difference—you're on the offense then."[586]

Manager Billy Martin credited not just the offensive support, but also some extra rest he had scripted out for his 37-year old veteran. Prior to winning his last two starts, Martin skipped Perry the first August turn through the rotation and he promised to do it again in order to keep Jim fresh.

"After his next outing he'll get something like seven days rest," promised the skipper, waving the sheet on which he had sketched out his projected pitching lineup through the end of the month.[587]

Even in this August 12 start by Perry, Martin was focused on getting rest for certain overworked hurlers. Chicago had plated a pair of ninth inning runs off of the starter, Perry, cutting the score to 6-2. They had runners on first and second with two outs when Martin made his only mound visit of the game.

His message to Perry? "I want to give (bullpen ace John) Hiller another day of rest."[588]

Message received. Just as Hiller got up in the bullpen and began to get loose, Jim promptly induced a routine grounder to second by Carlos May, ending the game.

Despite Martin's careful handling of his pitchers' workloads, the two-week road trip proved too much for the team, as the Tigers won only five of the 13 games. At the same time, the Baltimore Orioles went on a 13-game winning streak. After Detroit lost their first game back at home on August 28, they had gone from a game-and-a-half up to a full seven games back of Baltimore.

Jim captured one of Detroit's few road victories with a 4-2

win over Chicago on August 25 in a nationally televised Saturday afternoon Game of the Week. He scattered nine hits while walking no one and allowing just one run over the first eight innings. After Carlos May got to him for a solo home run to open the ninth, closer John Hiller came on to nail down the win for his 29th save.

Tigers Tension

Detroit hosted the Cleveland Indians for a four-game series beginning Thursday, August 30, but there was no rearranging of the pitching rotations to orchestrate a Perry brothers rematch. With a season that once held such high hopes quickly slipping away, the tension surrounding the Tigers and manager Billy Martin was running far too high for any kind of family frivolity. In fact, while Gaylord was in the midst of tossing a six-hit shutout in the first game of the series, Martin decided he had finally seen enough.

Just minutes after Gaylord had finished serving up a 3-0 defeat that pushed Detroit to seven-and-a-half games out, their greatest deficit of the season, Martin made a stunning announcement to the reporters gathered in his clubhouse office.

"Joe Coleman and Fred Scherman (Detroit's two pitchers in that game) were throwing spitballs the last two innings . . . on my orders," Martin shouted, his voice full of frustrated rage.

"They are making a mockery of the game, letting Perry get away with that spitter or greaser or whatever you want to call it. And as long as they let him get away with it I'm going to have my guys doing it too, only next time it will be from the first inning, not the eighth."[589]

Martin apparently had resorted to these drastic measures only after home plate umpire Red Flaherty failed to carry out a requested inspection of the perpetrator to the Detroit skipper's satisfaction.

"He didn't check him properly," Martin argued. "He puts the stuff in his eyebrows and his hair . . . I even know where he puts it on the ball—on the insignia. And you mean to tell me an umpire can't find the stuff?!?"[590]

"I'm trying to stay in contention in a pennant race and there's a pitcher out there cheating like hell and four umpires won't do anything to stop him," Martin continued. "I think I should do something to bring it to a head and I'm going to have my guys throw spitters every time Perry goes against us.

"If they take that pitch away from him, you won't see him around after the fifth inning because he'll be knocked off the box. He's a great competitor—I'll give him that—but without that pitch he'd be just another pitcher."[591]

The following morning, Martin was suspended without pay for three days by American League president Joe Cronin. Then, on the morning of Sunday, September 2, as Martin prepared to serve the final game of his suspension, he was suddenly fired. Detroit general manager Jim Campbell made the surprising announcement less than an hour before the team took the field for their final game of the series with Cleveland.

Doing the Job

Though he had just lost his friend, advocate, and respected boss, Jim Perry had a job to do. He was starting that day and, like the true professional that he is, he went out and did it. Jim held the Indians to one run over six innings, notching his 13th victory of the season in a 2-1 Tigers win.

Third base coach Joe Schultz, who filled in as manager during Martin's suspension, was named interim skipper for the remainder of the season, but the Tigers were just playing out the string at that point. Detroit went 13-12 the rest of the way, finishing a distant third, twelve games behind A.L. East champion Baltimore.

Unlike the Tigers, Jim did get some good news during the season's final month, as it was announced on September 21 that he and brother Gaylord would be inducted into the North Carolina Sports Hall of Fame on December 4. Perhaps buoyed by that news, Jim went out that night and beat the Boston Red Sox for the 31st time in his career. Jim gave up just one run on five hits before John Hiller came on with one out in the sixth for yet another multi-inning save, his 38th of the year—a new MLB record. It was a truly remarkable year for the Tigers bullpen ace, who posted a 1.44 ERA over 125 relief innings in 65 appearances. He finished fourth in both American League Cy Young and MVP voting.

While Jim finished the 1973 season with a disappointing 4.03

ERA, his record of 14-13 could have been better with some luck, or even just a little less misfortune. He also pitched 203 innings, which certainly carried value, not to mention his veteran leadership. With Detroit's "play for today" manager sent packing, however, the team was now focused on rebuilding with youth, and any remaining future for Jim Perry on the mound would likely not be with the Tigers. In an era still before free agency, however, it would be up to the team to dictate where Perry's future would be.

15

Brothers in Arms

More than 1,100 people crowded into Minges Coliseum on the East Carolina University campus Tuesday, December 4, 1973 to see Jim and Gaylord Perry inducted into the North Carolina Sports Hall of Fame. It was the largest crowd in the Hall's history to see the famous brothers inducted along with NASCAR legend Richard Petty and two-time Olympic decathlete bronze medal winner Floyd "Chunk" Simmons.

The banquet was classic North Carolina, featuring barbecue, fried chicken, brunswick stew, slaw, barbecue-boiled potatoes and hush puppies. It was a southern feast so fine that some attendees were reportedly moved to tears.

According to Gerald Martin of the *Raleigh News and Observer*, the event "was impressive without hoopla, a happening of importance for North Carolinians that prompted genuine pride among those inducted and those responsible for the success of the eleventh annual awards... Though none of the four inductees appeared awestricken by the ceremony, each was visibly moved, accepting the induction with sincerity and appreciation."[592]

"We both owe much to our father and mother," said Jim. "They sacrificed for the things we needed as kids."[593]

Moving Time

As the winter progressed, both Perrys saw their name connected to trade rumors. Though he had won the American League Cy Young award in 1972, his first season in Cleveland, Gaylord had slipped to a 19-19 record with a 3.38 ERA in '73. While he still threw a ridiculous 344 innings and hurled a league-leading 29 complete games, the Indians, who had finished in last place, 20 games under .500, were hoping that a trade of Gaylord for multiple pieces could somehow help them to improve.

"I keep waiting for the phone to ring," said Gaylord. "I'm very happy in Cleveland. I'd like to stay. But I can't blame them for trying to improve the club if they can."[594]

One reason Gaylord enjoyed playing for Cleveland was because it was in the same time zone, just a day's drive from his old hometown of Williamston, North Carolina, where his family had recently returned. They had been living in San Francisco during Gaylord's time with the Giants, but with the realization of the transiency of an MLB career following his first trade, he and wife Blanche decided having a more permanent "home base" in an area they both loved made sense.

"We decided we wanted to give the children a place they could always call home," Blanche explained. "We loaded up our car and a van with our two horses, and we gathered up the two cats and a dog and came back to Williamston."[595]

This led some to wonder why Jim, now no longer a member of the Twins, would keep his family up in the frozen winter tundra of Minnesota. Besides the easy access to many offseason hunting options, which Jim enjoyed, his family had established roots in the Edina, Minnesota community. Both daughters, Pam and Michelle, were becoming proficient ice skaters, but they weren't the only ones making the best of Minnesota's winter weather.

"My 12-year old boy is crazy about hockey," Jim explained of son Chris, who was already in his fourth year of involvement in the popular cold climate sport. "He just made what they call Beltline team in Edina. They only keep 17 boys out of about 85 who tryout. He could play 60 games this season if his team makes the playoffs."[596]

Not Done Yet

Although it had been assumed since Billy Martin's firing that Jim, along with many other veterans would be traded away amidst a Tigers youth movement, Jim found himself still with Detroit as spring training arrived. As the oldest pitcher in the league in terms of service and second-oldest by age (reliever Bob Veale of Boston, preparing for his final season, was two days older) Jim knew that he could not afford to provide an opening for a younger pitcher to grab his spot in the rotation. Despite that concern, Jim Perry reported to the Tigers spring training facility comfortable in his own skin.

"Management knows what us older guys can do," Perry stated confidently. "I know what I have to do to get ready and that's all I'm trying to do—get in shape as quickly as I can. I'm not trying to impress everybody. I'm just trying to impress myself.

"I want to be a starter," Perry continued. "I still can do the job as a starting pitcher. Whether it would be every four days or every five days, I don't know. But I wouldn't be here doing all this if I didn't think I could still do the job. And when I can't, I'll go ahead and stop. Nobody is going to have to tell me."[597]

Jim went to work having his normal solid spring. Tigers manager Ralph Houk mentioned Jim specifically as one of the veterans who had impressed him. When he wasn't refining his pitching skills, Jim was showing off his refined golf game.

In early March, Jim joined some 166 players, managers, coaches, front-office personnel, and local amateurs in the annual Pasadena Golf Club Major League Golf Tournament in St. Petersburg, Florida. Jim tied Tom Seaver of the New York Mets for low gross of 80, but under the Calloway system of scoring in the event of a tie (each golfer throws out his three worst holes), Jim was declared the winner. He received the Governor's Cup plus a portable television set for his efforts on a cold, windy afternoon, while Seaver settled for a set of irons.

Together Again

Just as Jim seemed to be settling in for a second season in the Tigers rotation, he received surprising news. On March 19, a little more than two weeks before the start of the 1974 regular season, Detroit announced a complicated three-team, five-player trade that would send Jim to Cleveland. Technically, Perry was traded along with fellow pitcher Ed Farmer from Detroit to the New York Yankees in exchange for catcher Jerry Moses. The Yankees then sent Perry to Cleveland in exchange for outfielder Walt Williams and rookie pitcher Rich Sawyer.

While it was not a surprise to see one of the Perry brothers traded, it was something of a shock that they would somehow end up together. Despite Cleveland's best efforts to extract a massive haul in exchange for Gaylord, potential trades during the 1973 World Series and again during the Winter Meetings all fell through. Though several clubs made offers, none were willing to send Cleveland what they felt was a suitable package for a pitcher capable of throwing 300+ innings.

The Perry brothers were suddenly reunited for the first time since they won the North Carolina state championship together at Williamston High School. In fact, Cleveland general manager Phil Seghi made it sound as if this was his master plan from the start.

"We've upgraded our pitching staff with a 14-game winner," Seghi stated in explaining his rationale for making the deal. "We're giving our farm system pitchers more time to develop and we've helped stabilize our lineup."[598]

Seghi claimed he had been trying to reunite the brothers for more than a year. "I was interested in Jim (when the Tigers traded for him), but we weren't able to satisfy the Twins," stated the Tribe general manager.[599]

Cleveland manager Ken Aspromonte was pleased with the sudden prospect of multiple Perrys on his pitching staff as opposed to none. "As far as I'm concerned I'd like to keep Gaylord to give us a kind of continuity," said the third-year skipper. "Our infield and outfield are stabilizing themselves. I don't want to trade Gaylord now."[600]

"I'm really excited to be joining Gaylord," said Jim. "We've talked over the phone so many times. I'd face a club and Gaylord would call me to find out who was hitting. It was a kind of scouting report between us.

"It'll be great going back to Cleveland, my old stomping grounds," Jim continued. "The trade is a complete surprise. I just hope Kenny (Aspromonte, Cleveland manager) is planning lots of work for me."[601]

If the trade was a complete surprise to Jim, such was not the case for Gaylord, who had an inkling something could be in the works. Cleveland general manager Phil Seghi had "talked to me about the possibility for the past three days," Gaylord revealed. "I told him Jim was in good shape and that I thought he could help us. Jim always has been dedicated. When a team gets in a slump it needs an experienced pitcher, and Jim will help. They need old guys like us to stabilize this staff."[602]

"I hope the brother combination can do a good job and get fans back in the park the way they used to come," said Jim, as he recalled coming up with a Cleveland team that regularly challenged for the pennant. "It'll be a challenge. Some will see it as brother fighting brother to see which is better—to see which one will win the most games. But that's good. We'll both be trying to win for the team."[603]

The one man who knew them best disagreed. "Gaylord made up his mind to out-do Jim," father Evan chuckled. "You just watch the family rivalry between those two boys this summer. If their arms hold up and the boys behind them help with their gloves, it wouldn't surprise me none to see 'em both win twenty."[604]

"Just let me say I'm sure we'll both do well," Jim clarified. We've both been around long enough to know what we've got to do without trying to over-do it. Naturally, I hope we both can become leaders, but we're not too old to listen and still learn."[605]

Jim touched on how the trade was especially good news for Mom and Dad. "I guess our parents are happiest about it because now they can root for the same team and visit both of us in one trip instead of having to make two."[606]

Same Ol' Jim

Tribe manager Ken Aspromonte immediately installed Jim as Cleveland's third starter after Gaylord and Dick Tidrow. The 27-year old Tidrow had gone 14-16 while throwing 275 innings over 40 starts the prior season.

Spending spring training in central Florida ever since joining the Twins, Jim returned to Arizona for his first spring action since 1963. His first appearance back in a Cleveland uniform came on March 26 in an exhibition game against the California Angels in Tucson. Though he allowed three runs on nine hits in five innings of work, his new manager was suitably impressed.

"Same old Jim Perry," said Tribe skipper Ken Aspromonte. "He's the kind of a guy you've got to hit to beat. They did, but I thought Jim pitched well, considering he's had an eight day layoff. (Jim had last pitched three shutout innings March 18 with the Tigers in West Palm Beach, Florida the day before the trade.)

"Jim showed me style . . . he pitched for the corners, moved the ball in and out and obviously, he knows how to pitch. He pitches the way you'd like to teach your kids how to pitch."[607]

> Jim Perry pitches the way you'd like to teach your kids how to pitch.
> — Ken Aspromonte
> CLEVELAND MANAGER

As the start of the 1974 season approached, Aspromonte penciled in another brotherly oddity, as he set up the answer to the question, what brother combination pitched two season openers in the same year for the same club? Gaylord was set to start the season opener against the New York Yankees in Shea Stadium, where they were playing while Yankee Stadium was undergoing a two-year long renovation. Although the Indians were scheduled to play three games there against the Yankees, Aspromonte felt that holding his third starter back to start the fourth game—the home opener in front of an expected 40,000 fans would be ideal.

"He has the experience and fits right into my rotation," Aspromonte explained of Jim Perry. "And I think the fans would like it too."[608]

The season did not get underway as the team or their fans hoped. After getting swept by the Yankees, Cleveland returned home to snow and freezing temperatures that saw their home opener, along with Jim's return, pushed back a day. When he finally took the mound to face the Milwaukee Brewers on Wednesday, April 10, it was in front of barely more than half of the expected crowd and in bitter cold conditions.

Jim pitched well, limiting Milwaukee to only two runs on five hits over eight innings. With the game tied at two in the ninth, Jim issued a one out walk to Darrell Porter followed by a single off the bat of Bob Coluccio. Concerned his veteran starter might be tiring, Aspromonte went to the bullpen. Restless fans took aim at the hapless Tribe skipper with catcalls and snowballs as he made his way to the mound.

Reliever Cecil Upshaw retired Pedro Garcia with a strikeout, but pinch-hitter Bob Sheldon worked an eight-pitch walk, bringing up veteran Don Money with the bases loaded. When Money pulled a 1-2 pitch over the left field wall for his first career grand slam, it prompted a barrage of snow and iceballs so heavy that home plate umpire Jim Evans was forced to raise his chest protector over his head in an act of self-defense.

Indians catcher Dave Duncan hit a home run in the bottom of the ninth, but it was not enough as Cleveland dropped their fourth straight game, 6-4. After the game, Duncan was upset about the behavior of the fans.

"I don't understand why they've gotta do it," he said. "It's stupid and immature. Someone could get hurt. You're talking about a career. A piece of ice could hit you in the eye. I'm sure no one meant any harm; it's all fun and games, but they ought to think."[609]

Turning his attention to the game action, Duncan added, "Perry threw good, in case anyone cares about something positive."[610]

While disappointed in the result, Jim took it in stride, as usual. "The walk could've gone either way," he reasoned, "and I had the next fellow set up pretty well. He just stuck out his bat and hit it.

"I've seen things like this before," said the philosophical veteran. "It's nothing to get upset about. You just go out and do your best next time."[611]

Cleveland finally got into the win column two games later, as Gaylord pitched a four-hitter. Jim likewise picked up his first win in his second start, again working into the ninth against the Brewers, this time in Milwaukee. He had allowed only one run on four hits and one walk until a pair of ninth inning singles led to the second run scoring after reliever Ken Sanders took over. The 3-2 win took just over two hours to complete, something that was not unusual when Perry was on his game.

"I don't like to take too much time," Jim explained. "When things are going good, you don't like to change your rhythm. I think it is easier to stay alert when things are happening all the time."[612]

Scared Straight

After snapping their season-opening five game skid, Cleveland won four out of five, but the Indians went right back to their losing ways. They had dropped three straight, falling to 4-9, when Jim took the mound for his third start April 21 in Boston. For the third straight time, Jim worked into the ninth inning and for the third straight time the bullpen allowed his runners to score as he watched helplessly from the dugout bench. This time, the Red Sox killer had his Indians in front 5-1 when he was lifted after the first two batters in the ninth reached on a walk and a single. Not only did a trio of Cleveland relievers fail to prevent Jim's runners from scoring, but they failed to hold the four-run lead. Boston tied it in the ninth and then won it in the tenth, prompting a postgame tirade by manager Ken Aspromonte. The clubhouse was closed for thirty minutes after the game, as Aspromonte aired out the 4-10 ballclub.

"I felt it had to be done," explained the exasperated Cleveland manager. "We have offense and we have defense. But I'm pleading with the pitchers. They have to wake up and do a job or they're going. These are veteran pitchers. They know what it takes. They have to deliver, is all. How can they blame anybody else? They are pitching, nobody else."[613]

Aspromonte did not say it, but he undoubtedly meant "pitchers not named Perry," most specifically those in the bullpen. Gaylord, who was 1-1 with a 2.67 ERA, gave Aspromonte 15 innings in his lone no-decision before relief pitcher Ken Sanders replaced him in the sixteenth inning and promptly served up a game-losing home run to the first batter he faced. Jim could have been even better with some help from the pen. Currently 1-1 with a 3.29 earned run average, he could just as easily have been 3-0 with a 1.47 ERA. Of nine runs charged to Jim through three starts, five had crossed the plate in the ninth inning while a reliever was on the mound.

Perhaps the tongue lashing did some good because the team bounced back the next day with a 2-1 win, although Gaylord left nothing to chance by going the distance. The win began a hot stretch in which Cleveland won 11 out of 14 games to climb all the way up into second place, just a game back of the first place Yankees.

It's A Business

Gaylord's April 23 win was the 179th of his career. Added to Jim's 195, the combined total of 374 made the brothers the winningest pair in modern day MLB history. While that is an undeniable fact, and was made mention of by many scribes of the day, the "accomplishment" was somewhat tongue-in-cheek. The previous record was held by the Mathewson brothers. Hall-of-famer Christy had 373 career wins while his brother Henry was winless in three career games covering 11 innings between 1906 and 1907. That the Perrys were the best brother combo was an undeniable fact that had been self evident for some time. Still, it was nice to make it official. The all-time record of 385 held by a trio from the Clarkson family, one of which was 1800s hall-of-famer John (328 wins), would go down before the summer was over.

"It means something that we set the record while we're on the same team," said Gaylord. "We can enjoy it together. But it's not something we thought about all the time we were growing up."[614]

While Jim said attaining the record was "great," he was most proud of his and Gaylord's work ethic and consistency. "The most important thing is having stayed healthy, taking good care of ourselves.

"I'm 37, and I can't throw like I did when I was 18," Jim continued. "But I've learned a lot more about pitching. We're both the same sort of pitcher, I think. We move the ball in and out, up and down. You can't let them get any kind of a pattern on you. You're always trying to think ahead of the batters.

"If you have real good stuff, you can just go at them—like Nolan

Ryan, for instance. If you don't have real good stuff, sometimes you can still get them out. Gaylord is more of a strikeout pitcher than I am, but we both like to make them hit the ball and not walk anybody. We both take pride in what we do.

"It's like being president of a company," the thoughtful veteran concluded. "There are a lot of eyes on you all the time. People watching, people across the country reading about you the next day. It's a business for us."[615]

Fastest Ever

Jim proceeded to take care of business in his next start April 27 against the Angels, contributing to Cleveland's late April hot streak by tossing the team's first shutout of the season. He allowed just four singles, didn't walk a batter, and permitted only two runners to get past first base. Most encouraging of all, Jim got better as the game progressed, retiring the last 15 California batters in order.

While the final score was 6-0, Jim had to nurse a 1-0 lead until the Tribe broke it open late. Charlie Spikes hit a solo home run in the eighth inning and Oscar Gamble capped off a four-run ninth inning rally with a two-run shot. Following the game, catcher Dave Duncan raved about Jim's masterful 104-pitch performance.

"I was trying to think of a time he didn't put the ball where I wanted it, and I can't," said Duncan. "Control's the name of the game. Some pitchers overpower you with velocity; he does it with control. If he needs the double play, he keeps the ball down. He knows how to pitch and his execution was excellent. It's easy to work with a guy like that. It makes the game fun."[616]

> Jim Perry knows how to pitch and his execution was excellent. It's easy to work with a guy like that. It makes the game fun.
> — Dave Duncan
> ALL-STAR CATCHER

The admiration was mutual. "Duncan's been calling a heck of a game," Perry pointed out. "He's a good catcher, and when he's not hitting it doesn't seem to bother his calling the ballgame. He shakes it off and goes about his business."[617]

With Perry (no walks) and opposing starter Bill Stoneman (one walk) both filling up the strike zone, the game was completed in a ridiculous one hour and 51 minutes. It was the tenth time in his career that Jim had finished off a complete game in less than two hours. He would pull off the amazing trick three more times before he was done. In fact, pitching fast complete games was Jim Perry's trademark.

Of 109 career complete games, 105 of them were nine innings (three went extra frames). Of those 105 nine-inning complete games, 42 (40%) were finished within two hours and 15 minutes. In fact, the career average for a Jim Perry nine inning complete game was two hours and nineteen minutes.

"I work pretty fast," reiterated Perry, "unless I'm getting hit all over the place. The guys like it better that way. I moved the ball around, changed speeds, hit spots, kept the ball down and got away with a few pitches. I felt good . . . felt strong. It was a nice day."[618]

Jim's characterization of "pretty fast" was an understatement, according to teammate Frank Duffy. "Jim Perry is the fastest working pitcher I've ever seen," exclaimed Cleveland's slick-fielding shortstop. "I love to work behind him. He runs to the mound, takes the two or three warmup pitches and almost before we get a chance to get the ball from the first baseman, he's ready to go.

"I would have said Gaylord before Jim came to us because he works relatively quick, too," Duffy continued. "But Jim works faster. You can count on him spending less than an hour in the first four or five innings. I can remember in the first year I was here, I'd look at the clock in center field and it would be something like two hours and ten minutes and we'd just be going into the sixth inning.

"It's tough when a pitcher goes to a full count on almost every batter, or goes to the resin bag, steps off the mound on every pitch. It's irritating. Your mind wanders and it's tough to stay in the game.

"Jim makes them hit the ball on the ground, he doesn't strike out many, there's always a lot of action. You have to be concentrating on the game all the time and he works so quick, it's easy to concentrate."[619]

> Jim Perry is the fastest working pitcher I've ever seen. I love to work behind him... He works so quick, it's easy to concentrate.
> — Frank Duffy
> 10-YEAR MLB SHORTSTOP

Perry x 2 = Right

Angels manager Bobby Winkles was among those impressed by the way Jim carved up his lineup. Winkles stated that Cleveland should be rated pennant contenders due to their improved pitching. "With the two Perry brothers pitching, how can you go wrong?" the Angels skipper asked rhetorically.[620]

When the Indians finished off a 7-2 West Coast road swing with a three-game sweep of the Angels in early May, however, Winkles was singing a different tune. Jim stymied the Angels for five shutout innings on May 7 before a defensive miscue allowed them to tie it, but Cleveland scored late to pull out a 5-3 win and a frustrated Winkles went into a post-game tirade with reporters.

"I'm not so sure (Gaylord's) brother didn't throw a few wet ones tonight," Winkles complained. "I know Gaylord throws the spitter. He's kidding us and the umpires if he wants us to think those are all his new forkballs. It looks like he's taught his brother a little something, too."[621]

Of course, Jim has long denied ever doing anything untoward to a baseball, and it's more than likely that Winkles was just venting frustration. In almost the next breath, the California skipper admitted as much. "Maybe it's mental," Winkles confessed of the Angels inability to beat Cleveland.[622]

Honoring Mom

Because the Perry brothers had been key to the hot start of the Indians, the team came up with a surprise to honor their work and achievements. The team announced that Ruby and Evan Perry were being flown in to Cleveland to celebrate Mother's Day with their boys. Jim was scheduled to pitch one game of a doubleheader on that day, May 12, with Gaylord due to follow the next day, so Mom and Dad would stay to see both.

"We can't pick up the Indians games on the radio very often down here," said the proud mother from her home back in Williamston, North Carolina. "But one of our neighbors, a blind lady, can pick up all the games. She always calls and tells me what happened.

"I can't believe (us coming to Cleveland to see the boys together) is going to happen," Ruby continued. "My boys always call me on

Mother's Day, but it's been 15 years since we've been together on Mother's Day."[623]

Unfortunately, Mother Nature did not cooperate with the best laid Mother's Day plans. A steady rain began in Cleveland shortly after the Indians got bombed by Baltimore, 12-1, on Saturday afternoon. The rain continued throughout the night and into the late hours of Mother's Day morning, leading to the postponement of both the doubleheader and the Perry matriarch festivities.

Ruby and Evan were able to stick around, fortunately, and watch Jim start the next day, followed by Gaylord the day after that. Both came up winners over Boston, vaulting the Indians into first place in the American League East. Jim's win was an emotionally-charged game, as an outstanding outing suddenly went awry late.

Cleveland cleanup hitter John Ellis blasted a first inning three-run homer to provide an early cushion. Jim gave one back in the second, but cruised after that, allowing just one single over the next five innings, though he did issue an uncharacteristic three free passes. Leading 4-1 as he went to work in the top of the eighth inning, Jim got Rick Miller to ground to shortstop Frank Duffy for what looked like a routine first out.

First baseman John Ellis was forced to tag Miller after Duffy's throw took him off the bag, but umpire Merlyn Anthony did not see the tag. Vociferous pleading by Cleveland manager Ken Aspromonte revealed that Anthony was only watching Ellis' feet, causing him to miss the tag. When Anthony finally asked home plate umpire Bill Kunkle for assistance, Kunkle claimed that he didn't see the play. Miller was safe, and when Jim walked the next hitter, Cecil Cooper, with Carlton Fisk, Carl Yastrzemski, and Bernie Carbo coming up, Aspromonte went to the bullpen.

A clearly frustrated Perry visibly gestured to the first base umpire as he walked off the field. "I don't usually say anything to umpires," Jim revealed. "But I told him I was bearing down and I wanted him to bear down, too."[624]

"If we had gotten Miller," Perry continued, "maybe I could have gone all the way. I tried to be too careful after that. I tried to keep the ball down to get the double play but it kept sinking and running away although all the pitches were close."[625]

"I had a good sinker and kept the ball down but I just kept missing the corners, which caused many three and two counts," Jim confessed.[626]

The full counts contributed to a pitch count that exceeded 100 in the first five innings, putting the starter on a tight leash by his manager. "Perry was getting tired," said Aspromonte. "He was throwing a lot of pitches. After he walked Cooper, I had to take him out. And I had a good man in the bullpen."[627]

That "good man" was Tom Buskey, recently acquired in a trade with the Yankees. Just as Aspromonte hoped, Buskey got out of the jam and retired the side in the ninth to preserve Jim's third win.

Solid Pro

Facing Detroit for the first time on May 18, Jim failed to get revenge against the team that traded him away two months prior, but he pitched another solid game. The Tigers had managed only one unearned run through six innings, but they finally broke through in the seventh. After Aurelio Rodriguez singled with one out, Ed Brinkman tied the game with an opposite-field liner that got down into the right field corner for a triple. Lefty-swinging John Knox then punched a soft single to left that brought home Brinkman with the third and eventual winning run.

"They were both good pitches," asserted dejected catcher Dave Duncan. "A fastball away to Knox and a slider away to Brinkman, right where we wanted them. Brinkman doesn't usually hit the ball on the line to right field. He's usually over more and up in the air when he hits to right."[628]

"Perry pitched real good," Detroit manager Ralph Houk agreed. "He's a good, solid professional pitcher."[629]

Jim suffered another tough-luck no-decision in a May 22 start at Baltimore. Locked in a scoreless pitching duel with Ross Grimsley, Cleveland got a runner to third with one out in the eighth inning. 24-year old Jack Heidemann, making his first start of the year, had beat out an infield hit to open the inning and advanced on an error followed by a sacrifice bunt. Mistakenly thinking a squeeze play was on, Heidemann excitedly took off for home on the 2-0 pitch to number two hitter John Lowenstein. When Lowenstein lofted a long fly ball to right field, Heidemann had to put on the brakes and scurry back to third base rather than tag up to score the easy go-ahead run.

After not allowing a runner past second base for ten innings of shutout pitching, Jim finally gave way to the bullpen in the eleventh inning. The Indians lost it when Baltimore scored a run in the bottom of the twelfth off of Tom Buskey, who had just saved Jim's previous win. Though he was not the losing pitcher, it was another missed opportunity, as Jim continued to do excellent work during his second tour in Cleveland.

No Rest for the Weary

In his next start, Jim was the victim of one of the unseen challenges of performing as a professional athlete. On Sunday, May 26, the Indians played a day game in Detroit, which they lost, 2-1. The game ended at 3:40 p.m., after which the team dressed and bussed to Detroit Metropolitan Airport, where they arrived around 5:30. Because they were flying commercial (not charter), the team could not book an early flight, just in case the game had gone extra innings or encountered some other delay. The only available flight did not leave until 11 p.m.

After the team finally boarded the American Airlines flight at 10:30 p.m., a mechanical problem was discovered and another plane had to be prepared. The team, along with various other commercial travelers, finally took off at 11:30 p.m. and landed in Indianapolis a little less than an hour later. Some passengers got off, but many more boarded, leading to a full flight to Dallas, Texas, the team's final destination.

The layover was quick, but the team did not land in Dallas until 2:30 a.m., central time, followed by an hour-long charter bus drive to the team hotel. By the time they got checked in, got to their rooms, and got to bed, it is likely that most players did not get to sleep until after 4 a.m. They then had to play a game against the Texas Rangers that evening. With that preparation, it is not surprising that the Rangers Jim Bibby tossed a three-hit shutout at the Indians. Though Jim was able to match Bibby for five innings, Texas finally got to him in the sixth, plating four runs on the way to a 6-0 defeat.

Cleveland manager Ken Aspromonte eventually came up with

the solution of sending the starting pitchers into a city one day ahead of the club when changing cities without the convenience of a charter flight. Gaylord was one of the vocal supporters of the sensible decision. "Now that we fly commercial, it's a great help to get a good night's sleep in the town you're going to work in."[630]

Lead by Example

As Cleveland remained a contender into the heat of summer, Jim's impact on the surprising Indians went beyond his exploits on the mound. His veteran leadership made a team-wide impact, which is no small tribute for a pitcher. A prime example was 26-year old part-time outfielder, Leron Lee. Though Lee entered the 1974 season with 1,274 MLB at-bats accumulated over 451 games in five seasons, he had never received a chance to prove himself on an everyday basis.

When third baseman Buddy Bell was disabled in late May with a knee injury, however, starting left fielder John Lowenstein was moved to replace Bell at third, opening up left for Lee to play every day. He responded by going on a tear, batting .424 with three home runs and ten RBIs over the first eight games of June. Lee's tear played a key role in a hot streak that helped the team recover from a late May slump and push them back into contention.

Lee was quick to credit Jim for helping him to stay ready while waiting for his chance. Of course, that had long been Jim Perry's specialty.

"Jim runs for about twenty minutes almost every day, so I figured if he can do it, so can I," the muscular Lee related.[631] So the two regularly ran together, part-time hitter and starting pitcher—a baseball odd couple.

"I've been telling Leron to stay ready," Perry explained. "Don't let up, and don't get down on yourself because we're going to need you sooner or later. It's hard for a guy in his position to stay in good shape. I know, because I've been in that spot myself. But you've got to push yourself all the time. Leron did, and when the time came, he was ready."[632]

"I owe Jim a lot for his encouragement," said the appreciative Lee.[633]

Two years later Lee would sign to play in Japan, becoming one of the first American players to do so during his prime. He starred for 11 seasons with the Lotte Orions, where he set the Nippon Pro Baseball record for career batting average with a lifetime .320 mark.

Lee hit two home runs on June 1, including a grand slam to account for all the Cleveland scoring in Jim's 5-2 complete game victory over Kansas City. The win evened Jim's record at 4-4, which belied his fine 2.51 ERA. The slugging outfielder bemoaned the lack of support his running mate had been receiving.

"It's been tough for him," said Lee. "Jim has been pitching so well and we haven't been getting any runs. If we had, he'd probably be 7-3 right now."[634]

Fight Night

"That was the closest you're ever gonna be to seeing someone get killed in this game of baseball."[635] That was Texas manager Billy Martin's assessment after the Indians were forced to forfeit their June 4, 1974 game to the Texas Rangers on "Ten Cent Beer Night" at Cleveland Municipal Stadium. Not surprisingly, gentleman Jim Perry was smack dab in the middle of it, trying to bring peace.

It all started the week before in Arlington when Lenny Randle made a hard slide into second base in the fourth inning. Indians second baseman Jack Brohamer called the "rolling block slide" a "cheap shot," which seemed to be the beginning of ill will between the two clubs. Randle singled and came around to score in the seventh inning without issue, but when he came up to bat again in the eighth inning, Cleveland relief pitcher Milt Wilcox put the first pitch slightly behind his feet, causing the left-handed hitting Randle to jump. The second pitch was also inside, but called a strike.

On the 1-1 pitch, Randle dragged a bunt up the first base line. As he was running down the line, Randle veered out of his way—and out of the baseline—directly into Wilcox, who was in the process of fielding the ball, delivering a forearm shiver that laid the pitcher out. Seeing this, first baseman John Ellis promptly left the bag and charged at the oncoming Randle, tackling him head-on before he reached the base. The benches immediately emptied with punches being thrown on both sides.

"Nobody runs at one of our pitchers like that and gets away with it," steamed Ellis.[636]

Just as order was restored among the players, fans behind the visiting dugout began showering Indians players with beer, obscenities, and assorted debris. This infuriated several players, including catcher Dave Duncan, who had to be restrained by teammates from climbing over the dugout roof and into the stands in pursuit of a particular fan he identified committing the offense.

Texas manager Billy Martin, who was knocked down twice as he wrestled with Cleveland third baseman Buddy Bell, was relatively matter-of-fact about the incident, though wary of where it might lead.

"Lenny believed Wilcox was pitching a little close to him," stated Martin. "I can't blame Ellis for trying to protect his pitcher. But I'll get the blame on ten-cent beer night, you can bet on that. They'll all be mad at me in Cleveland, that's for sure. I'm not exactly looking forward to it. On the other hand, they won't have enough fans to worry about."[637]

Martin was taking a jab at the Indians notoriously low attendance totals for typical weeknight games in cavernous Cleveland Municipal Stadium. After all, the last time Martin had been in Cleveland, a brief Monday-Tuesday series when he was managing the Detroit Tigers in '73, the attendance had averaged just over 7,000 for the two games played in the stadium with a capacity of 78,000.

Such would not be the case, however, for the June 4 "10-cent Beer Night" to which Martin referred. Thanks in part to local radio host Pete Franklin whipping fans into a frenzy against the Rangers throughout the week, more than 25,000 "fans" showed up on a pleasant early summer Tuesday evening for the first meeting between the Rangers and Indians since the Randle-Wilcox-induced melee the week before. They would collectively consume more than 60,000 ten-ounce cups of Stroh's 3.2 beer before the night was over. The Indians almost doubled the size of their normal 28-man police force in anticipation of a rowdy crowd, but no one could anticipate what was to come.

Under a full moon, signs of chaos first became evident early in the game. After the Rangers' Tom Grieve hit a second inning home run, a heavyset woman jumped the fence, ran to the Indians on-deck circle, and bared her substantial, unencumbered breasts to the crowd.

She then attempted to kiss third base umpire and crew chief Nestor Chylak, who was not in a kissing mood.

Grieve came up again in the fourth inning and belted another home run. As he rounded third base, a naked man jumped onto the field and slid into second base. The streaker immediately scampered back into the stands, somehow avoiding security, who likely already had their hands full. While uninhibited exhibitionism was the predominant theme throughout the early innings, conspicuous booing by the crowd accompanied each Rangers player who came to bat.

Turn for the Worse

An eerie sign that things could get ugly occurred in the bottom of the fourth inning when the Indians' Leron Lee smoked a liner back up the middle, catching Texas pitcher Ferguson Jenkins square in the stomach. As Lee raced to first and Jenkins lay on the ground writhing in pain, the crowd began to chant, "Hit him again, hit him again! Harder, harder!" Jenkins remained in the game, but he gave up a single to the next hitter, Charlie Spikes, which sent Lee racing to third, where he slid in just as the throw arrived. Lee was called safe on a bang-bang play. This drew Texas manager Billy Martin out of the third base dugout to argue the call, making his first appearance of the night.

This, of course, was the very moment for which the fans had been waiting—and drinking. Emulating their peers in Arlington the week before, fans hurled 10-cent plastic cups of beer out toward Martin. Never one to back away from a fight, Martin responded by blowing kisses to the crowd as he returned to the dugout. Then, as he reached the dugout steps, Martin scooped up a handful of gravel from the warning track in front of the dugout and flinged it into the stands.

The interaction with Martin plus the freely flowing suds seemed to energize the crowd, which became more emboldened from that point on. The frequency with which fans found their way onto the field grew exponentially by the inning, though most contented themselves with scurrying across the outfield and then right back into the stands. For every interruption on the field, however, there were multiple fist fights taking place in the stands. Amid plumes of marijuana smoke, there seemed to be no shortage of firecrackers, cherry bombs, knives, and bottles. Virtually any family in attendance soon had parents shielding their children and making their way toward the exits just as they might in preparation for an oncoming hurricane.

In the sixth inning, the tide of the mayhem suddenly took a turn for the worse. A random tennis ball was tossed into center field and a fan quickly jumped the fence and scrambled after it. He retrieved the tennis ball and then chucked it back into the stands. This brought a shower of debris out onto the field in response. With police in pursuit, the ball-retrieving fan then ran toward left field where another fan jumped the fence and greeted him with a hug. Police converged, successfully apprehending the first fan, much to the dismay of the booing crowd, while the other fan successfully scaled the right field fence. As the police ushered their captive off the field, the cups of beer raining down onto the field were joined by rocks, batteries, golf balls, and virtually any projectile that was not bolted down. A warning by the public address announcer to not throw things on the field only seemed to increase the quantity of debris.

Amazingly, the game continued with the grounds crew continually sweeping across the field in a fruitless effort to keep it playable. As the game incredibly proceeded amidst the mayhem into the seventh inning, one man jumped the fence, stopped at the right field line, took off his clothes, and streaked across the outfield (streaking was a not uncommon occurrence of the time). The streaker lost his footing and fell during the romp, but got up and dashed back to the right field fence, where he threw his clothes—which he had carried during the run—right into the hands of a policeman waiting on the other side of the fence.

When fans began trying to rip the padding from the outfield wall and pull it over into the seats, the grounds crew quickly abandoned their trash collection detail to save the padding. It was a battle the grounds crew would wage for the rest of the night. Meanwhile, the Texas Rangers bullpen was being peppered with firecrackers, leading umpire crew chief Nestor Chylak to order all Rangers relievers into the dugout for their own safety.

"I told (Martin) I'd give any (reliever) he put in as much time as he needed (on the game mound) to get ready," Chylak explained.[638]

Let's Go, Boys

The game went on even as the crowd was becoming undeniably more bold and hostile, with Chylak and his crew doing everything in their power to guide the game to an official conclusion. The Rangers led 5-3 going into the bottom of the ninth. Oscar Gamble grounded out to shortstop and just two outs remained before putting an end to the madness. As fortune would have it, however, the Indians started to rally. George Hendrick doubled to left. Indians manager Ken Aspromonte sent up three straight pinch-hitters who all singled. Throughout the ninth inning rally, there was no sign of life in the abandoned Texas bullpen. Billy Martin would not consider replacing pitcher Steve Foucault, even as he appeared to be losing effectiveness in his fourth inning of work.

"I wasn't going to send anyone out there to get hurt," said the Texas skipper.[639]

The late Tribe rally was like pouring gasoline on a fire, literally driving the agitated crowd into an uncontrollable frenzy. With the bases loaded, John Lowenstein hit a fly ball to center field that Joe Lovitto gloved for the second out, but Ed Crosby tagged up from third base and came home to score, which tied the game. As the crowd went wild, two more fans jumped onto the field and charged at Rangers right fielder Jeff Burroughs, intent upon stealing his cap.

"They grabbed my hat and grabbed at my glove, and then a guy hit me in the back of the head," said Burroughs. "I wasn't gonna take that. I got angry and went after him."[640]

The right fielder kicked at one of the men, and stumbled to the ground in the process. This was the first time that the night's chaos had directly involved a player, and it drew other youths onto the field toward the action.

From his perch on the top step of the Rangers dugout, Martin believed Burroughs had been knocked to the ground and was in danger. Armed with a fungo bat, Martin yelled, "Let's go, boys" and led the Rangers charging out onto the field, bats in hand, coming to their fallen comrade's aid. "No way we're gonna leave one of our men out there," stated Martin. "Burroughs was being surrounded and punched at."[641]

"If they hadn't come out, someone might have killed me,"

Burroughs attested. "I didn't have anything to protect myself with except my fists. I just feel sorry for the police. They were throwing cans at them, spitting on them, and they were highly outnumbered."[642]

As the Rangers charged across the field, hundreds of fans came pouring out of the stands and the full-fledged melee was on. Cleveland manager Ken Aspromonte could see that the Rangers, even armed with lumber, were quickly becoming outnumbered by fans who were wielding knives, chains, and makeshift clubs from pieces of stadium seats they had broken off. Aspromonte urged his players to grab a bat and he proceeded to lead a stream of Indians players out of their dugout toward the outfield to help the Rangers fend off the inebriated masses.

At some point, a metal folding chair was hurled onto the field, landing on the head and shoulders of Indians reliever Tom Hilgendorf. The Cleveland radio broadcast team of play-by-play man Joe Tait and former pitcher Herb Score remained on the air, giving a full accounting of the carnage...[643]

> **Tait:** Tom Hilgendorf has been hit on the head. Hilgy is in definite pain. He's bent over, holding his head ... Aw, this is an absolute tragedy ... I've been in this business for over 20 years, and I have never seen anything as disgusting as this ... And I'll be perfectly honest with you: I just don't know what to say.
>
> **Score:** I don't think this game will continue, Joe ... The unbelievable thing is people keep jumping out of the stands after they see what's going on!
>
> **Tait:** Well, that shows you the complete lack of brainpower on the parts of some people. There's no way I'm going to run out onto the field if I see some baseball player waving a bat out there looking for somebody. This is tragic ... The whole thing has degenerated now into just—now we've got another fight going with fans and ballplayers. Hargrove has got some kid on the ground and he is really administering a beating.
>
> **Score:** Well, that fellow came up and hit him from behind is what happened.
>
> **Tait:** Boy, Hargrove really wants a piece of him—and I don't blame him.

Score: Look at Duke Sims down there going at it.

Tait: Yeah, Duke is in on it. Here we go again.

With 50 angry professional athletes actively defending themselves and each other, the buzz of frivolity quickly began to dissipate. The two managers, Martin and Aspromonte, finally herded their players successfully back to their respective clubhouses, making sure there was no man left behind. With no players left to antagonize, the energy of the fracas slowly began to wane. As people dispersed, however, most did their best to avoid leaving empty handed. They pillaged the dugouts and the field, taking with them anything not nailed down as a souvenir. Tait and Score continued to describe the surreal scene, which lasted for another twenty minutes.

Score: They've stolen the bases.

Tait: The security people here are just totally incapable of handling this crowd. They just—well, short of the National Guard, I'm not sure what would handle this crowd right now. It's unbelievable. Just unbelievable.

Score: People go back into the seats and others jump down to take their place.

Tait: The bases are gone.

With both teams safely back in their respective clubhouses, they began to take stock of what they had just experienced. Hilgendorf thankfully emerged with only a bruise on the back of his head.

"I was in the middle of it," sighed an exasperated Jim Perry, leaning against the wall in the clubhouse. "Everybody was pushing everybody. I'll tell you, Alex (Johnson, Texas left fielder) was mad, real mad. So was Duke (Sims, Texas backup catcher and former teammate, likely in the compromised bullpen earlier in the game). But then we started back to the dugout, thinking it might be over. Then here came some more and then we had it all over again."[644]

"I was scared my players would get hurt," stated Martin. "The game had gone too far as far as I'm concerned. They were hanging over and throwing firecrackers in the bullpen—our dugout, too. They had knives and every damn thing. We're lucky we didn't get stabbed.

"I'm very proud of the Cleveland club, though, the way they

came out to protect us, and I called (Cleveland manager) Kenny (Aspromonte) and told him so. They showed me something."[645]

"Listen, if it hadn't been for the Cleveland players coming out there to help us, we might have been killed," insisted an obviously shaken Rangers pitcher Jackie Brown. "All the fans back in Texas should realize the Indians were the real heroes of this thing, and their guys got hurt the worst."

Though all statistics from the game counted, Cleveland was forced to forfeit by an official 9-0 score.

1-2 Punch

While Gaylord had been on an undeniable roll, winning ten straight decisions following his Opening Day defeat and leading the American League with a 1.43 ERA, Jim's dominance was more subtle. Despite ranking fourth in the league, just behind Gaylord with an earned run average of 2.48, Jim had struggled to manage a .500 record. The win total was due more to a lack of run support than an absence of proficient pitching.

Though Gaylord had started the first game of the season and Jim had originally been penciled in as the third starter, as the rhythm of the season evolved, they fell into a pattern of Jim followed the next day by Gaylord. Cleveland manager Ken Aspromonte explained that it was by design.

"I like to pitch them back to back," the skipper disclosed. "It's for psychological reasons. I know it would affect me if I had to face them. They're two different style pitchers. Gaylord is overpowering and Jim pitches with control, lets you hit the ball but it's never the pitch you really want."[647]

Control Magnifico

On June 11 in Chicago, Jim evened his record at 5-5 with a masterful 6-0 complete game shutout that Tribe manager Ken Aspromonte called "Jim's best game of the year." Although he allowed eight hits, all were singles and only twice did he allow a runner to reach second base. Jim issued no walks with pinpoint placement of his pitches.

"We went over the hitters before the game," said Aspromonte, "and he was in the right spot all night."[649]

"What is so gratifying to me is the way Jim Perry can pitch to a spot," Aspromonte continued. "As a matter of fact, there is no pitcher in baseball that can hit a spot as consistently as he can. What is unfortunate is that the American League umpires for the most part are not geared for Jim Perry because they are not in a position to watch where his ball goes. As far as I'm concerned, Jim Perry is the best control pitcher in baseball. He should be 8-2 if we had gotten him any runs."[650]

Jim was in a groove and he could feel it. "In the last ten years, I don't think I've pitched as good as I have this season," he confessed. "With some more runs my record could be a lot better."[651]

> There is no pitcher in baseball that can hit a spot as consistently as he can... As far as I'm concerned, Jim Perry is the best control pitcher in baseball.
> — Ken Aspromonte
> CLEVELAND MANAGER

"I wanted my 30th (career) shutout more than anything tonight," Jim continued. "There aren't too many goals that I had set for myself, but this was very important for me."[652]

At this point, the Perry brothers had accounted for 15 of Cleveland's 28 team win total. While Jim wished he had more wins than his five, he asserted there was no jealousy over Gaylord having twice that number.

"We're both pros and we're both competitors," Jim explained. "We both like to win and each goes out to do his best with every chance. We both give one hundred percent."[653]

"They're two individuals with competitive spirit," Aspromonte testified. "They're both Cy Young winners. They know how to pitch. They have great control of their pitches. They add another dimension in that our younger players look up to them. I'm just glad they're both on my side."[654]

White Sox manager Chuck Tanner, who was on the receiving end of Jim's surgeon-like work, sang his praises, as well. "Not much we could do against that kind of pitching," he stated. "I played with Jim Perry 15 years ago and he's as good a pitcher now as he was then."[655]

"He puts something on every pitch no matter where it goes," Tanner continued. "He can make it sink or make it rise. He has the ability to just miss a spot and then come back with the same pitch just an inch closer. To say the least, he was in full command tonight and we didn't get too many good pitches."[656]

Major Milestone

On June 27, 1974, Jim Perry became the 69th MLB pitcher to win 200 games in a career with a 2-1 nail-biter. It came, appropriately enough, against Boston, who he beat for the 33rd time. The Red Sox had knocked him out early in his previous attempt at number 200 five days prior, but Jim came right back, allowing just one run before getting help from the bullpen for the final two outs of the win. Jim shared another secret to his success as he explained his ability to bounce back from a tough outing.

"I like to let the past go," he explained, "and not worry about it. I just try not to make the same mistakes."[657]

While it wasn't Jim's best outing, he did not walk anyone and he got some help from his defense. When Rico Petrocelli singled with two outs in the seventh inning, center fielder George Hendrick made a perfect throw to the plate to gun down Carl Yastrzemski, who was trying to score from second with the tying run.

"They hit some line drives right at players," an appreciative Perry said after the game, "and George made a great throw to the plate. Things seem to be changing for me and going my way."[658]

Jim's analysis proved accurate, as that win began a string of four straight victories, while the offense suddenly provided 20 runs of support over his next three starts. Jim's 6-2 win on July 7 over California pushed Cleveland to ten games over .500 and into first place by a game-and-a-half. It would be the team's high-water mark, and the division lead would be short-lived.

The team suddenly went into a tailspin, dropping nine of their next ten games with their only win coming in another Jim Perry start. Even Gaylord, whose 15 consecutive winning decisions after the Opening Day loss fell one short of the American League record, suddenly hit the skids, losing six in a row.

Never Better

Jim's July 12 win in Minnesota not only proved to be Cleveland's lone win during a ten-game slump, but it snapped a five-game Twins winning streak. Staked to an early 5-1 lead, Jim ran into trouble in the fourth, allowing three Twins runs. With two runners on and only one out after four straight Twins singles, Indians manager Ken

Aspromonte made a visit to the mound, but he did not make a pitching change.

"We're still out in front by a run, 5-4, and I wanted to show (Jim) I had confidence in him," said Aspromonte. "He always gives 150 percent and I wanted to give him a chance to win the game."[659]

Aspromonte's faith was rewarded as Jim quickly gathered himself, retiring the next two batters. He would scatter three singles over three shutout innings after that, giving the Tribe time to pad their lead and cruise to a 9-5 win, keeping them in a tie for first place.

"Perry came back strong," said Twins manager and Jim's longtime teammate Frank Quilici. "He's been around and can be real tough on the hitters working the ball in and out."[660]

Though Jim's record was only 9-7 even after four straight wins, Gaylord believed that his brother could have had 14 wins under his belt by that point with any luck. "I don't believe I've ever seen my brother Jim pitch any better than he has this year," said Gaylord.[661]

Jim did not disagree. "I've been pitching the best ball I have in ten years," he contended. "I've been shut out twice this year. Another time I left a game in the tenth inning when neither team had scored and I lost one game 2-1. Early in the season I lost some tough games when we weren't scoring many runs. It adds up that my record could be much better with a break or two."[662]

Twins star Tony Oliva went 0-for-4 against his former teammate in Minnesota's July 12 loss. He marveled at his good friend. "I tell you something. Guy like Jim Perry never throw ball over plate. He just work corners, so you get no strikes from him anyway. But Perry so close all the time that umpires call all his balls strikes. He lucky man. No wonder he win all the time."[663]

Heartbreaker

In a season of coulda'-beens, a no-decision on July 17 versus California was as bad as any. Jim was cruising along with a 5-0 lead at home, working on a two-hit shutout in the eighth inning when things suddenly went south. Facing the 7-8-9 hitters in the Angels lineup, Jim got tagged for three straight fly balls that all landed in the right-centerfield alley and got through to the fence for doubles. In the blink of an eye, the shutout was gone and manager Ken Aspromonte was going to the bullpen. A trio of relievers failed to quash the rally and what was looking like a 5-0 Cleveland win turned into a 7-5 defeat.

After the heartbreaking loss that dropped Cleveland two games back of the first place Red Sox, you could hear a pin drop in the home clubhouse. A dejected Jim Perry spoke softly with reporters in front of his locker.

"Boy, I wanted that one bad," he sighed. "But it just doesn't work out sometimes."[664]

"I thought I'd pitched good enough this year to have a chance for the All-Star Game," he continued, his voice trailing off to the point that it was barely audible. "I think it would have been nice to be on the team with my brother . . . With some breaks, I believe I could have had 13, 14, or even 15 wins, too."[665]

With the third best ERA of any American League starting pitcher at the time, Jim certainly had the evidence to back up his claim. Jim's 2.73 ERA ranked only behind Catfish Hunter at 2.63 and brother Gaylord's phenomenal 1.48 mark.

"The bullpen has killed us the last two weeks," muttered frustrated manager Ken Aspromonte. "The Angels' speed helped a lot on some cheap hits, but by and large our bullpen is not being able to get batters out."[666]

"But it's one of those things about baseball," Perry philosophized. "When things are going bad, they keep going bad . . . and I've had more than a few like that this year."[667]

While his disappointment was personal, his empathy extended to his teammates. "One man can't do it alone," Jim asserted. "I can't do it with every pitch. George Hendrick can't carry the team every game with his bat. It's a team game. Our guys may be trying a little too hard now. They're a young group of players playing under a lot of pressure."[668]

Having shared all he could muster in the post-game morgue-like home clubhouse, Perry folded the towel that he chews on the bench when he pitches and wrapped it around his neck. "I sure wanted this one real bad," he reiterated even quieter. "I guess it just wasn't meant to be."[669]

Slump Buster

Cleveland ended their teamwide slump in spectacular fashion on July 19, as 30-year old Dick Bosman threw a no-hitter in a 4-0 win over the A.L. West-leading Oakland Athletics. No one was more excited than the man on the pitch chart that night, Jim Perry.

"I was getting more excited as the innings went by," Perry exclaimed. "Dick threw just 79 pitches! (60 for strikes.) He was ahead of most everybody. He had a lot of one, two and three-pitch hitters. His fastball was really sinking and his curve and slider were also real good and down. Everything was sinking, sinking, sinking."[670]

If Jim sounded something like a proud papa, it was rightly so. When Bosman got a chance to share his thoughts, Jim Perry, along with brother Gaylord, was one of the first targets to which he pointed in appreciation for his accomplishment. An original member of the 1974 Cleveland starting rotation, Bosman got bombed in his first start and was then bounced to the bullpen when the Indians pulled off a massive mid-April trade with the Yankees that brought in four pitchers. A frustrated Bosman suddenly found himself a forgotten man, languishing in the bullpen. He made only four appearances over Cleveland's next 44 games.

"You can't just (quit and) go home," the nine-year veteran explained. "I had to hang in there. Gaylord and Jim Perry kept encouraging me to be patient and things will break my way and they finally did after two months," smiled the happy pitcher.[671]

Give Away

Jim was keeping the chart because he was the following night's starter, and so it went from excitement back to disappointment for the hard luck pitcher of '74. As usual, Jim was cruising with a slim lead and not much margin for error, but error is precisely what the Indians encountered. Leading 2-1 through six innings, the only damage Jim had allowed was a solo home run by Joe Rudi.

Reggie Jackson began the seventh inning for Oakland by coaxing a walk from Perry on a borderline 3-2 pitch that brought howls from the Cleveland dugout and even drew a frustrated reaction from the normally unflappable pitcher. Rudi lofted a very catchable fly ball that somehow eluded outfielder George Hendrick before Gene

Tenace singled to left, loading the bases with nobody out. When Perry induced a tailor-made double-play grounder toward first baseman Tom McCraw, it looked like he might be able to wiggle out of the jam. McCraw fielded the ball, stepped on the bag for one out, and then fired home.

Catcher Dave Duncan, however, failed to see McCraw touch the base, which made it a tag play on Jackson, who was chugging down the third base line. Thus thinking it was a simple force out at the plate, Duncan took the throw from McCraw and let Reggie Jackson run right past him, touching home with the game-tying run. That opened the floodgates to a four-run rally and another Jim Perry hard luck loss.

"We gave the game away," a disgusted Perry grumbled. "That's what makes it so bad. You work hard and things like this happen. Five earned runs and they shoulda only had one. We all yelled at Duncan. He had plenty of time. Jackson was from here to the water cooler (on the other side of the room) . . . We shouldn't have been in that situation anyway," he sighed.[672]

"I hate to blame everything on the umpires," said manager Ken Aspromonte, "but Russ Goetz is not a good ball and strike umpire. I don't know what the hell he was looking at but he didn't make the call for us. We struck out Jackson and he didn't give it to us. When (Jackson) walked, that's when everything else happened. That's the one that really got Jim Perry excited."[673]

"There wasn't any question," Jim maintained of the ball four call on Jackson. "I had four inches of the plate."[674]

And so it went for the best spot pitcher in the game, having a great season masked by missed calls, missed opportunities and misplays that left him with a 9-8 record despite one of the league's best ERAs. Even his teammates felt bad about their role in Jim's perpetual disappointment. Reliever Tom Buskey was a prime example.

Payback Time

On July 27 against Detroit, Jim had pitched five shutout innings in hot, humid conditions while the Indians built a 3-0 lead. In the sixth inning, miscommunication between outfielders led to a pair of runs scoring. Manager Ken Aspromonte called on reliever Tom

Buskey with the tying run on second and the go-ahead run on first. As he was warming up in the bullpen, Buskey said he was thinking about Perry.

"A couple of times I came in and blew the lead for Jim," Buskey explained, "and I was thinking, 'today I can repay him.' But that was warming up. The minute you cross that white line, you forget it. You feel like you're the king of the hill. You've got to feel that way. You've got to feel you're the best out there."[675]

On this day, Buskey certainly was. He got Aurelio Rodriguez to pop up to first base and proceeded to set down ten Tigers in a row, successfully preserving Jim's tenth win of the year. Coming against Detroit, who had traded Jim away less than four months prior, made it particularly satisfying.

"The trade fired me up," Perry admitted. "I felt like I could still pitch. And I wanted to prove it. I was pitching better than anybody they had when they got rid of me. I think I know what they were trying to do. They wanted to go with their kids. But I felt then and I still feel like I can pitch for a couple of more years."[676]

Sheer Consistency

In a year during which he pitched as well as ever, featuring a bevy of excellent outings, Jim may have pitched his best game on August 17. At least that was the consensus throughout the Cleveland Municipal Stadium press box as pundits watched the crafty veteran dominate the Texas Rangers in a four-hit shutout. Though he only struck out one, Jim walked nobody and did not allow a runner as far as third base while completing the job in a crisp two hours and one minute. The Rangers only got seven balls out of the infield, none hit particularly hard.

Indians beat writer Bob Nold pointed out that Jim could have easily pitched a no-hitter based on the quality of balls put in play by Texas hitters. "It's necessary to establish early that the 37-year-old righthander WAS great," wrote Nold, "because all his games have a way of sounding alike when you talk to him. You could probably quote him without talking to him and not be incorrect . . . 'Kept the ball down, moved it around—in and out . . . fastballs, sliders, sinkers, a few changeups. The guys made some plays behind me.'

"Understand now, that's a composite from the season but it's pretty close to what he said Saturday. After watching him through the season, you begin to get the idea there's a lot more to those pitches than the words indicate—cunning, hard work, a lot of variations to boondoggle the hitters."[677]

First baseman and backup catcher John Ellis, who was dressing at his locker near Perry's felt compelled to comment in appreciation of the masterful performance. "I'll tell you about Jim Perry," said Ellis with a big grin. "What you think you see is not what you get. I know. I've hit against him."[678]

> *I'll tell you about Jim Perry. What you think you see is not what you get. I know. I've hit against him.*
>
> — John Ellis
> 13-YEAR MLB CAREER

Nold continued his story, reflecting on Jim's impressive season-long body of work. "Come to think of it," wrote Nold, "maybe (Jim's) comments are always the same because his games are so much the same. He didn't win 15 games in a row like brother Gaylord but for sheer consistency from the beginning, Jim is second to none.

"His victory Saturday made him 13-8 and with a little help from the bullpen earlier in the season, or maybe a chance to finish two or three of the games himself, he could easily have 17 or 18 wins."[679]

Alas, it was only his 13th victory, number 207 of his illustrious career. Added to Gaylord's 193, that gave the Perry brothers a remarkable 400 combined MLB wins.

Quiet Skid

The win was also significant because it pulled the Indians back to within 3.5 games of first place Boston. They would not be that close again. Losses in seven of their next eight games saw Cleveland fall from second to fourth, a full eight games out of first.

The skid started quietly. Fritz Peterson pitched a great game on August 18, the day after Jim's masterpiece, but Ferguson Jenkins was just a little better, shutting out the Indians for a 1-0 Rangers win. For Peterson, it was his first complete game in more than two months and the leadership of Jim Perry made its presence felt yet again.

"I tried what Jim does, only throwing three pitches between innings," Peterson explained. "It saves you for later in the game. I usually throw eight or nine warmup pitches but I had been getting tired in the seventh inning."[680]

When the Indians finally put an end to their slump on August 26, it was Jim doing the job with a five-hit complete game as Cleveland defeated the Royals, 5-1, in Kansas City. Another hard luck loss followed in his next outing, however, as the offense gave him no support in a 2-0 defeat at Texas.

Jim won his 15th game of the season on September 8 and Gaylord captured his 19th four days later. The wins bookended a four-game winning streak for the Tribe, leaving the team with a 71-70 record following Gaylord's victory. The team would win only four of their next 15 games, with Jim and Gaylord at one apiece accounting for half of those victories.

Stops Pulled

On September 12, the Indians made a surprising transaction that would have long-lasting ramifications not only for the organization, but for the Perry brothers, as well. Cleveland claimed 38-year old future hall-of-fame slugger Frank Robinson off waivers from the California Angels. It seemed curious that the Indians would add an aging high-priced veteran who was limited defensively with just three weeks left in a season that was quickly slipping away. It seemed even more curious that Cleveland general manager Phil Seghi immediately announced the team "came to an agreement" with Robinson on a contract for the 1975 season, a relatively aggressive move at the time.

Robinson was only 110 hits away from reaching the coveted 3,000 hit plateau and 28 home runs short of the 600-mark, so his interest in reaching those goals were seemingly reasonable motivations for the deal. However, there were rumors that Robinson, who had spent the previous five off-seasons managing in the Puerto Rican Winter League, had a strong interest in becoming MLB's first black manager.

Current Indians manager Ken Aspromonte was in the final year of a two-year contract and GM Seghi had not committed his support for another season at the helm. In addition, MLB Commissioner Bowie Kuhn was reportedly applying pressure on MLB owners to name a black man as manager for the first time. Robinson had also claimed in a recent interview that he felt it was possible for a man to serve in a dual capacity as designated hitter and manager. Seghi, however, denied any intention of acquiring Robinson as an ultimate player-manager.

"People can read into it what they want," asserted the Cleveland GM. "We got him to play. We're only five games behind in the loss column and we've got a chance to win. So we're pulling out all the stops."[681]

With the winds of change and potential controversy swirling inside the Cleveland clubhouse, the only "stop" Seghi managed to "pull" was stopping any hope of the Indians making a pennant drive in the season's final weeks. The team was swept in a doubleheader in Baltimore the next day and proceeded to lose nine of their next eleven games, quickly plummeting to ten games out of first place.

On Friday, September 27, as falling rain was in the process of forcing a postponement of that evening's home game with the Yankees, the boiling tumult finally came to a head. With the weather preventing any pregame on-field activity, an agitated Aspromonte went up to Phil Seghi's office and confronted the Indians' GM about the rumors. Aspromonte demanded to know if he was going to be retained as Cleveland manager for the 1975 season.

Seghi finally admitted that Aspromonte was not going to be retained, but felt that it would be best for all concerned to hold off on making an announcement until after the season concluded in just under a week. A dejected Aspromonte retired to his clubhouse office to reflect on the distressing news. Aspromonte's quiet contemplation was suddenly interrupted by shouting among players in the clubhouse.

Gaylord (earning approximately $100,000) had made a statement the previous day at a function with the Akron Press Club that made headlines in that morning's paper. Gaylord stated, "I want one more dollar than whatever Frank Robinson makes..."[682] Robinson (reportedly signed to a 1975 contract that would pay him $180,000) had approached Gaylord's locker to confront the pitcher about the statement, menacingly stating that he didn't appreciate being made the subject of Gaylord's public salary demands.

Though Gaylord remained seated as Robinson exploded, teammate Joe Lis, who had a locker between the two, stood up to Robinson, saying the team didn't need more trouble and advising

Robinson to take his problems with Perry outside. This led to an escalation of the confrontation that likely would have come to blows if Aspromonte hadn't emerged from his seclusion and quickly intervened.

With the knowledge of his dismissal now confirmed and seeing what the uncertainty was doing to the team, Aspromonte made an impromptu decision to unload the burdensome weight he was shouldering. He immediately called the team together and informed the players of his lame duck status.

Talking to the press after calm had been restored, Gaylord stated that he doubted he would be with the Indians in 1975 and that "a lot of it has to do with who the manager is."[683]

Playing to Win

Cleveland would lose four of Aspromonte's six lame-duck games. The two winners, not surprisingly, were Jim, his 17th, and Gaylord, his 21st. Jim's victory, a 2-1 nail-biter in Boston on September 30, was particularly emotional for two teams playing out the string. Boston had just been mathematically eliminated from playoff contention the day before and the Indians, with their lame duck manager, had been officially knocked out several days before that. Against that backdrop, the two respective skippers matched wits, managing the otherwise meaningless game as if it was the seventh game of the World Series.

With veteran lefthander Bill Lee trying for a career-best 18th win, Boston manager Darrell Johnson elected to go with his normal starting lineup. It was customary practice to give regulars a rest once a team was officially eliminated at the end of a grueling campaign, but Johnson felt he owed it to Lee to go hard for one more win. Perry and Lee traded zeroes, save for the fourth inning when Cleveland scratched a pair off Lee and Boston managed one off Perry. In the seventh, Indians manager Ken Aspromonte felt Jim was tiring and he went to the bullpen, replacing Perry with trusted reliever Tom Buskey.

As Lee remained in the game for the Red Sox, hoping for a lead to qualify for the win, Buskey held Boston in check until the bottom of the ninth. Still trailing 2-1 and trying everything he could possibly think of to manufacture a run, Boston manager Darrell Johnson began sending up a string of pinch-hitters. With two on and two outs, Buskey got behind in the count to pinch-hitter Tommy Harper, leading Aspromonte to bring on Tom Hilgendorf in the middle of the at-bat. When Hilgendorf was unable to avoid issuing a walk, Aspromonte turned to Milt Wilcox, the third reliever in the last two batters. With the bases now loaded, Wilcox induced a game-ending groundout off the bat of pinch-hitter Doug Griffin, preserving the win for Jim Perry, who ran his career record against the Red Sox to 34-19.

When the dust had settled, the final count saw the two managers combine to use three pitchers to fend off five pinch-hitters and a pinch-runner, all in the bottom of the ninth inning. Boston manager Darrell Johnson explained his approach in battling for his starting pitcher, who went the distance.

"We had a pitcher out there trying to win a game and it wouldn't have been fair to Bill Lee if we didn't do everything we could. He pitched a helluva game and it's a shame we couldn't win it for him."[684]

In the visitor's clubhouse, an elated Ken Aspromonte shared why he managed the end of the game so aggressively for the winning Tribe. "That was my thank you to Jim Perry for breaking his hump for me all year long," said Aspromonte. "Here's a 38-year-old guy who hasn't missed a starting turn all season. He's given me everything but his guts. I always play to win, but this one I wanted to save for Perry. He's just been great."[685]

> He's given me everything but his guts. I always play to win, but this one I wanted to save for Perry. He's just been great.
> — Ken Aspromonte
> CLEVELAND MANAGER

Men of the Year

Jim finished the 1974 season with a 17-12 record, pitching 252 innings in 36 starts, never once missing a turn, as his manager appreciatively pointed out. His 2.96 ERA ranked tenth best in the American League. In a later era, such a fantastic season by a veteran leader might garner a three-year multi-million dollar contract. In the mid-1970s, however, nothing was guaranteed.

The final game of the 1974 season was fittingly bizarre, as mercurial outfielder George Hendrick walked out on the team and left for his California home immediately after pre-game warmups despite being listed as the starting centerfielder. When asked about Hendrick's sudden exit, Aspromonte said, "I don't know anything about it. His name is in the lineup. Maybe you should ask number 20 (Frank Robinson). I'm finished here."[686]

Robinson would not be officially announced as manager until the following morning back in Cleveland, but even amidst the chaos, Gaylord pitched a complete game to capture his 21st win, as the Indians prevailed 8-6. With 38 wins between them, Jim and Gaylord accounted for almost half of the team's 77 victories.

In recognition of their joint contribution to the team, the Cleveland Chapter of the Baseball Writers Association of America voted the Perry brothers the Indians' Men-of-the-Year. Actually, it was co-Man-of-the-Year, which each had previously won individually—Jim in 1960, Gaylord in 1972—but the joint honor was no mistake.

"I'm excited about it," stated Jim of winning the honor for a second time. "There's a lot of guys on our team who are most valuable players. I got the award once before, and now. I'm pleased at winning it again with the brother. I know the brother and I couldn't have had our good years if we hadn't had the guys behind us to make the plays and get the runs for us."[687]

Gaylord, who had recommended acquiring his older brother, was pleased, as well. "Naturally I'm happy," said the younger Perry, "especially because both Jim and I were picked, and next year we all ought to be even better."[688]

Asked if he was concerned about his and brother Jim's (now 39 years old) advancing years, Gaylord (36) replied, "Our ages aren't important because we're both dedicated to the game and always determined to do our best."[689]

Jim echoed his brother's sentiment. "I feel that I pitched last season as well as I have in ten years, and if some breaks had gone the right way, I could have won as many as 24 games. Next year I hope to contribute even more, and it should be easier because we should have a better club. The young guys have a year's additional experience and I'm looking for good things from a lot of guys."[690]

16

Beginning of the End

Despite the celebration of the Perry brothers for their 1974 accomplishments, with Robinson now at the helm, 1975 was shaping up with a different vibe. To begin with, Gaylord's outspoken resentment of his massive salary differential with that of the player-manager continued to linger, as offseason trade rumors once again circulated involving the younger of the Perry brothers.

Gaylord was not dealt, however. In fact, prior to the December Baseball Winter Meetings, Gaylord reportedly agreed to a two-year contract at $150,000 per year. Though his salary failed to reach the "one dollar more than Frank Robinson" level of his initial demands, Gaylord claimed, "That's water under the bridge. I'm satisfied I've got a contract I can live with. I'm happy."[691]

The joy would not last long. For one thing, Jim and Gaylord's childhood North Carolina neighbor, Catfish Hunter, had been declared MLB's first "free agent" following the 1974 season. Oakland A's owner Charlie Finley was ruled to have breached Hunter's contract, which set off a bidding war for the star pitcher, who had just won the 1974 Cy Young award. Numerous teams, including Cleveland, made unprecedented offers before the 28-year old Hunter agreed to a stunning five-year guaranteed contract worth nearly $3.5 million with the New York Yankees. It was the beginning of a massive shift in the balance of power in the game away from the heavy-handed owners.

While many, particularly MLB team owners, tried to paint the bidding war for Hunter and his subsequent massive contract as a one-time anomaly, it was a huge development, thanks in large part to union head Marvin Miller and the work of player representatives like Jim Perry. Unfortunately, the men who helped pave the way, such as the 39-year old Perry, would never benefit directly from this monumental development. Jim entered 1975 in the second year of a two-year no-cut contract he had wrangled out of the Indians after he was traded from Detroit. Considered a rare luxury at the time, both the length and the five-figure salary would quickly become an afterthought compared to all the money that would be thrown around with the advent of organized free agency in the years to come.

Though Jim could see what was going on and expressed an interest in renegotiating his deal, Cleveland general manager Phil Seghi was not willing to enter into any such discussion. "Jim Perry has signed a contract for 1975," the GM responded to inquiries from the press. "It is an honorable one and one signed with full integrity and full satisfaction at the time it was signed."[692]

Getting the Runaround

As 1975 spring training neared, all appeared to be well with the Perry brothers penciled in as the top two starters in what was shaping up as a very thin Cleveland rotation. "We'll be looking for a fourth starting pitcher," Robinson admitted as he prepared for his first training camp at the helm. "There's no question who the first three will be . . . Gaylord Perry, Jim Perry, and, I guess, you'd have to put Fritz Peterson in there, too."[693]

Jim and Gaylord were both ready to go, as the brothers joined a handful of teammates in reporting to training camp four days early. New Indians pitching coach Harvey Haddix was a believer in letting established veterans with the track record of the Perry brothers be on their own program. Explaining what he expected from the anchors of his pitching staff in training camp, Haddix related his pre-camp conversation with the younger Perry.

"Gaylord is an old farm boy like me," Haddix explained. "He

takes wonderful care of himself and he's one of the great pitchers of our time. I told him to set his own pace in the spring and get himself ready as he always has."[694]

It did not take long, however, for the new manager to express different expectations than his pitching coach. Robinson mandated that all pitchers take part in an extensive daily foul line-to-foul line running program. Gaylord, who preferred his personal conditioning program that included a combination of sprints and pitcher's fielding practice, was less than enthused with the neophyte manager's decree. Dissatisfied with Gaylord's approach to the new running program, Robinson confronted his star pitcher.

"I was unhappy with his overall attitude as far as his work on the field was concerned, and I called him into my office," Robinson explained. "I didn't think he was putting enough effort into his work. I'm not saying he's not a hard worker. I just was not happy with his pace. I could have talked to him out on the field, but that's not the right way to do it."[695]

"Nobody establishes his own training program," the manager continued. "I want everybody on the team to feel the same. I want a rookie to look and see an established star like Gaylord Perry running and working just as hard as anybody else."[696]

After dressing, Gaylord went straight to Phil Seghi's office and told the Cleveland general manager of the confrontation and his disappointment in having his pre-season preparation dictated by a manager who had never pitched. "Perhaps it would be better for all concerned if I were traded to another team," suggested the disgruntled pitcher.[697]

Seghi quickly arranged a meeting with Gaylord, himself, and his manager, during which the three men hashed things out for an hour. All three emerged claiming the differences to be settled, but the disturbing trend was unmistakable. Esteemed national baseball writer Dick Young wrote, "It's only a matter of time before the Frank Robinson-Gaylord Perry situation explodes. They have made up twice publicly, but mutual resentments remain. The only way out of the sticky situation is for Gaylord to be traded."[698]

Let the Games Begin

Though Cleveland lost Robinson's exhibition game debut, 6-4 to San Francisco, the manager was delighted with the work of Jim and Gaylord, who combined to throw six shutout innings before the bullpen let the game slip away. The veteran aces "were very good," assessed Robinson. "Gaylord wasn't quite as sharp as usual (three walks), but he got the job done. And Jim just threw the ball in and got them out. He made it look easy."[699]

Robinson curiously piggy-backed his top two starters once again their next time out, leaving Jim perplexed. "This makes only six innings this spring," the veteran complained. "That's not enough. There are only 2½ weeks to go. I'm gonna pitch again in a couple of days; I've got to talk to them."[700]

Though he gave up five hits and a pair of runs in his three-inning outing, Jim was more concerned about the opportunity to refine his repertoire. "I'm just trying to get back the pitches I had last year," he explained. "They didn't hit much today—bloops and balls off the fist, but they got them all in a row."[701]

Always Working

Just as he promised, Perry did "talk to them" and he was back on the mound just three days later for a "B" game, normally the venue for young players not likely to make the team. Indians beat writer Bob Nold described the action:

"It may have been only a 'B' game on the program—but it was serious business to Jim Perry. He's always working—on the sideline, in batting practice or in the game. He requested the extra pitching time and this was it—as long as he wanted to go. It looked like all those games in Municipal Stadium last summer—ground balls and pop-ups; five harmless innings in which he gave up only two singles and two walks. Perry went directly from the mound to the sidelines and continued throwing hard—even harder than in the game."[702]

"I wanted to loosen up today and stretch it a little bit," Jim explained. "I could have gone another inning, but those other guys have to work, too. So I pitched on the sidelines . . . . threw probably an inning or an inning and a half there. Had good control. I was keeping the curveball down. I'm still not satisfied, but it's coming along and I feel all right."[703]

Jim explained his straightforward philosophy of pitching. "If a pitcher has two pitches—a good fastball and a good breaking ball—and changes speed on them, that's four pitches. I told Bert Blyleven that a lot of times when I was at Minnesota. I told him, 'You'd get everyone out if you did that.' A guy can win with that if he gets it down and over the plate."[704]

Though he threw two different kinds of breaking pitches, Jim explained why his slider was far superior to his curve. "I can throw my slider harder than my fastball," he revealed. "The off-speed curve is a good pitch if I keep it down. I got two or three of their hitters out with it today."[705]

In addition to changes in velocity, Jim detailed how his years of experience helped him to exploit a batter's weakness with location. "Today, I can pick up little things like when the batter changes his stance in the batter's box from one at-bat to the next right away where I couldn't do it when I first came up."[706]

He then proceeded to detail how he executed that knowledge with location and speed against Angels rookie John Balaz in the game earlier that day. In his first at-bat, Jim noticed Balaz did not like the ball in on him, so when Balaz set up further off the plate in his next at bat, Jim adjusted accordingly.

"I went in on him a little more and I got the ball down," Perry explained. "I made the pitch I wanted and he hit it on the ground. If the pitch had had a little more zip on it, it would've been a routine ground ball (instead of skipping through the infield for a single)."[707]

An old dog can still learn new tricks, according to the savvy veteran. "I'm working on some secret things," he claimed with a wink and a smile, nodding toward his brother's locker, "but no spitters."[708] Rather, it was the forkball that Gaylord had successfully demonstrated as his "super sinker" for league officials a year prior.

"It'll be a good changeup for me," Jim stated. "But I don't have the kind of fingers you can spread wide like some of the guys. Gaylord's fingers are bigger."[709]

Jim then proceeded to make a surprising claim. "I could still throw the knuckleball if I had to. I had a pretty good one in high school, but I don't use it up here because it makes your knuckle stiffen up and takes away from the fastball."[710]

The accomplished veteran wrapped up his impromptu pitching skull session with a state of his game. "I've lost a little off my fastball from when I started," he admitted. "You aren't gonna find too many guys who throw nine innings as hard as they did ten years ago. But I still do the same things. I still work hard. I'm smarter now."[711]

Bob Nold, in fact, noted the veteran's unwavering work ethic. "I don't know that anyone has worked harder than 39-year old Jim Perry," observed the Indians beat writer. "When the body finally betrays him, it won't be his fault."[712]

Jim's body certainly showed no signs of betrayal at this point. Harvey Haddix shared how the value of the Perry brothers' experience made up for the fact that the pair ranked far from the hardest throwers on the Cleveland pitching staff.

"Gaylord doesn't have outstanding stuff," stated the new pitching coach. "He knows how to pitch and he has a lot of pitches. He's able to hit the corners and read the hitters. He knows what the hitters are looking for. It takes experience.

"Jim doesn't have outstanding stuff either," Haddix continued. "But he can hit the corners. He doesn't have quite the assortment of pitches Gaylord does, though. The thing about the older guys is that they can take any pitch they've got and get it over the plate. That's what makes them good."[713]

Spahn and Sain, then Pray

Indeed, both of the "older guys" Perrys were looking so good as Opening Day approached that the Indians considered opening the season with only seven pitchers—Jim, Gaylord and Fritz Peterson as starters, to go with four relievers. Due to off days and potential rainouts, manager Frank Robinson had calculated he could give Gaylord four starts and both Jim and Peterson two apiece before expanding the staff in late April. It brought back memories of when the Boston Braves relied on their two great pitchers, Warren Spahn and Johnny Sain, to carry them to the 1948 World Series, prompting a local writer to quip, "Spahn and Sain, then pray for rain." There were skeptics of this strategy for the 1975 Indians, however, namely due to the age of the Perry brothers.

"Many think the two Perrys can not duplicate their combined 38 victories because of age and that's something they have to live with every year now," stated the *Akron Beacon Journal's* Bob Nold in his pre-season preview of the '75 Indians. "The Indians can only hope, but on the positive side, the Perrys are not ordinary 'old men.'"[714]

While Frank Robinson eventually elected to open the season with nine pitchers, that did not alter his rotation plan of "Gaylord, Jim, and Fritz, then hope bad weather hits." Gaylord (5) and Jim (3) combined to start eight of Cleveland's first ten games. It wasn't until an April 26 doubleheader forced manager Frank Robinson to turn to Dick Bosman in the team's eleventh game that anyone other than the opening trio made a start.

Seeds of Discontent

Jim's second start on April 19 resulted in his second loss and it was one with which he was none too pleased. More importantly, perhaps, he joined his younger brother in dissatisfaction with Robinson's handling of the pitchers. Specifically, it was the policy Robinson had implemented of sending pitching coach Harvey Haddix to the mound to carry out pitching changes. This was a frustrating deviation for a veteran accustomed to the opportunity for a man-to-man conversation with the man making the decision. To Jim, it now felt like he was dealing with the manager's messenger.

Locked in a pitcher's duel with Milwaukee starter Bill Champion even as a treacherous wind blew out at Cleveland's Municipal Stadium, Jim entered the top of the ninth inning trailing 1-0. After a one-out wind-blown home run by George Scott made it 2-0 in favor of the Brewers, Don Money lofted another wind-aided fly that dropped for a double. Robinson then ordered Jim to intentionally walk Darrell Porter before dispatching pitching coach Harvey Haddix to the mound for a pitching change. In a rare display of displeasure, Jim kicked the ground as he stalked off toward the dugout.

"What am I supposed to do, take it in stride?" the incredulous veteran steamed. "I don't want to come out of the game any more than anyone else. (Haddix) didn't say anything to me. He just said, 'I'm bringing in Buskey.' Hell, I'm no rookie. I think they shoulda asked me how I felt. I busted my rear out there today and I felt good.

That ball Scott hit was just a routine fly ball. And Money didn't hit the ball very good either. The wind helped it."[715]

As one who took great pride in his control, Jim also did not appreciate having a base on balls arbitrarily added to his record just before he was yanked from the game. "If they're going to walk the man, let Buskey walk him," said Jim angrily.[716]

"I'm honest," Jim continued. "If I feel tired late in the game, I'll tell 'em. But I have no opportunity to say anything and then I'm supposed to not be teed off. Sometimes you've gotta get teed off to shake up the team. We've got a better team than this."[717]

Cleveland was off to a 2-4 start and this loss was eerily similar to so many tough outings Jim suffered through in his hard-luck 17-win season the year before.

"We've got to hang in there; that's all," Jim reasoned. "The guys out there were trying. The wind did a lot of tricks. They're trying to do the job the same as I am."[718]

His manager concurred that the first run that scored on back-to-back doubles was due to a pair of fly balls that both fooled outfielders. "The wind carried the ball in the outfield," Robinson agreed, "but you've got to adjust to those things. We shoulda been nothin' to nothin' going into the ninth inning."[719]

Left fielder John Lowenstein, who was fooled by the wind on the first double off Perry, described the fluke ninth inning homer. "Scott's ball didn't drift over the fence. Nothing was propelling it. It was just waiting to come down. Then instead of coming down, a wind gust caught it and blew it over."[720]

Though Frank Robinson did not appreciate Jim venting to reporters about being removed from the game, the manager voiced support for his hard-luck pitcher. "Perry pitched well today," stated the skipper. "He's not as sharp yet as he's gonna be but he did a great job. If your team doesn't score any runs, though, the best you can be is tied."[721]

His third start on April 23 in Detroit brought Jim his first win of the young season, but it came in rainy, soggy conditions that forced him out of the game in the sixth inning. "I haven't had a good day to pitch yet," the frustrated pitcher reflected. "It's been raining, windy or cold every time I've been out. When you're pitching every four days and the weather is like that it's tough to get the soreness out. A guy can get hurt in weather like that.

"That last inning (as the steady rain picked up just before a lengthy delay) I couldn't believe I was pitching. The ball was so wet. You're slopping all over the mound. My hand was wet and the ball kept slipping out."[722]

Jim's frustrating inability to locate like he normally could led to a pair of solo home runs. The second homer of the inning by Bill Freehan cut the Tribe's lead to 4-3 and prompted Robinson to go to the bullpen. This time they held the lead, and Jim was rewarded with his 22nd career win over Detroit, the most of any active pitcher.

Frustrating Skid

A pair of first inning errors April 27 in Baltimore fueled an early Orioles rally that Cleveland could not overcome. It would be the first of four consecutive losing starts for Jim. The skid even included a pair of losses to Boston, the team he was known for beating. With the team struggling to get above .500, new manager Frank Robinson was feeling pressure to make a move to jump-start the ballclub. Following Jim's second loss to the Red Sox on May 5, Robinson made the decision to pull Jim from the rotation.

It was a frustrating development for the 39-year old who had performed so consistently well against Boston throughout his career. If you know Jim Perry, however, you know that he has a remarkably positive demeanor.

"I don't have any doubts about myself," the seasoned veteran stated amidst speculation that Father Time was catching up with him. "I know what I can do. When I begin to have doubts, I'll quit.

"I'm just walking too many people," Jim continued, acknowledging his un-Perry-like 14 walks over 30 innings to begin the season. "I've got to watch out for that. I'm not that far off from last year, though. I've been close when I've missed. There's been a lot of rain and cold, too, and I haven't been able to go like I want."[723]

Chicago White Sox manager Chuck Tanner, now in his sixth season managing against Perry, agreed with the veteran's self-assessment. "Jim Perry will pitch well," Tanner declared. "The season will continue and he'll get back in there. If you could wipe out the

0-5 record for some guys and say they're 4-1, I guarantee you they'd be better when they went out to pitch. I guarantee you that with success, your confidence is better and you do better."[724]

For a "spot" pitcher like Jim Perry, that confidence was especially important, yet the 1-5 record had to be weighing on his mind. In addition to dealing with confidence in executing his pitches, Jim also had to be questioning the confidence from his manager. Jim's name was beginning to appear in trade rumors, including one reportedly with the Indians sending Jim to Texas, where he would once again rejoin Rangers manager Billy Martin.

On May 15, Jim pitched for the first time in ten days. It was a five inning relief appearance during a 7-6 loss at Minnesota. After coming in to bail starter Don Hood out of a fourth inning jam, Jim allowed just two runs, one of which was unearned, while Cleveland battled back to tie the game. After the Indians knotted it up at six in the top of the sixth, Jim made quick work of the Twins, shutting them out into the ninth inning. When he issued a leadoff walk followed by a sacrifice bunt to open the ninth, however, Jim was ordered to serve up another intentional walk before he was replaced by Dave LaRoche. LaRoche struck out pinch-hitter Tony Oliva, but Rod Carew lined a game-winning single off the reliever, putting Jim on the hook for another loss.

While the defeat dropped Jim's record to 1-6 and Cleveland fell to 12-17, manager Frank Robinson was encouraged. "I'm certainly not pleased about the outcome," said the skipper, "but I was happy about some of the guys who did come through and Jim Perry threw better than he has in quite awhile."[725]

Opportunity Knocks

As Cleveland focused on giving more of an opportunity to young pitchers like 20-year old rookie Dennis Eckersley and with first-year manager Robinson feeling increased pressure to shake things up, Oakland A's owner Charlie Finley smelled an opportunity. World Series winners each of the past three seasons, the 1975 A's were struggling to recover from the unexpected and devastating loss of free agent Catfish Hunter. Youngsters that Oakland were hoping would help offset Hunter's absence had been either hurt or ineffective.

On May 20, the A's traded struggling pitcher John "Blue Moon" Odom and cash (estimated $15,000) to Cleveland in exchange for Jim Perry and fellow pitcher, 31-year old Dick Bosman. "I think this trade will put us into the playoffs," Finley announced triumphantly.[726]

"Pitching is what we need," confirmed A's manager Alvin Dark. "I don't want to use either of these guys in the bullpen."[727]

"We got them to start for us," Dark continued, "and I definitely think they'll help our club. I know they haven't done much this year, but they have good credentials."[728]

Anxious for a fresh start with the defending champs, Jim said, "I'd like to come here and pick up the club. I'm healthy and I'm throwing good."[729]

"We were so excited," Jim's wife Daphne recalled. "We couldn't believe that we were going from a bottom-place club to the top, joining the three-time defending champs. What a thrill!

"We would spend the summer with Jim in California as soon as the children were out of school. It was an exciting summer for the family. We got to see so many beautiful spots and visit friends (in California) that we rarely could see otherwise."

As for speculation that lingering problems between brother Gaylord and Cleveland manager Frank Robinson might have been a factor in the deal, Jim refused to point fingers. "I don't know what's happening over there," he said. "Gaylord, himself, might not be there long. I'm just sorry I didn't pitch better for Frank."[730]

Just as his big brother surmised, Gaylord was dealt to the Texas Rangers less than a month later. It was a deal that also involved cash going back to Cleveland, as rumors of a cash flow crunch swirled around the Indians franchise.

At the time of his trade, Gaylord said, "I think another big factor in my being traded was that the Indians needed money, which they got in the deal, and also because they wanted to get rid of my high salary. I also think it's the reason they got rid of my brother Jim earlier."[731]

Ironically, the A's, who were in the midst of a ten-day road trip, were headed to Cleveland next, so their two newest pitchers were told to just move their belongings over to the visitor's clubhouse and wait for the team to arrive.

"Both Bosman and Perry will pitch in the doubleheader (against Cleveland) Sunday," Alvin Dark announced. "We'll pitch them in batting practice on (the off day) Thursday, start them on Sunday, then have to feel their way around (on how to use them)."[732]

Shaking Off the Rust

Making just his third appearance in almost three weeks, the rust on Jim's game was apparent in his first start for the A's, as he allowed eight baserunners in two-plus innings. "Perry won't pitch in a game for awhile," announced manager Alvin Dark afterward. "He needs work so we'll have him throw batting practice Tuesday and Friday."[733]

Those plans were quickly shelved, however, as the team returned to Oakland to begin a 12-game homestand with a series against Baltimore. When starter Ken Holtzman ran into trouble to begin the sixth inning, Dark decided that Perry could best get his "needed work" on the game mound. A two-run homer by Jim Northrup, the second batter Jim faced, was the only hit he allowed in three effective innings of work, leaving Alvin Dark encouraged.

After the A's pulled the game out in extra-innings, Oakland's skipper complimented the bounce-back effort of his newest acquisition. "Jim pitched well, even on the home run ball," said Dark. "He gave (Northrup) a pitch that wasn't more than 12 or 14 inches off the ground. He just hit a good pitch out, that's all."[734]

Another start and another relief appearance each showed periods of encouragement offset by moments of frustrating inconsistency. A's manager Alvin Dark was determined one way or another to give Perry enough work to get sharp.

"Perry has to pitch a lot—all pitchers do—to be effective," Dark pointed out. "And, there's only two ways for a pitcher to stay sharp. They have to pitch in a lot of games, or they have to pitch batting practice."[735]

Jim's determination remained similarly steadfast. "As long as they don't lose faith in me, I'll keep working hard and things will have to change," the veteran pitcher rationalized. "I'm still throwing the ball good, but they're hitting balls just out of somebody's reach. Some day those line shots are going to be at somebody."[736]

No one could have predicted that "some day" would be Jim Perry's next start.

One-Hit Wonder

On June 10 in Baltimore, Dark's faith in his trusty veteran was rewarded, as Jim hurled one of the best games of his storied career. After walking leadoff hitter Al Bumbry to begin the game, Perry proceeded to retire 17 consecutive Orioles batters. With two outs in the sixth inning, the same hot-hitting Bumbry slapped a grounder up the middle that escaped Jim's outstretched glove and bounced over second base into center field for Baltimore's first hit of the game. Jim followed the hit with a wild pitch and then walked Paul Blair, his only other walk of the game, but he quickly recovered to strike out Tommy Davis.

Perry would not allow another Baltimore batter to reach base, retiring the final ten men he faced, including five by strikeout. In fact, only one of the final ten Orioles hitters managed to get the ball out of the infield as Jim closed out a fabulous one-hit shutout in dominant fashion.

Despite barely missing his first career no-hitter, Jim was his typical matter-of-fact self in reflecting on the clean hit that eluded him. "I wasn't disappointed in that," he revealed. "I just wanted to get on the winning way. It was a good pitch, down to make him hit it on the ground."[737]

"It was out of my reach," Jim continued. "It was off to my left and hit on the corner of the dirt."[738]

"I knew I had a no-hitter going but I'm just trying to win games," Jim explained. "I was ahead of the hitters all night, which was a big change from the way I was going. I wasn't discouraged but being 1-7 didn't look good. Things had to turn around for me and I'm glad they finally did."[739]

Oakland catcher Gene Tenace, whose two-run homer in the fourth inning broke open a scoreless game and gave his pitcher all the runs he would need, revealed how Jim finally turned things around. "His secret tonight," Tenace explained, "was mixing up his pitches, keeping the ball down and throwing strikes."[740]

Jim needed only 99 pitches as he struck out seven batters in the 3-0 whitewashing. He punched out the final two batters of the game to finish off the gem. It was the 32nd shutout of Jim's career and it would be the final one he would record.

"I'm not a no-hit pitcher," Jim explained. "I don't think I've ever pitched a one-hitter before. I've had a lot of two-hitters (five). I knew I could pitch better than I have. I had no doubts about what I could do."[741]

After his great game, the pitching star celebrated in classic Jim Perry fashion—a quiet dinner with 38-year old teammate and fellow pitcher Sonny Siebert.

Irregular Regular

While he was no longer used as a reliever after that great game, Jim's starting assignments were somewhat irregular. Team ace 25-year old Vida Blue and 29-year old Ken Holtzman pitched every fourth or fifth day, with some combination of youngster Glenn Abbott (24 years old) and veterans Stan Bahnsen (30), Dick Bosman (31), Sonny Siebert (38), and Perry (39) mixed in between based on the schedule, as well as the whims of the manager. Jim made only four starts over the next month, as he averaged six days off between each start.

Oakland manager Alvin Dark explained how the loss of Catfish Hunter had changed the way he handled the rotation. "Last year, we had three starting pitchers and we were never concerned about what the rotation was. When the time came, they pitched. This year, it's a little different situation. We have seven starting pitchers. We go with Vida Blue and Ken Holtzman and then we have five other starting pitchers we can use at a time when one of them is most well rested.

"It's this balance of our pitching staff that makes our club as strong as it is this year," Dark continued. "We have good names, winners on this staff. It's great to have this number, but we can't know just what's going to happen from day to day."[742]

Even when Perry did get an opportunity, the manager was quick to turn to the bullpen by the midway point in the game. "Unless it's Ken (Holtzman) or Vida (Blue)," explained frequently used reliever Paul Lindblad, "we (the bullpen) know we're coming in around the fifth inning. Even those two are afraid to go 3-2 or 3-1 on a batter.

"There's been a couple games this year where Jim Perry was lifted before completing the fifth inning," Lindblad added in amazement.[743]

It was a tough time for a veteran like Perry, who took pride in not only finishing what he started, but who had also worked so hard to become a rotation anchor. Still, he kept working, kept battling.

Last Hurrah

On July 7 against Cleveland, Jim pitched into the seventh inning for only the second time since coming to Oakland, mainly because he was pitching too well to take out. He allowed only two harmless singles over the first five innings, while the A's built a 5-0 lead. When the Indians managed a pair of singles in the seventh, however, A's skipper Alvin Dark could not resist going to his trusty bullpen. Reliever Rollie Fingers allowed one of Jim's inherited runners to score, before finishing up Jim's third victory of the season and his first in almost a month.

"A long time in between," Jim sighed.[744] "I'm happy the manager let me stay around long enough to win the game. I wanted to win real bad."[745]

"We don't figure him to go nine innings," said Oakland manager Alvin Dark of his 39-year old veteran.[746] "He's pitching exactly the way we hoped he would. Five to six solid innings, and then the bullpen can finish up."[747]

"He did very well and I'm proud of him," Dark continued. "He knows how to pitch."[748]

Asked if he took any particular satisfaction in beating the team that recently traded him away, Jim explained that his focus was on helping the A's. "I've got some good friends on that team," he said. "But pitching against them is nothing special. It's just nice to beat anyone."[749]

"I wasn't trying to prove anything to anyone," Perry continued. "I'm on a new team and I want to help. That's all."[750]

Jim's next start came five days later against the Baltimore Orioles and the manager not only let him stay in long enough to get the win, but let him finish what he started. Matched up against league ERA leader Jim Palmer, Perry limited Orioles hitters to just a pair of harmless singles over eight shutout innings while his offense piled up seven runs of support against the Baltimore ace. After a one-out walk to Ken Singleton in the ninth, Bobby Grich lofted a high fly ball that center fielder Billy North lost in the blinding Saturday afternoon sun. By the time North could corral it, Grich had an RBI-triple, spoiling the shutout effort. Perry retired the next two batters, Al Bumbry and Lee May to strand Grich at third and finish off the three-hit complete game victory.

"That's overtime," kidded teammate Reggie Jackson, in reference to the complete game effort. "They oughta pay you overtime for those last three innings, Jim."[751]

It was the 109th complete game and the 215th win of Jim's career. "I'd like to have a shutout," he admitted, but I can't get greedy. It was a good win."[752]

At this point, Jim was now 3-1 since coming to Oakland, with a very respectable 3.08 ERA, but something still was not right. At 39 years old, in his 17th year in the big leagues, his resilient right arm had a lot of mileage on it. The best "spot" pitcher in the game was finding it increasingly difficult to hit his spots with the regularity that had once made him one of the best pitchers in the game. Years later, Perry would be diagnosed with a torn rotator cuff of unknown origin. It is highly likely that the subtle tear had begun by this point and was beginning to impact the pitcher's trademark pinpoint accuracy.

Sudden Slump

Coming out of the all-star break, Jim suddenly encountered another slump. It started quietly enough. On July 19 in Baltimore, a series of defensive miscues keyed an Orioles rally that broke open a 1-1 deadlock and led to a 5-1 defeat. In his next start five days later in Detroit, Perry was lifted with two on and nobody out in the fourth inning. He was charged with four runs in the eventual 5-2 loss.

Back home against the Texas Rangers on July 29, the frustrating disappearance of Perry's signature pinpoint command proved costly. The Rangers opened the game with back-to-back singles. After a pair of fly outs, a walk to Jim Spencer brought Toby Harrah to the plate.

"You never think about grand slam homers when you first go to the plate with the bases loaded," Harrah explained. "But when the count was 2-0, I thought I might get a pitch to hit. Then I started thinking about it. I looked for a fastball and tried to hit it hard."[753]

Harrah succeeded, lofting a long fly ball into the left field stands for what he called "the first grand slam homer of my life." Though Jim recovered to pitch five more innings while allowing only one run, he issued six walks in five-and-two-thirds innings of work in a 6-1 Oakland loss. Perry's three-game skid coincided with fellow starter Sonny Siebert's return from a six-week stint on the disabled list. The combination was enough to get Jim bounced from the rotation.

He relieved on back-to-back days August 4-5 but was hit hard mopping up a pair of lopsided Oakland losses. Jim's spot on the pitching staff was suddenly in jeopardy. He would not appear in any of Oakland's next eight games.

The first place A's had been struggling in August, seeing their 11-game lead cut in half in just a matter of days. When outfielder Joe Rudi suffered a mysterious and possibly season-ending thumb injury, the team was in need of reinforcements and owner Charlie Finley swung a deal to acquire veteran outfielder Tommy Harper. The team needed a roster spot, and Jim's was the one they chose. On August 13, 1975, Jim Perry was given his outright release.

Packing Tears

In addressing the media about the move, Oakland A's manager Alvin Dark went out of his way to pay Jim a compliment that summed up the veteran star's 17-year career. "I want to say that Perry showed me some class," the skipper pointed out. "He was willing to throw long relief, anything to help the club."[754]

The release came as a shock. "He had endured other struggles in his career," said wife Daphne, "and we figured he would pull out of this one just like he always had in the past."

> I want to say that Perry showed me some class... He was willing to throw long relief, anything to help the club.
>
> — Alvin Dark
> Oakland Manager

This time, the veteran would not get the chance to work through his struggles. After telephone calls to various teams came up empty, Jim faced the harsh reality that he was unemployed.

"I can remember sitting up in the stands after we got out to Oakland," recalled Daphne, "and looking out at all the championship banners, thinking how great it was going to be to experience another World Series together. Now we had suddenly been turned out. I just can't explain the shock we felt.

"As we began to pack up the apartment for our return to our home in Minnesota, the tears fell into each box of dishes, linens, and clothes that I put together. Oh, God, where are you? Where is that strength that you are supposed to be giving me? Why have you let this happen to us?

"On the night of August 14, I took my Bible and my Meditation Moments (a Christian Women's Club publication), knowing it was the last night in the apartment. I needed strength. Two verses spoke to me in this time of need."

Deuteronomy 31:8, And the Lord, it is He that doth go before thee. He will be with thee, he will not fail thee, neither forsake thee. Fear not, neither be dismayed.

Jeremiah 29:11, "For I know the plans I have for you," declares the Lord, "plans to prosper you and not to harm you, plans to give you hope and a future."

"What a peace this put in my heart," said the ever supportive wife and mother.

Homeward Bound

The next morning, Jim and Daphne, along with kids Chris, Pam, and Michelle, embarked on a multi-day drive back to their house in Minnesota. Their faith that the Lord was watching over them provided both strength and hope during the long journey home...

Proverbs 3:5-6, "Trust in the Lord with all your heart, and lean not on your own understanding; In all your ways acknowledge Him, and He shall direct your paths."

Never one to waste time or an opportunity, Jim took advantage of this rare late-summer break to see some sights with his family during the trip home. The family caught a couple shows in Las Vegas and heard the Mormon Tabernacle Choir practicing in Salt Lake City. Even as he looked for distractions during the more-than-2,000 mile journey, however, Jim understood the reality of the situation. As they trekked through the Rocky Mountains and made their way home, there were no messages from MLB teams waiting for him at any of the Howard Johnsons or Holiday Inns along the way.

For the first time in his 17-year major league career, Jim Perry did not have a team. Though he never had arm problems and still felt confident in his ability to get major league hitters out, Jim was in the midst of his worst statistical season. At 39 years old, the prospects of him continuing were grim.

17

Dialing Up Success

Even during the prime of his baseball career, Jim was always working on an off-season business venture of some sort. A 1971 feature in *Sports Illustrated* explained how he was "into promotions and public relations (for shopping center openings and a home-delivery orange juice concern), connections with a boat company and a snowmobile company, part ownership of a mobile home concern in Cincinnati and the directorship of a bank in St. Paul. Lately it seems he's always on a plane heading somewhere, to meet some people on business or to make an appearance.

"'I say the only time I get to relax is in the dentist's chair,' said Jim at the time, 'and that's about the truth. I've got a poor dog I haven't even taken out duck hunting. But I like to stay busy, I like to meet people, and these are things you have to do.'"[755]

Jim had been involved with everything from auto dealerships, to mobile homes to even an innovative mobile-houseboat project. He was a manufacturer's rep for a juice company called Home Juice. Jim was so involved with business interests during baseball's off-season, in fact, that it once prompted young daughter Pam to announce confidently to a reporter, "My dad is a jelly smucker!"

With his baseball future now especially in doubt, Jim wasted little time after getting the family unpacked back at their Edina, Minnesota home. He quickly hooked up with longtime friend Ray Antonen, who had regularly organized trips for busloads of underprivileged and disabled South Dakota kids to Minnesota Twins games. Jim and Ray had been introduced by Jim's former teammate Dean Chance back in Jim's early years with the Twins and the two became friends.

Even before the 1975 baseball season was over, Jim and Ray had already formed a company called JR Distributing that sold probiotics for livestock. "Probiotics is a whole new concept in feeding poultry and livestock," explained Antonen. "Basically, what it does is crowd out harmful bacteria and give the poultry or livestock a chance to gain weight while feeding less."[756]

The pair set up the home office of JR Distributing in a run-down barber shop, paying ten dollars for the windowless building on the main street of Lake Norden, South Dakota, about 100 miles north of Sioux Falls. Jim would spend the next few years splitting time between Lake Norden and Edina, Minnesota, where his family continued to make their home.

Though he originally had hopes of securing an invite to '76 spring training with an MLB team or even hooking on with one of the MLB expansion teams (Seattle Mariners and Toronto Blue Jays) that were to begin play in 1977, the value his experience offered was not enough to offset concerns about his 40-year old age. Both Jim and Daphne had strong hopes of a return for one more run with the Twins that would enable him to be home much of the summer, but the Twins surprisingly showed no interest. Twins owner Calvin Griffith felt greatly impacted by the sudden rise in player salaries and rumors persisted that he never completely forgave Jim for his instrumental role in the early days of solidifying the MLB players' union.

Jim remained active, of course. To keep in baseball playing shape, he joined a local team in the South Dakota Amateur Baseball Association, of which Antonen was president. Jim played on the Lake Norden team, both as a pitcher and a switch-hitting outfielder, often helping the team win more with his bat than his arm. Also on the team was Ray Antonen's son Mel, who was a young sportswriter, eventually to become a national baseball correspondent for *USA Today*. Antonen's daughter, Kathy, had also worked for the Perry family as a "summer girl" in the early '70s, helping Daphne manage the hectic schedule of three growing and very active children.

When he wasn't working or keeping his baseball skills sharp, Jim was either speaking at local charity events, pheasant hunting, or playing golf in celebrity pro-ams. Though he did not begin playing golf until he reached the major leagues in his early 20s, Jim had become quite proficient on the links. He won several club championships and regularly contended for top prize at the many celebrity outings in which he appeared.

Jim's son, Chris, the oldest of three children, was likewise becoming a renowned golfer in his own right. "He's got good size, hits the ball well, is a good putter and has a good touch with the irons," stated Edina West High School golf coach Bart Larson of 16-year old Chris following his sophomore year of high school. "He's got a super future."[757]

Chris Perry would go on to become the first three-time winner of the Minnesota Class AA High School Boys' State Golf Tournament before a hall-of-fame career at Ohio State University. He would play 17 years on the PGA Tour. In 1992, Jim and Chris got the rare opportunity to team up together in the PGA Pebble Beach Pro-Am. The father-son duo not only made the cut, but combined for a top-20 finish.

"Without the name," Chris said of growing up in his star father's shadow, "I might not have been anything. But (Dad) has always let me make the choice of what I've wanted to do. Both of my parents have let me decide what sport I wanted to play. They've never tried to force me into anything."[758]

Out of Gas

As his efforts with JR Distributing continued, sometimes even involving an occasional shift behind the wheel of a tractor, Jim continued to seek additional forms of income. The travel back and forth between Edina and Lake Norden—a four hour drive one way—was taking a toll on him both physically and mentally. When brother Gaylord told him of an investment opportunity, Jim was all ears.

Gaylord invited Jim to invest in a company that was making automobile gas caps with a special flap that enabled drivers to add fuel without ever unscrewing the cap. While likely a bit ahead of its time, the concept made sense and many promises were made about advertising that was lined up and retail opportunities. People that Jim and Daphne trusted agreed that it seemed like a sound investment and was a product that would "sell like crazy." After much prayer and contemplation, Jim decided to go forward with the investment.

"I can remember boxes of those gas caps stacked up in the basement," his daughter Pam later recalled.

Unfortunately, though the underlying product may well have been solid, promises about other aspects of the business were not. As the business went south, Jim was frustrated to realize that he had little say in trying to right the ship. It was a mistake he would learn from, but one that also set him back financially.

Baseball Redux

Jim continued to yearn for a return to the game that had been such a big part of his life for so long. If it would not be as a player, he would explore other options.

In 1978, Jim served a stint in the Texas Rangers' spring training camp. "I ran and worked with the pitchers and I certainly enjoyed it and was very impressed with the entire organization," he said.[759]

Told that pitching coach Sid Hudson welcomed Jim's input on anything he observed from Rangers pitchers, both right and wrong, the long-time hurler downplayed his insights. "I guess after 17 years in baseball, I should be able to spot a few things," Perry remarked.[760]

Three years later, a full-time opportunity to return to the game finally presented itself. In 1980, irascible Billy Martin had taken the helm of his fifth team, leading the Oakland A's to a winning record and a 29-win improvement from the prior year. Martin had rejuvenated the A's with an aggressive style of play that fans affectionately called "Billy Ball."

With Martin seeking players that fit the mold of his intense persona, he asked Oakland owner Charlie Finley to procure the services of highly respected scout Dick Wiencek. Billy had become close with Wiencek when both were with the Minnesota Twins and the scout spent time teaching Martin the finer points of his craft. (Before his legendary 53-year career was over, Wiencek would sign 72 future big league players, including Bert Blyleven, Mark McGwire, Jim Kaat, and Graig Nettles—an unofficial record.) Following the 1980 season, Finley hired Wiencek away from the Detroit Tigers and gave him the title of Director of Scouting and Minor League Personnel.

Just as Martin was impacted by Wiencek with the Twins, Wiencek never forgot the determined, studious pitcher he watched during his prime in Minnesota. Prior to the 1981 season, Wiencek hired Jim Perry as a roving minor league pitching instructor. Martin was thrilled to have his first ace pitcher aboard and frequently counted on Jim's input scouting major league opponents.

Perry also scouted local amateur players for the draft. In 1983, he recommended that the A's draft University of Minnesota junior third baseman Terry Steinbach. Oakland selected Steinbach in the ninth round and Jim negotiated a $15,000 signing bonus. Steinbach was converted to catcher and became a three-time all-star during a 14-year big league career.

In 1981, Oakland won the first half of the season that was split into two parts due to the mid-season strike that interrupted play for two months. The A's swept Kansas City in the first round of the playoffs, but then lost three straight to the New York Yankees. By the following year, as was his unfortunate pattern, Martin's intense approach had run its course in Oakland with the A's dropping back to fifth place and a losing 68-94 record. By this time, a costly divorce from his wife had forced Charlie Finley to sell the team. Having no sentimental attachment to Martin, the new owners fired him and he was quickly scooped up for a third run with George Steinbrenner's New York Yankees. The departure of one of Jim's biggest boosters would prove a precursor to big changes in Jim's professional career.

1984 brought more honors for Jim Perry. When his alma mater, Campbell University, decided to formally institute a hall of fame for its athletic program, it was only natural that the Perry brothers be recognized. Jim was joined by brother Gaylord as the first inductees into the Campbell University Sports Hall of Fame on April 26, 1984.

Destiny Calls

After five years coaching and scouting for the Oakland A's, Jim forged another opportunity that would soon demand his time and attention. While he had always worked some other job during baseball's offseason, the mid-1980s brought a more urgent need for additional income. Son Chris was attending Ohio State University on an athletic scholarship for his golf, but in the fall of 1984 daughter Pam had enrolled at Miami University in Oxford, Ohio. With another daughter, Michelle, not far behind, Jim and wife Daphne were facing some difficult life decisions. Jim knew he needed to earn more than he was paid as a scout and minor league coach for the A's. As fortune would have it, a seismic shift in the telecommunication industry was about to present a life-changing opportunity.

The breakup of the AT&T Bell Telephone monopoly in the early 1980s led to the creation of seven Regional Bell Operating Companies, often referred to as "Baby Bells." These Baby Bells were required to offer any long-distance company access to local switching and transmission facilities equivalent to AT&T's access.

This led to the creation of a sudden throng of long-distance "resellers"—middlemen who would buy long-distance WATS lines (Wide Area Telephone Service) in bulk from major carriers and then resell access to these lines. At the same time, the evolution of modern computing allowed for the creation of a routing system that could automatically seek the cheapest long-distance service available to a given area at a given time. While this concept is long forgotten in the days of seamless cell phone communication, it was a revolutionary development that transformed telecommunications in the mid-'80s. While AT&T still had the advantage of experience and seamless nationwide access, they were no longer able to arbitrarily hold rivals at bay.

In addition to working for Ray Antonen in the late '70s, Jim had been very active in the Sioux Falls, South Dakota area. Not only did he play baseball on the local team, but Jim was an avid hunter, another sport popular in the Dakotas. Through his time and involvement in the region, Jim became friends with a local sports coach named Gus Bartholow who was active in the community and knew lots of people. Aware that Jim was interested in exploring new business opportunities, Gus suggested he look into this burgeoning industry with a man he knew named John Dennis.

Dennis, a former marketing executive with Northwestern Bell Telephone, had decided to go out on his own after the Bell breakup. He had started a new company he called Republic Telcom and was attempting to recruit new salesmen. The "qualifications" did not require technical expertise. Dennis was looking for people who met a simple standard:[761]

- Ambitious
- Aggressive
- Energetic and excited about personal growth and high earnings
- Interested in rapid advancement

For a man who had excelled for almost two decades at the highest level of professional sports and was determined to provide for his family, this opportunity was heaven sent. In fact, you might say Jim Perry was *overqualified* for this role. At least that must have been the conclusion of Dennis when the two first met.

In order to recruit salesmen, Dennis had rented a meeting room at a Minneapolis hotel where he and an engineer named Don Szymik were teaching a sales training class that explained the business opportunity. Dennis had expertise in the telecommunications industry from his time with Northwestern Bell and Szymik had great technical knowledge of how to use switches to capitalize on the new availability of WATS lines. The only problem is the pair lacked money. Though they had an idea of what they wanted to do and how to do it, they were trying to start up Republic Telcom on a shoestring budget, and a "baby boot shoestring," at that. They also were light on leads for their new business. Imagine their delight when a local sports hero walked in the door. There is no better way to break the ice than talking sports, and there are few easier talkers than Jim Perry.

For his part, Jim could immediately see the potential. "With all the people I knew in this area, I had no doubt that I could sell this," he recalled. But there was one problem. "They had no money," he explained. With only one child left at home, Jim had an idea of how he could come up with some cash, but the tough part was breaking it to his loving, supportive wife.

Forging New Ground

"I remember we were down in Florida for some baseball event," Daphne recalled. "Jim told me, 'When you go home, you know what you've got to do. You've got to start getting that house ready to sell.' I thought that was one of the worst things he could do to me, but I knew in my heart he was right."

Jim and Daphne quickly sold the beautiful Edina home where they had raised their family, but they still needed more if they were going to do this right. Jim shared the opportunity with Tom Lovett, his longtime personal attorney and friend. Lovett was good friends with another attorney who represented Wilbur Peters, the owner of Minnesota Fabrics. Not only was Peters seeking other investment opportunities, but he had tremendous respect for the hard-working pitcher he had enjoyed watching during Perry's great seasons with the Twins. The two attorneys arranged a meeting between Peters and Perry where Jim convinced Wilbur to become an investor in a new company.

With money he had from the sale of his house, Jim put up $25,000 and he lent $25,000 each to both John Dennis and Don Szymik for them to put up the same. Wilbur Peters put up $50,000 plus he made a loan of $250,000 dollars to become a partner with a forty-percent share in a new long distance telephone company they would call Dial-Net. Perry, Dennis, and Szymik each retained a twenty-percent share in the new venture.

While the more established long-distance competitors, AT&T, Sprint, and MCI, were fighting for market share in major metropolitan areas like New York, Chicago, and Los Angeles, there was far less competition in smaller cities. Even Minneapolis might be a tough starting ground, but the trio quickly determined there was a potential gold mine right next door.

"We knew that (in) South Dakota, there was a need for economical long-distance services," Dennis explained, "because South Dakota had basically been ignored."[762]

While the trio gave some thought to setting up their home office in Rapid City on the western side of the state, Jim successfully argued in favor of Sioux Falls, located toward South Dakota's southeast corner, due to its closer proximity to Minneapolis. With a more manageable four hour drive, at least Jim would be able to make it home some weekends.

With Sioux Falls decided upon as a home base, Dennis, Szymik, and Perry set out with a local realtor to decide upon a suitable place for their first office. The only catch was they needed a location near a junction that would house incoming and outgoing telephone lines for AT&T and Northwestern Bell. In the process of their discussions with the realtor, one of the men mentioned that they could also use the help of an accountant to help with some of the more complex financial aspects of the new business. Of course, they didn't want an expensive accountant from some big-time firm. The trio was more interested in an accountant from a boutique firm that they could afford.

As luck would have it, the realtor informed the threesome, both needs could be found at the same location. The realtor called his friend, accountant Fred Thurman, and told him he was bringing some businessmen over that he thought Fred should meet.

"Three guys came bursting into my office," Thurman recalled, "and told me how they were going to take on AT&T, MCI, and Sprint, who were already considered the titans of the new long distance industry. I thought they were crazy!"

Nevertheless, Thurman agreed to help them out and the trio set up shop in a small hole-in-the-wall office in the Western Surety building, formerly the United National Bank building, located on 9th and Phillips in downtown Sioux Falls.

"Our first office was a tiny 10-by-12 room," said Jim. We had three guys and one phone. We couldn't afford another phone. We made friends with the guy across the hall and one of us was always running over to borrow his phone."

"As the business got going, I could see we had a great opportunity to make an impact in this industry," Jim explained. "I had to drive four hours from our home in Edina, Minnesota to the office in Sioux Falls, so I rented a house near the office where I usually stayed during the week. A lady there had gone to Arizona for the winter, so she rented out her house. I told Daphne, 'For the next two years you might not see me too much.' I often didn't make it home more than every other weekend."

Eventually, Jim had to get his own place, however, and he found a small studio apartment near the office suitable for his tight budget. Jim's youngest daughter, Michelle, recalled the difficulties of this time.

"Dad was gone a lot," said Michelle, "usually only making it back home to Edina for the weekend, sometimes not even then. One time Mom and I drove out to visit him in Sioux Falls and I remember being so sad that he was living all alone in this tiny apartment with only a recliner and a small black-and-white TV. On the way back home, I cried to Mom because I felt so bad for him, but she assured me Dad was just doing what needed to be done for our family."

As a three-sport star, playing volleyball, basketball, and softball in high school, Michelle was often lucky if she could get even one parent to her games. "Mom was working a ton at the mall where she worked for a friend at Dahlstrom, a ladies clothing retailer. She would come straight from work to see me play. If I was really lucky, we might have an occasional weekend game where Dad could see me, too."

"One thing I will never forget," added Michelle, "was that no matter how tough times got, Dad always had that positive attitude."

Mo' Money

Though he was basically a silent partner, Wilbur Peters had a significant interest in not only his stake in the new company, but also his very sizable loan. About six months after they got started, Peters checked in with Perry to see how his investment was coming along. "How's things going, Jim?' Peters asked.

"Things are going good," Jim replied, "but it's getting tight." As start-ups often do, even when they are going well, Dial-Net was burning through money faster than it was coming in at this early stage. Not only were they buying needed lines and switches, but they had to pay salesmen to sell them. "We're gonna need some more money," Jim confessed.

"Well, how much do ya' need?" Peters matter-of-factly inquired.

And just like that, the young company had another loan to work with, this one for a million dollars. The second cash infusion provided a boost that would help propel the company to great things.

"Wilbur Peters was a key figure in the success of Dial-Net," asserted Fred Thurman. "And the reason he did it was because he trusted and had faith in Jim Perry."

Road Warrior

By the summer of '86, Jim was on the road so much between Dial-Net meetings, charity golf events, and old-timers baseball games that even making it home every other weekend was a challenge. That spring, he laid out his extensive upcoming travel schedule and explained his strategy in a letter to his partners.

"The places I will be traveling in the upcoming months in many ways will benefit Dial-Net. Television and radio coverage along with newspaper articles will be inquiring as to what Jim Perry has been doing outside baseball. Given this opportunity, I will always be selling Dial-Net as the best long distance company around, along with the help from Northwestern Bell and AT&T.

"We are all in the game of business to be winners. By being winners we will end up on top where we want Dial-Net to be at all times. Representing Dial-Net in all the places I travel means being a businessman as well as a helper to charitable organizations. I enjoy helping out others as well as Dial-Net salesmen when help is needed. I hope that all Dial-Net customers will be pleased at our efforts to be the best in the areas we service."

Indeed, Jim's help to charitable organizations and his help to Dial-Net salesmen would prove to make huge impacts in the days ahead. As the business got going, the opportunity was opening up exactly as they hoped, but the company was still lacking resources until Wilbur Peters stepped up with the second very sizeable loan.

Explosive Growth

The loans from Wilbur Peters made an enormous impact on Dial-Net's ability to grow its business. Not only could they buy more lines, but they were able to get more and bigger switches that would allow Don Szymik and his team of engineers to better route calls to the most efficient available lines.

"We were able to pay Wilbur back within a year," said Jim. "He was thrilled!"

As part of the breakup of AT&T, Northwestern Bell was required to offer any long-distance company access to local switching and transmission facilities. In early spring of '86 Northwestern Bell mailed out a ballot to more than 30,000 Sioux Falls residences and another 17,000 businesses that allowed customers to choose their long-distance carrier. Dial-Net was listed, along with AT&T, GTE Sprint, MCI Telecommunications, MidCo Communications, and Muth Communications. Even if a customer failed to return their ballot, they would be assigned a carrier on a percentage basis of the initial return, so this was a huge opportunity for the smaller carriers to gain ground.

Dial-Net used telephone calls, personal contact, and even some direct mailings to campaign for votes. It was uncharted waters which left many customers confused about what was going to happen if they left the lifelong "security" of Ma Bell and AT&T.

Jim shared the difficulty of explaining the new long-distance options to customers. "Some people would ask, 'Are you gonna take my phone away?'"

Under the guidance of chief engineer Don Szymik, Dial-Net had built a system that could consistently route calls through the cheapest available lines. The fact that many of these lines comprised new fiber optic cable technology, giving them improved sound quality was an added bonus. This gave Dial-Net an advantage over an established company like AT&T, which used only its own lines. Szymik was also very good at fighting for the best possible price on lines he was able to procure. As a result, Dial-Net could compete aggressively with a cheaper price point and often a better quality product.

As the ballots were distributed throughout the region, Dial-Net president John Dennis confidently stated, "We are guaranteeing Sioux Falls we are the lowest priced of all the companies."[763]

It was no lie. For more than a year, Dial-Net had been running ads urging area businesses to "Take the Sioux Falls Challenge." The promotion stated, "Dial-Net challenges all businesses to allow us to analyze their current long distance phone bill. If we can't show your business a savings on direct dial calls, Dial-Net will give you $50.00 FREE . . . NO QUESTIONS ASKED."[764]

For young Dial-Net, the equal access balloting was a huge success.

By mid-summer of '86, Dial-Net had gained more than 6,000 new customers. "We received over ten percent of the people who filled out ballots," stated a thrilled Dennis. "We doubled our business."[765]

Perhaps just as important was the fact that both MidCo and Muth withdrew from equal access before the new system was hooked up, leaving Dial-Net to do battle with the big three of AT&T, MCI, and Sprint. These big three, as previously explained, were more focused on major markets, leaving the field wide open for Dial-Net to gain ground in smaller markets.

Star Power

The Dial-Net founding triumvirate comprised a perfect combination of experience and talents. John Dennis, named president of the company, brought industry experience and excelled in training new salesmen. Don Szymik, chief engineer, possessed technical know-how and insight that capitalized on both the increased access that the Bell breakup provided, plus technology that was advancing at an almost exponential rate. Finally, Jim Perry brought not only star power and name recognition, but an unmatched ability to break the ice with anyone and instantly break down their defenses. It was a virtually unstoppable combo.

Sales manager Brad VanLeur, who joined Dial-Net in 1989, explained the advantage of having Perry on his team.

"What Jim did for us was he was a great 'people person.' He was great socially. People would want to see him and talk to him. We loved to bring him with us on sales calls because he would break the ice for us. If they wanted to talk baseball or play golf—and who doesn't want to do that—they just gravitated to him. He was just a really good asset for us to have to bring people in. And he could really close a deal, too."

Jim, who was named chairman of the board, almost immediately became the face of Dial-Net, with his name and likeness featured in newspaper print ads, as well as billboard campaigns throughout the region.

"Billboards were everywhere featuring Dad looking larger than life!" marveled his youngest daughter, Michelle.

One early ad campaign featuring Jim in a three-piece suit and wearing a Twins cap was headlined, "Jim Perry's striking out the competition again." On one side of his likeness was a chart showing Dial-Net's cost savings for Sioux Falls calls to various destinations, while the other side carried the following quote: "When I was pitching in the major leagues, there was nothing more satisfying than going the distance and shutting out the competition. Well, that's exactly what Dial-Net is doing. Using state-of-the-art telecommunications equipment, we're providing long distance service that is guaranteed to cost you less than the competition. Just check the chart in this ad. Then, give us a call to find out how much we can save you. I think you'll like our pitch."[766]

The play on both Perry's athletic achievements, as well as his reputation as an honest, hard-working team player was a brilliant success. The company would continue to promote Perry's sterling reputation and his leadership throughout its existence.

Win-Win-Win

Not only did Dial-Net have a technological edge, but they had a "win-win-win" approach to doing business. That is, if the customer "wins" with better service at a lower price and the salesman "wins" with a good incentive plan, the company will "win" with growth and profits. The plan worked to perfection.

"We strived to treat our customers right," VanLeur explained. "If they had a line go down or had problems with their billing, we would go and talk to them. Even if they didn't have a problem, we made it a point to check in regularly to see how everything was going. We made sure our clients knew we cared about them and were there to help them solve their problems."

The company also strived to treat their salesmen right. They implemented a residual commission structure that not only rewarded salesmen for acquiring new accounts, but also for keeping and growing current accounts. This not only allowed salesmen to earn better and more consistent pay, but it provided encouragement to make sure existing customers were satisfied customers. Many Dial-Net accounts came from referrals.

"I spent a lot of time in the field with our salesmen," Jim related. "I always tried to treat them the way I would like to be treated. I took them out to dinner and got to know them. I went with them on sales calls. We would naturally start out talking baseball with a prospect, but then I would say, 'we've got to talk business.' I'd get them to give us a copy of their phone bill and we would take it back and analyze it.

I would get a customer to a certain point and then turn it over to the salesman. I would say, 'You handle it. I've got him this far, it's yours now.' When our salesman went back and showed them how much money we could save them, he was able to close the sale more often than not."

"I told our salesmen, never be late to an appointment. Be 15 minutes early. We're selling them, they're not selling you. Also, when you go into an office, you treat the secretary as nice as you would treat the boss there, because the secretary usually did a lot of the phone stuff anyway. One time, the guy we were meeting with asked his secretary, 'Do you like what you hear from these people?' She said, 'Oh yeah.' So he says to her, 'Okay, we'll go with them, but if anything happens, I'm coming for you!'"

"Boy, he was competitive," said VanLeur of Perry. "He would say, 'Let's get this guy. Okay, now let's get the next guy.' He was always pushing the salesmen to do more. He drove us to be our best."

While most were men, a couple of Dial-Net's best salespeople were women, according to Jim. "We even had some couples—husband-and-wife teams—who worked sales together. Our product was so good and our incentive structure was so strong that we had no trouble finding good people who wanted to sell for us."

Booming Blooms

With success came growth and with growth came more success. "By midway through their second year, I decided maybe they weren't so crazy," Thurman confessed. Though the company was not yet profitable, Thurman could see that it was only a matter of time with their steadily increasing sales numbers.

Dial-Net finally turned in their first profitable month at the end of their second year in business. "I knew then that we were going to make it," Jim recalled. By the end of 1986, Dial-Net had established a regional office in Rapid City, giving them full coverage of more than 100 cities throughout South Dakota. They had also initiated expansion into Colorado Springs and Denver, Colorado.

In early December of that year, Dial-Net announced another regional headquarters to be located in Grand Island, Nebraska. They projected their revenues of $8 million in 1986 would grow to $11 million in 1987 as they unleashed 35 salesmen selling long distance service to 57 cities throughout Nebraska's 308 area code. Although the service was offered primarily to businesses, residential customers could also make the switch.

While most other telecommunications companies had moved into major metropolitan areas to offer discount long-distance rates for business, Company president John Dennis explained Dial-Net's approach. "We're going to offer the little guy the same thing as in the major metros," he promised.[767]

"We had received many inquiries from Nebraska cities about our long distance service," stated Dennis.[768]

He also credited Northwestern Bell's updated equipment to go with the already excellent working relationship between the two companies, plus aggressive recruiting by the Grand Island Chamber of Commerce.

Rod Bates, Director of the Department of Economic Development for the state of Nebraska explained the state's reasoning for aggressively courting Dial-Net. "Telecommunications is predicted to be a trillion dollar industry by the 1990s and Nebraska wants to exploit it. Dial-Net is proof that deregulation doesn't mean geography will be a barrier to good service. Their interest in rural areas is very encouraging."[769]

By this time, Dial-Net had also upgraded its home office in Sioux Falls, and Jim Perry was using it to full advantage. "If our office opened at 8 o'clock, I was always in by 7:30," he explained. "I was always in early and my door was always open. I had a nice office. We built a trophy case in my office where I had a nice display of bats and other baseball memorabilia that made great conversation starters. I told my secretary if somebody comes into our building and wants to see the display, you take them in there."

Key Additions

As Dial-Net continued to grow, they gained the resources to purchase some smaller companies that could be helpful to their cause. In early 1989, they purchased BTI/Executone, which made Dial-Net a single-source supplier for all telecommunication needs. For the first time, Dial-Net could offer a "complete telecommunication package: long distance services, incoming 800 service, basic phone systems, sophisticated PBXs, switching hardware, pay phones and cellular phones."[770]

Soon after that, Dial-Net bought a small competitor called Computel. This not only added accounts to their stable, but also some top salesmen, including Brad VanLeur, who quickly formed a close working relationship with Jim. Though VanLeur had met Perry briefly prior to joining Dial-Net, this was the first opportunity for him to really get to know the former baseball star.

"I had met Jim Perry at a couple Twins functions and I knew he was a good guy, but nothing more. After coming aboard at Dial-Net, I could see right away he was a good people person. He would talk to everybody. I knew this would work great for clients.

"I never asked for his autograph until I got to Dial-Net," VanLeur confessed. "Once I got to know him, I asked for some autographed baseballs. I kept one for myself and gave some to the family. Before long, Jim and I would go to all these chamber functions. All the sales managers liked it when Jim would be at a trade show. We always tried to get him to come to the booth because he was a big draw.

"They would say, 'come and meet former Cy Young award winner Jim Perry at booth such and such,' and people would naturally gravitate to our booth. He would shake hands, sign an autograph, and that would open the door to talking about what we had to offer, which quite often led to making a sale."

"I spoke to 98 chamber of commerce meetings in one year throughout South Dakota," Jim confirmed. "And I had to arrange my schedule myself. When a conflict came up, I had to coordinate changes with the salesman in the area, but I always tried to get there because I knew how much it helped sales. The chambers liked us being a part of their events, too. For one event at a Holiday Inn, they made a giant ice sculpture in the shape of a phone and put it right out in front!"

Bonus Time

One of the keys to Dial-Net's success was their sales force and Dial-Net's leadership team recognized this. In addition to the residual commission structure, the company paid out handsome bonuses to top salesmen.

"At Christmas parties, we tried to honor our salesmen and give them generous cash bonuses for their hard work," Jim explained. "Our first Christmas, our top salesman, from Rapid City, got a ten thousand dollar sales bonus. He was a good salesman. I told the other guys, see, this guy worked hard and this year we only had one winner. Next year we might have two or three different winners."

Dial-Net continued to expand, opening more regional offices in Boise, Idaho and San Jose, California, where John Dennis had roots. Though Dial-Net faced more competition from "the big three" out in California, there was also abundant opportunity, with businesses of all sizes looking for long-distance access back toward the east. The potential was so vast, in fact, that Jim's wife Daphne felt compelled to speak up.

"We were at a Christmas party in California where Dial-Net had offices on the 15th floor of a big 16-floor office building," recalled Daphne. "Ron Hooper, who was the sales manager of the San Jose office, said 'Jim Perry's wife Daphne is on this trip. Maybe she would like to say something to the group.' I thought, 'Oh, Lord.' Well, the top salesman that year was from a small town in southern Minnesota, so I said, 'All of you salesmen out here should be ashamed of yourselves. You have more potential customers in this one building than a person in South Dakota or southern Minnesota. They have to drive for hours and hours just to find as many as you have right here in one building.'"

Perhaps due to Daphne's "encouragement," California eventually accounted for almost half of Dial-Net's business, as the company continued its fabulous growth. By 1990, Jim was making almost as much money in one month than he ever earned in a full season playing major league baseball.

Key Technology

A mishap with AT&T early in 1990 illustrated the technological advantage Dial-Net held over its more established competitor. As a Dial-Net ad that ran in the *Argus-Leader* newspaper explained, "The AT&T long distance network broke down, leaving its customers paralyzed for nine long hours. Millions of businesses came to a screeching halt! Deadlines were missed. Sales were lost.

"When your business is dependent upon a single long distance network," the ad continued, "it's like putting all your eggs in one basket. If that long distance network goes down, *you're out of business*. DIAL-NET provides access to *multiple* nationwide long distance networks. If there's a problem, DIAL-NET'S state-of-the-art equipment will *automatically* select another long distance network to make sure every call you make is completed. This type of service reliability is just one reason thousands of businesses across our region have chosen DIAL-NET as their long distance company. Another reason is savings—savings that can add up to a *better* bottom line for your business."[771]

While it was admittedly a biased account of AT&T's problem, the ad provided key insight into what made the more nimble and progressive Dial-Net better able to capitalize on emerging technological innovations. Dial-Net's sales teams appreciated not only the value of what they were selling, but also the high-quality product. Sales manager Brad VanLeur explained:

"We had a great team of engineers, led by Don Szymik," said VanLeur. "AT&T had its own network. Dial-Net would buy lines with several carriers—MCI, Qwest, Southwestern Bell, and the like. We built a good redundant network. If part of our network went down, we always had another part that was working."

Key Recognition

Dial-Net received national recognition in November of 1990 when they were included in *Inc.* magazine's list of the 500 fastest growing privately held companies. The rankings were based on the percentage of increases in sales between 1985 and 1989. Dial-Net had grown from $300,000 in 1985 sales to more than $27 million in '89—a whopping 7,979-percent increase. The phenomenal growth ranked Dial-Net 23rd on the Inc. magazine list.

Making the *Inc.* magazine list had been a goal at Dial-Net and company president John Dennis was thrilled. "It's going to give us a visibility in all of our new markets," he attested.[772]

With more than 300 employees serving customers in nine states, Dial-Net was off and running. Their explosive growth would continue for two more years, reaching a peak of $80 million in sales while serving customers in 16 states. Things were going almost too well.

"John and Don started talking about buying a private jet for the company," said Perry. "That's when I knew we were starting to get carried away with our success. John and Don were just becoming too extravagant."

Too Good To Pass Up

Though Dial-Net had amazingly grown to become the ninth largest long distance company in the U.S., their tremendous success was dwarfed by another upstart rival from Jackson, Mississippi. Long Distance Discount Services (LDDS), led by a brash dealmaker named Bernie Ebbers, was set on amassing enough capacity to dominate the exploding growth of data and internet traffic on not only a local and long-distance basis, but even international. LDDS was doing this by aggressively buying up rivals and smaller companies.

It was only a matter of time, and when LDDS finally came after Dial-Net in early 1993, they came with an offer that was too good to refuse. Perry's concern immediately turned to the hard-working sales staff that had helped to fuel the company's incredible growth.

"When we first started talking about selling," Jim recalled, "I told John that we need to honor the people who have put us where we are. We always tried to treat our people right. We gave our salesmen extra bonuses before we sold the company. Several salesmen told me 'We'll never work for another company that treats people as well as you have.' Some of our key employees got a year's pay when we sold."

"Dial-Net treated its people really well," Brad VanLeur concurred. "They were very generous with their employees."

Melinda Agre, who lost her position taking new orders at Dial-Net, shared similar feelings. "The hardest thing was it was a good company to work for," she told the *Argus Leader* following the sale.[773]

"We took Bernie Ebbers around to six different offices to show him our operation," said Perry. "He liked everything he saw. The deal got done quickly."

18

Giving Back

Despite more time on his hands and suddenly blessed with more money than he ever dreamed of, Jim Perry did not slow down. Far from it. He continued to pour his energy into charitable work, as he had done consistently since his playing days. One of the first things he and Daphne did with their windfall from the sale of Dial-Net was to set aside money in a trust for what is now Campbell University.

Campbell had transitioned from a junior college to a four-year institution in 1961 before becoming a full-fledged university in 1979. With the school in the midst of major academic growth, Jim and Daphne looked to help the athletic program keep pace at the institution that first brought them together.

"If it weren't for Campbell, we wouldn't have met," said Jim. "Our children, our grandchildren... none of that would have happened if it hadn't been for Campbell."[774]

Jim also credited the school for giving him the opportunity to fulfill his hopes and dreams. "For as long as I can remember, I dreamed of playing baseball. This college gave me the opportunity to chase my dreams."[775]

With significant funding from the Perry trust, major renovations to Campbell's baseball facility began in 2011. On November 12, 2012, Campbell announced it would rename the stadium in honor of Jim Perry. On February 15, 2013, Jim Perry Stadium was officially dedicated. The Jim and Daphne Perry Pavilion, housing new offices for the entire baseball staff plus a state-of-the-art locker room was added in 2017.

"We're fortunate that we're able to do the things we can do for Campbell," Jim said. "We decided a long time ago to do this. Campbell helped me to get to where I am today. Why can't I turn around and help them now? I've been looking forward to this for a long time."[776]

Golfing for Dollars

Jim Perry has always been one to step up and help with a charitable cause, and more often than not his method of choice has been raising money for charity via celebrity golf outings. Jim has not only been a reliable participant, but also a major organizer. If he does not hold the unofficial record for playing in the most charity outings, he may well hold the title for helping to organize more than any celebrity in history. The story of the Jim Perry Celebrity Classic illustrates his impact.

Jim was looking to go hunting in the Central Montana area and to visit his friend Mike McLaughlin, a former Minnesota stock broker who had moved to Lewistown, Montana several years earlier. Sitting in the Elks Club bar, McLaughlin turned to his buddy, Hank Hanson, an experienced fund-raiser, and said, "Hey Hank, let's bring in the Per and put on a golf tournament.

"The who?" asked a confused Hanson.

"Jim Perry, the former Minnesota Twins great," McLaughlin replied. He proceeded to explain how Perry was a friend of his and that he had been involved in many celebrity golf tournaments for charities around the country and he would probably be up for one in Lewistown.

"Let's go for it," said an excited Hanson, and the Jim Perry Celebrity Classic was born.[777]

The first event teed off on September 21, 1985 with 46 golfers and Jim Perry the only notable "celebrity" on hand. Braving 29-degree temperatures, the players were forced to quit after nine holes when snow began to accumulate on the greens. The event raised a grand total of $800 which went to buy equipment for Lewistown's youth baseball program. Was Jim Perry frustrated by the relatively small size of an event bearing his name? Of course not. He was simply determined to help grow it.

The following year, Jim urged Hanson and McLaughlin to make the event bigger and better. For one thing, he insisted that the Special Olympics be included as a beneficiary and he also suggested that they go after a major sponsor for the event. The Jim Perry-Savin Corporation Celebrity Classic went off in 1986 with 70 golfers, including nearly 20 celebrity athletes, both professional and collegiate, past and present, from baseball, football, basketball, boxing, and wrestling.

By its tenth year in 1994, the Perry Classic was sold out months in advance and featured several big-name celebrities, including NFL hall-of-famers Johnny Unitas of the Baltimore Colts and Kansas City Chiefs great Bobby Bell. Unsurprisingly, Jim Perry made it a point to personally invite every celebrity participant in order to be sure they realized the importance of the fundraiser.

In 1995, the Jim Perry Celebrity Golf Classic expanded to a second event in South Dakota at the Spring Creek Country Club just south of Sioux Falls. The state that had been so good to Jim was facing a crisis and he wanted to help. A lack of available scholarships was hampering enrollment at technical schools in the state, leading high-tech firms to expand elsewhere.

"There is every year not a big enough pool of graduates to satisfy the industries in our state," said Leo Hartig, a former Sioux Falls newscaster who helped organize the scholarship drive that money from the event would fund.[778]

Enter Jim Perry, who gladly got on the phone to recruit athletes from baseball, football, basketball, boxing, and even rodeo. Event coordinator Bud Olson marveled at Perry's networking ability. "He must have a lot of friends," Olson remarked, "because all it took was a phone call to get them here."[779]

Twenty four celebrity athletes came out to Sioux Falls in support of Jim Perry and the event's charities, including baseball hall-of-famers Bob Feller, Gaylord Perry, and Tony Oliva, as well as basketball greats Cazzie Russell and Darral Imhoff. Other notables included baseball's Dave Kingman, Ryne Duren, Donn Clendenon, Jim Merritt, Bernie Allen, Jim Maloney, Roy Sievers, Mudcat Grant, and Bert Campaneris.

"The celebrities have been remarkable," Olson said. "Their enthusiasm and readiness for this has really been outstanding."[780]

With a $300 entry fee and one hundred spots to golf and rub elbows with sports legends, the event raised approximately $150,000 to go toward the scholarships in South Dakota's four technical schools located in Sioux Falls, Rapid City, Mitchell, and Watertown.

Hall-of-fame pitcher Bob Feller explained the importance of Jim Perry's name on the event. "I do a lot of these things when I'm not suspicious of the charity," Feller stated. "Sometimes you run into people who are just out to make a profit, and you have to be careful of those guys. But Jim's a good friend of mine and I know this is a worthwhile charity."[781]

Jim's Montana event would run twenty consecutive years with his leadership, raising close to $200,000 for a variety of youth sports programs in central Montana. "We thought if we could get to where we were making $20,000 from this small town, that would be very good. Well, we've done that," stated Perry.[782]

Other charity events included the Jim Perry Legends Golf Classic, which ran for ten years in Ohio from 2003-2012, presented by the Ohio Masonic Home. Over the years, these events raised money for various charities. Among Jim's favorites were the Boys' Ranch and Habitat For Humanity.

Ron Noble, who ran the Celebrity Golf Classic at Plantation Golf & Country Club in Venice, Florida was thankful for 15 years of Jim's involvement. "We call Jim Perry the Ambassador of Goodwill," Noble said. "He would shake everyone's hand. If he didn't know somebody, he would go right up and meet them."

The sports celebrities who came out to support the cause felt such a loyalty to Jim Perry that it was not uncommon for them to make a return engagement the following year. George Geise, sports editor for the *Great Falls Tribune*, once wrote that "Perry plays in so many celebrity golf events across the country that he has built a network of old pros he can call on for appearances. The popular veterans who keep coming back each summer make Perry's bash more like a family reunion than a celebrity affair."[783]

Money Never Sleeps

None of the Dial-Net founders were retained by LDDS following the sale, and all three were restricted by a two-year non-compete clause as part of the deal. While Jim's short-term business exploits were put on a brief hold, he kept abreast of developments in the telecommunications industry.

Former sales manager Brad VanLeur was one of the people still in the business who Jim kept in touch with. Besides forming a great team working together, the two had formed a bond through their mutual love of pheasant hunting. Shortly after he joined Dial-Net and found out Perry was a hunter, VanLeur asked him if he ever did any pheasant hunting in the Sioux Falls area.

"I've been out with some guys up near Madison," Jim told him, "but they aren't a very experienced group. Once the shootin' starts, I do more ducking (for safety) than hunting."

After he stopped laughing, VanLeur invited Jim out to hunt at his family farm where Brad's father ran a tight ship as far as making sure all hunters followed proper hunting safety protocol. The opening of pheasant hunting season in South Dakota comes on the third Saturday of October at high noon. Jim would not miss spending this day on the VanLeur family farm for the next 26 consecutive years.

Though VanLeur initially remained with LDDS following their purchase of Dial-Net, he did not stick around for long. "I didn't like some of the things LDDS did, the way they did business. Their primary concern was just growing as fast as possible. Product quality and customer satisfaction—two keys to Dial-Net's success—simply did not get the same emphasis. They just didn't seem like the right organization for me, so I left after about three months."

VanLeur soon wound up at FirsTel, a small telecom company that was starting up in Sioux Falls following the Dial-Net sale. FirsTel founder, Rick Law, said, "I wouldn't have started this company if it hadn't been for the sale of Dial-Net. I think that there are a lot of people that are disappointed that Dial-Net was sold."[784]

Marshall Damgaard, executive director of the state's public utility commission, noticed a growing number of companies requesting permission to specialize in portions of the long-distance market, hoping to fill some of the gaps left behind by Dial-Net's disappearance. "There is an incredible growing number of niche companies like FirsTel that serve a very tiny, but they hope growing niche," said Damgaard.[785]

Once Jim's non-compete agreement ran out, he got involved with FirsTel, serving something of a role similar to that which Wilbur Peters once served in the early stages of Dial-Net. He provided the company with needed capital as an investor, as well as occasional input. The company was successful enough to be bought up a few years later, similar to what happened with Dial-Net. Just as Peters had benefited from his investment in Dial-Net, Perry did the same with FirsTel.

As the telecommunications industry continued its rapid metamorphosis, some other aspects changed, leading to increased "access." Companies that had their own lines could sell access for other companies to use their lines. Feeling he could take advantage of this development, VanLeur struck out on his own and started Orbit Com, a company that specialized in access, long distance, local, and even a little bit of cellular service. Once again, Jim stepped in as a key early-stage investor, and once again it was a profitable investment. Orbit Com was in business from 2002-2015.

Brad VanLeur was not the only Dial-Net employee who found their way to FirsTel and then Orbit Com. He later explained how that migration helped with the success of the two later companies.

"We always placed a high priority on customer satisfaction with Dial-Net," said VanLeur. "When we went back to those same people with FirsTel and then Orbit Com, they remembered how we treated them and they stuck with us."

Good Vibrations

A hallmark of Jim's post-playing business success has been to surround himself with good people—businessmen and advisors with high character, much like that of himself, and rely on them for sound advice. Fred Thurman, one of those people, explained, "Jim listens to people that he trusts."

It is interesting to note that Jim's manager, Billy Martin, made a similar observation back in 1969 when he said "one of Perry's greatest assets is that he listens to advice."[786]

Terry Elgethun was another one of those people Jim trusted and who gave good advice. A former portfolio manager with Dean Witter and then Wells Fargo, Terry formed his own company, Elgethun Capital Management in 2003. In addition to serving as Jim's frequent golf partner, Terry handled several investments for the Perry family and was a trusted friend. Terry passed away unexpectedly in 2012 and Elgethun Capital Management was left in the capable hands of John Barker, who has since played a key role in expertly advising the Perry family.

It is not uncommon to hear of athletes who made a fortune during their playing careers only to see it disappear following their playing days with bad financial decisions based on poor advice. Fred Thurman, Terry Elgethun, and John Barker have done a fantastic job of helping Jim and Daphne to make the most of what they worked so hard for. They have each been blessed friends and advisors to Jim Perry and his family.

Match Made in Heaven

One important aspect of the strong marriage Jim and Daphne Perry share is their mutual love and devotion to the Lord. Raised by Mamma Ruby to make attendance at Sunday School a priority, Jim compiled an admirable record of several years without a miss. As was the practice in many churches of the time, Jim was awarded a badge following each year of perfect attendance. Not surprisingly, the dutiful young man had amassed quite a collection of attendance badges by the time he arrived at Campbell, an achievement for which Coach McCall gave him a good natured razzing on a regular basis.

While they had always given to the church, following the sale of Dial-Net, Jim and Daphne made it a priority to give back to the home churches that had been so instrumental in providing them with a strong Christian foundation during their formative years. For Jim this was the same Maple Grove First Christian Church back in Farm Life, N.C. where he had piled up the perfect attendance badges. For Daphne, it was Roper (N.C.) Baptist Church. They would also become generous supporters of David Jeremiah's Turning Point for God ministry.

Jim's faith provided a guiding light through some of his toughest challenges when he was fighting to reestablish himself in Minnesota. This faith was not limited to quiet prayer alone in his room. In the mid-1960s, Al Worthington, along with fellow pitchers Jim Perry and Jim Kaat led the Twins in becoming one of the first teams to arrange for a local Christian leader to lead a regular Bible study and worship with Twins players when the team was on the road. The trio campaigned and eventually was successful in changing the location of these Sunday morning gatherings from the team hotel to the ballpark, which made it much easier for more players to participate.

Daphne, of course, had been performing in front of church congregations since before she was big enough to be seen over the choir rail. She carried her singing talents on to the renowned formal Campbell Touring Choir and then the church choir for many years into adulthood.

With a beautiful voice and lifelong experience performing in front of a crowd, it was only natural that Daphne would become an influential Christian leader. In addition to volunteering as a Sunday School teacher while her kids were growing up, Daphne became active in Christian Women's Club. A national organization with chapters in cities around the country, Christian Women's Club held monthly meetings in which a guest speaker would make a presentation that would be of interest and enlightenment to women in the area. Daphne's involvement in CWC included a term as president of the Minneapolis chapter, which provided a wonderful opportunity to share her testimony.

"We would hold meetings in small towns throughout Minnesota, as well as parts of South Dakota and Iowa," said Daphne. "While I enjoyed the opportunity to share my testimony, it could also be quite nerve-wracking. In order to calm myself, I would start off with a few simple questions, usually about the Twins and baseball. (Of course, my favorite was 'What Twins player won the Cy Young award in 1970?') I then transitioned with a baseball analogy:

"The tension I feel right now might be a lot like Jim feels when he has the bases loaded and a 3-2 count on a top hitter. As you know, I'm the wife of a professional baseball player. I am also a housewife, the mother of three, and I'm certainly no speaker, but the need to witness to tell others of Jesus

Christ is my reason for coming. What a joy and a thrill it is to be used by God.

"'Too many of us seldom open our mouths for Christ. We open them to eat, to gossip, to criticize, and to cheer for our favorite team, but not to present the Gospel. We often feel inadequate and know there are others that can do a better job, so we sit back, but remember, all of us can witness. Do not minimize the value of your personal individual witness. "'To paraphrase what Paul wrote in *2 Timothy 1:8, If you will stir up this inner power, you will never be afraid to tell others about our Lord.*

"God tells us in *Romans 10:10, For it is by believing in his heart that a man becomes right with God; and with his mouth he tells others of his faith, confirming his salvation.*

"And in *Mark 16:15, Go ye into all the world and preach the Gospel.*

"Now, I'm not here to preach, but to share how God has worked in my life."

"I would proceed to share how being a baseball wife is not all glitz and glamour. I would talk about the ups and downs of Jim's career and my struggles to be supportive even as I sometimes wondered why God would not step in and let his managers give him a chance. Then I would typically finish with another baseball analogy:

"As I close, I'd like to leave you with this baseball illustration, which shows how each of us can experience an abundant life here, and later eternal life with God. Picture a baseball diamond…

"God tells us that salvation through Jesus Christ is as simple as A-B-C, or as running the bases, 1st to 2nd to 3rd:

"FIRST BASE: **A**ccept Christ. *John 3:16, For God so loved the world that He gave His only begotten Son, that whosoever believeth in Him should not perish but have everlasting life.*

"SECOND BASE: **B**elieve in Jesus Christ as your personal savior. *John 14:6, I am the way, the truth, and the life. No man cometh unto the Father but by me.*

"THIRD BASE: **C**onfess your sins. Be sorry for your sins and being out of fellowship. *1 John 1:9, If we confess our sins, He is faithful and just to forgive us our sins and to cleanse us from all unrighteousness.*

"When you've run the bases, you have:
  • **A**ccepted Christ, admitted you are a sinner (1st Base)
  • **B**elieved in Jesus Christ as your savior and that he died on the cross to save you from your sins (2nd Base)
  • **C**onfessed your sins to God and make it public (3rd Base)
"Once we have accomplished all of these, we have "run the bases," but in order to score a run, we must advance from third base to home. In the same way, we must complete our A-B-C's by *personally receiving Jesus as Lord of our lives.* We must let go and allow Him to take control.
"**Accept, Believe, Confess, Receive**... *John 1:12, But to all who received Him, He gave the right to become the children of God.*"

"Now, you've touched all the bases and you have eternal life—you are *home safe!*"

For years even after she was no longer actively speaking at events, Christian Women's Club would receive letters periodically from women who said Daphne Perry's testimony had moved them and changed their lives.

Baseball Hall

Even during the height of his businessworld success, Jim Perry always remained connected to the game that made him famous. For every appearance or interview he made on behalf of Dial-Net, the conversation inevitably turned back to baseball. Whether it was reminiscences of his career or his thoughts on present-day developments, Jim's perspective was frequently in demand.

One such occasion was a sad one on Christmas Day, 1989 when a key figure in Jim's rise to baseball fame was lost. Billy Martin died in a one-vehicle crash near his Binghamton, New York home. Back in Edina, Minnesota, the news hit Jim hard.

"I'm sad," he said. "I loved Billy Martin. He was a great guy. He told me I could win twenty. He had faith in me. In tight games, he would come to the mound and tell me, 'You're as good as I got. Go get 'em.'

"Some people didn't like Billy, but he was great for baseball. He got people to the ballpark. He loved to win. He caused excitement. If he didn't win, you would see him over in the corner pouting. That is the way he was."

Though many considered Martin hard to get along with, Jim recalled their special relationship. "I knew when I could talk to him and I knew when not to. I am going to miss him."[787]

One of the difficult aspects of taking care of yourself and having the good fortune to live a long, healthy life is that you begin to lose many of those who made a difference in that life. Fortunately, plenty of those difference-makers were on hand when Jim received one of his greatest honors.

On June 11, 2011, Jim Perry was inducted as the 23rd member of the Minnesota Twins Hall of Fame. Even for a man who had accomplished so much, Jim said he considered the honor to be "one of the better things that has happened in my life. This is super, a thrill."[788]

The honor was undoubtedly special because of the way the move to The Land of 10,000 Lakes had impacted Jim's life. "My career really started jumping in Minnesota," he said. "I was in Cleveland to start my career, but when we went to Minnesota, I told my wife, 'You'll like the people there, the park there, the players there.' And you know what? We spent thirty years up there. All our children went to the same grammar school and high school and finished there. That tells you what we think about Minnesota."[789]

Charley "Shooter" Walters, a sports columnist for the *Pioneer Press,* profiled the 75-year old former star prior to his induction. "Perry spends summers in North Carolina, winters in Florida. He's extremely fit and, despite his age, is a three-handicap golfer who has won the Super Senior division at his Old North State course near Charlotte the last half-dozen years. He's got the enthusiasm of a teenager."[790]

While many former teammates would be on hand in Minnesota to celebrate this honor, the passage of time was already taking its toll on Perry's contemporaries almost 40 years after his last Twins pitch. "I'm really looking forward to seeing the guys up there from a long time ago," Perry said prior to traveling to Minnesota from his home, now in North Carolina. "You know what, though? I'm going to miss Harmon. I really miss Harmon."[791]

Harmon Killebrew, who was in many ways the heart and soul of the first great Twins teams in the 1960s, had succumbed to cancer at age 74 less than a month prior to Jim's ceremony.

"When I came to the Twins after being traded by Cleveland," Jim recalled, "Harmon was the first guy who said to me, 'Welcome to the team, Jim. Pitch good, and we'll try to get some runs. And let's have a good time and win.'

"Harmon always called me 'Mother Perry.' That was because I always took care of him, made sure he didn't get hurt. I told him I needed him out on the field. 'Mother Perry.' Just him being on the field made a difference."[792]

Bert Blyleven, who broke in as a rookie during Jim's 1970 Cy Young award-winning season, presented Perry for the on-field induction ceremonies. "There's no telling what he might say," Jim laughed before the ceremony, alluding to Blyleven's well-earned reputation as a prankster.[793]

"You know what? Bert says I was a big thing in his career, but it goes the other way around, too. I told him, 'You might have put some spirit in me, too, because you came in at 19 and threw that hard fastball and that great curveball.' I was thinking that maybe he was coming up here to take my spot. I told him he made me have a good year that year."[794]

When Blyleven was inducted into the National Baseball Hall of Fame later that same summer, his thoughts turned back to his early days playing for a great team in a modest stadium in a small market that may have left many of the stars overlooked.

"I look at the guys in the Twins Hall of Fame, and I played with all of them," Blyleven said proudly. "That's pretty special. It was a great group of guys, a great group of players, and I think more of them should be recognized."[795]

Blyleven also echoed Harmon's feelings about their well-respected teammate. "I was just thinking back to Jim Perry, and his induction into the Twins Hall of Fame. He wasn't just a father figure to me. He was a mother figure, too. He was my first roommate, and I couldn't do anything for myself."[796]

Great Pitcher, Greater Man

In 2011, the *Cleveland Plain Dealer* published a series of essays they called "Tribe Memories." The stories were submitted by area readers and one particular entry perfectly encapsulated the essence of Jim Perry the great pitcher and the even greater man.

The story was submitted by Stu McAllister, a resident of Crestline, Ohio, located about 95 miles to the southwest of Cleveland:[797]

"In 1959 in Crestline, Ohio, my 16-year old brother Fritz was to be the starting pitcher in the town's Pony League championship game. On the last day of practice, Fritz was riding his bike home when he was hit by a train and lost his left leg.

"Soon after the accident, I took a train to Cleveland with a special purpose in mind. I wanted autographs for my brother from our favorite team. I walked from Terminal Tower to Municipal Stadium, bought a game ticket and a program, turned to the scorecard in the program, and marched through the concourse until I found the Indians dressing room.

"I introduced myself to the security guard and stated my reason for being there. He listened politely, then he smiled and said, 'Wait here a minute, son.' Then he went inside and closed the door.

"Soon after, the door opened again and I was greeted by the pitcher Jim Perry, who would start the game that day. He escorted me into the clubhouse.

"I stood there awestruck just inside the door while Jim Perry did the legwork. I remember Tito Francona giving me a smile and a wave as he signed the scorecard. I was too shocked in the moment to remember anything else about being in the presence of my beloved Tribe, in the privacy of their dressing room, so up-close and personal. I do remember this: They were much bigger and muscular than they appeared on TV, or even in the ballpark.

"Every Tribe player signed the scorecard for Fritz, and Jim Perry wrote, 'Fritz, this game's for you,' and then **he won the game!**"

Notes

1. Nichols, Max. "'I rate starting job,' declares Twins' Perry, tired of bull pen." *The Sporting News*, December 31, 1966, p. 30.
2. Ibid.
3. Briere, Tom. "Perry, Allison pace Twins." *Minneapolis Tribune*, August 11, 1967, p. 23.
4. Hartman, Sid. *Minneapolis Tribune*, August 11, 1967, p. 24.
5. Staff. "Kaat set by opener?" *Minneapolis Tribune*, March 21, 1968, p. 34.
6. Cullum, Dick. *Minneapolis Tribune*, April 1, 1968, p. 32.
7. Staff. "Perry—journeyman pitcher." *Minneapolis Tribune*, April 15, 1968, p. 36.
8. Ibid.
9. Ibid.
10. Ibid.
11. Ibid.
12. Ibid.
13. Cullum, Dick. *Minneapolis Tribune*, April 17, 1968, p. 34.
14. Mona, Dave. "Indians, Tiant blank Twins; Kaat arm ok." *Minneapolis Tribune*, May 4, 1968, p. 16.
15. Hartman, Sid. *Minneapolis Tribune*, May 15, 1968, p.26.
16. Hartman, Sid. *Minneapolis Tribune*, May 29, 1968, p. 22.
17. Hartman, Sid. *Minneapolis Tribune*, June 17, 1968, p. 11.
18. Mona, Dave. "Rain halts Twins, Perry no-hitter." *Minneapolis Tribune*, May 18, 1968, p. 11.
19. Ibid.
20. Ibid.
21. Netland, Dwayne. "Twins rained out; Harmon, Carew on stars." *Minneapolis Tribune*, June 26, 1968, p. 28.
22. Ibid.
23. Netland, Dwayne. "Bauer can't help but remember 1966." *Minneapolis Tribune*, June 27, 1968, p.34.
24. Netland, Dwayne. "McDowell stifles Twins." *Minneapolis Tribune*, July 2, 1968, p.26.
25. Ibid.
26. Ibid.
27. Ibid., 25.
28. Ibid.
29. Ibid.
30. Ibid., 26.
31. Hartman, Sid. *Minneapolis Tribune*, July 22, 1968, p. 28.
32. Ibid.
33. Mona, Dave. "A's nullify Twin rally in 8-7 win." *Minneapolis Tribune*, July 28, 1968, p. 1S.
34. Mona, Dave. "Perry, Chisox errors end Twin loss string." *Minneapolis Tribune*, August 2, 1968, p. 23.
35. Mona, Dave. "Indians Trip Twins in 12th." *Minneapolis Tribune*, September 12, 1968, p. 30.
36. Mona, Dave. "Twins Carew 'best actor' in baseball nummy awards." *Minneapolis Tribune*, September 23, 1968, p. 30.
37. Mona, Dave. "It's official—Martin Twins' pilot." *Minneapolis Tribune*, October 12, 1968, p.17.
38. Ibid.
39. Mona, Dave. "Tovar signs to complete Twin roster." *Minneapolis Tribune*, October 12, 1968, p.17.

40. Lamey, Mike. "Jim Perry hankers for series duel against brother Gaylord." *The Sporting News*, August 23, 1969, p. 15.

41. Hartman, Sid. "Boswell back; Martin hasn't set starters." *Minneapolis Tribune*, April 5, 1969, p. 11.

42. Hartman, Sid. "Twins beaten by Mets 'Once+.'" *Minneapolis Tribune*, April 7, 1969, p. 33.

43. Hartman, Sid. *Minneapolis Tribune*, April 3, 1969, p. 34.

44. Hartman, Sid. "Short's Senators clobber Chance, Twins, 7-2." *Minneapolis Tribune*, April 4, 1969, p. 29.

45. Hartman, Sid. "Twins beaten by Mets 'Once+.'" *Minneapolis Tribune*, April 7, 1969, p. 31.

46. Mona, Dave. "Perry shuts out Kansas City 4-0." *Minneapolis Tribune*, April 29, 1969, p. 21.

47. Ibid.

48. Ibid.

49. Ibid.

50. Ibid., 22.

51. "Chance, Reese nurse arm, leg ailments." *Minneapolis Tribune*, May 22, 1969, p. 34.

52. Hartman, Sid. *Minneapolis Tribune*, May 24, 1969, p. 16.

53. Mona, Dave. "Worthington glad to be back, ready to face 'dumb' hitters." *Minneapolis Tribune*, May 30, 1969, p. 17.

54. Hartman, Sid. *Minneapolis Tribune*, June 17, 1969, p. 26.

55. "Practice makes Perry and Oliva perfect." *The Sporting News*, July 5, 1969, p. 34.

56. Foss, Paul. "Monday morning quarterback." *Minneapolis Tribune*, June 30, 1969, p. 26.

57. Mona, Dave. "Killebrew, Twins rip A's 13-1." *Minneapolis Tribune*, July 6, 1969, p. 3S.

58. Ibid.

59. Ibid., 1S.

60. Mona, Dave. "Twins post 'divine' win." *Minneapolis Tribune*, July 11, 1969, p. 32.

61. Mona, Dave. "Reese, Twins rap Seattle for 11-1 win." *Minneapolis Tribune*, July 13, 1969, p. S1.

62. Haft, Chris. "After moon landing, Gaylord Perry shocked everyone." https://www.mlb.com/news/gaylord -perry-first-career-homer-moon- landing

63. Ibid.

64. Bluth, Jack. "Speaking of sports." *San Mateo Times*, August 27, 1969, p. 41.

65. Price, S.L. "Moon magic: the Apollo 11 landing wasn't the only fantastical event of July 20, 1969." *Sports Illustrated*, July 15, 2019, p. 17.

66. Hartman, Sid. *Minneapolis Tribune*, July 22, 1969, p. 20.

67. Hartman, Sid. *Minneapolis Tribune*, July 27, 1969, p. 3S.

68. Ibid.

69. Hartman, Sid. *Minneapolis Tribune*, July 30, 1969, p. 28.

70. Ibid.

71. Ibid.

72. Staff. "Twins start longest, most vital road trip." *Minneapolis Tribune*, August 4, 1969, p. 31.

73. Ibid.

74. Cullum, Dick. "Twins, Perry top Tigers 3-1." *Minneapolis Tribune*, August 7, 1969, p. 29.

75. Ibid.

76. Foss, Paul. "Monday morning quarterback." *Minneapolis Tribune*, August 18, 1969, p. 36.

77. Mona, Dave. "Twins rout Yanks; Perry wins 5th." *Minneapolis Tribune*, August 24, 1969, p. 3S.

78. Ibid., 1S.

79. Ibid.
80. Ibid., 3S.
81. Ibid.
82. Mona, Dave. "Twins stop Nats for Perry's 16th." *Minneapolis Tribune*, August 28, 1969, p. 37.
83. Mona, Dave. "Perry beats Royals 3-0 for 18th." *Minneapolis Tribune*, September 13, 1969, p. 13.
84. Mona, Dave. "Twins rout A's 11-3." *Minneapolis Tribune*, Sept. 17, 1969, p.27.
85. Mona, Dave. "Perry takes 20th." *Minneapolis Tribune*, Sept. 21, 1969, p. 1S.
86. Ibid., 5S.
87. Mona, Dave. "Blair bunts Birds past Twins in 12." *Minneapolis Tribune*, October 5, 1969, p. 3S.
88. Blount, Roy Jr. "Return of the natives." *Sports Illustrated*, March 29, 1971,p.66.
89. Perry, Gaylord. *Me and the Spitter*, Clarke, Irwin & Company, 1974, p. 59.
90. Ibid., 48.
91. Fowler, Bob. "20 is the name of Perrys' game." *The Sporting News*, October 3, 1970, p. 3.
92. Ibid.
93. Smith, Seymour S. "Perrys first brothers to win 20 each in same season." *Baltimore Sun*, October 3, 1970, p. B5.
94. Schneider, Russell. "Gaylord, now mr. kleen, cleans up victories." *The Sporting News*, June 15, 1974, p. 3.
95. "Sentiment growing for Henderson Co. farm life school." *The Western Democrat and French Broad Hustler*. August 13, 1914. https://ruralnchistory.blogspot.com/2014/08/farm-life-high-schools-established-in.html
96. Perry, Gaylord. *Me and the Spitter*, Clarke, Irwin & Company, 1974, p. 48.
97. Ibid., 55.
98. Blount, Roy Jr. "Return of the natives." *Sports Illustrated*, March 29, 1971,p.64.
99. Perry, Gaylord. *Me and the Spitter*, Clarke, Irwin & Company, 1974, p. 55.
100. Blount, Roy Jr. "Return of the natives." *Sports Illustrated*, March 29, 1971,p.75.
101. Perry, Gaylord. *Me and the Spitter*, Clarke, Irwin & Company, 1974, p. 75.
102. Ibid., 85.
103. Blount, Roy Jr. "Return of the natives." *Sports Illustrated*, March 29, 1971, p. 69.
104. Shapiro, Hal. "Surveying the scene." *Carteret County News-Times*, June 7, 1955, p. 2.
105. Blount, Roy Jr. "Return of the natives." *Sports Illustrated*, March 29, 1971, p. 69.
106. Breibart, Jack. "Jim fond of Campbell College." *Raleigh News and Observer*, July 19, 1959, p. II-3.
107. "Cy Young Award winner Jim Perry says his major league dream became reality thanks to Campbell University." *Campbell University Magazine*, December 28, 2012. https://magazine.campbell.edu/articles/dreaming-big/
108. Breibart, Jack. "Jim fond of Campbell College." *Raleigh News and Observer*, July 19, 1959, p. II-3.
109. Ibid.
110. Ibid.
111. "Cy Young Award winner Jim Perry says his major league dream became reality thanks to Campbell University." *Campbell University Magazine*, December 28, 2012.

https://magazine.campbell.edu/articles/dreaming-big/

112. Ibid.

113. Ibid.

114. Associated Press. "Perry earns role as Tribe starter." *Tampa Times*, July 27, 1959, p. 10.

115. Quincy, Bob. "A bonus that went to pappy." *Charlotte News*, August 24, 1959, p. 8.

116. Associated Press. "North Platte wins." *Lincoln Star*, August 18, 1956, p.12.

117. McAuley, Ed. "The character who isn't one." *Baseball Digest*, September, 1960. P. 30.

118. Fitzgerald, Eugene. "Good overall balance may pull Twins out of cellar." *St. Cloud Daily Times*, April 23, 1957, p. 20.

119. Perry, Gaylord. Me and the Spitter, Clarke, Irwin & Company, 1974, p. 98.

120. Breibart, Jack. "Perry brothers: they keep close tab." *Raleigh News and Observer*, July 19, 1959, p. II-3.

121. Associated Press. "Indians take bigger lead in loop race." *Daily Intelligencer Journal*, August 16, 1958, p. 13.

122. Porter, Carl. "Tribe departs smiling as Jim Perry sizzles." *Tucson Citizen*, April 3, 1959, p. 17.

123. Breibart, Jack. "Game against Cubs landed Perry job with Tribe." *Raleigh News and Observer*, July 19, 1959, p. II-3.

124. Lebovitz, Hal. "Tribe whoops it up for Perry in rookie of year showdown." *The Sporting News*, Sept. 30, 1959, p. 24.

125. Schlemmer, Jim. "Lane withdraws bids for Jones and Lopez." *Akron Beacon Journal*, March 28, 1959, p. 18.

126. Porter, Carl. "Tribe departs smiling as Jim Perry sizzles." *Tucson Citizen*, April 3, 1959, p. 17.

127. Associated Press. "Perry finds he's no. 1 in 'family'." *Spokesman-Review*, June 7, 1959, p. 6.

128. Porter, Carl. "Tribe departs smiling as Jim Perry sizzles." *Tucson Citizen*, April 3, 1959, p. 17.

129. Schlemmer, Jim. "Indians are 'wild about Perry." *Akron Beacon Journal*, April 3, 1959, p. 37.

130. Ibid.

131. Ibid.

132. Porter, Carl. "Tribe departs smiling as Jim Perry sizzles." *Tucson Citizen*, April 3, 1959, p. 17.

133. Blount, Roy Jr. "Return of the natives." *Sports Illustrated*, March 29, 1971, p. 66.

134. "Cy Young Award winner Jim Perry says his major league dream became reality thanks to Campbell University." *Campbell University Magazine*, December 28, 2012. https://magazine.campbell.edu/articles/dreaming-big/

135. Schlemmer, Jim. "Gordon lacks many answers." *Akron Beacon Journal*, April 7, 1959, p. 20.

136. Associated Press. "Rookie to receive first starting job." *Marion Star*, April 22, 1959, p. 20.

137. United Press International. "Big Yank error was in getting Jim Perry mad." *Coshocton Tribune*, May 13, 1959, p.12.

138. Grayson, Harry. "Gordon's full of fight, and so are his Indians." *Lima News*, May 24, 1959, p. D3.

139. Ibid.

140. Bang, Ed. "Dodgers' miracle rated top thrill." *The Sporting News*, December 30, 1959, p. 32.

141. Young, Dick. "Lane says sked juggling to Yank fear of Indians." *New York Daily News*, May 14, 1959, p. 87.

142. Ibid.

143. Lebovitz, Hal. "Perry's whiff pitch dazzled Yanks on first visit to N.Y." *The Sporting News*, May 20, 1959, p. 12.

144. Mozley, Dana. "Perry's pinch-pitching rewards Gordon's faith." *New York Daily News*, May 14, 1959, p. 80.

145. Farrington, Frank. "The Fanning Mill." *St. Cloud Daily Times*, May 22, 1959, p. 12.

146. Lebovitz, Hal. "Tribe whoops it up for Perry in rookie of year show-down." *The Sporting News*, Sept. 30, 1959, p. 24.

147. Hoobing, Bob. "Perry saves Grant; Indians prevail 4-3." *Marion Star*, May 16, 1959, p. 15.

148. Ibid.

149. United Press International. "Biggest win of season—Gordon." *Sandusky Register*, July 24, 1959, p. 14.

150. Associated Press. "Harder, McLish 'polished' Perry." *Massillon Evening Independent*, July 27, 1959, p. 16.

151. United Press International. "Slim Jim shines bright on Indian pitching staff." *Zanesville Times Recorder*, July 29, 1959, p. 10.

152. Hand, Jack. "Cleveland shoots for sixth in row." *East Liverpool Review*, July 27, 1959, p. 15.

153. Hand, Jack. "Joe Gordon elated over Perry's 2-hit shutout." *East Liverpool Review*, July 27, 1959, p. 15.

154. Ibid.

155. Ibid.

156. Schlemmer, Jim. "Gordon starts Score ... on swing shift!" *Akron Beacon Journal*, August 7, 1959, p. 30.

157. Schlemmer, Jim. "Heat wave still gripping Cleveland." *Akron Beacon Journal*, August 27, 1959, p. 45.

158. McAuley, Ed. "The character who isn't one." *Baseball Digest*, September, 1960. P. 30.

159. Ibid.

160. Schlemmer, Jim. "The voice from the grandstand." *Akron Beacon Journal*, November 8, 1959, p. 3B.

161. Lebovitz, Hal. "Tribe whoops it up for Perry in rookie of year show-down." *The Sporting News*, Sept. 30, 1959, p. 24.

162. Ibid.

163. Ibid.

164. Ibid.

165. Ibid.

166. Daniel, Dan. "Over—the fence." *The Sporting News*, November 11, 1959, p. 10.

167. Schlemmer, Jim. "Lane, Gordon 'harmonizing'." *Akron Beacon Journal*, Jan. 28, 1960, p. 34.

168. Schlemmer, Jim. "Woodie's big mole upsets infield." *Akron Beacon Journal*, Mar. 14, 1960, p. 23.

169. Ibid.

170. Jones, Harry. "Piersall silences clown capers, makes big noise with bludgeon." *The Sporting News*, March 23, 1960, p. 26.

171. Associated Press. "Gordon names rookie to hurl against Athletics." *Marion Star*, April 22, 1960, p. 18.

172. Associated Press. "Held slams two home runs as Indians win." *Massillon Evening Independent*, April 30, 1960, p. 16.

173. Schlemmer, Jim. "Kuenn's throw saves Perry." *Akron Beacon Journal*, May 26, 1960, p. 37.

174. Associated Press. "Jim Perry tosses third win; Cleveland Indians move west." *Lancaster Eagle-Gazette*, May 26, 1960, p. 22.

175. Schlemmer, Jim. "Kuenn's throw saves Perry." *Akron Beacon Journal*, May 26, 1960, p. 37.

176. Ibid.

177. Lebovitz, Hal. "Frankie faces music; Tribe's boss refuses to duck fans' barks." *The Sporting News*, August 31, 1960, p. 6.

178. Lebovitz, Hal. "Peerless Perry sends Dykes to history books." *The Sporting News*, Aug. 24, 1960, p. 7.

179. Ibid.

180. Ibid.

181. Ibid.

182. *The Sporting News*, November 9, 1960, p. 33.

183. Associated Press. "Perry to marry college sweetheart." *Lima Citizen*, December 2, 1960, p. 23.

184. Associated Press. "Cleveland baseball writers to honor Jim Perry tonight." *Salem News*, January 23, 1961, p. 6.

185. Schlemmer, Jim. "A real spot for 'truth serum!'." *Akron Beacon Journal*, January 24, 1961, p. 20.

186. Lebovitz, Hal. "Perry's new pitch helps stitch patch on Wigwam mound." *The Sporting News*, June 16, 1962, p. 7.

187. Ibid.

188. Ibid.

189. Ibid.

190. Dolgan, Bob. "Funk's '61 lesson: 'don't get careless'." *The Sporting News*, March 7, 1962, p. 18.

191. Lebovitz, Hal. "Perry's new pitch helps stitch patch on Wigwam mound." *The Sporting News*, June 16, 1962, p. 7.

192. "Tribe's Perry provides Tiger tranquilizer." *Akron Beacon Journal*, June 2, 1962, p. 12.

193. Lebovitz, Hal. "Perry's new pitch helps stitch patch on Wigwam mound." *The Sporting News*, June 16, 1962, p. 7.

194. Durbin, Joe. "Rookie sparkles as Perry blanks Nats." *Mansfield News-Journal*, September 12, 1962, p. 27.

195. Briere, Tom. "Perry gets a 'warm' greeting from Twins." *Minneapolis Tribune*, May 3, 1963, p. 21.

196. Briere, Tom. "Perry welcomes Twin starting job on 'club that wants me.'" *Minneapolis Tribune*, May 3, 1963, p. 21.

197. Ibid.

198. Ibid.

199. Ibid.

200. "Ex-teammate Power says Perry will help." *Minneapolis Tribune*, May 3, 1963, p. 23.

201. Ibid.

202. Lebovitz, Hal. "Brown chases Injun blues with red-hot bat and cool glove." *The Sporting News*, August 10, 1963, p. 19.

203. Hartman, Sid. *Minneapolis Tribune*, November 7, 1970, p. 14.

204. Briere, Tom. "Perry welcomes Twin starting job on 'club that wants me.'" *Minneapolis Tribune*, May 3, 1963, p. 21.

205. Staff. "Battey: Perry's big asset sharp control." *Minneapolis Star*, May 8, 1963, p. 59.

206. Ibid.

207. Hartman, Sid. "Hartman's roundup." *Minneapolis Tribune*, May 9, 1963, p. 26.

208. Staff. "Battey: Perry's big asset sharp control." *Minneapolis Star*, May 8, 1963, p. 59.

209. Hartman, Sid. "Hartman's roundup." *Minneapolis Tribune*, May 9, 1963, p. 26.

210. Staff. "Battey: Perry's big asset sharp control." *Minneapolis Star*, May 8, 1963, p. 59.

211. Nichols, Max. "Allison only Twin to escape slump." *Minneapolis Star*, May 13, 1963, p. 28.

212. Associated Press. "Twins' Perry justified if he is gaunt." *St. Cloud Times*, May 13, 1963, p. 16.

213. Nichols, Max. "Allison only Twin to escape slump." *Minneapolis Star*, May 13, 1963, p. 28.

214. Netland, Dwayne. "Perry baffled, but 'the runs will come'." *Minneapolis Tribune*, May 13, 1963, p. 33.

215. Staff. "Allison, Killebrew join select homer company." *Minneapolis Tribune*, May 18, 1963, p. 15.

216. Ibid.

217. Staff. "Power talks... so does Vic's bat." *Minneapolis Star*, May 22, 1963, p. 59.

218. McGrane, Bill. "Commodore Perry winds up 42 days in drydock." *Minneapolis Morning Tribune*, August 10, 1963, p. 10.

219. Ibid.

220. Thornton, Ralph. "Suburban Neighbors." *Minneapolis Star*, September 7, 1963, p. 11A.

221. Nichols, Max. "'Bomb under every slugger,' Cal vows." *The Sporting News*, October 24, 1964, p. 12.

222. Ibid.

223. Ibid.

224. Ibid.

225. Briere, Tom. "Martin: 'Twins have men to beat Yanks.'" *Minneapolis Tribune*, February 3, 1965, p. 19.

226. Hartman, Sid. "Hartman's roundup." *Minneapolis Tribune*, March 7, 1965, p. 45.

227. Staff. "Twins trim 11 more players; Dailey goes." *Minneapolis Tribune*, July 11, 1965, p. 45.

228. Briere, Tom. "Tutor Sain: 'all credit to Perry'." *Minneapolis Tribune*, July 11, 1965, p. 1S.

229. Nichols, Max. "Reliever Perry strikes it rich after weeks of toil for Twins." *The Sporting News*, June 19, 1965, p. 11.

230. Ibid.

231. Ibid.

232. Ibid.

233. Nichols, Max. "Perry patches Twins leaking dike." *The Sporting News*, August 14, 1965, p. 5.

234. Nichols, Max. "Reliever Perry strikes it rich after weeks of toil for Twins." *The Sporting News*, June 19, 1965, p. 11.

235. Ibid.

236. Ibid.

237. Nichols, Max. "Perry patches Twins' leaking dike." *The Sporting News*, August 14, 1965, p. 5.

238. Hengen, Bill. "Mele's wish turns into fact with 17-inning feat." *The Minneapolis Star*, July 6, 1965, p. 36.

239. Briere, Tom. "Perry finishes in spite of headache." *Minneapolis Tribune*, July 6, 1965, p. 24.

240. Nichols, Max. "Perry patches Twins' leaking dike." *The Sporting News*, August 14, 1965, p. 5.

241. Ibid.

242. Nichols, Max. "Sain's spring projects pay off in July." *Minneapolis Star*, July 6, 1965, p. 35.

243. Briere, Tom. "Tutor Sain: 'all credit to Perry'." *Minneapolis Tribune*, July 11, 1965, p. 5S.

244. Ibid., 1S.

245. Ibid., 5S.

246. Ibid.

247. Ibid.

248. Briere, Tom. "Twins win skein severed at nine." *Minneapolis Tribune*, July 11, 1965, p. 48.

249. Briere, Tom. "The champs! Twins win 2-1." *Minneapolis Tribune*, September 27, 1965, p. 29.

250. Ibid.

251. Staff. "Pride? It's spelled T-W-I-N-S." *Minneapolis Tribune*, September 27, 1965, p. 32.

252. Ibid.

253. Briere, Tom. "'Why wait for seven to win?' asks Mele." *Minneapolis Tribune*, October 5, 1965, p. 21.

254. "Twin starters: Pascual, Boswell, Perry, Merritt." *Minneapolis Star*, March 29, 1966, p. 2D.

255. Ferguson, Lew. "Mele: we're ready, now all we have to do is win." *St. Cloud Daily Times*, April 9, 1966, p. 11.

256. Wiebusch, John. "Mantle: 'we're the same Yanks'." *Minneapolis Tribune*, May 10, 1966, p. 20.

257. Ibid.

258. Martel, Bob. "M&M boys back in business." *St. Cloud Daily Times*, May 10, 1966, p. 16.

259. Hartman, Sid. "Hartman's roundup." *Minneapolis Tribune*, May 14, 1966, p. 14.

260. Wiebusch, John. "Perry: being ready matter of conscience." *Minneapolis Tribune*, May 16, 1966, p. 29.

261. Ibid., 30.

262. Ibid., 29.

263. Ibid., 30.

264. Nichols, Max. "Wife worries, not Perry." *Minneapolis Star*, May 16, 1966, p. 10B.

265. Ibid.

266. Ibid.

267. Nichols, Max. "Mele, Stanky stir up spicy beanball rhubarb." *The Sporting News*, June 4, 1966, p. 9.

268. Briere, Tom. "Hall, Oliva spark 5th straight win." *Minneapolis Tribune*, May 20, 1966, p. 22.

269. Fowler, Bob. "Mele, Stanky square off in beanball 'war'." *Minneapolis Tribune*, May 20, 1966, p. 21.

270. Ibid.

271. Associated Press. "Stanky is 0-5 as White Sox-Twins feud grows." *Fergus Falls Daily Journal*, May 20, 1966, p. 8.

272. Nichols, Max. "Mele, Stanky stir up spicy beanball rhubarb." *The Sporting News*, June 4, 1966, p. 9.

273. Associated Press. "Stanky is 0-5 as White Sox-Twins feud grows." *Fergus Falls Daily Journal*, May 20, 1966, p. 8.

274. Ibid.

275. Nichols, Max. "Mele, Stanky stir up spicy beanball rhubarb." *The Sporting News*, June 4, 1966, p. 9.

276. Levitt, Ed. "Designated Targets." *Oakland Tribune*, July 10, 1975, p. 35.

277. Nichols, Max. "Twins' pennant dreams fading—but they still hold key to crown." *The Sporting News*, July 23, 1966, p. 18.

278. Briere, Tom. "Martin, Fox 'both wrong.'" *Minneapolis Tribune*, July 20, 1966, p. 19.

279. Staff. "'Best game for me,' claims Twins' Perry." *Minneapolis Tribune*, July 20, 1966, p. 21

280. Ibid.

281. Nichols, Max. "Twin pitchers serious at bat, too." *Minneapolis Star*, August 17, 1966, p. 1D

282. Ibid.

283. Ibid.

284. Nichols, Max. "Twin hill staff best in A.L. in using bats, Mele chortles." *The Sporting News*, September 3, 1966, p. 15.

285. Nichols, Max. "'I rate starting job,' declares Twins' Perry, tired of bull pen." *The Sporting News*, December 31, 1966, p. 30.

286. Nichols, Max. "Dropped by Twins, Sain and Naragon join Tigers." *The Sporting News*, October 15, 1966, p. 15.

287. "Jim Kaat decries Sain, Naragon loss." *Minneapolis Tribune*, October 6, 1966, p. 1.

288. Ibid., 7.

289. Nichols, Max. "'I rate starting job,' declares Twins' Perry, tired of bull pen." *The Sporting News*, December 31, 1966, p. 30.

290. Nichols, Max. "Perry priming Twins' pennant pump." *The Sporting News*, September 2, 1967, p. 11.

291. Associated Press. "Grant, Perry help Twins sweep pair." *Winona Daily News*, July 5, 1967, p. 19.

292. Ibid.

293. Nichols, Max. "Perry priming Twins' pennant pump." *The Sporting News*, September 2, 1967, p. 11.

294. Ibid.

295. Ibid.

296. Ibid.

297. Ibid.

298. Hengen, Bill. "No job too lowly on Twins." *Minneapolis Star*, September 12, 1967, p. 6E.

299. Goethel, Arno. "Weary of relief, Perry sets sight on starter's $$$." *The Sporting News*, November 11, 1967, p. 32.

300. Netland, Dwayne. "Rod Carew takes 2-way walk..." *Minneapolis Tribune*, July 3, 1968, p.1.

301. Ibid.

302. Ibid.

303. Goethel, Arno. "All-star Rod Carew escapes Twins' doghouse." *The Sporting News*, July 20, 1968, p. 12.

304. Ibid.

305. Netland, Dwayne. "Rod Carew takes 2-way walk..." *Minneapolis Tribune*, July 3, 1968, p.1.

306. Ibid., 8.

307. Goethel, Arno. "All-star Rod Carew escapes Twins' doghouse." *The Sporting News*, July 20, 1968, p. 12.

308. Ibid.

309. Lamey, Mike. "Billy Martin fired." *Minneapolis Star*, October 13, 1969, p. 1.

310. Lamey, Mike. "Twins' skipper Rig taps relievers Ron, Stan for heavy duty." *The Sporting News*, February 7, 1970, p. 32.

311. Cullum, Dick. *Minneapolis Tribune*, March 3, 1970, p. 27.

312. Staff. "Twins' spring not the worst." *Minneapolis Star*, March 25, 1970, p. 63.

313. Roe, Jon. "Ratliff, Twins beat Reds 4-0." *Minneapolis Tribune*, March 25, 1970, p. 25.

314. Ibid.

315. Ibid., 28.

316. Hartman, Sid. "Astros' rally rips Williams." *Minneapolis Tribune*, March 29, 1970, p. 1S.

317. Ibid., 2S.

318. Roe, Jon. "Rigney eager for regular season debut." *Minneapolis Tribune*, April 7, 1970, p. 19.

319. Roe, Jon. "Perry, Alyea club White Sox." *Minneapolis Tribune*, April 8, 1970, p. 25.

320. Ibid., 26.

321. Ibid.

322. Ibid., 25.

323. Ibid.

324. Cullum, Dick. *Minneapolis Tribune*, April 9, 1970, p. 32.

325. Lamey, Mike. "Alyea's 'sacrifice fly' turns into a grand slam." *Minneapolis Star*, April 16, 1970, p. 1D.

326. Lamey, Mike. "Perry: forgotten man to Twins' pitching ace." *Minneapolis Star*, April 20, 1970, p. 14B.

327. Lamey, Mike. "At last . . . Twins' Jim Perry can claim ranking as ace." *The Sporting News*, May 9, 1970, p. 8.

328. Associated Press. "Owners to renew offer players vetoed 505-89." *Minneapolis Tribune*, May 16, 1970, p. 15.

329. Ibid.

330. Ibid.

331. Briere, Tom. "Perry, Twins batter Nats." *Minneapolis Tribune*, June 17, 1970, p. 25.

332. Ibid.

333. Hartman, Sid. "Rose, Fosse both come up limping." *Minneapolis Tribune*, July 15, 1970, p. 21.

334. Staff. "Weaver took it easy on Perry...Cuellar, too." *Minneapolis Tribune*, July 16, 1970, p. 34.

335. Hartman, Sid. "Rose, Fosse both come up limping." *Minneapolis Tribune*, July 15, 1970, p. 22.

336. Briere, Tom. "Twins 'preside,' hold off Tigers 2-1." *Minneapolis Tribune*, July 23, 1970, p. 29.

337. Jackman, Phil. "HR-hittin' Harm vulnerable to bunt." *Baltimore Evening Sun*, July 27, 1970, p. 25.

338. Ibid.

339. Briere, Tom. "Powell, Orioles 'get well' on slam." *Minneapolis Tribune*, July 27, 1970, p. 23.

340. Stoneking, Dan. "Happy Tiant was edgy." *Minneapolis Star*, August 4, 1970, p. 2D.

341. Hartman, Sid. *Minneapolis Tribune*, August 4, 1970, p. 20.

342. Ibid.

343. United Press International. "Twins tip A's as Perry wins 17th." *St. Cloud Daily Times*, August 8, 1970, p. 9.

344. Ibid.

345. Associated Press. "Perry blanks Yankees 3-0." *Fergus Falls Daily Journal*, August 20, 1970, p. 12.

346. Roe, Jon. "Perry, Twins zip past Yanks 3-0." *Minneapolis Tribune*, August 20, 1970, p. 29.

347. Associated Press. "Sox bomb Boston with 11-run 9th." *Tri-City Herald*, August 20, 1970, p. 36.

348. Roe, Jon. "Perry, Twins zip past Yanks 3-0." *Minneapolis Tribune*, August 20, 1970, p. 29.

349. Associated Press. "Perry blanks Yankees 3-0." *Fergus Falls Daily Journal*, August 20, 1970, p. 12.

350. Fowler, Bob. "20 is the name of Perrys' game." *The Sporting News*, October 3, 1970, p. 3.

351. Greene, Bob. "Brewers, Perry's 20th victim." *Winona Daily News*, September 2, 1970, p. 22.

352. Fowler, Bob. "20 is the name of Perrys' game." *The Sporting News*, October 3, 1970, p. 3.

353. Roe, Jon. "Perry hits, pitches Twins past Oakland." *Minneapolis Tribune*, September 10, 1970, p. 33.

354. Frizzell, Pat. "Gaylord joins brother: each boasts 20 wins." *The Sporting News*, September 26, 1970, p. 5.

355. Associated Press. "Perry brothers first to win 20 same year." *Minneapolis Tribune*, September 12, 1970, p. 17.

356. Fowler, Bob. "20 is the name of Perrys' game." *The Sporting News*, October 3, 1970, p. 3.

357. Ibid.

358. Smith, Seymour S. "Perrys first brothers to win 20 each in same season." *Baltimore Sun*, October 3, 1970, p. B5.

359. Fowler, Bob. "20 is the name of Perrys' game." *The Sporting News*, October 3, 1970, p. 3.

360. Ibid.

361. Ibid.

362. United Press International. "Perry wins 24h, defeats Royals 1-0." *St. Cloud Daily Times*, September 26, 1970, p. 10.

363. Briere, Tom. "Perry two-hitter blanks K.C. 1-0." *Minneapolis Tribune*, September 26, 1970, p. 15.

364. Ibid.

365. Fowler, Bob. "Weather spurs Perry." *The Sporting News*, October 10, 1970, p. 10.

366. Bordman, Sid. "Royals parade by Twins, 14-13." *Kansas City Times*, September 30, 1970, p. 2B.

367. Hartman, Sid. *Minneapolis Tribune*, October 3, 1970, p. 18.

368. Trimble, Joe. "Twins, Bird Tied in 3d." *New York Daily News*, October 4, 1970, p. 41C.

369. Roe, Jon. "Orioles breeze by Twins." *Minneapolis Tribune*, October 4, 1970, p. 12S.

370. Elliot, Jim. "24-game winners treated roughly." *Baltimore Sun*, October 4, 1970, p. A11.

371. Ibid.

372. Roe, Jon. "Orioles breeze by Twins." *Minneapolis Tribune*, October 4, 1970, p. 12S.

373. Ibid., 1S.

374. Elliot, Jim. "24-game winners treated roughly." *Baltimore Sun*, October 4, 1970, p. A11.

375. Roe, Jon. "Orioles breeze by Twins." *Minneapolis Tribune*, October 4, 1970, p. 12S.

376. Briere, Tom. "Wind made hit with Orioles." *Minneapolis Tribune*, October 4, 1970, p. 12S.

377. Ibid.

378. Ibid.

379. Maisel, Bob. "The Morning After." *Baltimore Sun*, October 4, 1970, p. A1.

380. Eyewitness Reports. "Cuellar's homer lacks artistry." *Baltimore Evening Sun*, October 5, 1970, p. C8.

381. Bock, Hal. "Twins stung by Orioles." *Winona Daily News*, October 4, 1970, p. 7b

382. Eyewitness Reports. "Cuellar's homer lacks artistry." *Baltimore Evening Sun*, October 5, 1970, p. C8.

383. Elliot, Jim. "24-game winners treated roughly." *Baltimore Sun*, October 4, 1970, p. A11.

384. Ibid.

385. Recht, Mike. "Jim Perry gets Cy Young Award." *Hagerstown Daily Mail*, November 6, 1970, p. 14.

386. United Press International. "Perry: like winning 2 World Series games." *St. Cloud Daily Times*, November 6, 1970, p. 12.

387. Ibid.

388. Ibid.

389. Nichols, Max. "Faith kept Jim Perry going…" *Minneapolis Star*, November 7, 1970, p. 7A.

390. Hengen, Bill. "Cookies, donuts for celebration." *Minneapolis Star*, November 6, 1970, p. 10B.

391. Nichols, Max. "Faith kept Jim Perry going…" *Minneapolis Star*, November 7, 1970, p. 7A.

392. Fowler, Bob. "In Twin Cities, Perry synonym for class." *The Sporting News*, November 28, 1970, p. 39.

393. Stoneking, Dan. "Twins' Perry named Cy Young winner." *Minneapolis Star*, November 6, 1970, p. 10B.

394. Ham, Tom. "Tributes flow at 'Perry brothers day'." *Rocky Mount Telegram*, November 11, 1970, p. 2D

395. Ibid.

396. Ibid.

397. Ham, Tom. "Tributes flow at 'Perry brothers day'." *Rocky Mount Telegram*, November 11, 1970, p. 5D

398. Ibid.

399. Ibid.

400. Ibid.

401. Hartman, Sid. *Minneapolis Tribune*, November 27, 1970, p. 36.

402. Briere, Tom. "Mays to Aaron to Perry." *Minneapolis Tribune*, January 18, 1971, p. 31.

403. Stoneking, Dan. "Perry seeking $100,000 pact?" *Minneapolis Star*, February 3, 1971, p. 3D.

404. Gordon, Dick. "Calvin 'fishing' holdouts -- Martin after bass." *Minneapolis Star*, February 16, 1971, p. 2D.

405. Associated Press. "Pascual happy to be 'home.'" *Minneapolis Tribune*, February 20, 1971, p. 3B.

406. Lamey, Mike. "Last offer? Oliva burns." *Minneapolis Star*, February 23, 1971, p. 1D.

407. "Griffith, Perry talk; 'far apart.'" *Minneapolis Star*, February 24, 1971, p. 3F.

408. Associated Press. "Perry, Twins $30,000 apart." *Winona Daily News*, February 25, 1971, p. 5b.

409. "Twins' Perry agrees to $65,000 pact." *Minneapolis Tribune*, February 27, 1971, p. 1B.

410. Roe, Jon. "Woodson 'psyched up' for Twins rotation spot." *Minneapolis Tribune*, March 3, 1971, p. 2C.

411. Briere, Tom. "Twins slumping 'out of picture.'" *Minneapolis Tribune*, April 17, 1971, p. 1B.

412. Ibid.

413. Thompson, Pat. "Three run eighth frame kills Perry, Twins 4-1." *Fergus Falls Daily Journal*, April 17, 1971, p. 8.

414. Briere, Tom. "Twins edge Royals 5-4." *Minneapolis Tribune*, April 21, 1971, p. 1C.

415. Roe, Jon. "Twins shake off Boston outburst." *Minneapolis Tribune*, May 2, 1971, p. 1S.

416. Ibid.

417. Briere, Tom. "Twins edge Royals 5-4." *Minneapolis Tribune*, April 21, 1971, p. 1C.

418. Fowler, Bob. "Twin Jim not so gentle this season." *The Sporting News*, April 24, 1971, p. 26.

419. Briere, Tom. "Patek, Kansas City ambush Twins 6-3." *Minneapolis Tribune*, July 10, 1971, p. 1B.

420. Gordon, Dick. "Shoes fit—so does Harper in steal 'if' role." *Minneapolis Star*, April 7, 1971, p. 5D.

421. Roe, Jon. "Twins Perry, a student of the game, still learning." *Minneapolis Tribune*, April 4, 1971, p. 1S.

422. Fowler, Bob. "Twin Jim not so gentle this season." *The Sporting News*, April 24, 1971, p. 26.

423. Briere, Tom. "Perry maintains hold over Tigers in 3-1 win." *Minneapolis Tribune*, June 2, 1971, p. 1C.

424. Briere, Tom. "Twins turn tables on Tigers 5-4." *Minneapolis Tribune*, June 13, 1971, p. 3C.

425. Briere, Tom. "Oliva's bat, Perry's arm stop Tribe." *Minneapolis Tribune*, June 15, 1971, p. 1C.

426. Associated Press. "Twins clip Indians in 3-1 contest." *Marion Star*, June 15, 1971, p. 14.

427. Briere, Tom. "Oliva's bat, Perry's arm stop Tribe." Minneapolis Tribune, June 15, 1971, p. 1C.

428. Associated Press. "Twins clip Indians in 3-1 contest." *Marion Star*, June 15, 1971, p. 14.

429. Stoneking, Dan. "Perry finally catching up to old Cleveland mates." *Minneapolis Star*, June 15, 1971, p. 4D.

430. Roe, Jon. "Perry wins 11th on Twin homers." *Minneapolis Tribune*, June 23, 1971, p. 1C.

431. Ibid.

432. Hengen, Bill. "Twins 'ran out' Perry in 10 shutout innings." *Minneapolis Star*, July 16, 1971, p. 8B.

433. Roe, Jon. "Petrocelli, Red Sox top Twins." *Minneapolis Tribune*, July 16, 1971, p. 1C.

434. Roe, Jon. "Twins fall, thank God for Brewers." *Minneapolis Tribune*, July 25, 1971, p. 6C.
435. Ibid.
436. Mooshil, Joe. "Perry backed up by 15 hits but Twins fall." *Winona Daily News*, August 3, 1971, p. 4b.
437. Lamey, Mike. "Falling behind kills Perry." *Minneapolis Star*, August 3, 1971, p. 1D
438. Mooshil, Joe. "Perry backed up by 15 hits but Twins fall." *Winona Daily News*, August 3, 1971, p. 4b.
439. Fowler, Bob. "Twins' tattered hill staff due for a major overhaul." *The Sporting News*, August 21, 1971, p. 21.
440. Lamey, Mike. "Perry's 13th ends slump." *Minneapolis Star*, August 21, 1971, p. 16A.
441. Associated Press. "Twins' rally finally nets Perry No. 13." *Winona Daily News*, August 22, 1971, p. 8b.
442. Ibid.
443. Associated Press. "Twins' rally finally nets Perry No. 13." *Winona Daily News*, August 22, 1971, p. 8b.
444. Fowler, Bob. "Will the real Jim Perry please stand?" *The Sporting News*, September 11, 1971, p. 14.
445. Ibid.
446. Paladino, Larry. "Perry's 4-hitter stops Detroit 3-1." *Winona Daily News*, August 25, 1971, p. 4b.
447. Ibid.
448. Cullum, Dick. "Perry hurls Twins to win over Detroit." *Minneapolis Tribune*, August 25, 1971, p. 1C.
449. Hartman, Sid. *Minneapolis Tribune*, September 4, 1971, p. 2B.
450. Briere, Tom. "Twins split with Royals; Tovar gets 200th hit." *Minneapolis Tribune*, September 27, 1971, p. 9C.
451. Briere, Tom. "Perry settling for 17-17; Blyleven wants 16th victory." *Minneapolis Tribune*, September 28, 1971, p. 1C.
452. Ibid.
453. United Press International. "Perry not too hurt." *Ukiah Daily Journal*, November 30, 1971, p. 6.
454. Addie, Bob. "addie's atoms." *The Sporting News*, December 25, 1971, p. 12.
455. Griffin, John. "Big names are expendable." *Ukiah Daily Journal*, November 30, 1971, p. 6.
456. Schneider, Russell. "'Great feeling!' says Fosse; Tribe catcher is injury-free." *The Sporting News*, May 13, 1972, p. 11.
457. United Press International. "Twins sign Kaat, Perry." *St. Cloud Daily Times*, January 14, 1972, p. 13.
458. Lamey, Mike. "Perry pitches back under control." *Minneapolis Star*, March 16, 1972, p. 6D.
459. Fowler, Bob. "Worthington given task of rebuilding Twin hill." *The Sporting News*, November 27, 1971, p. 50.
460. Lamey, Mike. "Perry pitches back under control." Minneapolis Star, March 16, 1972, p. 6D.
461. Briere, Tom. "Griffith claims Twins players disturbed about strike." *Minneapolis Tribune*, April 1, 1972, p. 1B.
462. Hartman, Sid. *Minneapolis Tribune*, March 31, 1972, p. 2C.
463. Briere, Tom. "Griffith claims Twins players disturbed about strike." *Minneapolis Tribune*, April 1, 1972, p. 1B
464. Ibid.
465. Lamey, Mike. "Twins train at St. Olaf." *Minneapolis Star*, April 3, 1972, p. 10B.

466. Ibid.
467. Miller, Marvin. *A Whole Different Ball Game: The Sport and Business of Baseball.* Carol Publishing Group, 1991. p. 218-219.
468. Lamey, Mike. "Perry weathering storm." *Minneapolis Star,* April 6, 1972, p. 1D.
469. Ibid.
470. Ibid.
471. Ibid.
472. Ibid.
473. Thompson, Pat. "Twins continue daily workouts at St. Olaf." *Winona Sunday News,* April 9, 1972, p. 7b.
474. "Perry says strike went 5 extra days." Minneapolis Tribune, April 14, 1972, p. 2C.
475. Holtzman, Jerome. *The Sporting News,* May 13, 1972, p. 20.
476. "Perry says strike went 5 extra days." *Minneapolis Tribune,* April 14, 1972, p. 2C
477. United Press International. "Twins club Boston." *St. Cloud Daily Times,* April 26, 1972, p. 42.
478. Ibid.
479. Briere, Tom. "Twins B-B shot blasts Boston 12-0." *Minneapolis Tribune,* April 26, 1972, p. 1C.
480. Briere, Tom. "Perry beats Yanks 2-0." *Minneapolis Tribune,* May 11, 1972, p. 1C.
481. Lowitt, Bruce. "Perry brothers do their thing." *Winona Daily News,* May 11, 1972, p. 5b.
482. Lamey, Mike. "Twin Perry at crafty best." *Minneapolis Star,* May 11, 1972, p. 1D.
483. Ibid.
484. Ibid.
485. Roe, Jon. "Loss spoils Harmon's homer." *Minneapolis Tribune,* June 4, 1972, p. 1C.
486. Hartman, Sid. *Minneapolis Tribune,* June 13, 1972, p. 2C.
487. Roe, Jon. "Twins beat rain, Tigers." *Minneapolis Tribune,* June 14, 1972, p. 1C.
488. Ibid.
489. Jackle, John. "Perry isn't worried about possible trade." *St. Cloud Daily Times,* June 16, 1972, p. 12.
490. Ibid.
491. Ibid.
492. Briere, Tom. "Twins bow 5-0 before Royals." *Minneapolis Tribune,* June 24, 1972, p. 1B.
493. Ibid.
494. Ibid., 3B.
495. Ibid., 1B.
496. Associated Press. "Twins' pitchers starving for runs." *Winona Daily News,* July 6, 1972, p. 12.
497. Associated Press. "Perry foils Rangers with 3-hitter, 9-1." *Winona Daily News,* August 4, 1972, p. 4b.
498. Briere, Tom. "Perry, Twins confuse Texas." *Minneapolis Tribune,* August 8, 1972, p. 1C.
499. Stoneking, Dan. "Perry pace like night and day." *Minneapolis Star,* August 8, 1972, p. 1D
500. Briere, Tom. "Perry, Twins confuse Texas." *Minneapolis Tribune,* August 8, 1972, p. 2C.
501. Fowler, Bob. "Running around puts Twins' Perry on winning road." *The Sporting News,* August 26, 1972, p. 17.
502. *Minneapolis Tribune,* June 19, 1972, p. 2C.
503. Fowler, Bob. "Running around puts Twins' Perry on winning road." *The Sporting News,* August 26, 1972, p. 18.
504. Ibid.
505. Ibid.
506. Ibid.

507. Stoneking, Dan. "Twins mess up record chance." *Minneapolis Star,* September 4, 1972, p. 12B.

508. Ibid.

509. Briere, Tom. "Twins don't execute, get executed by Tribe." *Minneapolis Tribune,* September 4, 1972, p. 1C.

510. Briere, Tom. "Perry first in wins." *Minneapolis Tribune,* September 21, 1972, p. 3C.

511. Schneider, Russell. "'I'll split my award with Fosse,' says Gaylord." *The Sporting News,* November 18, 1972, p. 49.

512. Hartman, Sid. *Minneapolis Tribune,* September 4, 1972, p. 1C.

513. Stoneking, Dan. "Stalemate hurts; no key Twins signed." *Minneapolis Star,* February 12, 1973, p. 12B.

514. Ibid.

515. Hengen, Bill. "Baseball in fourth quarrel." *Minneapolis Star,* February 13, 1973, p. 1D.

516. Netland, Dwayne. "Baseball owners accused of lockout." *Minneapolis Tribune,* February 13, 1973, p. 4C.

517. Ibid.

518. Chass, Murray. "Key issues still block baseball negotiations." *Minneapolis Tribune,* February 18, 1973, p. 1C.

519. "Mum's the word in baseball." *Minneapolis Star,* February 19, 1973, p. 6B.

520. Ibid.

521. Hartman, Sid. *Minneapolis Tribune,* February 27, 1973, p. 2C.

522. Netland, Dwayne. "Pact pleases Quilici, Griffith; Killebrew, others still unsigned." *Minneapolis Tribune,* February 26, 1973, p. 2C.

523. Boeck, Greg. "Reggie: call the season off." *Sioux Falls Argus-Leader,* July 29, 1981, p. 1B.

524. Netland, Dwayne. "Pact pleases Quilici, Griffith; Killebrew, others still unsigned." *Minneapolis Tribune,* February 26, 1973, p. 2C.

525. Netland, Dwayne. "Griffith gives newcomer raise." *Minneapolis Tribune,* March 1, 1973, p. 2C.

526. Netland, Dwayne. "Oliva unhappy about contract cut to $96,000." *Minneapolis Tribune,* March 2, 1973, p. 1C.

527. Hartman, Sid. *Minneapolis Tribune,* March 2, 1973, p. 2C.

528. Hawkins, Jim. "Tigers deal for Jim Perry." *Detroit Free Press,* March 28, 1973, p. 1-D.

529. Paladino, Larry. "Billy beams; Tigers land 4th starter." *Lansing State Journal,* March 28, 1973, p. C-1.

530. Hawkins, Jim. "Tigers deal for Jim Perry." *Detroit Free Press,* March 28, 1973, p. 1-D.

531. Hawkins, Jim. "Tigers finally fool Twins." *Detroit Free Press,* March 30, 1973, p. 4-D.

532. Netland, Dwayne. "Perry traded to Detroit." *Minneapolis Tribune,* March 28, 1973, p. 1C.

533. Ibid.

534. Ibid., 2C.

535. Paladino, Larry. "Pitching help." *Battle Creek Enquirer,* March 28, 1973, p. B-2.

536. Hawkins, Jim. "Tigers celebrate Billy's return – win." *Detroit Free Press,* April 1, 1973, p. 5-E.

537. Hartman, Sid. *Minneapolis Tribune,* April 1, 1973, p. 3C.

538. Ibid.

539. Hartman, Sid. *Minneapolis Tribune,* April 2, 1973, p. 2C.

540. Cullum, Dick. "Twins tip A's; Hisle homers." *Minneapolis Tribune,* April 8, 1973, p. 1C.

541. Hawkins, Jim. "Tiger bats boom… new guy Perry benefits, 8-2." *Detroit Free Press*, April 15, 1973, p. 1-E.

542. Paladino, Larry. "'Admiral' Perry scuttles Indians, 8-2." *Lansing State Journal*, April 15, 1973, p. E-1.

543. Ibid.

544. Associated Press. "Lolich and Tigers ready for opener in Cleveland." *Battle Creek Enquirer and News*, April 7, 1973, p. B-1.

545. Hankins, Jim. "17 hits! 3 HRs!… Tigers demolish Bosox again, 7-1." *Detroit Free Press*, April 19, 1973, p. 1-D.

546. United Press International. "Tigers pound Bosox, move into 2nd place." *Traverse City Record-Eagle*, April 19, 1973, p. 23.

547. Ibid.

548. Hawkins, Jim. "17 hits! 3 HRs!… Tigers demolish Bosox again, 7-1." *Detroit Free Press*, April 19, 1973, p. 1-D.

549. United Press International. "Tigers' Perry phones his praise." *Port Huron Times Herald*, April 28, 1973, p. 1B.

550. Ibid.

551. Associated Press. "Bats fly, Detroit wins." *Manhattan Mercury*, May 10, 1973, p. B1.

552. Ibid.

553. Associated Press. "Tigers handle KC, bat and beer can." *Lansing State Journal*, May 10, 1973, p. C-3.

554. Paladino, Larry. "Tigers master Red Sox 1-0." *Battle Creek Enquirer*, May 18, 1973, p. B-2.

555. Associated Press. "Tigers beat Oakland in 13-inning duel." *Benton Harbor News-Palladium*, May 26, 1973, p. 14.

556. Hawkins, Jim. "Tigers lose, fall into 2d." *Detroit Free Press*, June 10, 1973, p. 1C.

557. United Press International. "Tigers belt Indians with long ball, 5-1." *Traverse City Record-Eagle*, June 19, 1973, p. 15.

558. Bilotti, Richard. "Tigers' homers win for Perry." *Lansing State Journal*, June 19, 1973, p. C-1.

559. "Duncan out with break." *Mansfield News Journal*, July 3, 1973, p. 22.

560. Hawkins, Jim. "Help! Tigers lose 8th in row, 2-1." *Detroit Free Press*, June 26, 1973, p. 1-C.

561. "Perry lone 'star' in Yankees movie." *Tacoma News Tribune*, June 27, 1973, p. C-11.

562. Associated Press. "Perry brothers to duel." *Lansing State Journal*, July 2, 1973, p. C-1.

563. Ibid.

564. Ibid.

565. "Duncan out with break." *Mansfield News Journal*, July 3, 1973, p. 22.

566. Ibid.

567. United Press International. "Perry brothers face-off tonight." *Bowling Green Daily Sentinel-Tribune*, July 3, 1973, p. 11.

568. Ibid.

569. Jupiter, Harry. "Giants drop sixth in row, 5-4; McCovey cracks pair of homers." *San Francisco Examiner*, March 31, 1963, p. IV-1.

570. Perry, Gaylord. *Me and the Spitter*, Clarke, Irwin & Company, 1974, p. 121.

571. Ibid.

572. Jupiter, Harry. "Giants drop sixth in row, 5-4; McCovey cracks pair of homers." *San Francisco Examiner*, March 31, 1963, p. IV-1.

573. Perry, Gaylord. *Me and the Spitter*, Clarke, Irwin & Company, 1974, p. 121.

574. Jupiter, Harry. "Giants drop sixth in row, 5-4; McCovey cracks pair of homers." *San Francisco Examiner*, March 31, 1963, p. IV-1.

575. Ibid.

576. United Press International. "Perry brothers face-off tonight." *Bowling Green Daily Sentinel-Tribune*, July 3, 1973, p. 11.

577. Ibid.

578. Ibid.

579. Ibid.

580. Associated Press. "Perrys' meeting gets in league record book." *Newark Advocate*, July 4, 1973, p. 15.

581. Ibid.

582. Ibid.

583. Ibid.

584. Ibid.

585. *Dayton Daily News*, July 4, 1973, p. 16.

586. Hawkins, Jim. "Tigers Cash in on Norm's day… beat Sox, 6-2." *Detroit Free Press*, August 13, 1973, p. 1-D.

587. Ibid., 2-D.

588. Ibid.

589. Vincent, Charlie. "Billy orders spitter." *Detroit Free Press*, August 31, 1973, p. 1-D.

590. Ibid.

591. Ibid., 7-D.

592. Martin, Gerald. "Special Night." *Raleigh News and Observer*, December 6, 1973, p. 39.

593. Quincy, Bob. "The Gaylord Perrys decided North Carolina really home." *Charlotte Observer*, December 6, 1973, p. 1B.

594. Tiede, Joe. "Gaylord Unconcerned." *Raleigh News and Observer*, December 9, 1973, p. II-2

595. Quincy, Bob. "The Gaylord Perrys decided North Carolina really home." *Charlotte Observer*, December 6, 1973, p. 1B.

596. Tiede Tiede, Joe. "Gaylord Unconcerned." *Raleigh News and Observer*, December 9, 1973, p. II-2.

597. *Detroit Free Press*, March 2, 1974, p. 6-C.

598. "Gaylord still No. 1." *Akron Beacon Journal*, March 20, 1974, p. C15.

599. Schneider, Russell. "Reunited Perrys promise big things for family and Tribe." *The Sporting News*, April 13, 1974, p. 25.

600. "Gaylord still No. 1." *Akron Beacon Journal*, March 20, 1974, p. C15.

601. Ibid.

602. Associated Press. "Perrys team up with Indians." *Port Huron Times Herald*, March 20, 1974, p. 1D.

603. Ibid.

604. Schneider, Russell. "Reunited Perrys promise big things for family and Tribe." *The Sporting News*, April 13, 1974, p. 25.

605. Ibid.

606. Ibid.

607. Associated Press. "Jim Perry debut impresses Aspro." *Port Clinton News Herald*, March 27, 1974, p. 9.

608. "Both Perrys to open." *Akron Beacon Journal*, March 30, 1974, p. A-9.

609. Nold, Bob. "Tribe's problems snowball." *Akron Beacon Journal*, April 11, 1974, p. C-1.

610. Ibid., C-2.

611. Ibid.

612. Associated Press. "Sanders' fielding helps preserve Tribe victory." *Akron Beacon Journal*, April 17, 1974, p. D-4.

613. "Tribe ponders trades after bullpen failure." *Akron Beacon Journal*, April 22, 1974, p. A-16.

614. United Press International. "Perry brothers top Major League record." *Zanesville Sunday Times Recorder*, April 28, 1974, p. 4-B.

615. Ibid.

616. Nold, Bob. "Duncan, Perry swap praise after 6-0 win over Angels." *Akron Beacon Journal*, April 28, 1974, p. C-1.
617. Ibid.
618. Ibid.
619. Kozloski, Hank. "Frank Duffy 'loves to work behind' Jim Perry." *Mansfield News Journal*, February 18, 1975, p. 16.
620. "Winkles calls Tribe contender." *Minneapolis Star*, April 29, 1974, p. 9B.
621. Associated Press. "Jim Perry joins Gaylord." *Port Clinton News Herald*, May 8, 1974, p. 10.
622. Ibid.
623. Associated Press. "Tribe schedules reunion of mother, pitching sons." *Marion Star*, May 10, 1974, p. 13.
624. Nold, Bob. "Buskey again superb as Indians top Bosox." *Akron Beacon Journal*, May 14, 1974, p. C1.
625. Ibid.
626. United Press International. "Boos turn to cheers as Indians triumph 4-1." *Bucyrus Telegraph-Forum*, May 14, 1974, p. 12.
627. Associated Press. "Ellis' homer lifts Indians to 4-1 victory over Red Sox." *Daily Reporter*, May 14, 1974, p. B-2.
628. Nold, Bob. "Lolich slims down Tribe 3-2." *Akron Beacon Journal*, May 19, 1974, p. B-2.
629. Ibid.
630. "A.L. flashes." *The Sporting News*, July 20, 1974, p. 22.
631. Schneider, Russell. "Leron's hot bat revives injury-plagued Tribe." *The Sporting News*, June 29, 1974, p. 15.
632. Ibid.
633. Ibid.
634. Nold, Bob. "Indians beat Royals as Lee has grand day." *Akron Beacon Journal*, June 2, 1974, p. B1.
635. Nold, Bob. "Beer and blood at the old ball game." *Akron Beacon Journal*, June 5, 1974, p. A1.
636. Associated Press. "Martin is flattened twice during brawl with Indians." *Akron Beacon Journal*, May 30, 1974, p. C12.
637. Ibid.
638. *Akron Beacon Journal*, June 5, 1974, p. A1.
639. Ibid., A8.
640. Ibid.
641. Ibid.
642. Ibid.
643. Jackson, Paul. "The night beer and violence bubbled over in Cleveland." http://www.espn.com/espn/page2/story?page=beernight/080604
644. "Crowd didn't care about us." *Akron Beacon Journal*, June 5, 1974, p. C1.
645. Ibid., A8.
646. Shropshire, Mike. "Indians, Rangers united against rioters." Fort Worth Star-Telegram, June 5, 1974, p. 2-E.
647. "Perry rewards heroes with steaks." *Mansfield News Journal*, June 18, 1974, p. 22.
648. "White Sox hope act II not as tough." *Akron Beacon Journal*, June 12, 1974, p. E1.
649. Ibid.
650. United Press International. "Jim Perry Whitewashes Chisox on pitching cue from Gaylord." *Coshocton Tribune*, June 12, 1974, p. 8.
651. "White Sox hope act II not as tough." *Akron Beacon Journal*, June 12, 1974, p. E1.
652. "Perrys are the berries." Detroit Free Press, June 13, 1974, p. 5-D.
653. *Akron Beacon Journal*, June 12, 1974, p. E1.
654. Ibid.
655. Ibid.

656. United Press International. "Jim Perry Whitewashes Chisox on pitching cue from Gaylord." *Coshocton Tribune*, June 12, 1974, p. 8.

657. Nold, Bob. "Torres Realistic." *Akron Beacon Journal*, June 28, 1974, p. B6.

658. Associated Press. "Jim Perry collects 200th career win." *Lima News*, June 28, 1974, p. 17.

659. Kallestad, Brent. "Tribe smacks Twins, 9-5." *Mansfield News Journal*, July 13, 1974, p. 9.

660. Associated Press. "Tribe leaps back into first place." *Marion Star*, July 13, 1974, p. 9.

661. Hartman, Sid. *Minneapolis Tribune*, July 13, 1974, p. 2B.

662. Ibid.

663. "Oliva hits like Caruso sings." *Port Huron Times Herald*, July 7, 1974, p. 3C.

664. Nold, Bob. "Jim dandy until eighth, then has double trouble." *Akron Beacon Journal*, July 18, 1974, p. C-15.

665. Kozloski, Hank. "Jim Perry disappointed after losing." *Mansfield News-Journal*, July 18, 1974, p. 23.

666. Kozloski, Hank. "Tribe 'gives' Angels series sweep, 7-5." *Mansfield News-Journal*, July 18, 1974, p. 22.

667. Kozloski, Hank. "Jim Perry disappointed after losing." *Mansfield News-Journal*, July 18, 1974, p. 23.

668. Ibid.

669. Ibid.

670. Kozloski, Hank. "Jim Perry 'more excited' about Bosman's no-hitter." *Mansfield News-Journal*, July 20, 1974, p. 14.

671. United Press International. "Near-perfect . . . Indians' Bosman no-hits A's." *Detroit Free Press*, July 20, 1974, p. 1-C.

672. Nold, Bob. "Jim Perry says it all: 'we gave game away.'" *Akron Beacon Journal*, July 22, 1974, p. A-16.

673. Ibid.

674. Ibid.

675. Nold, Bob. "Buskey repays Jim Perry, Indians collect dividend." *Akron Beacon Journal*, July 28, 1974, p. D-1

676. Hawkins, Jim. "Too old, eh? Jim Perry haunts Tigers, 3-2." *Detroit Free Press*, July 28, 1974, p. 1-E.

677. Nold, Bob. "Ho hum, it's another Jim dandy for Perry." *Akron Beacon Journal*, August 18, 1974, p. C-1.

678. Ibid.

679. Ibid.

680. Nold, Bob. "Memory key for Jenkins." *Akron Beacon Journal*, August 19, 1974, p. A-23.

681. Nold, Bob. "Robinson's '75 status with Tribe unclear." *Akron Beacon Journal*, Sept. 13, 1974, p. B-4.

682. Patterson, Jack. "Gaylord boils, hints at trade." *Akron Beacon Journal*, September 27, 1974, p. A-1.

683. "Gaylord, Robinson argue." *Akron Beacon Journal*, September 28, 1974, p. A-11.

684. O'Hara, Dave. "Jim Perry gains 17th victory as Indians edge Boston, 2-1." *Marysville Journal-Tribune*, October 1, 1974, p. 5.

685. Ibid.

686. "Hendrick walks out." *Akron Beacon Journal*, October 3, 1974, p. E-4.

687. Kozlowki, Hank. "Jim Perry seeks better season." *Mansfield News-Journal*, February 9, 1975, p. 2-E.

688. Schneider, Russell. "Perry brothers plan even bigger whoopee in tepee." *The Sporting News*, January 4, 1975, p. 43.

689. Ibid.

690. Ibid.

691. Ibid.

692. "Arbitration no problem." *Akron Beacon Journal*, March 30, 1975, p. E-8.

693. Kozloski, Hank. "Robinson seeks fourth Indians starting pitcher." *Mansfield News Journal*, February 25, 1975, p. 18.

694. Collett, Ritter. "Haddix won't tinker with Gaylord Perry." *Dayton Journal Herald*, February 19, 1975, p. 14.

695. Nold, Bob. "Gaylord, Robinson in 'running feud.'" *Akron Beacon Journal*, March 5, 1975, p. E-2.

696. Schneider, Russell. "Robinson and Perry clear air after spring squabble." *The Sporting News*, March 29, 1975, p. 42.

697. Ibid.

698. Young, Dick. "young ideas." *The Sporting News*, March 29, 1975, p. 14.

699. Associated Press. "Robbie's debut spoiled by 6-4 loss to Giants." *Fremont News-Messenger*, March 14, 1975, p. 14.

700. Nold, Bob. "Bell's knee ok after first test." *Akron Beacon Journal*, March 18, 1975, p. C-4.

701. Ibid.

702. Nold, Bob. "Jim Perry makes his work count." *Akron Beacon Journal*, March 21, 1975, p. B-4.

703. Ibid.

704. Ibid.

705. Ibid.

706. Kozloski, Hank. "Veteran Jim Perry is 'ready.'" *Dover-New Philadelphia Times Reporter*, March 21, 1975, p. C-1.

707. Nold, Bob. "Jim Perry makes his work count." *Akron Beacon Journal*, March 21, 1975, p. B-4.

708. Kozloski, Hank. "Veteran Jim Perry is 'ready.'" *Dover-New Philadelphia Times Reporter*, March 21, 1975, p. C-1

709. Nold, Bob. "Jim Perry makes his work count." *Akron Beacon Journal*, March 21, 1975, p. B-6.

710. Kozloski, Hank. "Veteran Jim Perry is 'ready.'" *Dover-New Philadelphia Times Reporter*, March 21, 1975, p. C-1

711. Nold, Bob. "Jim Perry makes his work count." *Akron Beacon Journal*, March 21, 1975, p. B-6.

712. Nold, Bob. "Indians expecting to win." *Akron Beacon Journal*, March 30, 1975, p. C-8.

713. Nold, Bob. "The pitch." *Akron Beacon Journal*, March 23, 1975, p. C-8.

714. Nold, Bob. "Tribe in AL's top six— maybe." *Akron Beacon Journal*, April 6, 1975, p. C-4

715. Nold, Bob. "Robby's move is criticized by Jim Perry." *Akron Beacon Journal*, April 20, 1975, p. C-1.

716. Ibid., C-2.

717. Ibid.

718. Ibid.

719. Ibid.

720. Ibid.

721. Ibid.

722. Associated Press. "Rain plagues Perry, but Tigers all wet." *Akron Beacon Journal*, April 24, 1975, p. C-1.

723. Nold, Bob. "Jim Perry: I don't have any doubts." *Akron Beacon Journal*, May 13, 1975, p. C-1.

724. Ibid.

725. Associated Press. "Twins grab pieces in the nick of time." *Winona Daily News*, May 16, 1975, p. 11.

726. Schwarz, Glenn. "A's cool to Odom trade for Perry, Bosman." *San Francisco Examiner*, May 21, 1975, p. 53.

727. Bergman, Ron. "Finley swings deals to prop up A's hill staff." *The Sporting News*, June 7, 1975, p. 11.

728. Schwarz, Glenn. "A's cool to Odom trade for Perry, Bosman." *San Francisco Examiner*, May 21, 1975, p. 53.

729. Bergman, Ron. "Finley swings deals to prop up A's hill staff." *The Sporting News*, June 7, 1975, p. 11.

730. Ibid.

731. Schneider, Russell. "Wad of cash seen as big item in Perry deal." *The Sporting News*, June 28, 1975, p. 13.

732. Spudich, Pete. "Tribe sends Perry, Bosman to A's." *Coshocton Tribune*, May 21, 1975, p. 10.

733. Schwarz, Glenn. "Bosman happy— and so are A's." *San Francisco Examiner*, May 26, 1975, p. 44.

734. Hickey, John. "Tired Tenace on hitting tear." *The Argus*, May 27, 1975, p. 9

735. Hall, Mike. "A's needed Blue, bullpen—had neither." *Berkeley Gazette*, June 4, 1975, p. 8.

736. Schwarz, Glenn. "A's lose faith in Perry as starter." *San Francisco Examiner*, June 4, 1975, p. 53.

737. Bergman, Ron. "A's 38-year-old retread one-hits Orioles." Oakland Tribune, June 11, 1975, p. F37.

738. Associated Press. "Jim Perry steals Ryan's thunder." *Bakersfield Californian*, June 11, 1975, p. 25.

739. United Press International. "Perry one hitter gives A's 3-0 win over Birds." *Oroville Mercury Register*, June 11, 1975, p. 17.

740. Bergman, Ron. "A's 38-year-old retread one-hits Orioles." *Oakland Tribune*, June 11, 1975, p. F37.

741. Ibid.

742. Schoenfeld, Ed. "Yanks, A's in AL Playoffs?" *Oakland Tribune*, July 7, 1975, p. EE33.

743. Hall, Mike. "Lindblad-led relievers keep A's on top." *Berkeley Gazette*, July 5, 1975, p. 4.

744. Bergman, Ron. "A's bounce back on family night." *Oakland Tribune*, July 8, 1975, p. EE33.

745. O'Connor, Dick. "Perry premium pays off for A's." *Palo Alto Times*, July 8, 1975, p. 38.

746. Ibid.

747. United Press International. "Robinson-Barnett feud sizzles." *Napa Valley Register*, July 8, 1975, p. 8.

748. O'Connor, Dick. "Perry premium pays off for A's." *Palo Alto Times*, July 8, 1975, p. 38.

749. Ibid.

750. United Press International. "Robinson-Barnett feud sizzles." *Napa Valley Register*, July 8, 1975, p. 8.

751. Hickey, Lowell. "A's rack Palmer, 7-1." *The Argus*, July 13, 1975, p. 18.

752. Ibid.

753. O'Connor, Dick. "Ungrateful Harrah slams Oakland A's." *Palo Alto Times*, July 30, 1975, p. 27.

754. Schwarz, Glenn. "Happy surprise for Tommy Harper." *San Francisco Examiner*, Aug. 14, 1975, p. 51.

755. Blount, Roy Jr. "Return of the Natives." *Sports Illustrated*, March 29, 1971, p. 68.

756. Antonen, Mel. "'Sales pitch' added to Jim Perry's repertoire." *Sioux Falls Argus-Leader*, December 14, 1975, p. 7D.

757. Brothers, Bruce. "Pitcher Perry's son pitches, putts to title." *Minneapolis Tribune*, June 9, 1978, p. 1D.

758. Roe, Jon. "Golf." *Minneapolis Tribune*, May 25, 1980, p. 4C.

759. *Minneapolis Star*, April 4, 1978, p. 2D.

760. Ibid.

761. *Minneapolis Tribune*, April 8, 1984, p. 27M.

762. Schmidt, Brenda Wade. "2 S.D. firms make fastest-growing list." *Sioux Falls Argus-Leader*, November 28, 1990, p. 9D.

763. Jurgens, Dave. "Sioux Falls to ring in new phone system." *Sioux Falls Argus-Leader*, February 16, 1986, p. 1E.

764. Argus Leader, May 2, 1985, p. 3B.

765. Rasmussen, Jim. "Phone companies call new 1-plus system a success." *Sioux Falls Argus-Leader*, July 2, 1986, p. 1B.

766. *Sioux Falls Argus-Leader*, January 5, 1986, p. 6C

767. Reutter, Harold. "Dial-Net announces plans to move into Grand Island." *Grand Island Daily Independent*, December 4, 1986, p.2.

768. "Dial-Net chooses Grand Island for its Nebraska headquarters." *Grand Island Business In Action*, December 15, 1986, Volume 1, Issue 3, p.1.

769. Ibid, p.4.

770. *Sioux Falls Argus-Leader*, February 12, 1989, p. 2E.

771. *Sioux Falls Argus-Leader*, January 22, 1990. 3A.

772. Schmidt, Brenda Wade. "2 S.D. firms make fastest-growing list." *Sioux Falls Argus-Leader*, November 28, 1990, p. 9D.

773. Schmidt, Brenda Wade. "DialNet to reduce office space." *Sioux Falls Argus-Leader*, August 11, 1993, p. 6B.

774. "Dreaming Big." *Campbell Magazine*, December 28, 2012. https://magazine.campbell.edu/articles/dreaming-big/

775. Ibid.

776. Ibid.

777. 1986 Jim Perry-Savin Celebrity Golf Classic program, p. 8.

778. Schmidt, Brenda Wade. "And now, it's golfing for dollars." *Sioux Falls Argus-Leader*, June 23, 1995, p. 6B.

779. Haller, Doug. "Ex-athletes pitch in." *Sioux Falls Argus-Leader*, September 7, 1995, p. 1C.

780. Ibid.

781. Haller, Doug. "Trading memories." *Sioux Falls Argus-Leader*, September 9, 1995, p. 1D

782. Geise, George. "Can-do attitude mark of Perry tournament." *Great Falls Tribune*, June 8, 2004, p. 1S.

783. Ibid.

784. Schmidt, Brenda Wade. "Long-distance field increases." *Sioux Falls Argus-Leader*, August 20, 1993, p. 6B.

785. Ibid.

786. Mona, Dave. "Perry takes 20th." *Minneapolis Tribune*, September 21, 1969, p. 1S.

787. Kranz, David and Deselms, Jen. "Perry: loss is personal." *Sioux Falls Argus-Leader*, December 26, 1989, p. 1B

788. Walters, Charley. "Shooter now: Jim Perry joining Twins Hall 'just as important' as brother's Cooperstown induction." *Pioneer Press*. https://www.twincities.com/2011/06/07/shooter-now-jim-perry-joining-twins-hall-just-as-important-as-brothers-cooperstown-induction/

789. Ibid.

790. Ibid.

791. Ibid.

792. Ibid.

793. Ibid.

794. Ibid.

795. Souhan, Jim. "Will Hall be taking more old-time Twins?" *Sioux Falls Argus-Leader*, July 24, 2011, p. 5C.

796. Ibid.

797. *Crestline Advocate*, June 22, 2011, p.1

Index

Aaron, Henry 209
Adair, Jerry 166
All-Star Game 88, 91, 141, 170, 183-186, 228, 231, 308
Allen, Bernie 17, 362
Allen, Dick 185
Allison, Bob 6, 13-15, 48, 102, 108, 129, 146, 156, 173, 196
Alomar, Sandy 214-215
Alou, Felipe 270
Alston, Walter 143, 146
Alvis, Max 13-14
Anthony, Merle (umpire) 271, 293
Antonen, Kathy 339
Antonen, Mel 338
Antonen, Ray 338-339, 342
Aparicio, Luis 185, 215
Alyea, Brant 179
Andrews, Mike 166
Aspromonte, Ken 284-288, 293-295, 300-317
Astrodome 218, 232
Atlanta Braves 23, 257
Balaz, John 323
Baltimore Colts 361
Baltimore Orioles 11, 28, 40-41, 48-49, 99, 105, 108 115, 119, 131, 154, 158, 168, 173, 183, 186-187, 197-203, 219, 223-224, 227, 255, 259, 275, 276-278, 293-295, 314, 327, 330-331, 333-334
Bando, Sal 15-16, 30, 191
Barker, John 365
Bartholow, Gus 342-343
Battey, Earl 114, 128, 145-146, 156
Bauer, Hank 31
Bavasi, Buzzie 144
Becquer, Julio 114
Belanger, Mark 17, 28, 48-49, 199-201
Bell, Bobby 361
Bell, Buddy 296, 298

Bell, Gary 94, 97, 98, 104-106, 114-115, 129
Bench, Johnny 186
Berra, Yogi 27, 100-101
Berry, Ken 16
Bertaina, Frank 18
Bethea, Bill 136
Billings, Rich 246
Blair, Paul 49, 198, 331
Blasingame, Don 157
Blue, Vida 194, 226, 259, 332
Blyleven, Bert 203, 214, 235, 238, 253, 257, 323, 341, 370
Bock, Wally 114
Bolin, Bobby 34
Bolling, Frank 99
Borbon, Pedro 30
Borgmann, Glenn 248
Bosman, Dick 309, 325, 328-329, 332
Boston Braves 134
Boston Red Sox 3, 42, 44, 101, 106, 113, 125, 126, 130, 131, 138, 139, 153, 163-167, 181, 189, 190, 215, 222, 238-239, 245, 259, 261, 265, 278, 283, 288, 293, 306, 312, 315, 316, 327
Boswell, Dave 7, 11, 13, 23-25, 32, 38, 40, 48-49, 135, 139, 145, 147-149, 161, 165, 173, 174, 176, 214
Boyer, Clete 141
Brabender, Gene 36
Braun, Steve 220
Brewer, Tom 106
Bridges, Rocky 98
Briggs, John 226
Brinkman, Ed 262, 294
Brodowski, Dick 103
Brohamer, Jack 297
Brown, Gates 7, 220, 241, 261
Brown, Hal 120

Brown, Ike 260
Brown, Jackie 304
Brown, Jimmy 62
Brown, Johnny Mack 62
Buford, Don 198
Bumbry, Al 331, 333
Bunning, Jim 131
Burkot, A.R. 73, 80
Burroughs, Jeff 301-302
Busby, Steve 259-260
Buskey, Tom 294-295, 310-311, 315-316, 325-326
Buzhardt, John 151-153
California Angels 3, 10, 15, 25, 29, 148, 158, 164-165, 174, 179, 191, 194, 214-215, 234, 238, 275, 286, 290, 292, 306, 307, 313, 316
Campaneris, Bert 16, 189, 362
Campbell College/University 72-74, 78-83, 85, 117, 341, 359-360, 365-366
Campbell, Jim 255-256, 278
Carbo, Bernie 293
Cardenas, Leo 40, 198-200, 224, 226, 271
Carew, Rod 1, 15, 29, 31, 36, 38, 46, 49, 166-170, 180, 233, 234, 253, 328
Carey, Andy 100
Carr, Roy 224
Casanova, Paul 9
Cash, Norm 113, 122, 271-272, 274
Cater, Danny 30-31
Cepeda, Orlando 270
Cerv, Bob 96
Champion, Bill 325
Chance, Dean 2, 4, 23-29, 33, 40, 161, 164-165, 167, 174, 176, 338
Chicago Cubs 17, 116, 250
Chicago White Sox 7, 8, 11-12, 16, 26, 27, 32, 35, 47, 71, 95, 97, 99-101, 105-107, 138, 150-153, 165, 169, 177, 226, 244, 276-277, 304, 327

Chylak, Nestor (umpire) 151-153, 262, 299-301
Cicotte, Al 103
Cincinnati Reds 99-100, 121, 136, 175, 192
Clark, Ron 46-47
Clarke, Horace 190
Clarkson, John 289
Clendenon, Donn 361
Cleveland Indians 8, 12-13, 18, 27, 38-39, 43, 44, 73, 83-127, 129-130, 132-133, 135, 158, 161, 168, 174, 176, 181, 183, 188, 203, 220, 225, 228, 239, 241, 248-249, 258, 263, 265, 267-271, 277-278, 282-329, 333, 369-371
Cleveland Municipal Stadium 267, 298, 311, 322, 325
Cloninger, Tony 90
Colavito, Rocky 94-95, 106-107, 112-113, 119
Coleman, Joe 44, 261, 265, 277
Coluccio, Bob 287
Cooper, Cecil 293-294
Corbin, Ray 226
Cosell, Howard 236, 265
Cronin, Joe 251, 278
Crosby, Ed 301
Cuellar, Mike 41, 48, 197-203, 211, 227
Cullen, Tim 8, 18
Curtis, John 261
Dark, Alvin 12, 35, 37, 269, 329-335
Davis, Brock 245
Davis, Hargrove "Hoggie" 73
Davis, Tommy 331
Dean, Dizzy 249
Dean, Paul 249
Dempsey, Rick 233
Dennis, John 343-356
Denver Bears 15, 22, 136, 162
Designated Hitter 6-7, 244, 254, 270-271, 314

Detroit Tigers 7, 18, 28, 39-40, 98, 101, 103, 112, 115, 116, 119, 122, 130, 131, 153, 159, 165, 167, 168, 180, 186, 212, 219, 225, 241, 242, 255-279, 283-284, 294-295, 298, 310-311, 320, 326-327, 334, 341
Dietz, Dick 186
Dimick, Jim 234
Dobson, Chuck 191
Dobson, Pat 227
Dolin, Nate 109
Donaldson, John 16
Donovan, Dick 107
Drabowski, Moe 95
Drysdale, Don 143-145
Duffy, Frank 228, 291, 293
Duncan, Dave 15-16, 287, 290, 294, 298, 310
Duren, Ryne 106, 361
Dykes, Jimmy 115-116
Eckersley, Dennis 328
Elgethun, Terry 365
Elliot, Sonny (umpire) 274
Ellis, John 271, 293, 297-298, 312
Epstein, Mike 17
Ermer, Cal 6-21, 162-170
Estrada, Chuck 115
Evans, Jim (umpire) 287
Fahey, Bill 246
Fargo-Moorhead Twins 86-88
Farmer, Ed 271, 275, 284
Farnell, Ed 206
Feeney, Chub 251
Feller, Bob 84, 97, 119, 361-362
Fenway Park 102, 125, 222, 239
Fife, Dan 255-256
Fingers, Rollie 31, 261, 333
Finley, Charlie 319, 328-329, 335, 340-341
Fischer, Bill 113
Fisk, Carlton 245, 265, 293
Flaherty, Red (umpire) 277
Ford, Whitey 84, 140
Fosse, Ray 184, 186, 229

Foucault, Steve 301
Fox, Charlie 228
Fox, Howard 155-156, 170, 232
Franklin, Pete 298
Freehan, Bill 327
Fryman, Woodie 261, 274
Funk, Frank 119
Gaherin, John 252
Gamble, Oscar 271, 290, 301
Garcia, Mike 84, 97, 119
Garcia, Pedro 287
Gardner, Slim 56
Gaston, Cito 185
Gebhard, Bob 226
Gelnar, John 36
Gibson, Bob 185, 205, 210
Gibson, Russ 166
Goetz, Russ 310
Goldstein, Harold "Spud" 107
Gooddale, Elmore 230
Gordon, Joe 27, 94-115
Goryl, John 169
Grabarkewitz, Billy 185
Granger, Wayne 239, 245
Grant, Jim "Mudcat" 105, 115, 135, 137, 142, 144-148, 154, 158, 161-163, 362
Green Bay Packers 161
Green, Dick 45
Green, Gene 123
Green, N.C. 206
Grich, Bobby 333
Grieve, Tom 298-299
Grimsley, Ross 294
Griffin, Doug 316
Griffith, Calvin 7, 21-22, 24, 28, 32, 127, 133-135, 147, 159, 173, 181-182, 210-214, 229, 232-235, 242, 249-250, 253-254, 256-258, 338
Haddix, Harvey 320-321, 324-325
Hall, Jimmy 140
Hall, Tom 24-26, 29, 33, 175, 188, 202, 214, 227

Haller, Tom 269

Hands, Bill 256

Haney, Larry 30

Hanson, Hank 360

Harder, Mel 105, 109, 121, 122

Hardy, Carroll 95

Hargrove, Mike 302

Harper, Tommy 218, 316, 335

Harrah, Toby 334

Harrelson, Bud 185

Harrelson, Ken 166

Harris, Gail 98-99

Harris, Morgan 73

Haydel, Hal 225

Hegan, Mike

Held, Woodie 95, 269

Hendrick, George 271, 301, 306, 308-309, 316-317

Hendricks, Elrod 41, 199-200

Heidemann, Jack 294

Hickman, Jim 185-186

Hilgendorf, Tom 302, 316

Hiller, John 260-262, 276-278

Hinton, Chuck 38

Hodges, Gil 183-185

Holman, Gary 17

Horlen, Joel 150

Holt, Jim 189, 191

Holtzman, Ken 330, 332

Hood, Don 328

Hooper, Ron 354

Horton, Tony 8

Horton, Willie 40, 180, 185

Houk, Ralph 149, 155, 283

Houston Colt .45s 121

Hovley, Steve 47

Howard, Elston 100-101, 106

Howard, Frank 17, 25, 29, 156-157, 274

Hudson, Sid 340

Huggins, Miller 94

Hunter, Jim "Catfish" 15, 65, 185, 213, 261, 308, 319-320, 328, 332

Imhoff, Darral

Jackson, Reggie 30, 32-33, 180, 226, 253, 309-310, 334

Jenkins, Ferguson 299, 312

Johnson, Alex 214, 303

Johnson, Darrell 315-316

Johnson, Davey 199-200

Johnson, Lou 13

Jones, Dalton 166

Josephson, Duane 216

Jupiter, Harry 35

Kaat, Jim 4-7, 12, 14, 23-40, 48, 125, 132-139, 144-148, 151, 154-166, 174, 176, 202, 211, 214, 227, 229, 233-234, 238, 240, 248-249, 253, 254, 256, 341, 366

Kaline, Al 7, 99, 113, 220, 225, 265

Kansas City Athletics 95-97, 113, 121-122, 125, 129-130, 139, 147, 153-154, 165

Kansas City Chiefs 361

Kansas City Royals 25-27, 32, 34, 45, 47, 195-196, 215-217, 226-227, 244, 253, 259-260, 272-273, 275, 297, 313, 341

Keller, Ron 15

Kelly, Pat 196

Kennedy, John 46, 223

Kenworthy, Dick 16

Killebrew, Harmon 7, 10, 15, 42, 45, 114, 143-146, 156, 166, 187, 189, 194, 198, 199, 209, 234, 243, 253, 370

Kindall, Jerry 140

King, Carolyn 273

Kingman, Dave 361

Kirkpatrick, Ed 47, 197, 217

Kline, Ron 166

Klippstein, Johnny 145-146, 148

Knowles, Darold 261

Knox, John 294

Konga, Wayne 204

Kosco, Andy 136, 157

Koufax, Sandy 143-146

Kralick, Jack 26, 125, 132

Kubek, Tony 100-101
Kubiak, Ted 30
Kuenn, Harvey 98, 103, 113
Kuhn, Bowie 206, 210, 313
Kunkle, Bill (umpire) 293
Lane, Frank 96, 106, 112, 114-115
LaRoche, Dave 244, 328
Larsen, Don 84
Larson, Bart 339
Lee, Bill 265, 315-316
Lee, Leron 296-297, 299
Leek, Gene 95
Lemon, Bob 84, 97
Lemon, Jim 114
Lentz, Doc (trainer) 16
Lindblad, Paul 332
Lis, Joe 314
Lombardi, Vince 161
Lolich, Mickey 7, 39-40, 261, 265
Lopez, Hector 106
Lovett, Tom 344
Lovitto, Joe 301
Lowenstein, John 271, 294, 296, 301, 326
Maddox, Elliott 186
Maloney, Jim 362
Maltzberger, Gordie 134
Manning, Helen 78-79
Mantle, Mickey 27, 33, 100-101, 134, 141, 148-149
Martin, Billy 21-49, 67, 98, 100, 134-135, 140, 144, 155-156, 173, 191, 233, 241-242, 255-278, 283, 297-304, 328, 340-341, 364, 368-369
Martin, J.C. 151-152
Martinez, Tony 270
Mathewson, Christy 289
Mathewson, Henry 289
Maxwell, Charlie 103, 116
Mayberry, John 244, 260
Mayer, Jacqueline 127
May, Carlos 276-277
May, Lee 333

Mays, Willie 209, 268-270
McAuliffe, Dick 180, 220, 241, 261
McCall, Fred 72-73, 80-82, 365
McCovey, Willie 185, 268-270
McCoy, Larry (umpire) 262
McCraw, Tom 310
McCullough, Clyde 119
McDowell, Sam 13-14, 168, 183-185, 188, 203, 228
McGaha, Mel 121-123
McGuire, Mark 341
McKinney, Rich 240
McLain, Denny 39
McLaughlin, Mike 360
McLish, Cal 101, 105
McMullen, Ken 17-18
McNally, Dave 49, 187-188, 197-198, 203, 211, 227, 253
Mee, Tom 156
Mele, Sam 2, 125, 128-129, 131, 133, 138-154, 158-162, 205
Menke, Denis 185
Merritt, Jim 145-148, 158, 161, 165-166, 184, 362
Messersmith, Andy 179, 253
Metropolitan Stadium 33-34, 42, 49, 99, 127, 141, 144, 160, 197, 234
Michael, Gene 4
Miller, Bob 31, 49
Miller, Marvin 22, 181-182, 211, 231-236, 250-252, 320
Miller, Rick 265, 293
Milwaukee Braves 90
Milwaukee Brewers 181, 188, 190, 218, 226, 240, 245, 261, 287-288, 325
Mincher, Don 142, 144, 157
Minges Coliseum 281
Minneapolis Millers 99
Minnesota Twins 1-49, 125-259, 282, 284, 286, 306-307, 328, 338, 340-341, 344, 350, 353, 360, 366, 369-370
Minnesota Vikings 247

Mitterwald, George 44, 49, 178, 182-183, 199-202, 221, 226, 244

Monbouquette, Bill 4

Monday, Rick 16, 31, 180

Money, Don 287, 325

Monzon, Danny 233

Moss, Dick 252

Motton, Curt 49

Munson, Thurman 265

Murcer, Bobby 43

Murchison, Tim 71

Murphy, Tom 29

Napp, Larry (umpire) 4

Naragon, Hal 126-127, 139, 150, 159-161

Narleski, Ray 98

Nelson, Dave 246

Nettles, Graig 18, 31, 341

Neudecker, Jerry (umpire) 276

New York Mets 24, 183, 188, 238, 250, 283

New York Yankees 4, 6, 17, 21, 27, 42-43, 67, 83, 84, 90, 94, 100-101, 104, 106, 116, 127, 130, 131, 133-135, 140-142, 144, 148-149, 154-156, 162-163, 190, 206, 218, 229, 239, 263-266, 284, 286, 289, 294, 309, 314, 319, 341

Newsome, Eley 79

Nischwitz, Ron 91

Nixon, Richard 206

Noble, Ron 362

North, Billy 333

North Platte Indians 73, 85, 87

Northrup, Jim 180, 225, 274, 330

Norton, Tom 233

Nossek, Joe 140

O'Phelan, Harvey 23

Oakland A's 14-15, 19, 29-32, 41-42, 44-45, 153, 173, 179, 183, 189, 191, 194, 219, 221, 225, 226, 237, 240, 249, 259, 261, 262, 309, 319, 328-335, 340-342

Odom, John "Blue Moon" 328

Oldis, Bob 19

Oliva, Tony 1, 7, 13, 15, 31-32, 46-49, 143-144, 150-152, 168-169, 199, 201, 212, 214-215, 220, 241, 244-245, 249, 253-254, 307, 328, 361

Oliver, Bob 216

Olson, Bud 361

Oopsy the Clown 274

Osborn, Dave 247

Osteen, Claude 37, 143, 145

Otis, Amos 186, 273

Pagliaroni, Jim 36

Palmer, Jim 183-185, 202, 227, 333

Pappas, Milt 250

Pascual, Camilo 4, 125, 132-139, 144-148, 153, 158, 161

Patek, Freddie 217-218, 272

Pattin, Marty 188, 245

Paul, Gabe 121

Pebble Beach Pro-Am 339

Pelekoudas, Chris (umpire) 269

Pena, Roberto 180

Perranoski, Ron 7, 18, 25-28, 30-31, 36, 38-39, 41, 44, 49, 176, 180, 182, 186-188, 191, 196, 202, 211-212, 215, 219, 223, 227

Perry, Blanche 228, 282

Perry, Chris 120, 126, 132, 155-156, 235, 243, 274, 282, 336, 339, 342

Perry, Daphne 35-36, 51, 75-82, 117-118, 120, 126-127, 132, 143, 150, 155-156, 203-204, 211-212, 234-235, 243, 329, 335-336, 338-340, 342-344, 346, 354, 359-360, 365-368

Perry, Evan 18, 52-67, 75, 89, 119, 193, 207, 215, 285, 292

Perry , Gaylord 17-18, 34-38, 51-72, 89-90, 143, 183-186, 190, 192-194, 205-207, 209, 211, 222, 228-229, 239-241, 249, 258, 263, 265-272, 274, 277, 278, 281-325, 329, 339-341, 361

Perry, Michelle 243, 273, 282, 336, 342, 346, 349

Perry, Pam 143, 155-156, 243, 273-274, 282, 336, 337, 340, 342

Perry, Ruby 18, 52-59, 63, 67, 79, 207, 215, 292, 365

Peters, Gary 7, 86, 151, 216

Peters, Wilbur 344, 346-347

Peterson, Fritz 312, 320, 324

Petrocelli, Rico 222, 306

Petty, Richard 281

Pianowski, Tony 86

Piersall, Jim 102

Piniella, Lou 47, 197, 217, 244, 260-261

Pinson, Vada 225

Porter, Darrell 287, 325

Postove, Harry 71

Powell, Boog 41, 48-49, 198-199, 202, 224

Power, Vic 98, 126

Price, Jim 39

Quilici, Frank 9, 168, 212, 248, 307

Ramos, Pedro 227

Randle, Lenny 297-298

Ratliff, Paul 220-221

Reading Indians 82, 88-89, 91, 119

Reagan, Ronald 206

Reese, Rich 15, 199, 211, 220

Richards, Paul 108

Richardson, Bobby 141, 206-207

Rigney, Bill 174-196, 212, 214, 219-228, 238-241, 245

Riverfront Stadium 183

Robinson, Brooks 185, 199-200, 236-237, 250, 253

Robinson, Frank 28, 48, 197, 199, 224, 313-329

Rodriguez, Aurelio 182, 219, 241, 294, 311

Rojas, Cookie 195, 217, 272

Roland, Jim 17, 132

Rollins, Rich 8

Roof, Phil 33, 232-233

Rose, Pete 175, 184-186

Roseboro, John 25, 32, 47, 49

Rowe, Ralph 233

Rudi, Joe 309, 335

Russell, Cazzie 361

Ryan, Nolan 238, 275, 289

San Diego Padres 93, 268

Sain, Johnny 134-142, 149-150, 159-161, 230, 324

Sanders, Ken 288

Santiago, Jose 166

Sawyer, Rich 284

Scherman, Fred 265, 277

Schultz, Joe 38, 278

Score, Herb 84, 94-95, 119, 302-303

Scott, George 166, 325-326

Scott, Robert 206

Seattle Mariners 338

Seattle Pilots 1, 34-38, 46-47

Seaver, Tom 183-184, 188, 237, 250, 283

Seghi, Phil 284-285, 313-314, 320-321

Segui, Diego 46

Sheldon, Bob 287

Short, Bob 237

Siebert, Sonny 332, 334

Sievers, Roy 108, 362

Simmons, Floyd "Chunk" 281

Sims, Duke 38, 261, 303

Singleton, Ken 333

Skowron, Moose 27

Slaughter, Enos 100, 106

Smith, Reggie 166, 215, 223

Snell, Laura 77

Snell, Mack 76-77

Soderholm, Eric 233

Spahn, Warren 116, 324

Spencer, Jim 334

Spikes, Charlie 271-272, 290, 299

Splittorff, Paul 244

Springstead, Marty 246

St. Olaf College 233-236, 240, 247

Stange, Lee 132

Stanky, Eddie 152
Stanley, Mickey 261-262, 272
Steinbach, Terry 341
Stengel, Casey 21, 101
Stevens, John (umpire) 200
Stigman, Dick 94, 125, 132, 135
Stoke (the dog) 224
Strickland, Jim 224, 226, 245
Stoneman, Bill 290
Stottlemyre, Mel 42
Stuart, Dick 131
Sturdivant, Tom 84
Szymik, Don 343-356
Tait, Joe 302-303
Tanner, Chuck 305, 327
Taylor, Tony 261
Tebbetts, Birdie 12, 123, 125
Tenace, Gene 226, 309-310, 331
Texas Rangers 237, 246, 248, 273, 295, 297-304, 311-312, 328-329, 334, 340
Thompson, Danny 199, 220, 253
Thrift, Roger 85
Thurman, Fred 345, 347, 364-365
Tiant, Luis 174, 176, 211, 214, 222
Tidrow, Dick 286
Tornay, Frank 87
Toronto Blue Jays 338
Torre, Joe 251
Tovar, Cesar 30, 41, 44-45, 151, 156-157, 180, 197, 198, 212, 220, 233, 245
Tresh, Tom 4
Turley, Bob 84
Uhlaender, Tom 29, 35, 36, 43, 46, 48
Unitas, Johnny 361
Upshaw, Cecil 287
Valentine, Fred 157
VanLeur, Brad 349-356, 363-364
Veale, Bob 283
Versalles, Zoilo 140, 142, 144, 150, 166

Walton, Danny 46-47
Washington (D.C.) Senators 2, 9, 17, 25, 29, 41, 44, 90, 102, 104-105, 107-108, 113, 123, 127, 130, 138, 142, 144, 149, 150, 154, 156-157, 163, 165, 168, 182, 190, 210, 215, 249
Weaver, Earl 183-187, 198, 255
Webster, Ray 95, 102
Weis, Al 151-153
Wert, Don 18, 186
Westgate Park 268-269
Wiencek, Dick 340-341
Wilcox, Milt 297-298, 316
Wilhelm, Hoyt 56
Williams, Dick 166, 261
Williams, Stan 168, 176, 191, 194, 196, 219, 222, 224, 227
Williams, Walt 284
Wilson, Red 116
Winkles, Bobby 292
Woodson, Dick 47, 204, 213, 230, 232-233, 238
World Series 3, 67, 84, 133, 142-145, 158-159, 162, 165, 197, 231, 249, 284, 328
Worthington, Al 5, 7-9, 18, 22, 28-29, 38, 40, 142, 145-146, 148, 205, 229-230, 366
Wynn, Early 3, 24, 84, 97, 120, 161, 164
Yastrzemski, Carl 42, 44, 131, 166, 184-185, 215, 293, 306
York, Jim 217
Yost, Eddie 98-99
Zepp, Bill 196-197, 202, 212
Zimmerman, Jerry 164